The Methuen Drama
Anthology of Irish Plays

The Methuen Drama Anthology of Irish Plays

The Hostage
Brendan Behan

Bailegangaire
Tom Murphy

The Belle of the Belfast City
Christina Reid

The Steward of Christendom
Sebastian Barry

The Cripple of Inishmaan
Martin McDonagh

Edited and introduced by
Patrick Lonergan

Bloomsbury Methuen Drama
An imprint of Bloomsbury Publishing Plc

B L O O M S B U R Y
LONDON · NEW DELHI · NEW YORK · SYDNEY

Bloomsbury Methuen Drama

An imprint of Bloomsbury Publishing Plc

Imprint previously known as Methuen Drama

50 Bedford Square	1385 Broadway
London	New York
WC1B 3DP	NY 10018
UK	USA

www.bloomsbury.com

BLOOMSBURY, METHUEN DRAMA and the Diana logo are trademarks of Bloomsbury Publishing Plc

This collection first published in Great Britain in 2008 by Methuen Drama
Reprinted by Bloomsbury Methuen Drama 2014

The Hostage first published in 1958 by Methuen & Co. A revised and reset edition was published in 1962.
Copyright © 1958 and 1962 by Theatre Workshop
Bailegangaire first published in 1986 by The Gallery Press, Dublin, Ireland
Reprinted in a revised version in 1988 by Methuen London Ltd
Reprinted, with revisions, in Tom Murphy Plays: 2 in 1993 and 2005 by Methuen Drama
Copyright © 1986, 1988, 1993, 2005 by Tom Murphy
The Belle of the Belfast City first published as a Methuen New Theatrescript in 1989
Copyright © 1989, 1997 by Christina Reid
The Steward of Christendom first published in Great Britain in 1995 in the
Royal Court Writers Series by Methuen Drama. Reprinted 1996 as a Methuen Modern Play.
Copyright © 1995, 1997 by Sebastian Barry
The Cripple of Inishmaan first published in Great Britain in 1997 by Methuen Drama
Copyright © 1997 by Martin McDonagh

Introduction copyright © Patrick Lonergan, 2008

The authors and editor have asserted their rights under the Copyright, Designs and Patents Act, 1988,
to be identified as authors and editors of this work.

British Library Cataloguing-in-Publication Data
A catalogue record for this book is available from the British Library.

ISBN: PB: 978-1-4081-0678-5

Library of Congress Cataloging-in-Publication Data
A catalog record for this book is available from the Library of Congress.

Series: Play Anthologies

Contents

Introduction

And if we finished it, that would be something at least, wouldn't it?
Tom Murphy, *Bailegangaire*

Since the early 1990s, Ireland has been completely transformed – almost beyond recognition. Devastated by famine in the nineteenth century, it is now one of the world's richest nations; blighted by military conflict and terrorism in the twentieth century, it is now at last at peace. This new-found prosperity has rightly been celebrated, but it has provoked both new questions and new challenges.

Economic growth means that Ireland now seems in many ways indistinguishable from other countries in the West, prompting a growing sense of uncertainty about national identity: 'we' may be wealthier, but it's not clear what the word 'we' refers to any more. As peace takes root in Northern Ireland, other divisions are becoming apparent throughout the island – in terms of class, gender, race and other characteristics. Perhaps most importantly, there is a growing fear that the country is developing a strange form of collective amnesia, a reluctance to acknowledge that its history is dominated by failure: by mass emigration, military defeat, economic stagnation and underdevelopment. So as we move into the second decade of this century, Ireland is faced with difficult questions. How can we reconcile the memory of that troubled past with the desire to enjoy an apparently successful present? And if we let go of our histories, will we still remember who we are?

The five plays collected in this book point us towards possible solutions to these and other problems. From Brendan Behan in 1958 to Martin McDonagh in 1996, each writer presented here repeatedly challenges and transgresses the boundaries that define national identity. In doing so, they also push against the conventions of theatrical form: by asking what it means to be Irish, they are also exploring how identities can be represented theatrically. Along the way, they cross and redraw many other borders. The dramatic merges with different literary forms and with other media, from storytelling to music to cinema. The distinction between high art and popular culture is repeatedly blurred, and often rejected. And, most importantly, these five plays argue persuasively that the distance between past, present, and future may not be as clear cut as we had imagined.

That chronological tension is made instantly obvious in Brendan Behan's *The Hostage* (1958) – a play that starts with the line 'Thank God, that's over' (implying that the past has been left behind) and ends with the words 'I'll never forget you . . . till the end of time' (implying that the past will never be left behind). Like that other great Irish play of the 1950s, Samuel Beckett's *Waiting for Godot* (1955), *The Hostage* presents a group of characters who are trapped in a cycle of eternal recurrence: they might think that something has finished, but it will be repeated, again and again, becoming worse each time. Where Behan differs from Beckett, however, is in his determination to root that idea in a political context. The cycle being repeated here is Anglo-Irish violence which, his play shows, is always self-perpetuating and ultimately self-defeating.

   This argument is made through the characterisation of the eponymous hostage, Leslie Williams, a British soldier being held prisoner in a Dublin boarding house (which is really little more than a brothel). He has been kidnapped by the IRA because one of their members has been arrested and sentenced to death; if that execution goes ahead, they will shoot Leslie in reprisal. The problem, however, is that the Englishman has formed close relationships with many of the people in the house – notably with Teresa, a young countrywoman who works there as a maid. His fate will be determined by the willingness of the house's inhabitants to help him to escape, by their seeing him not as a soldier from a foreign army but as an individual whom they know and like. The play's dramatic momentum is therefore generated by the conflict between Leslie's public and private identities, a tension captured well in Behan's stage directions, which refer to him as 'Soldier' on some occasions, but by his Christian name at other times.

By focusing on the relationship between Leslie and Teresa, Behan is tapping into a long-standing tradition in Irish literature, in which Anglo-Irish relations are explored symbolically through the presentation of a romance between an English soldier and a young Irish woman. When relations between the two countries are perceived to be positive, that relationship will thrive – as we see in plays like Dion Boucicault's *The Shaughraun* (1874). But when the two countries are in conflict, it will usually come to a tragic conclusion – as shown in Brian Friel's *Translations* (1980), and indeed in *The Hostage* itself.

Behan's play is different from such works in one crucial respect, however. Whereas writers like Boucicault and Friel suggest that Irish and English identities should be seen as opposites that may be harmonised, Behan instead celebrates difference, dissonance and discord. *The Hostage* operates effectively as tragedy, but it's also a disarmingly light-hearted musical. It celebrates romantic love while (with a wink and nudge) considering the commodification of sex through prostitution. It gives us Monsewer, an Irish-speaking patriot who, it turns out, is actually an Englishman. It's written by a noted Irish nationalist, but its hero is an English soldier. And most importantly, it challenges the notion that Ireland and England are locked in a cycle of antagonism. When Behan's characters directly address the audience (as they frequently do), they are stepping out of the Ireland represented on stage and into the England where this version of the play was originally performed: the two national spaces are thus shown not to be separate, but intertwined. This powerfully disrupts the audience's sense of the distinction between 'us' and 'them', between 'here' and 'there', between 'then' and 'now'.

Like *The Hostage*, Tom Murphy's *Bailegangaire* (1985) dramatises an attempt to break free from a cycle of eternal recurrence. Each night, a senile old woman called Mommo begins a story about how the (fictitious) town of Bailegangaire received its name – which, it emerges, occurred as a result of a laughing contest that concluded tragically. Pronounced *bawl-yah-gone-goy-rah* (with the emphasis on the second and fourth syllables), the word means 'the place without laughter', a name that could also be applied to the Ireland presented in the play, which seems a bleak and hopeless environment – until the final moments of the action.

Again, the play is dominated by the theme of memory. We gradually realise that Mommo is both obsessed with and terrified of the past. She is compelled to repeat her story endlessly, but seems equally compelled to avoid concluding it, since doing so would require her to face a trauma that she seems determined to forget. As her astonishing monologue develops, storytelling is simultaneously deployed as a strategy of revelation and a technique for evasion. Murphy maintains that tension between giving and taking masterfully: the poetry of Mommo's speech reveals hidden truths, even as its density obscures unbearable realities; her exuberance demands our admiration, even as the actions she describes horrify and alienate us.

Murphy also presents Mommo's granddaughters Mary and Dolly, whose lives contrast with and occasionally mirror events in the monologue. They too are trapped by the past, both desperately attempting to reject the only roles available to them – wife, nurse, mother, whore – but seeming unable to forge an alternative sense of who they might become.

Murphy's ability to bring the two strands of his play into harmony gives *Bailegangaire* lasting significance. He forces his audience to acknowledge the tragic elements of Mommo's monologue. Then, as it moves towards its conclusion, he gradually tears apart our sense of normality – our awareness of the gap between storytelling and real life, between the irrational and the real, between the past and the present. And then, almost miraculously, in the play's dying moments, he offers us a glimpse of hope, leaving us with an image that makes sense of everything that has come before. Like many of Murphy's other great plays, *Bailegangaire* thus forces us to acknowledge the genuinely tragic elements of our own lives, but it does so only to teach us how we can begin to move on once the tragic has finally occurred. It is for this reason that Murphy is indisputably one of the great Irish dramatists of the twentieth century – and it also explains why *Bailegangaire* may be his greatest play.

Christina Reid's *The Belle of the Belfast City* (1989) is much closer in form and spirit to *The Hostage* than *Bailegangaire*, but it's motivated by a similar awareness of how the past can both anchor and restrain us. It presents three generations of women from a Belfast family, whose domestic difficulties are mirrored in the social unrest caused by the implementation of the 1985 Anglo-Irish Agreement. That deal would later be regarded as an important step in the development of the Peace Process, but at that time was seen by many Unionists as an act of betrayal by the British government. Reid aims to analyse and historicise the resultant sense of anger and anxiety.

Where Murphy's play presents an old woman who tells stories, Reid's gives us an old woman who sings – Dolly Horner, formerly a music-hall star known as the Belle of Belfast City. Reid's inclusion of popular songs, many of them performed by Dolly and the other characters, imbues the play with an air of nostalgia, thus inviting audiences to compare the representation of the past through music with the representation of the present through naturalistic performance.

That contrast shouldn't be seen as a naive celebration of an idyllic past, however, because Reid also shows that many of her characters' problems are rooted in their histories. This is particularly true of Jack and Janet, Dolly's nephew and niece, whose dysfunctions as adults appear to stem from a childhood filled with anxiety and sexual repression. As her play develops, Reid makes clear that we can't deny where we have come from – our lives *are* determined by politics, race, religion, class, gender, culture and, above all, by family. We don't have to define ourselves exclusively in terms of our histories, however, as we're also free to form other allegiances, to forge new identities. This argument is made most explicitly through the characterisation of Janet, who is eventually forced to consider how much she really owes her brother, but it's an important feature of the entire play.

In some respects, *The Belle of the Belfast City* has been overtaken by history. Its analysis of the anxieties of Northern Ireland's Unionist community has ongoing relevance, but much of the play's energy arises from the fear that power-sharing between the North's Catholic and Protestant communities would never happen – a suggestion that has been disproved by subsequent events. Yet, in other ways, *Belle* is remarkably prescient, giving us one of the earliest treatments of racism on the Irish stage, an issue that is becoming increasingly important as both parts of Ireland become more multicultural. That theme is developed through the presentation of Dolly's granddaughter Belle, a young black woman who is visiting her Northern Irish relatives for the first time. Reid establishes a relationship between the racism experienced by Belle and anti-Catholic prejudice, and she interweaves that theme with a challenging subplot in which Jack manipulates Davy, a disabled youth, for political gain. She therefore places the issue of Irish sectarianism in an international and historical context, drawing on the American Civil Rights movement and international popular culture to transcend her play's chronological and geographical setting. That global perspective makes *Belle* challenging for audiences (indeed, it received a negative response from some quarters during its 1989 Belfast premiere). But, by showing that the expression of one form of identity may ultimately lead to prejudice against others, Reid's play acquires urgency today – in Ireland and elsewhere.

If history is always written by the victors, perhaps one function of literature is to remind us that the vanquished deserve our attention too. That argument is made brilliantly by Sebastian Barry's *The Steward of Christendom* (1995), a compassionate and richly poetic memory play that focuses on a man whose life has been destroyed by politics, his future snatched from him, his past written out of history.

Barry's protagonist, Thomas Dunne, is a former superintendent of the Dublin Metropolitan Police, the force that held the peace when Ireland was still a part of the United

Kingdom. He joined the police, he tells us, from love of king and country, from a sense of duty – from the noble desire to protect the vulnerable, from a need to uphold justice. The achievement of Irish independence in 1922, however, has turned him suddenly from pillar of the community to social outcast. He finds himself recast as a 'Castle Catholic' – an Irishman who was loyal to Dublin Castle (the seat of British authority before independence), when he ought to have supported the nationalist cause. Dunne thus finds himself in the curious position of being rendered metaphorically homeless without ever having gone anywhere. The Ireland he lived in (and for) has disappeared beneath his feet.

Once again, we see that there is a surprisingly strong relationship between the personal and the political in Irish drama. As his life draws to a close, Dunne is isolated from his family as well as his country. Institutionalised and losing his sense of reality, he struggles to express the love that he so evidently feels for his daughters and grandchildren. He also circles endlessly around the tragedies that have dominated his life: the loss of his wife, and the death of his only son Willie during the First World War – a story that Barry would later return to in his heartbreakingly beautiful novel *A Long Long Way* (2005).

There are clear links between *The Steward* and the other plays collected in this book. Betrayed by the state whose rule he upheld, Dunne has suffered the fate that many of Christina Reid's characters fear. There are also clear echoes of *Bailegangaire* in Barry's suggestion that Dunne's ramblings may ultimately be more rational than some of the statements made by the play's supposedly sane characters. But Barry's work also represents a departure from the past, an emergence of a new direction in Irish drama. Where Irish playwrights once gave us a speech that had been heightened and poeticised, Barry instead celebrates the eloquence of the everyday, finding a strange beauty in the apparently inarticulate. In doing so, he develops a style of writing that is generous and evocative – an approach that would later become evident in the works of many younger Irish writers, such as Conor McPherson and Enda Walsh.

*

If the conflict between England and Ireland could be
presented in terms of a doomed romance in Behan's *The
Hostage*, perhaps it's a sign of how much things have changed
that in Martin McDonagh's *The Cripple of Inishmaan* (1996),
the relationship of the two countries is re-imagined as a
sadistic but hilarious game involving broken eggs. At first
glance, everything about the play seems just as frivolous
as that unique perspective on Anglo-Irish relations but, as
with all of McDonagh's works, we must look beyond surface
appearances before we form any conclusions.

The action is set on one of the three Aran Islands that
lie off Ireland's west coast – places that have repeatedly
been presented to the world as the site of the 'real' or
authentic Ireland, not only in plays like Synge's *Riders to
the Sea* (1904), but also in such documentaries as Robert
Flaherty's celebrated *Man of Aran* (1934), the filming of which
acts as the backdrop to this play. Ostensibly, McDonagh is
using this setting to serve up a standard comic tale about a
likeable country lad called Cripple Billy, who sees a chance
to escape his restrictive and dull home by running away to
Hollywood with Flaherty's film-crew. And (again ostensibly)
Billy's story is told in an occasionally crude but essentially
good-natured comedic style that seems to recall Behan,
while nodding towards Quentin Tarantino. It's therefore
entirely possible for some audiences to misunderstand the
play, to see it as enjoyable, superficial and forgettable.

But if McDonagh works only with surface appearances,
that's probably because he wants to reflect the audience's
gaze back upon itself. In *The Cripple*, we find ourselves
watching a group of Irish characters who are themselves
watching and evaluating the performance of Irishness in
Man of Aran. Their reactions to that film are intensely funny,
but they should also be seen as inspirational. When we are
confronted with the islanders' willingness to analyse, interpret
and reject the Ireland they see on screen in 1934, we're
being reminded of our obligation to analyse the version
of Ireland being constructed on McDonagh's stage in the
present. This treatment of the clash between representation

and reality allows us to critique the impulse of filmmakers and dramatists to create images of an 'authentic' Ireland for global consumption.

The Cripple therefore forces us to confront questions that are not so much about Ireland as ourselves. What values, presuppositions and stereotypes did we bring with us to the theatre? How and why has McDonagh challenged those assumptions? And what should we take with us, after a performance of this play has concluded? In this way *The Cripple of Inishmaan* is another example of how Irish drama is setting off in exciting new directions – largely because it challenges our notion that there was something called 'Irish drama' in the first place.

In making this case, McDonagh raises questions that dominate all of the plays in this volume. Is there a risk that, like Johnnypateenmike in *The Cripple*, Irish dramatists might eventually find themselves trading in stories that purport to be authentic, but which are really just cynical attempts to generate an income? If so, what happens when national identity becomes a commodity, a brand to be traded on the global culture market? Should audiences accept unthinkingly the images of Ireland that they see on stage, page and screen? After all, isn't there something paradoxical about an audience's desire to experience the authentic in (of all places) a theatre – a space which should be a site for fantasy and play, as these five dramas show so persuasively? These questions are firmly rooted in the history of Irish theatre, but, as reformulated by McDonagh, they look set to dominate our stage throughout the years ahead.

Patrick Lonergan
Galway, May 2008

Brendan Behan

The Hostage

The Hostage was first presented by Theatre Workshop at the Theatre Royal, Stratford, London E15, on 14 October 1958. A revised version was presented by Theatre Workshop at the Théâtre des Nations Festival, Paris, on 3 April 1959, and in conjunction with Donmar Productions Ltd at Wyndham's Theatre, London, on 11 June 1959. The text in this edition is of this later production. The cast, on this occasion, was as follows:

Pat	Howard Goorney
Meg Dillon	Eileen Kennally
Monsewer	Glynn Edwards
Rio Rita	Stephen Cato
Princess Grace	Roy Barnett
Mr Mulleady	Brian Murphy
Miss Gilchrist	Ann Beach
Colette	Yootha Joyce
Ropeen	Leila Greenwood
Leslie Williams	Alfred Lynch
Teresa	Celia Salkeld
IRA Officer	James Booth
Volunteer	Clive Barker
Russian Sailor	Dudley Sutton
Kate	Kathleen O'Connor

Produced by   Joan Littlewood
Setting designed by   Sean Kenny

Characters

Pat, *the caretaker of a lodging-house*
Meg Dillon, *his consort*
Monsewer, *the owner of the house*
Rio Rita, *a homosexual navvy*
Princess Grace, *his coloured boyfriend*
Mr Mulleady, *a decaying civil servant*
Miss Gilchrist, *a social worker*
Colette, *a whore*
Ropeen, *an old whore*
Leslie Williams, *a British soldier*
Teresa, *the skivvy, a country girl*
IRA Officer, *a fanatical patriot*
Volunteer, *Feargus O'Connor, a ticket-collector*
Russian Sailor
Kate, *the pianist*

[handwritten notes:]

nonlinear. unreal places. characters are just types.
language is derailyed.

what kind of people?
sex workers. russian. oxford man.

Act One

*The action of the play takes place in an old house in Dublin that has
seen better days. A middle-aged man wearing carpet slippers, old
corduroys and using a walking-stick is holding court. He runs the house.
He doesn't own it, although he acts as though he does. This is because
the real owner isn't right in his head and thinks he's still fighting in the
Troubles or one of the anti-English campaigns before that.
Since the action of the play runs throughout the whole house and it isn't
feasible to build it on stage, the setting is designed to represent one room
of the house with a window overlooking the street. Leading off from this
room are two doors and a staircase leading to the upper part. Between
the room and the audience is an area that represents a corridor, a landing,
or another room in the house and also serves as an extension of the room
when the characters need room to dance and fight in.*

The middle-aged man is **Patrick**, *an ex-hero and present-time
brothel-keeper. During the first act of the play* **Patrick**, *with the
aid of* **Meg Dillon**, *his consort, is preparing the room that we can
see for a guest. It contains a table, two chairs and a brass bedstead.
During the action of the play the other inhabitants of the house, in
search of stout, physical comfort or the odd ballad, drift in and out of
the room according to their curiosity and the state of* **Pat**'s *temper.
Like the house, they have seen better times. As the curtain rises, pimps,
prostitutes, decayed gentlemen and their visiting 'friends' are dancing
a wild Irish jig, which is a good enough reason for* **Meg** *and* **Pat**
*to stop their preparations and sit down for a drink of stout. During the
act these rests and drinks occupy more time than the actual work of
preparation.*

The jig reaches its climax and the dancers swing off the stage leaving
Pat *and* **Meg** *sitting at the table in the room.*

Meg   Thank God, that's over!

*From the end of the passage comes the blast of an off-key bagpiper. The
noise recedes into the distance.*

Meg   In the name of God, what's that?

Handwritten annotations:

- city *(above "Dublin")*
- acts as tho
- he does bc.
- the real owner is mad
- kinda odd.
- who gave him power?
- we know this is really "action"
- = plough & stars *(above "window overlooking the street")*
- un-realism.
- Monsewer is still alive?
- all provide some chance at authentic. esp. song/dance
- of time *(beside "Like the house, they have seen better times")*
- ad. *(margin)*
- As ensure when the reality begins.
- immediately more music.
- → what does it mean that Meg doesn't like music, Pat thinks music is akin to fighting?
- → Meg & Pat reinforce each other & contradict. as if truth doesn't matter. they're stuck in their "type" and do not want to move.

6   The Hostage

Annotations (handwritten): why keg? "evidence" of his ex-hero identity → doesn't quite matter if it's real. It's all past + done.

practice = anticipating death. like the wake for Leslie.

Pat   It's Monsewer practising his music. He's taken it into his head to play the Dead March for the boy in Belfast Jail when they hang him in the morning. You know, the one that got copped for his IRA activities. *this is also nonspecific. we never know what he—*

Meg   I wish he'd kept it in his head. Those bagpipes get on me nerves. *a little bit of ambiguity. that boy should have kept to himself...*

Pat   Get us a drink.

Meg   Get it yourself.

Pat   I can't move my leg. *we're never given whether it's real injury. also he can walk.*

Meg   There's nothing wrong with your leg. *(contradiction?)*

She reaches him a bottle of stout.

Here you are, you old scow.

A homosexual navvy, **Rio Rita**, *attempts to get through the room and up the stairs without* **Pat** *seeing him. He is accompanied by a negro with a kit-bag,* **Pat** *spots them.* *road construction worker. = soldiers bag.*

Pat   Hey! Where's your rent?

Rio Rita   Give me a chance to earn it. *→ how long has he been here.*

They scuttle upstairs.

Meg   Do you think they will hang him?

Pat   Who, him?

He indicates **Rio Rita**'s *disappearing backside.*

Pat   They bloody well ought to! *→ for not paying rent? for being gay?*

Meg   No, the boy in Belfast Jail. *→ now "he" actually returns to the boy.*

Pat   There's no think about it. Tomorrow morning at the hour of eight, he'll hang as high as Killymanjaro.

Meg   What the hell's that?

Pat   It's a noted mountain off the south coast of Switzerland. It would do you no good to be hung as high as that, anyway. *→ no "south coast". ignorance o... wild. → why?*

heroism, actual war = authentic experience = Charleston. → now gone. not allowed.

↔ Monsewer, playing music, somehow knows a secret plan... → revival !

Meg   Do you know what he said? 'As a soldier of the Irish Republic, I will die smiling.'

? direct disillusioning of Clitheroe etc.

Pat   And who asked him to give himself the trouble? *he's lived time & knows better.*

Meg   He only did his duty as a member of the IRA.

? only "real" time when he was a hero himself. → heroism = Charleston.

Pat   Don't have me use a coarse expression, you silly old bitch. This is nineteen-sixty, and the days of the heroes are over this forty years past. Long over, finished and done with. The IRA and the War of Independence are as dead as the Charleston. *now they're not allowed in Pat's world.*

→ "decolonizing" is done. ... but the boy is in Belfast, N. Ireland, now UK.

→ dance?

Meg   The old cause is never dead. 'Till Ireland shall be free from the centre to the sea. Hurrah for liberty, says the Shan Van Vocht.'

Pat (*to the audience*)   She's as bad as that old idiot out there. (*He indicates* **Monsewer**.) It's bad enough he hasn't got a clock, but I declare to Jesus, I don't think he even has a calendar. And who has the trouble of it all? Me! He wants to have the New IRA, so-called, in this place now. Prepare a room for them, no less.   *→ "pimping" patriots/heroes. we must greet & host them.*

Colette, *an attractive young whore, enters propelling a* **Sailor** *before her. The* **Sailor** *obviously speaks no English or Gaelic, and seeing the bed in the room starts to take his trousers off.* **Colette** *drags him away upstairs.*

a room for revival of real experience

Colette   I've got a right one here, this time.   *→ almost overtaken by sex. or already is.*

They go upstairs.

Sex is the only living allowed

Pat   It's bad enough trying to run this place as a speak-easy and a brockel –

Meg   A what?

contd misinformation.

Pat   A brockel. That's English for whorehouse.

Meg   I will be thankful to you to keep that kind of talk about whorehouses to yourself. I'm no whore for one.

→ feigned "dignity"!

Pat   Why? Are you losing your union card?

*The **Sailor** sings lustily upstairs.*

Meg   Well, if I'm a whore itself, you don't mind taking the best part of my money. So you're nothing but a ponce.

Pat   Well, I'm saving up to be one. And a long time that will take me with the money you can earn.

Meg   Well, you know what you can do. And shut that bloody row up there.

Colette (*off*)   And you.

Pat (*to* **Meg**)   You ought to know better than to abuse a poor crippled man that lost his leg, three miles outside of Mullingar.

Meg   There's nothing the matter with your leg.

Pat   And how do you think we could keep the house going on what we get from Monsewer? And who would look after him in England or Ireland if I didn't?

Meg   Not me for one.

Pat   Well, I'll stick by him because we were soldiers of Ireland in the old days.

*There is a **Pianist** at one end of the passage area with the piano half on stage and half off.* **Pat** *signals to her and he sings:*

On the eighteenth day of November,
Just outside the town of Macroom,
The Tans in their big Crossley tenders,
Came roaring along to their doom.
But the boys of the column were waiting
With hand grenades primed on the spot,
And the Irish Republican Army
Made shit of the whole mucking lot.

*The foreign **Sailor** sings on.*

Rio Rita   Oh shut up, you dirty foreign bastard.

H-bomb: annihilation.
what is annihilated? living.

→ hungry for a drink of authenticity.

song → draws ppl. triggers curiosity.

While **Pat** *is singing* all the other inhabitants come on to the stage,
join in the song, and stay for a drink.

Meg   You stand there singing about them ould times and
the five glorious years, and yet you sneer and jeer at the
boys of today. What's the difference?

= Belfast boy, Leslie.

Pat   It's the H-bomb. It's such a big bomb it's got me)→?
scared of the little bombs. The IRA is out of date –

→ admits he doesn't like the IRA bc. he's scared.

All   Shame. No.

Pat   – and so is the RAF, the Swiss Guards, the Foreign
Legion, the Red Army –

Sailor   *Niet.*

Pat   – the United States Marines, the Free State Army, the
Coldstream Guards, the Scots Guards, the Welsh Guards,) *guards.*
the Grenadier Guards and the bloody fire guards.
= defence

both are pointless vs. army
when all are dead = offence
already.

Meg   Not the Horse Guards?

→ not himself? other-defined.

A blast on the bagpipes *and* **Monsewer** *enters along the passage*
looking like Baden Powell *in an Irish kilt and flowing cloak. The noise* → *lack of*
from the bagpipes is terrible. Everyone but **Meg** *springs smartly to* *response to*
attention as **Monsewer** *passes and salutes.* **Monsewer** *lives in* *music*
a world of his own, peopled by heroes and enemies. *He spends his time*
making plans for battles fought long ago against enemies long since
dead.

→ but they are populating his world for him.
why play along? → music naturally dictates their action.

Monsewer   *(greets him in Gaelic)*   Cén caoi ina bfuil tu.

Pat   Commandant-General.

Monsewer   As you were, Patrick.

Pat   Thank you, Monsewer.   → *name? pronoun? ambiguous.*

Pat *stands at ease. The rest,* except for **Meg**, *drift away.*

Monsewer *addresses* **Pat** *with a great* show of secrecy.

→ contradictory.

Monsewer   Patrick – preparations.   *Meg doesn't matter.*

Pat   Everything's ready for the guest.   *New IRA.*

Pat: responds clearly to Monsewer's world.
Meg: actively refuses Monsewer.
kinda the same. refusing to live in present vs refusing to understand annihilation.

Monsewer   Good, good. The troops will be coming quite soon.

Pat (*aside*)   The troops! Good God! (*To* **Monsewer**.) How many of them are expected, then?

Monsewer   There will be the two guards and the prisoner.

Pat   The prisoner?

Monsewer   Yes. Yes, we only have the one at the moment, but it's a good beginning.

Pat   Yes, indeed, as the Scotchman says, 'Many a mickle makes a muckle.'

Monsewer   And as we Irish say, 'It's one after another they built the castle. *Iss in yeeg a Kale-ah shah togeock nuh cashlawn.*'

Pat (*to the audience*)   Do you hear that? That's Irish. It's a great thing, an Oxford University education! Me, I'm only a poor ignorant Dublin man, I wouldn't understand a word of it. (*To* **Monsewer**.) About this prisoner, Monsewer.

Monsewer   Yes. An English laddie to be captured on the Border.

Pat   Armagh?

Monsewer   Only one at first, but soon we'll have scores of them.

Pat (*aside*)   I hope to God he's not going to bring them all here.

Monsewer   What's that?

Pat   I say, it's a great thing, the boys being out again, sir.

Monsewer   Absolutely first class. Carry on.

Monsewer *marches off to make more plans.* **Pat** *retires defeated to have another stout.*

Meg   He's a decent old skin, even if he has got a slate loose.

Pat   Did you hear that? It's bad enough turning this place into an IRA barracks. Monsewer wants to make a glasshouse out of it now.

Meg   A what?

Pat   A kind of private Shepton Mallet of his own.

Meg   We should be proud to help the men that are fighting for Ireland. Especially that poor boy to be hanged in Belfast Jail tomorrow morning.

Pat   Why are you getting so upset over Ireland? Where the hell were you in nineteen-sixteen when the real fighting was going on?

Meg   I wasn't born yet.

Pat   You're full of excuses. Where were you when we had to go out and capture our own stuff off of the British Army?

Meg   Capture it? You told me that you bought it off the Tommies in the pub. You said yourself you got a revolver, two hundred rounds of ammunition, and a pair of jodhpurs off a colonel's batman for two pints of Bass and fifty Woodbines.

Pat   I shouldn't have given him anything. But I was sorry for him.

Meg   Why?

Pat   He got my sister in the family way.

Meg   Well, she was a dirty no good . . .

The conversation is interrupted by the rush of feet on the stairs. The **Sailor** *enters, minus his trousers, pursued by* **Colette** *in a dressing gown. The rear is brought up by* **Mulleady**, *a decaying civil servant. The row brings the other people in and the* **Sailor** *is chased into a corner, where a menacing ring of people surrounds him.*

Mulleady   Mr Pat, Mr Pat, that man, he – he's a Russian.

Pat   A what?

[handwritten: religion as type?
↳ acting in the name of Catholiz, but really just
manipulated at their whim.
↳ Teresa = outwardly most Catholic... a sybol f
Mary.]

Mulleady   A Russian. *[handwritten: ↗ doesn't care abt. Russian*
but cares abt. gay.]

Pat   Well, is he dirty or something?

Mulleady   He's a Communist.

Meg   A Communist. *[handwritten: another "type"-ing.]*

[handwritten: Communism = anti-Catholic?]

Colette   Oh now, Pat, it's against my religion to have *[handwritten: but she's a]*
anything to do with the likes of him. *[handwritten: this is another "type" prostitute*
→ to defy this type?]

Pat   You have to pick up trade where you can these days.
The only reason I know for throwing a man out is when he
has no money to pay. *[handwritten: → tolerates only when they can pay. or rather,]*

Meg   Has he got any? *[handwritten: bitchy about poors only.]*

Pat   I'll find out. Have you got any money? Any gelt?
Dollars? Pound notes? Money?

Pat *makes a sign for money.*

Sailor   *Da! Da!*

He produces a big wad of notes. *[handwritten: unspecified?*
in any case he understands English too goo]

Meg   Do you see the wad he has on him?

*The **Sailor** throws the money in the air and beams. They all dive for
the money.*

Meg   Sure, pound notes is the best religion in the world.

Pat   And the best politics, too.

*As they all scrabble and fight for the money on the floor, a voice
thunders from the stairs:*

Monsewer   *[handwritten: interruption.]*
Hark a voice like thunder spake,
The west awake, the west awake.
Sing Oh Hurrah, for Ireland's sake,
Let England quake.

Sailor   *Mir y drushva!* *[handwritten: → this is wrong*
... evidence that he's not Russian!]

[handwritten: Monsewer's song: patriotic.
→ why does the sailor reply?]

Monsewer   *Cén caoi ina bfuil tu.* (*He compliments* **Colette**.)
Carry on, my dear. Ireland needs the work of the women as
well, you know. (*Exit.*)

Colette   Is it all right now?

Pat   Yes, go on.

Colette   Well, I've been to <u>confession</u> three times already
and I don't want to make a mistake about it.

Colette *takes the* **Sailor** *upstairs to bed. The excitement over,
everyone drifts off, leaving* **Mulleady** *with* **Pat** *and* **Meg**.

Mulleady   I'm sorry, Mrs M – I mean about the Russian.
I felt that as a God-fearing man I could shut my eyes no
longer.

Meg   Anybody would think you was doing God a good
turn speaking well of him.

Mulleady   Oh, and another thing – about my laundry,
Miss Meg. It was due back three days ago.

Pat   It walked back.

Mulleady   I have to go to one of my committees this
evening and I haven't a shirt to my name.

Meg   Go and ask the <u>Prisoners' Aid Society</u> to give you
one.

Mulleady   You know very well that is the committee on
which I serve.

Meg   Well, go and wash one.

Mulleady   You know I can't –

Meg   Get going, or I'll ask you for the money you owe me.

Mulleady   Please don't bring all that up again. You know
that at the end of the month . . .

Meg   Are you going?

She drives him out.

Fine thing to be letting rooms to every class of gouger and bowsey in the city.

Pat   Dirty thieves and whores the lot of them. Still, their money is clean enough.

Meg   It's not the whores I mind, it's the likes of that old whited sepulchre that I don't like.

Mulleady *comes downstairs with a filthy shirt and scoots through the room and out of the kitchen door.*

Pat   You don't mean Monsewer?

Meg   No, I don't. I mean that old Mulleady geezer, though Monsewer is bad enough, giving out about the Republic and living in a brockel.

Pat *(hushing her)*   Monsewer doesn't know anything about these matters.

Meg   Course he does, Pat.

Pat   He doesn't.

Meg   He must know.

Pat   No. He thinks everybody in this house are gaels, patriots or Republicans on the run.

Meg   He doesn't, the old idiot! He's here again.

Monsewer *enters, on secret service, carrying a sheaf of despatches and plans.*

Monsewer   Patrick!

Pat   Sir!

Monsewer   As you were.

Pat *stands at ease.*

Pat   Thank you, Monsewer.

Monsewer *(in great confidence)*   Patrick, I trust we may rely on the lads in the billet if anything should go wrong tonight?

Pat   We may put our lives in their hands, Monsewer.

so. strong. betrayal moment.

Meg   God help us.

Monsewer   There was a bit of a rumpus in here a minute ago, wasn't there?

Pat   Strain of battle, Commandant. *→ he deliberately lies.*

Monsewer   Yes, yes. The boys are bound to be a bit restless on a night like this. It's in the air, Patrick – can you smell it?

Like Wellington on the eve of Waterloo, **Pat** *sniffs.*

Pat   No, sir, I'm afraid I can't.

Monsewer   The coming battle. I think you should have a copy of this, Patrick. Battle orders. Plenty of fodder in?

Pat   For the horses, Commandant?

Monsewer   For the men, damn you! The men.

Pat   Oh yes, Monsewer. This is in Irish, Monsewer.

Monsewer   At a time like this, we should refuse to use the English language altogether. *→ the "old" tactic.*

↳ not "use Irish".   *"but then what common language is left? none.*

Monsewer *surveys his imaginary battlefield, planning how he will deploy his forces.*

Pat   Well, you've done your bit on that score, Monsewer. For years Monsewer wouldn't speak anything but Irish.

Chooses to refuse English.

Meg   Most people wouldn't know what he was saying, surely.

Pat   No, they didn't. When he went on a tram or a bus he had to have an interpreter with him so the conductor would know where he wanted to get off. *↳ carry on. does he ever get off the train? well...*   *"trapped"*

Meg   Ah, the poor man. *→ trapped by his choice.*

Monsewer   Patrick. (*He draws him aside.*) Any letters arrived for me from England lately?

Pat   No, sir.

Monsewer   Oh dear. I was relying on my allowance for a few necessities.

Pat   Ah, never mind, sir, we'll keep the kip going somehow.

Meg (*to the audience*)   Sure, he hasn't had a letter from England since they naturalised the Suez Canal.

Monsewer   There's another matter: <u>fellow patriot</u> of ours calls himself <u>Pig-eye</u> – code name, of course. Just served six months in prison for the cause. I told him that, in return, he shall billet here, at our expense, <u>till the end of his days</u>. Carry on.

Monsewer *marches off.*

Pat (*to the audience*)   Pig-eye! He's just done six months for robbery with violence. 'Till the end of his days.' If he doesn't pay his rent, he'll reach the end of his days sooner than he expects.

Meg   Don't you talk to me about that Pig-eye. He's as mean as the grave. A hundred gross of <u>nylons</u> he knocked off the other day, from the Hauty Cotture warehouse, and <u>not one did he offer to a girl in the street</u>. No, bejasus, not even to the one-legged girl in Number 8. The old hypocrite.

Pat   Who? Pig-eye?

Meg   No. Monsewer. He's not as green as he's cabbage-looking. Calling himself 'Monsewer', blowing the head off you with his ould pipes, and not a penny to his name.

Pat   Well, he's loyal to the old cause, and he's a decent old skin.

As **Pat** *begins to tell his story other people from the house edge in:* **Kate**, *the pianist,* **Rio Rita** *in a faded silk dressing gown and his coloured boyfriend,* **Mulleady**, **Colette** *and the* **Sailor** *and* **Old Ropeen**, *a retired whore. They egg* **Pat** *on or mock him, if they dare.*

[handwritten top margin: funny irony. Meg = modern Irish struggle, knows Irish, doesn't like M. Pat = old Irish, doesn't care, no Irish speaker, loves M.]

Meg   Where did he get that monniker for a start? Is it an English name?

Pat   What?

Meg   Monsewer.

Pat   It's French for 'mister', isn't it?

Meg   I don't know. I'm asking you.

Pat   Well, I'm telling you, it is. At one time all the toffs were going mad, talking Irish and only calling themselves by their Irish names.

Meg   You just said it was a French name.

Pat   Will you let me finish for once? What's the Irish for mister?

Ropeen   *R. Goine Vasal.* *[handwritten: → very bastardized version of the actual word.]*

Meg *starts laughing.* *[handwritten: → why? Meg knows.]*
Pat   Yes, well it was too Irish for them, too, so they called themselves Monsieur or Madame as the case might be. *[handwritten: Why is the resolution "French"? revolution? What is "too" Irish?]*

Meg   Ah, they're half mad, these high-up ould ones.

Pat   He wasn't half mad the first time I saw him, nor a quarter mad, God bless him. See that? (*He produces a photo.*) Monsewer on the back of his white horse, the Cross of Christ held high in his right hand, like Brian Boru, leading his men to war and glory. *[handwritten: like magic. again, a mimicked personality. Monsewer = mythical.]*

Meg   Will you look at the poor horse? *[handwritten: = Pat. power, glory… irony.]*

Pat   That was the day we got captured. We could have got out of it, but Monsewer is terrible strict and honest. You see, he's an Englishman. *[handwritten: facing enemy with strict morality.]*

Meg   An Englishman, and him going round in a kilt all day playing his big Gaelic pipes.

Pat   He was born an Englishman, remained one for years. His father was a bishop.

[handwritten bottom margin: Monsewer's definition: either explicit English or mythical Irish.]

Meg   His father was a bishop.

All good Catholics, they start to leave.

Well, I'm not sitting here and listening to that class of immoral talk. His father was a bishop, indeed!

Pat   He was a <u>Protestant bishop</u>.

Meg   Ah well, it's different for them.

They all come back.

Rio Rita   They get married, too, sometimes.

Pat   He went to all the biggest colleges in England and slept in the one room with the King of England's son.

Meg   Begad, it wouldn't surprise me if he slept in the one bed with him, his father being a bishop.

Pat   Yes, he had every class of comfort, <u>mixed</u> with dukes, marquises, earls and lords.

Meg   <u>All sleeping in the one room</u>, I suppose?

Ropeen   <u>In the one bed.</u>

Pat   Will you shut up? As I was saying, he had every class of comfort until one day <u>he discovered he was an Irishman.</u>

Meg   Aren't you after telling me he was an Englishman?

Pat   He was an Anglo-Irishman.

Meg   In the name of God, what's that?

Pat   A Protestant with a horse.

Ropeen   Leadbetter.

Pat   No, no, an ordinary Protestant like Leadbetter, the plumber in the back parlour next door, won't do, nor a Belfast Orangeman, not if he was as black as your boot.

Meg   Why not?

Anglo-Irish: by definition privileged, double-sided.
  → traitor for either side.

Pat   Because they work. An Anglo-Irishman only works at riding horses, drinking whisky and reading double-meaning books in Irish at Trinity College. *double-language.*

Meg   I'm with you he wasn't born an Irishman. He became one.

Pat   He didn't become one – he was born one – on his mother's side, and as he didn't like his father much he went with his mother's people – he became an Irishman.
  ↳ smth about mother > father also   *contradictory.*
Meg   How did he do that? *repeats. by birth/nature but also by nurture/choice.*

Pat   Well, he took it easy at first, wore a kilt, played Gaelic football on Blackheath.

Meg   Where's that?

Pat   In London. He took a correspondence course in the Irish language. And when the Rising took place he acted like a true Irish hero. *not just Irish "man". Irish "hero".* *double meaning. true*

Meg   He came over to live in Ireland. *true*

Meg gets slightly wrong just slightly every time.

Pat   He fought for Ireland with me at his side.

Meg   Aye, we've heard that part of the story before.

Pat   Five years' hard fighting. *duplicity*

Colette   Ah, God help us. *of identity too.*

Ropeen   Heavy and many is the good man that was killed.

Pat   We had the victory – till they signed that curse-of-God *?* treaty in London. They sold the six counties to England and Irishmen were forced to swear an oath of allegiance to the British Crown.

Meg   I don't know about the six counties, but the swearing wouldn't come so hard on you. *banter.*

Ropeen   Whatever made them do it, Mr Pat?

Pat   Well, I'll tell you, Ropeen. It was Lloyd George and Birkenhead made a fool of Michael Collins and he signed an agreement to have no more fighting with England.

Meg   Then he should have been shot.

Pat   He was.

Meg   Ah, the poor man. *full of contradiction. she's heard it yet she "doesn't know"*

Pat   Still, he was a great fighter and he fought well for the ould cause.

Ropeen   They called him 'The Laughing Boy'. *why?*

Pat   They did. *→ Ropeen also already knows, but still asks*

Rio Rita   Give us your song, Pat.

General agreement. *they've all heard the story & know "LB" song.*

Pat   Give us a note, Kate.

He sings the first verse and the others join in, naturally, as they feel moved, into the choruses and the following verses.

Pat

'Twas on an August morning, all in the morning hours,
I went to take the warming air all in the month of flowers,
And there I saw a maiden and heard her mournful cry,
Oh, what will mend my broken heart, I've lost my
    Laughing Boy.

Meg

So strong, so wide, so brave he was, I'll mourn his loss
    too sore
When thinking that we'll hear the laugh or springing step
    no more.

All

Ah, curse the time, and sad the loss my heart to crucify,
Than an Irish son, with a rebel gun, shot down my
    Laughing Boy.
Oh, had he died by Pearse's side, or in the GPO,
Killed by an English bullet from the rifle of the foe,

civil conflict.

Pat's song: Laughing Boy.

Or forcibly fed while Ashe lay dead in the dungeons of
Mountjoy,
I'd have cried with pride at the way he died, my own dear
Laughing Boy.

[handwritten: same death. but enemy death is proud.]
[handwritten: traitor death is mournful.]
[handwritten: fighting tgt for Ireland is pride but betrayal stings.]

Rio Rita   Now one voice.

[handwritten: → this is also out of place. odd.]

Meg
My princely love, can ageless love do more than tell to you
Go *raibh mile maith Agath*, for all you tried to do,
For all you did and would have done, my enemies to
destroy –

All
I'll praise your name and guard your fame, my own dear
Laughing Boy.

[handwritten: ↳ also prison-like.]

Pat   It's a great story.

[handwritten: → I mean in a way imprisonment is like guarding against what you would do.]

Meg   It's better than that show that used to be on the
television below in Tom English's Eagle Bar, *This is Your
Life*.

[handwritten: what is written in your name.]

Pat   It wasn't the end of the story. Some of us wouldn't
accept the treaty. We went on fighting, but we were beat.
Monsewer was loyal to the old cause and I was loyal to
Monsewer. So when the fighting was done we came back
together to this old house.

Meg   This dirty old hole.

Pat   A good hole it was for many a decent man on the run
for twenty years after that.

[handwritten: ↳ actually used as sanctuary!]

Meg   Who the hell was still running twenty years after
that?

[handwritten: → 20 yrs of "disillusionment".]

Pat   All the Republicans who wouldn't accept the treaty.
We put Cosgrave's government in and he had the police
hunting us.

Rio Rita   Then you put de Valera in, and he started
hunting us too.

[handwritten: ?]

Pat   I put de Valera in – what the hell are you talking about?

Rio Rita   I ought to know what I'm talking about – I was Michael Collins's runner in the old days.

Pat   He must have had a thousand bloody runners if you were another one.

Rio Rita   Are you calling me a liar?

Pat   Oh get out.

Rio Rita   You know I was Michael Collins's runner.

Mulleady   That was over thirty years ago – you weren't even born.

Rio Rita   I did my bit in O'Connell Street, with the rest of them.

Ropeen   He did his bit up in O'Connell Street.

Rio Rita   You shut your bloody row – you want to take a bucket of water out with you when you go out the back, you do.

Ropeen   Get out, will you.

She chases him upstairs.

Rio Rita   There you are – look – she's picking on me again. I haven't said a word to her. I won't argue with her – I only upset meself if I argue with that one. I'll go and have a lie down. (*Exits.*)

Meg   Carry on with the coffin, the corpse'll walk.

Pat   Hiding hunted Republicans was all very well, but it didn't pay the rent, so in the end we had to take in all sorts of scruffy lumpers to make the place pay.

Rio Rita (*from the top of the stairs*)   You wouldn't say that to my face.

Pat   This noble old house, which housed so many heroes, was turned into a knocking shop. But I'd you to help me.

Meg   You had me to help you! The curse of God meet and melt you and your rotten lousy leg. You had me to help you, indeed! If I'm a whore itself, sure I'm a true patriot.

Pat   Course you are, course you are. Aren't we husband and wife – nearly? *doesn't quite*

Meg   Well, nearly. *fit the word.*

Pat   Sure, I wasn't referring to you. I was talking about old Ropeen and that musician, and Colette, there's another one.

Colette   I don't have to stay here.

Meg   Don't you talk to me about that Colette, not after what she done to the poor old civil servant out of the Ministry of Pensions.   *↳ why so many civil servants?*
civil servant → serving the public?
we see stupid & hypocrites.

Pat   Never mind that now.

Meg   There was the poor old feller kneeling by the bedside saying his prayers. For Colette to go robbing him   *?* of all his money and him in the presence of Almighty God, so to speak.   *we never hear the full story.*
↳ introduction of another story, another emotion.
The sound of hymn-singing comes from upstairs. Down the stairs **Rio**   *↳ lustful* **Rita** *flies into the room, followed by the* **Negro**, *now in boxing kit*   *Russian* *with gloves on. The other people in the house flood into the room and*   *singing.* *listen to the din.*   *↳ again it's Meg.*

Meg   What the hell's that? What's going on?

Rio Rita *silences the room and tells his story.*   *↳ but actually* *Mulleady's story.*

Rio Rita   I've seen everything, dear. I've seen everything. I was upstairs doing a bit of shadow boxing with my friend.   *euphemism? clearly, but its turned literal too.*

Meg   Where the hell's that row coming from?   *concealment by literality.* *reality.*

Rio Rita   It's that man in the third floor back. He has a strange woman in his room.

Meg   Old Mulleady?

Rio Rita   Three hours he's had her in there, and the noises, it's disgusting. It's all very well you laughing, but it doesn't say much for the rest of <u>us girls</u> in the house.

Ropeen   No, it doesn't, does it?

Meg   Has he got that one-legged girl from Number 8 in there?

Rio Rita   No, she's not even out of the street, let alone the house. A complete stranger – I don't know the woman.

Meg   Well, what sort of woman is it?

Rio Rita   A female woman. *that's enough explanation.*

Meg   Well, the dirty low degenerate old maniac, what does he take this house for?

Colette   They're coming.

Mulleady *and* **Miss Gilchrist** *appear on the stairs, kneeling and* <u>*singing their prayers*</u>*. Their shoes are beside them.*

Mulleady   Let us say a prayer, Miss Gilchrist, and we will be forgiven.

just throwing christian phrases. but deliberate ignoring of what they're saying.

Mulleady'*s hand* <u>*strays*</u> *and gooses* **Miss Gilchrist**.

Miss Gilchrist   *In nomine* – please, Mr Mulleady, let us not fall from grace again.

Mulleady   I'm very sorry, Miss Gilchrist, let not the right hand know what the left hand is doing. Miss Gilchrist, can you –

The hand <u>*strays*</u> *again and strokes* **Miss Gilchrist**'*s tail.*

Meg (*calling*)   Mr Mulleady.

Mulleady   – feel our souls together?

Meg   Mr Mulleady.

The praying and the stroking stop. **Mulleady** *puts on his shoes,* **Miss Gilchrist** *smooths her hair and dress. She looks very prim and proper.*

Mulleady & Gilchrist's song: hymn / prayer. anti-living.

Mulleady   Is that you, Mrs M?

→ respect term again. apology /scared.

Meg   Is it me? Who the hell do you think it is? Will you come down here and bring that shameless bitch down with you?

Mulleady   What do you want? Did you call me, Mrs M?

Meg   If Mulleady is your name, I called you, and I called that low whore you have up there with you. I didn't call her by her name, for I don't know what it is, if she's got one at all. Come down from there, you whore, whoever you are.

Meg *shoos everyone out of the room and hides behind the door.*
Mulleady *enters, sees no one and turns to go, only to find* **Meg** *blocking his path. She thrusts her bosom at him and drives him back onto one of the chairs.*

Mulleady   Mrs M, she might have heard you.

Meg   Who's she when she's at home, and what's she got that I haven't got, I should like to know.   *offence comes from the fact that he chose an outside*

Mulleady   She is a lady.   *"whore" when this B literally a whorehouse.*

Meg   The more shame to her, and don't you go calling me your dear Mrs M. Nor your cheap Mrs M either. What do you mean by bringing whores into this house?

Pat   And it's full of them, coals to Newcastle.

Colette, Ropeen, Rio Rita *and* **Meg** *crowd* **Mulleady** *and sit on his knees, ruffle his hair and tickle him. The* **Negro** *shadow boxes, the* **Sailor** *falls asleep with a bottle of vodka and* **Pat** *takes no part in this.*

Meg   Now, Mr Mulleady, Mr Mulleady, sir, don't you know you could have got anything like that, that you wanted, here?

Rio Rita   Yes, anything.

Meg   I'm surprised at you, so I am. God knows I've stuck by you. Even when that man there was wanting to cast you out into the streets for the low-down dirty old hypocrite that you are.

Mulleady   Thank you, Mrs M. Your blood's worth bottling. →almost passive aggressive.

Meg   Are you all right now?

Mulleady   Oh yes, indeed, thank you.

Meg   Right then. Bring down that brassitute.

Mulleady   Oh, is there any need?

Meg   Fetch her down.

Mulleady (*feebly*)   Miss Gilchrist.

Meg   Louder.

Mulleady   Miss Gilchrist.

Miss Gilchrist   Yes, Mr Mulleady?

Mulleady   Will you come down here a minute, please?

Miss Gilchrist   I haven't finished the first novena, Mr Mulleady.

Meg   I'll give her the first bloody novena!

Mulleady   Mrs M, please. I'll get her down.

Mulleady *climbs the stairs and helps* **Miss Gilchrist** *to her feet. Together they prepare to meet their martyrdom and they march resolutely down the stairs singing (to a corrupt version of Handel's Largo).*

Mulleady *and* **Miss Gilchrist** (*together*) ∂ she refers to herself as
    We are soldiers of the Lord, Miss Gilchrist, 3rd person. odd.
    Forward to battle, forward side by side,
    Degenerates and layabouts cannot daunt us.
    We are sterilised. de-sexualised. =not really living.

Miss Gilchrist *takes a firm stand, whilst* **Mulleady** *hands out religious tracts.* such a show. performance.

Mulleady & Gilchrist sing again: martyrdom! but corrupt. unholy.

Miss Gilchrist   Save your souls, my brothers, my sisters, save your souls. One more sinner saved today. Jesus lives.

Mulleady   This is Miss Gilchrist.   *converting people that are already catholic!*

Meg   In the name of all that's holy, what kind of a name is Gilchrist?   *→ gives definition.*

Miss Gilchrist   It is an old Irish name. In its original form 'Giolla Christ', the servant or gilly of the Lord.   *she's got authenticity. acts very Irish (= religious) in her own way too.*

even her name is such a "type". → Teresa?

Meg   You're a quare-looking gilly of the Lord, you whore.

Miss Gilchrist   I take insults in the name of our blessed Saviour.

Meg   You take anything you can get like a good many more round here. You've been three hours up in his room.

Mulleady   A quarter of an hour, Mrs M.

All   Three hours.   *→ I mean they can't quite verify either.*

Miss Gilchrist   We were speaking of our souls.

Mulleady *and* **Miss Gilchrist** (*together, singing*)
Our souls. Our souls. Our souls.   *→ he says that when stroking her butt p.24.*

This is slurred to sound: 'Our souls. Are souls. Arse-holes.'

Meg   You can leave his soul alone, whatever about your own. And take yourself out of here, before I'm dug out of you.

Miss Gilchrist   I will give you my prayers.

Meg   You can stuff them up your cathedral.   *= ass.*

Miss Gilchrist   I forgive her. She is a poor sinful person.

Meg   And you're a half-time whore.

Pat   Compliments pass when the quality meet.

Miss Gilchrist   Mr Mulleady, come away. This is Sodom and Gomorrah.   *Gilchrist doesn't live here.*

why does she stick around til Act 3?

Meg (*stops him*)   Don't leave us, darlin'.

Mulleady   I can't, Miss Gilchrist, I haven't paid my rent.

Miss Gilchrist   I will pray for you, Eustace. My shoes, please.

Mulleady (*fetching her shoes*)   Will you come back, Miss Gilchrist?

Miss Gilchrist   The Lord will give me the strength. God go with you.

The **Russian Sailor** *goes to grab her. She runs out.*

Mulleady   Evangelina!

Pat   Ships that pass in the night.

Meg   Did you ever see anything like that in you life before? Now are you going to ask for an explanation, or am I?

Pat   Leave me out of it. You brought him here in the first place.

Meg   So I did, God help me. And you can take your face out of here, you simpering little get.

Mulleady *starts to go.*

Meg   Not you, him.

Rio Rita   Me – well, there's gratitude for you. Who told you about him in the first place? I always knew what he was, the dirty old eye-box.

Mulleady   Informer! Butterfly! You painted maypole!

Rio Rita   You filthy old get!

Pat   Hey, what about some rent?

The room clears as if by magic. Only **Rio Rita** *is trapped on the stairs.*

Rio Rita   I wish you wouldn't show me up when I bring a friend into the house.

Pat   Never mind all that. What about the rent? What's his name, anyway?

Rio Rita   Princess Grace.

Pat   I can't put down Princess Grace, can I?

Rio Rita   That's only his name in religion.

Meg   Don't be giving out that talk about religion.

Pat   Well, what's his real name?

Rio Rita   King Kong. (*Exit.*)

A row erupts in the kitchen between **Mulleady** *and* **Ropeen** *and* **Mulleady** *enters, holding his dirty shirt.*

Mulleady   Mr Pat, Mr Pat, she has no right to be in there all morning washing her aspidistra. I only wanted to wash my shirt. (*He recovers his dignity.*) All this fuss about Miss Gilchrist. She merely came to talk religion to me.

Meg   That is the worst kind. You can take it from me.

Pat   From one who knows.

Mulleady   You don't seem aware of my antecedents. My second cousin was a Kilkenny from Kilcock.

Meg   I'll cock you. Take this broom and sweep out your room, you scowing little bollix – take it before I ruin you completely.

She throws a broom at him and he disappears, flicking the old whore with the broom as he goes. Things quieten down and **Pat** *and* **Meg** *take a rest.*

Pat   If the performance is over I'd like a cigarette.

Meg   I sent the skivvy out for them half an hour ago. God knows where she's got to. Have a gollywog.

Pat   What in the hell's name is that?

Meg   It's a French cigarette. I got them off that young attaché case at the French Embassy – that one that thinks all Irishwomen are his mother.

Pat   I don't fancy those. I'll wait for me twenty Afton. Meanwhile I'll sing that famous old song, 'The Hound That Caught the Pubic Hair'. *weird title.*

Meg   You're always announcing these songs, but you never get round to singing them.

↗ somehow announcing ⇔ singing.

↗ he's always gotten around to singing here tho.

Pat   Well, there is a song I sing sometimes.

There's no place on earth like the world
Just between you and me.
There's no place on earth like the world,
Acushla, astore and Mother Machree.

↳ 1910's song/play, 1920s movie. Irish immigrant to US.

Teresa, *the skivvy, runs in. She is a strong, hefty country girl of nineteen, and a bit shy.*

Teresa   Your cigarettes, sir.

Pat   A hundred thousand welcomes. You look lovely. If I wasn't married I'd be exploring you.

"nearly". → always possible.

Teresa   I'm very sorry I was so late, sir.

Meg   Were you lost in the place? *inside the house? or shop?*

↓ very odd.

Teresa   I was, nearly. Shall I get on with the beds, Meg?

Meg   Yes, you might as well.

Pat   Don't be calling me 'sir', there's only one sir in this house and that's Monsewer. Just call me Pat.

Teresa   Pat, sir, there's a man outside.

Meg   Why doesn't he come in?

Teresa   Well, he's just looking around.

Pat   Is he a policeman?

Teresa   Oh no, sir, he looks respectable. *lol.*

Pat's song: the Hound that caught the Pubic Hair.
↗ love, "world just btwn you and me".

Pat Where is he now?

Teresa *goes to the window.*

Teresa He's over there, sir.

Pat I can't see without me glasses. Is he wearing a trench coat and a beret.

Teresa He is, sir. How did you know!?

Meg He's a <u>fortune-teller</u>.

Teresa And he has a <u>badge to say he only speaks Irish</u>.

Pat Begod, then him and me will have to use the deaf and dumb language, for the only bit of Irish I know would get us both prosecuted. That badge makes me think he's an officer.

Teresa He has <u>another to say he doesn't drink</u>.

Pat That means he's a higher officer.

Meg Begod, don't be bringing him in here.

Pat He'll come in, in his own good time. Now, Teresa girl, you haven't been here long but you're a good girl and you can keep your mouth shut.

Teresa Oh yes, sir.

Pat Well, someone's coming to stay here and you'll bring him his meals. Now, if you don't tell a living sinner about it, <u>you can stay here for the rest of your life</u>.

Meg Well, till she's married anyway.

Teresa Thank you, sir. Indeed, I'm very happy here.

Pat You're welcome.

Teresa And I hope you'll be satisfied with my work.

Pat I'd be more satisfied if you were a bit more cheerful and not so serious all the time.

Teresa I've always been a very serious girl.

Sings:

Open the door softly,
Shut it – keep out the draught,
For years and years, I've shed millions of tears,
And never but once have I laughed.

'Twas the time the holy picture fell,
And knocked me old granny cold,
While she knitted and sang an old Irish song,
'Twas by traitors poor old Ulster was sold.

So open the window softly,
For Jaysus' sake, hang the latch,
Come in and lie down, and afterwards
You can ask me what's the catch.

Before these foreign-born bastards, dear,
See you don't let yourself down,
We'll be the Lion and Unicorn,
My Rose unto your Crown.

Meg   Hasn't she got a nice voice, Pat?

Pat   You make a pretty picture. Do you know what you look like, Meg?

Meg   Yes, a whore with a heart of gold. At least, that's what you'd say if you were drunk enough.

*Two men enter and begin examining the room, stamping on the boards, testing the plaster and measuring the walls. The first is a thin-faced fanatic in a trench coat and black beret. He is a part-time **Officer** in the IRA. The second man is Feargus O'Connor, a **Volunteer**. He wears a rubber mackintosh and a shiny black cap. The **IRA Officer** is really a schoolmaster and the **Volunteer** a railway ticket-collector. They survey all exits and escape routes.*

Rio Rita   Is it the sanitary inspector, Pat?

Officer   Filthy – filthy. The whole place is filthy.

*He sees the **Sailor** asleep.*

Handwritten annotations:
- gruesome song
- open → closed
- = Northern Ireland province
- open → open
- sensual. contradictory!
- Meg — Teresa = Meg. confusing.
- you [circled]
- disguise → multiple. part-time officers, sanitary inspector.
- we know why they're really doing this
- → when did he come in? Teresa's song ...
- Teresa's song: also patriotic ... but vulgar. death. (Nor. Ireland lament)

Officer   Get rid of that, will you?

Pat   Who does this belong to?

Colette   That's mine. [handwritten: people = belonging]

Rio Rita   Let me give you a hand with him.

Colette   Keep your begrudging hands off him.

She exits with the **Sailor**.

Officer   Who's in charge here?

Pat   I am.

Officer   Your cellar's full of rubbish.

Pat   Oh, there's no rubbish there. No, I'll tell you what there is in there. There's the contents of an entire house which nearly fell down a couple of weeks ago. [handwritten: this is so random.]

Officer   What are these people doing here? [handwritten: we never even use the cellar.]

Pat   Well, that's Meg and that's Teresa . . .

Officer   Get 'em out of here.

Pat   You'd better go – get out.

Meg   Come on, Teresa – if they want to play toy soldiers we'll leave them to it.

All leave except **Pat**, **IRA Officer** *and* **Volunteer**.

The **Volunteer** *makes lists.*

Officer   You'll have to get that cellar cleared; it's an escape route.

Pat   Yes, sir.

Officer   Here's a list of your instructions; it's in triplicate, one for you, one for me and one for HQ. When you've read and digested them, append your signature and destroy your copy. Do you have the Gaelic?

Pat   No, I'm afraid I don't.

Officer   Then we'll have to speak in English. Have you food sufficient for three people for one day?

Pat   There's always plenty of scoff in this house.

Officer   May I see your toilet arrangements, please?

Pat   Oh yes, just through that door – no, not that one – there. There's plenty of paper, and mind your head as you go in.

*The **IRA Officer** goes.*

Monsewer (*off*)   I'm in here.

He comes out.

No damned privacy in this house at all. Laddie from HQ?

Pat   Yes, sir.

Monsewer   Damned ill-mannered.

*Exit. The **IRA Officer** returns.*

Officer   Who the hell was that?

Pat   My old mother.

Officer   Can we be serious, please?

Pat   Can I offer you any refreshment?

Officer   I neither eat nor drink when I'm on duty.

Pat   A bottle of stout?

Officer   Teetotal. I might take a bottle of orange and me after dancing the high caul cap in a Gaelic measurement at an Irish ceilidh, but not at any other time.

Pat   Well, no one would blame you for that.

Officer   Rent book, please.

Pat   Are you thinking of moving in?

Officer   I wish to see a list of tenants.

Pat *takes out a very old, dilapidated rent book.*

Pat   Well, there's Bobo, The Mouse, is Ropeen still here?
– Mulleady.

The people of the house look round the doors and whisper at **Pat.**

Get out, will you?

Goes back to book.

Colette – ey, this one's been dead for weeks, I hope he's not
still there. Rio Rita, Kate, Meg . . . Well, that's all I know
about – there might be some more about somewhere.

Officer   If it was my doings, there'd be no such thing as us
coming here at all. And the filthy reputation this house has
throughout the city.

Pat   Can't think how you came to hear about it at all,
a clean-living man like yourself.

Officer   I do charitable work round here for the St
Vincent de Paul Society. Padraig Pearse said, 'To serve a
cause that is splendid and holy, the man himself must be
splendid and holy.'

Pat   Are you splendid, or just holy? Rent in advance, four
pounds.

Officer   Is it money you're looking for?

Pat   We're not all working for St Vincent de Paul.

Officer   Will you leave St Vincent out of it, please.

Pat   Begod, and I will. (*To the audience.*) St Vincent de Paul
Society! They're all ex-policemen. In the old days we
wouldn't go anywhere near them.

Officer   In the old days there were nothing but
Communists in the IRA.

Pat   There were some. What of that?

Officer   Today the movement is purged of the old dross. It has found its spiritual strength.

Pat   Where did it find that?

Officer   'The man who is most loyal to the faith is the one who is most loyal to the cause.' → *pseudo-religious feel.*

Pat   Haven't you got your initials mixed up? Are you in the IRA or the FBI?

Officer   You're an old man, don't take advantage of it.

Pat   I was out in 1916.

somehow an important thread.

Officer   And lost your leg, they tell me.

well-known tale.

Pat   More than that. You wouldn't recall, I suppose, the time in County Kerry when the agricultural labourers took over five thousand acres of land from Lord Tralee?

Officer   No, I would not. *Pat lives in a diff. memory space from other*

Pat   1925 it was. They had it all divided fair and square and were ploughing and planting in great style. IRA HQ sent down orders that they were to get off the land. That social question would be settled when we'd won the thirty-two-county republic.

Officer   Quite right, too.

Pat   The Kerry men said they weren't greedy, they didn't want the whole thirty-two counties, their own five thousand acres would do 'em for a start.

Officer   Those men were wrong on the social question.

Pat   It wasn't the question they were interested in, but the answers. Anyway, I agreed with them. I stayed there and trained a unit. By the time I'd finished we could take on the IRA, the Free State Army, or the British bloody Navy, if it came to it.

self-defence against IRA.

Officer   That was mutiny. You should have been court-martialled.

Pat   I was. Court-martialled in my absence, sentenced to death in my absence. So I said, right, you can shoot me – in my absence.

Officer   I was told to come here. They must have known what I was coming to. You can understand their reasons for choosing it, the police would never believe we'd use this place. At least you can't be an informer.

English police is the enemy. ↳ *bc. pat is so antagonistic to the cause. only doing it. bc. prisoner is doing it.*

Pat   You're a shocking decent person. Could you give me a testimonial in case I wanted to get a job on the Corporation?

Officer   I was sent here to arrange certain business. I intend to conclude that business.

Pat   Very well, let us proceed, shall we? When may we expect the prisoner?

Officer   Tonight.

Pat   What time?

Officer   Between nine and twelve.

Pat   Where is he now?

this is somewhat contradictory. we can't tell the time

Officer   We haven't got him yet.

Pat   Are you going to Woolworth's to buy one?

Officer   I have no business telling you more than has already been communicated to you. The arrangements are made for his reception.

raised it lol.

Pat   All except the five pounds for the rent.

Officer   I told you I haven't got it.

Pat   Then you'd better get it before your man arrives, or I'll throw the lot of you, prisoner and escort, out – *shun*!

Officer   I wouldn't be too sure about that if I were you.

Meg *and* **Teresa** *come in.*

Meg   Can we come in now, Pat?

Pat   What do you want?

Meg   We want to put the sheets on the bed.

There is a blurt of mechanical sound and a commotion upstairs.
Everyone in the house rushes in to listen to a portable radio that
Colette *is carrying.*

Rio Rita   Mr Pat, Mr Pat!

Pat   What is it?

Rio Rita   It's about the boy in the Belfast Jail. They've
refused a reprieve.

Mulleady   The Lord Lieutenant said tomorrow morning,
eight o'clock. No reprieve final.

Ropeen   The boy – the boy in the Belfast Jail?

Mulleady   Yes – made on behalf of the Government of
Northern Ireland.

Colette   I've lost it now.

The radio blurts out music.   interjection attempted
                                    ↓ failed.
Pat   Turn the bloody thing off.
                         → living cannot be mixed w. dead.
Silence.

Meg   God help us all.

Teresa   The poor boy.

Ropeen   Eight o'clock in the morning, think of it.

Meg   Ah sure, they might have mercy on him yet.
Eighteen years of age –

Officer   Irishmen have been hanged by Englishmen at
eighteen years of age before now.

Pat   Yes, and Cypriots, Jews and Africans.
                    oh wow, Pat "universalizes" first. Ireland is not
Meg   Did you read about them black fellers? Perhaps Mr   special
de Valera could do something about it.
                                    ↓
                              not worth
                              fighting
                    → but maybe it's
                       worth bc. of

Pat *and* **Officer** *(together for once, and with great contempt)*   Mr de Valera!

Meg   I'm sure he could stop it if he wanted to. They say he's a very clever man. They say he can speak seven languages.

[handwritten: → why say this? what reference?]

Pat   It's a terrible pity that English or Irish are not among them, so we'd know what he was saying at odd times.

Rio Rita   Quiet everybody, something's coming through.

Colette *repeats the news item from the radio and is echoed by* **Mulleady**, **Ropeen**, **Rio Rita**, *and* **Teresa**:

[handwritten: → they have got him already! I guess the news didn't reach yet.]

'Early today, a young British soldier was captured as he was coming out of a dance hall in Armagh by the IRA. He was put into the back of a car and when last seen was speeding towards the border. All troops have been alerted . . .'

Officer   Turn it off, Patrick, get these people out of here.

Pat   I can't do that without making a show of ourselves.

Officer   Then come outside with me.

Pat, **IRA Officer** *and* **Volunteer** *go out.*

Rio Rita   Who is that man, anyway?

[handwritten: → that's not true. covering? or confused.]

Meg   He's just come about the rent. He's an IRA Officer.

Mulleady   That poor boy waiting all night for the screws coming for him in the morning.

Meg   Shut up, will you?

Mulleady   I know just how he feels.

Meg   How do you know?

Mulleady   Well, I was in prison myself once.

Meg   Oh, yes, he was. I forgot. *[handwritten: Meg agrees. why?]*

Rio Rita   Mountjoy?

Mulleady   As a matter of fact, it was.

Rio Rita   So was I – I'll get you a drink.

They all sit at **Mulleady**'s *feet.*

Mulleady   I was in a cell next to a condemned man.

Rio Rita   What were you in for?

Mulleady   It was the *Pall Mall Gazette* in 1919.

Colette   The what?

Mulleady   The *Pall Mall Gazette*.

Colette   What's that?

Mulleady   A magazine. There was an advertisement in it for an insurance company and I put all my savings into it. And in return I was to receive an annuity of twenty pounds a year.

Meg   Well, that's not such a vast sum.

Ropeen   It was in those days.

Mulleady   Yes, that's the point. When the annuity was due the value of money had declined, so I ran off with the church funds.

[handwritten: remembering church money. religion is the first to go when things go away.]

Meg   That was a filthy thing to do.

Mulleady   They put me into prison for that.

Rio Rita   What about the boy in the condemned cell? What had he done?   *[handwritten: slight difference, condemned man.]*

Mulleady   Yes, now this is interesting. Flynn, I think his name was. He disposed of his wife and a chicken down a well. Said it was an accident. Said his wife fell down the well trying to retrieve the chicken, but, unfortunately, the police found the wife under the chicken.   *[handwritten: stupid police.]*

Colette   How long were you in for?

Mulleady   Three years.

Rio Rita   You don't look it, dear.

Mulleady   All this time my younger brother was travelling all over the world.

Rio Rita   They do – don't they?

Mulleady   Visited every capital in Europe, saw Cardiff, Liverpool, Middlesbrough, went to London – saw Marie Lloyd every night, at the Tivoli.

Ropeen   Marie Lloyd! She was lovely.

Mulleady   She may have been, but all that time I was in prison. It broke my poor mother's heart. *he never gets anywhere with his story. Meg takes it.*

Meg   Well, I never caused my poor mother any sorrow, for I never <u>knew</u> her.

Mulleady   You never <u>had</u> a mother. How very sad. *distortion. there are lots of these.*

Meg   I never heard of any living person that didn't have a mother, though I know plenty that don't have fathers. I had one, but I never saw her. *↳ this is untrue but the sentiment is true.*

All   How sad – <u>I never knew my mother</u> – Never to know <u>your mother</u>. *collective emotion.*

Meg   Are you lot going to sit there all night moaning about your mothers? Did you sweep out your room? *→ Meg is literally his mother, why?*

Mulleady   Well, no.

Meg   Well, go out and get us twelve of stout.

Mulleady *goes and <u>talks with</u>* **Kate***, the pianist.* *about what? only time... she retrieves booze?*

Meg   We've run dry by the look of it. And if you're going to sit there you can give us a hand with the beds.

Colette   Do you mind – I've been flat on my back all day.

Mulleady   Kate says the credit has run out.

Meg   Oh Kate, I've got a terrible drought on me.

Rio Rita   I'll tell you what I'll do – I'll run down to the docks and see if I can pick up a sailor – and I'll bring back a crate of Guinness. (*Exit.*)

→ sexual appeal = drink.
pleasures entangled together: all living.

Meg   Bring the beer back here.

Ropeen   And the sailor.

Ropeen, **Mulleady** *and* **Colette** *go.* **Teresa** *and* **Meg** *start to make the bed.*

Teresa   There's some very strange people in this house.

Meg   There's some very strange people in the world.

Teresa   I like that big feller. There was no one like him in the convent. *all gender norms & division, this house = place of free norms are broken.*

Meg   Do you mean Rio Rita?

Teresa   Yes, it's a gas name, isn't it?

Meg   How long have you been out of the convent?

Teresa   I've just had the one job with the family in Drumcondra.

Meg   Why did you leave there? Did you half-inch something?

Teresa   What did you say?

Meg   Did you half-inch something?

Teresa   I never stole anything in my whole life.

Meg   There's no need to get so upset about it. I never stole anything either. The grand chances I had, too! God doesn't give us these chances twice in a lifetime.

Teresa   It wasn't that; you see, there was a clerical student in the house. *irony of religion, religious → more bad*

Meg   Well, as far as that's concerned, you'll be a lot safer here. Do the nuns know you left that job in Drumcondra?

Teresa   Oh, no, and they wouldn't be a bit pleased. → *a bit of "m's chief" in her life.*

Meg   Well, don't say anything to Pat about it. It doesn't do to tell men everything. Here he comes now – don't forget.

Pat *and* **Monsewer** *enter from* <u>*opposite sides*</u> *along the passageway.*

[like officer + volunteer marching & guarding in Act 2.]

Meg   Oh, isn't it terrible, Pat? About that poor young man. There's to be no reprieve. Wouldn't it break your heart to be thinking about it?

Monsewer   It doesn't break my heart.

Pat (*softly*)   It's not your neck they're breaking either.

Monsewer   It doesn't make me unhappy. It makes me proud; proud to know that the old cause is not dead yet, and that there are still young men willing and ready to go out and die for Ireland.

Pat   I'd say that young man will be in the presence of the Irish martyrs of eight hundred years ago just after eight o'clock tomorrow morning.

Monsewer   He will. He will. With God's help, he'll be in the <u>company of the heroes</u>. [< his house is also that]

Pat   My life on yer!

Monsewer   I would give anything to stand in that young man's place tomorrow morning. For Ireland's sake I would hang crucified in the town square. [BS.] [talk ever]

Pat   Let's hope it would be a fine day for you.

Monsewer   I think he's very lucky.

Pat   Very lucky – it's a great pity he didn't buy a sweepstake ticket. (*Coming to* **Monsewer**.) You were always a straight man, General, if I may call you by your <u>Christian</u> name. Well, everything is ready for the guest. [↳ doesn't mean anything. rather, Christian name = old title. eusbative.]

Monsewer   Good. (*Exit.*)

Exit **Pat** *slowly, singing to himself the third verse of '<u>The Laughing Boy</u>' – 'Oh, had he died by Pearse's side, or in the GPO.'* [↳ Irish betrayal. →Belfast by 13 no]

Teresa   Wasn't that ridiculous talk that <u>old one</u> had out of him? [so real.] [diff? ↳ Teresa doesn't know Monsewer?]

[Pat's song: Laughing Boy (again – hummed).]

Meg   Well, Monsewer doesn't look at it like an ordinary person. Monsewer is very given to Ireland and to things of that sort.

Teresa   I think he's an old idiot. → Teresa has frankness.

Meg   Monsewer an old idiot? I'll have you know he went to all the biggest colleges in England, → same definition as before. did he jump around or what.

Teresa   It's all the same where he went. He is mad to say that the death of a young man will make him happy. but that doesn't guara tee anyth

Meg   Well, the boy himself said when they sentenced him to death that he was proud and happy to die for Ireland.

Teresa   Ah, but sure, Meg, he hasn't lived yet. yeah.

Meg   Have you? → existence as a patriot onl B not living. (Meg is keen hanging w.

Teresa   A girl of eighteen knows more than a boy of eighteen. "strange people

Meg   You could easy do that. That poor young man, he gave no love to any, except to Ireland, and instead of breaking his heart for a girl, it was about the Cause he was breaking it.

Teresa   Well, his white young neck will be broken tomorrow morning anyway. too descriptive. vulgarity.

Meg   Well, it's no use mourning him before his time. Come on, Kate, give us a bit of music; let's cheer ourselves up. s but they can't help.

The pianist plays a reel and **Meg** *and* **Teresa** *dance. Gradually everyone else in the house hears the music and comes to join in, until* all of them coming together *everyone is caught up in a swirling interweaving dance. Through this dance the* **Soldier** *is pushed by the two IRA men. He is blindfolded. The dancing falters and the music peters out as the blindfold is whipped from his eyes.* → dropped in the midst of "living"!

Soldier   Don't stop. I like dancing. oddly cheerful.

Officer   Keep your mouth shut, and get up there.

The **Soldier** *walks slowly up into the room, then turns and sings.*

Soldier

There's no place on earth like the world,
There's no place wherever you be.

All

There's no place on earth like the world,
That's straight up and take it from me.

Women

Never throw stones at your mother,
You'll be sorry for it when she's dead.

Men

Never throw stones at your mother,
Throw bricks at your father instead.

Monsewer

The South and the North Poles are parted,

Meg

Perhaps it is all for the best.

Pat

Till the H-bomb will bring them together,

All

And there we will let matters rest.

Curtain.

[handwritten: → annihilation. death as unter... for all martyrs?]

[handwritten bottom: Leslie's song: Hound & Pubic Hair... but variation with their persons. not a love & patriotic song anymore.]

Act Two

*Later in the same day. The **Soldier** is confined in the room. The passage is dark and the lights in the rest of the house are low. The **IRA Officer** and the **Volunteer** march along the passage on alternating beats, peering out into the darkness and waiting for a surprise attack that they fear may come. The **Volunteer** carries an old rifle.*

*The house appears to be still, but in the dark corners and doorways, behind the piano and under the stairs, people are hiding, waiting for an opportunity to contact the prisoner, to see what he looks like and to take him comforts like cups of tea, Bible tracts, cigarettes and stout. As soon as the **IRA Officer** and the **Volunteer** turn their backs, a scurry of movement is seen and hisses and low whistles are heard. When the IRA men turn to look there is silence and stillness. The IRA men are growing more and more nervous.*

Soldier (*as the **Volunteer** passes him on his sentry beat*)   Psst!

*The **Volunteer** ignores him, marks time and marches off fast. He re-enters cautiously and marches along his beat.*

Soldier   Psst!

*The **Volunteer** peers into the darkness and turns to go.*

Soldier   Halt!

*The **Volunteer** drops his rifle in fright, recovers it and threatens the **Soldier** as the **IRA Officer** comes dashing in. In the corners there is a faint scuttling as people hide away.*

Officer   What's going on here?

Soldier   Any chance of a cigarette?

Officer   I don't smoke.

Soldier   How about you?

Volunteer   I don't indulge meself.

*He waits until the **IRA Officer** has left.*

Volunteer   Ey, you'll get a cup of tea in a minute.

He marches off.

Soldier   Smashing.

'I'll get a nice cuppa tea in the morning,
A nice cuppa tea . . . '

Officer (*rushing back*)   What's the <u>matter</u> now?

Soldier   Nothing.

The **Volunteer** *reappears.*

Officer   What's all the noise about?

Soldier   I just wondered if she might be bringing my tea.

Officer   Who's she?

Soldier   You know, the red-headed one – the one we saw
first. Bit of all right.

Officer   Guard, keep him covered. I'll go and see about
his tea.

The **IRA Officer** *goes to see about the* **Soldier**'s *tea. The*
Volunteer <u>resumes his beat</u>. *As he turns to go, all hell breaks loose
and everyone tries to get to the* **Soldier** *at once. People hare through
the room at breakneck speed, leaving the* **Soldier** *with stout, hymn
sheets, aspidistras, and words of comfort.*

Colette   Five minutes – upstairs – I won't charge you.

The **Volunteer** *attempts to stop them all at once and only gets more
and more confused until* **Pat** *enters and drives everyone offstage. The
lines of this scene are largely improvised to suit the situation.*

Pat   Come on, out of here, you lot. Get out, will you!

Ropeen   I'm only going to the piano.

They all go and **Pat** *calls* **Teresa**. **Pat** *and the* **Volunteer** *leave
as* **Teresa** *comes downstairs with the* **Soldier**'s *tea on a tray. She
goes to leave straight away, but he stops her.*

Soldier   Ey! <u>I liked your dancing</u> . . . you know, the <u>old</u>
knees-up . . . Is that mine?

Teresa   Yes, it's your tea – sure you must be starving. Your belly must be stuck to your back with hunger. ✓ same thing twice.

Soldier   A bit of all right, isn't it?

Teresa   You're lucky. Meg gave you two rashers. bacon.

Soldier   Did she now?

Teresa   She said you must have double the meal of a grown person.

Soldier   Why's that? guessing game. for what reason?

Teresa   Because you have two jobs to do.

Soldier   What are they?

Teresa   To grow up big and strong like all lads.

Soldier   Here, I'm older than you, I bet.

Teresa   I think you look like a young lad.

Soldier   You look like a kid yourself. How old are you?

Teresa   I'm nineteen. ~ unsure if this is a lie too. and she imply she's 18? she's 19.

Soldier   Are you? I'm nineteen, too. When's your date of birth?

Teresa   January. Twenty-fifth of January. When were you born?

Soldier   August. (*He is shamed.*)

Teresa   So you see, I'm older than you.

Soldier   Only a few weeks. half a year.

Teresa   What name do we call you? → Who? people of the house? Ireland? why ask like this? "others"? what is your preferred name

Soldier   Leslie. What's yours?

Teresa   Teresa.

Soldier   Teresa. That's proper Irish, ain't it?

Teresa   Well, it is Irish. Leslie "types" her.

vs. what name do we call you. → present. active.

Soldier   Yeah, <u>that's what I said</u>. Teresa, you haven't got a fag have you?

Teresa   A what?

Soldier   A fag.

He makes a gesture with his fingers for a fag, which **Teresa** *thinks is an <u>invitation to bed</u>.*

Smoke – cigarette.

Teresa   No, thank you. I don't smoke.

Soldier   No, not for you – for me.

Teresa   Oh, for you. Wait a minute. Look, it's only a bit crushed. Pat gave it to me.

She gives him a crumpled cigarette.

Soldier   Have you got a match? They took mine.

Teresa *gives him matches.*

Soldier   Hey, don't go. I suppose you couldn't get me a packet?

Teresa   I'll get you twenty Afton.

Soldier   Oh no. I mean – thanks, anyway. Ten'll do.

Teresa   You don't fancy the Irish cigarettes?

Soldier   What? The old Aftons? I love 'em. Smoke 'em by the barrer-load.

Teresa   I'll get you twenty. You've a <u>long night</u> ahead of you.

Teresa *gets <u>money from</u>* **Kate**, *the pianist, who is standing offstage. The* **Soldier**, *left completely alone for the first time, has a quick run round the room, looking through doors and windows. He lifts the clothes and looks under the bed.* **Teresa** *returns.*

Teresa   Are you looking for something.?

Soldier   No. Yes, an ashtray.

Teresa   Under the bed?

Soldier   Well, I might have been looking for the in and the out, mightn't I?

Teresa   What?

Soldier   The way out. I'm a prisoner, ain't I?

Teresa   I'd better go.

Soldier   You'll be back with the fags?

Teresa   I might. I only work here, you know.

She goes, and the **Soldier** *moves to all the doors in turn and calls out:*

Soldier   Hey! Charlie! Buffalo Bill!

The **Volunteer** *rushes on, thinking an attack has started, does not see the* **Soldier** *in the corner of the room and prepares to defend the front. The* **Soldier** *calls him back and whispers to him.* **Pat** *comes downstairs.*

Pat   What's he saying?

Volunteer   He wants to go round the back, sir.

Pat   Well, he can, can't he?

Volunteer   No, sir. I'm in the same plight myself, but I can't leave me post for two hours yet.

Pat   Why don't you both go?

Volunteer   We'll have to ask the officer.

Pat   Well, I'll call him. Sir, St Patrick, Sir.

The **IRA Officer** *enters in a panic.*

Officer   What the hell's going on here?

Pat   It's your man here . . .

The **IRA Officer** *silences him and leads him out into the passage.* **Pat** *whispers in his ear. The* **IRA Officer** *comes to attention.*

Pat (*to the audience*)   A man wants to go round the back and it's a military secret.

Officer   Right. Prisoner and escort, fall in.

Pat *and the* **Volunteer** *fall in on either side of the* **Soldier**.

Officer   Prisoner and escort, right turn. By the front, quick march . . . Left . . . right.

They march right round the room to the lavatory door.

HALT! Prisoner, fall out. You two, guard the door.

Teresa *rushes into the room with the twenty Afton, sees the* **IRA Officer** *and starts to rush out again, but he spots her.*

Officer   You girl, come back here. What are you doing here?

Teresa   I was just going to give him his cigarettes, sir.

Officer   What is this man to you?

Teresa   Nothing, sir.

Officer   Give them to me.

Teresa   But they're his.

Officer   Give them to me.

She gives him the cigarettes. The parade returns.

Pat   Fall in. Quick march – left right, etc. Halt. One man relieved, sir.

Volunteer   What about me?

Officer   Silence.

Teresa   Where has he been?

Pat   Doing a job that no one else could do for him.

Teresa   Leslie, I got you . . .

Officer   That's enough. Get along with you, girl. About your business.

Exit **Teresa**. **IRA Officer** *watches her go.*

Officer   Patrick, is that girl all right?

Pat   Oh, come on, sir. You don't want to be thinking about that, and you on duty, too.

[handwritten: ↳ what does he imply. oh Teresa's "quality" as prostitute.]

Officer   I mean will she keep her mouth shut?

[handwritten: this is also a type.]

Pat   Sure now, you know what women are like. They're always talking about these things – did you have a bit last night? But I don't think she'd fancy you somehow.

Officer   I'm asking you if she's to be trusted.

Pat   You mean would she help your man to escape?

Officer   Now you have it.

[handwritten: ↳ her integrity, but also she's a "runaway" in a sense]

Pat   She'd do nothing to bring the police here. And as for helping him get away, she's all for keeping him here. They're getting along very well, those two.

Officer   Yes, a bit too well for my liking.

[handwritten: like the song, cigarette, story ...]

Pat   Well, <u>she's passing the time for him.</u> Better than having him fighting and all. Sure, they're getting along like a couple of budger<u>iguards.</u>

[handwritten: ↳ wordplay on budgerigar, type of parrot, guarding each other? Aim who ...]

Officer   This is no laughing matter, you idiot.

Pat   You know, there are two kinds of gunmen. The earnest, religious-minded ones like you, and the <u>laughing boys.</u>

[handwritten: ↳ who got shot fellow Irishman]

Officer   Like you.

Pat   Well, you know, in the time of the troubles it was always the laughing boys who were most handy with the skit.

Officer   Why?

Pat   Because <u>it's not a natural thing for a man with a sense of humour to be tricking with firearms and fighting.</u> There must be something <u>wrong</u> with him.

[handwritten: pronouns = categorization. → laughing boys = one screw loose.]

Officer   There must be something the matter with you, then.

Pat   Of course there is. Ey, what about the money for the rent?

Officer   At this moment the hearts of all true Irishmen are beating for us, fighting as we are to save the Belfast martyr, and all you can think about is money.

grand name.
— are they fighting? nobody cares

Pat   Well, you see, I'm not a hero. I'm what you might call an ex-hero. And if we get raided . . .

abt. Leslie.
"ex" is another powerful term. he says that another time.

Officer   I refuse to envisage such a possibility.

Pat   All the same, if we are raided. You can say I only did it for the money.

Officer   We shall fight to the death.

Pat   You're all in the running for a hero's death.

Officer   I hope I would never betray my trust.

Pat   You've never been in prison for the cause.

Officer   No. I have not.

Pat   That's easily seen.

Officer   You have, of course.

Pat   Nine years, in all.

Officer   Nine years in English prisons?

Pat   Irish prisons part of the time.   *betrayer. laughing boy.*

Officer   The loss of liberty is a terrible thing.

↳ but these ppl. are already un-liberated. what diff. does it make?

Pat   That's not the worst thing, nor the redcaps, nor the screws. Do you know what the worst thing is?

Officer   No.

Pat   The other Irish patriots in along with you.

Officer   What did you say?

Pat   Your fellow patriots, in along with you. There'd be a split straight away.

↳ of the two types?

Officer   If I didn't know you were out in 1916 . . .

Bagpipes have been playing in the distance and the sound comes steadily nearer. Everyone in the house crowds down into the passage area and stares out front as though they are looking through two windows, straining to get a sight of the procession in the street.

Meg   Teresa – Teresa – it's a band!

Pat   What's going on?

Meg   They're marching to the GPO over the boy that's being hung in the Belfast Jail.

Pat   It's like Jim Larkin's funeral.

Volunteer   Plenty of police about.

Monsewer   By Jove, look at those banners. 'Another victim for occupied Ireland.'

Meg   'England, the hangman of thousands. In Ireland, in Kenya, in Cyprus.'

Mulleady   'Release the Belfast martyr!'

Meg   The world will see a day when England will be that low you won't be able to walk on her.

Rio Rita   'Eighteen years of age, in jail for Ireland.'

Ropeen *and* **Colette**   Ah, the poor boy.

Meg   Oh, the murdering bastards.

*The **Soldier** comes down to the front of the stage and tries to explain to the audience what is happening.*

Soldier   You know what they're on about, don't you? This bloke in the Belfast Jail who's going to be topped tomorrow morning. You read about it, didn't you? Papers were full of it over here – headlines that big. He's only eighteen, same age as us National Service blokes. Anyway, they got him, and tomorrow they're going to do him in – eight o'clock in the morning.

The pipes fade away and the groups break up. [handwritten: crowd comes in w music again.]

Meg   That's the end of it.

Pat   Thanks be to God we don't all go that way. [handwritten: → way of marching & martyrdom.]

Monsewer   It was a good turn-out, Patrick. [handwritten: → as if he organized it.]

He leaves.

Pat   It was, sir. [handwritten: → answering to nobody.]

Miss Gilchrist   I shan't sleep a wink all night.

Rio Rita   Ah, you murdering bastard. Why don't you go back home to your own country? [handwritten: → this is another generalization.]

Soldier   You can take me out of it as soon as you like. I never bloody well asked to be brought here.

The first person to take advantage of the **IRA Officer**'s *absence and the* **Volunteer**'s *confusion is* **Miss Gilchrist**. *While the* **Volunteer** *is striving to keep* **Mulleady** *and* **Colette** *out of the room,* **Miss Gilchrist** *slips behind his back, the* **Volunteer** *turns, and soon* **Mulleady**, **Colette** *and* **Ropeen** *are inside the room with* **Miss Gilchrist**. *They crowd round the* **Soldier** *and paw and stroke him.* [handwritten: → Miss Gilchrist → very Christian, also very determined actor.] [handwritten: → he's also in the crowd. homoerotic foreshadowing? why is he obsessed?]

Miss Gilchrist   Is this the English boy? May I give him a little gift? [handwritten: another generalization.]

Pat   What is it?

Miss Gilchrist   It's an article from a newspaper and as it's about his own dear Queen, I thought it might comfort him.

Pat   Come here.

Miss Gilchrist   No, Mr Pat, I insist. (*She reads from a paper.* *) It's from the *Daily Express* and it's called 'Within the Palace Walls'. 'Within the Palace Walls. So much is known

[handwritten: → on one level it's just a word salad. any language will do, since he himself is a nondescript identity.]

* The extract was varied to keep it as topical as possible within the context of the scene.

[handwritten: on another level, privacy/exposure. life... feeding him in artificial life.]

of the Queen's life on the surface, so little about how her life is really run. But now this article has been written with the active help of the Queen's closest advisers.' *It's nother tho. one degree removed.*

Soldier   No, thank you, ma'am, I don't go in for that sort of mullarkey. Haven't you got something else?

Mulleady   Evangelina!

Miss Gilchrist   Who calls? *grand. as if she doesn't hear.*

Mulleady   Me! Me! Me! Me! Bookie, please! Please!

Miss Gilchrist   Well, if the boy doesn't want it . . .

Soldier   Quite sure, thank you, ma'am.

Mulleady   May I read on, please?

Miss Gilchrist   Go on, Eustace. *(stop* *why?? it's like he's adding more w*

Mulleady (*savouring and drooling over each phrase*)   'Because it *to his* is completely fresh, probing hitherto unreported aspects of *ident* her problems, this intriguing new serial lays before you the *literal* true pattern of the Queen's life with understanding, intimacy *consum* and detail.' Oh, may I keep it, Miss Gilchrist? *word* *filling*

Pat   Give it here. *unionist? "secrecy" reveated?* *what fac* *fetishising?*

He snatches the paper from **Mulleady**.

Pat   We don't go in for that sort of nonsense.

He looks at the article.

Would you believe it. It's by an Irishman. Dermot Morrah!

Rio Rita   I don't believe it.

Meg   Never! And she calls herself an Irishwoman, the silly bitch. *who? Gilchrist? why is the writer being Irish an issue?*

The Irish patriots leave the stage. Those remaining in the room are pro-English, sentimental, or both. **Miss Gilchrist** *comes down to address the audience.*

Miss Gilchrist   I have nothing against the Royal Family.
I think they're all lovely, especially that Sister Rowe and
Uffa Fox. I get all the Sunday papers to follow them up.
One paper contradicts another, but you put two and two
together – and you might almost be in the yacht there with
them. And there's that Mrs Dale, she's a desperate nice
woman. I always send her a bunch of flowers on her birthday.
They even have an Irishman in it, a Mr O'Malley. He keeps
a hotel, like you, Mr Pat.*

Pat *has gone long ago.*

Mulleady (*picking up the paper from where* **Pat** *threw it*)   I'll get
this paper every day. It will be my Bible.

Soldier   Well, personally mate, I'd sooner have the Bible.
I read it once on jankers.

Miss Gilchrist   Is this true?

Soldier   It's blue, ma'am.

Miss Gilchrist (*enraptured*)   My favourite colour.

Soldier   You'd like it then, ma'am. All you've got to do is
sort out the blue bits from the dreary bits and you're laughing.

Miss Gilchrist   May we sing to you?

Soldier   If you like.

Miss Gilchrist *and* **Mulleady** *assemble themselves on either
side of the table and pose.* **Ropeen** *places an aspidistra in the centre
of the table. They sing to the tune of 'Danny Boy'.*

Miss Gilchrist
    You read the Bible, in its golden pages,
    You read those words and talking much of love.
    You read the works of Plato and the sages,
    They tell of hope, and joy, and peace and love.

* Uffa Fox and Sister Rowe were two examples of people whose names
were so closely linked with royalty that the distinction became blurred.
Other names used were Armstrong-Jones before his marriage, several
Maharajahs and Billy Wallace.

all the sings
→ just saying what they want to say
in a borrowed format.

Mulleady

But I'm afraid it's all a lot of nonsense,
About as true as leprechaun or elf.

Both

You realise, when you want somebody,
That there is no one, no one, loves you like yourself.

Mulleady

I did my best to be a decent person,
I drove a tram for Murphy in thirteen.
I failed to pass my medical for the Army,
But loyally tried to serve my king and queen.
Through all the troubled times I was no traitor, *"to the Brits.*
Even when the British smashed poor Mother's Delft.
And when they left, I became a loyal Free-Stater.
But I know there is no one, no one loves you like yourself.

What does this have to do with that?

Mulleady *with* **Miss Gilchrist** (*crooning in harmony*)

I really think us lower-middle classes,
Get thrown around just like snuff at a wake.
Employers take us for a set of asses,
The rough, they sneer at all attempts we make
To have nice manners and to speak correctly,
And in the end we're flung upon the shelf.
We have no unions, cost of living bonus,

Both

It's plain to see that no one, no one loves you like yourself.

Pat *catches them singing and drives everyone off the stage except the* **Soldier**.

Pat   Come on, get out, will you? (*To the* **Soldier**.) Never mind that old idiot, if you want to go round the back again, just give me a shout.

Soldier   What if you're asleep?

Pat   I haven't slept a wink since 8th May 1921.

Soldier   Did you have an accident?

Leslie sees it's "trauma-related".

Pat   I had three. I was bashed, booted and bayoneted in Arbourhill Barracks.

Soldier   Redcaps. Bastards, aren't they?

Pat   They are, each and every one.

He goes off.

Teresa (*entering*)   Leslie, Leslie, hey, Leslie.

Soldier   Hello, Ginger — come into me castle.

Teresa   Did you get your cigarettes?

Soldier   No.

Teresa   Did the officer not give them to you?

Soldier   No.

Teresa *swears in Irish.*

Soldier   'Ere, 'ere, 'ere, you mustn't swear. Anyway, you should never trust officers.

Teresa   Well, I got you a few anyway.

There is a mournful blast off from **Monsewer**'s *pipes.*

Soldier   What's that?

Teresa   It's Monsewer practising his pipes.

Soldier   He's what?

Teresa   He's practising his pipes. He's going to play a lament.

Soldier   A lament?

Teresa   For the boy in Belfast Jail.

Soldier   You mean a dirge. He's going to need a lot of practice.

Teresa   Don't make a jeer about it.

The bagpipes stop.

Soldier   I'm not jeering. I feel sorry for the poor bloke, but that noise won't help him, will it?

Teresa   Well, he's one of your noble lot, anyway.

Soldier   What do you mean, he's one of our noble lot?

Teresa   Monsewer is – he went to college with your king.

Soldier   We ain't got one.

Teresa   Maybe he's dead now, but you had one one time, didn't you?

Soldier   We got a duke now. He plays tiddlywinks.

Teresa   Anyway, he left your lot and came over here and fought for Ireland.

Soldier   Why, was somebody doing something to Ireland?

Teresa   Wasn't England, for hundreds of years?

Soldier   That was donkey's years ago. Everybody was doing something to someone in those days.

Teresa   And what about today? What about the boy in Belfast Jail? Do you know that in the six counties the police walk the beats in tanks and armoured cars.

Soldier   If he was an Englishman they'd hang him just the same.

Teresa   It's because of the English being in Ireland that he fought.

Soldier   And what about the Irish in London? Thousands of them. Nobody's doing anything to them. We just let them drink their way through it. That's London for you. That's where we should be, down the 'dilly on a Saturday night.

Teresa   You're as bad as the Dublin people here.

Soldier   You're one of them, aren't you?

Teresa   I'm no Dubliner.

Soldier   What are you – a country yokel?

Teresa   I was reared in the convent at Ballymahon.

Soldier   I was reared down the Old Kent Road.

Teresa   Is that where your father and mother live?

Soldier   I ain't got none.

Teresa   You're not an orphan, are you?

Soldier   Yes, I'm one of the little orphans of the storm.

Teresa   You're a terrible chancer.

Soldier   Well, actually, my old lady ran off with a Pole, not that you'd blame her if you knew my old man.

The bagpipes are heard again, louder and nearer.

is parents that he's known but less than existent

b. parents never met but still existing. (meg?)

Teresa   He's coming in.

both.

Monsewer *and* **Pat** *enter from opposite sides of the stage and slow march towards each other.*   →this happened before...

Soldier   Cor, look at that, skirt and all.

Monsewer *stops to adjust the pipes and continues.*

Soldier   You know the only good thing about them pipes? They don't smell. what does that mean.

Pat *and* **Monsewer** *meet and halt. The bagpipes fade with a sad belch.*

Monsewer   Not so good, eh, Patrick?

Pat   No, sir.

Monsewer   Never mind, we'll get there.

7 in 8 hrs?

Pat   Yes, sir.

Monsewer (*gives* **Pat** *the pipes*)   Weekly troop inspection, Patrick.

→this language means something to them. to all.

Pat   Oh, yes, sir. (*Shouts.*) Come on, fall in. Come on, all you Gaels and Republicans on the run, get fell in.

when he calls from by this name they all fall into the role.

beginning of new "role."

*Everyone in the house, <u>except</u> **Meg** <u>and the</u> **IRA Officer**, rushes on and lines up.*

Soldier   Me an' all?

Pat   Yes, get on the end. Right dress.

The 'troops' stamp their feet and someone shouts 'Olé'.

Attention. All present and correct, sir.

Monsewer   Fine body of men.

He walks down the line inspecting.

(*To* **Princess Grace**.) Colonials, eh? (*To* **Rio Rita**.) Keep the powder dry, laddie.

Rio Rita   I'll try, sir.

Monsewer (*to* **Colette**)   You're doing a great job, my dear.

Colette   Thank you, sir.

Monsewer (*to the* **Volunteer**)   Name?

Volunteer   O'Connor, sir.

Monsewer   Station?

Volunteer   Irish State Railways, Central Station, No. 3 Platform.

Monsewer (*to the* **Soldier**)   Name?

Soldier   Williams, sir, Leslie A.

Monsewer   Station?

Soldier   Armagh, sir.

Monsewer   Like it?

Soldier   No, sir, it's a dump, sir. (*To* **Pat**.) It is, you know, mate, shocking. Everything closes down at ten. You can't get a drink on a Sunday.

The parade dissolves into a shambles.

Pat   Can't get a drink?

Soldier   No.

Monsewer   Patrick, is this the English laddie?

Pat   Yes, sir.

Monsewer   Good God! We've made a bloomer. Dismiss
the troops.

why mistake? what's wrong?
his honesty? talks too much?

Pat   Troops, dismiss. Come on, there's been a mistake.
Get off.

They go, except **Teresa**.

Soldier (*to* **Pat**)   She don't have to go, does she?

Pat   No, she's all right.

forbidden friendship.

Monsewer   What's that girl doing, fraternising?

Pat   Not at the moment, sir. She's just remaking the bed.

Monsewer   I'm going to question the prisoner, Patrick.

Pat   Yes, sir.

Monsewer   Strictly according to the rules laid down by
the Geneva Convention.

Pat   Oh yes, sir.

Monsewer (*to the* **Soldier**)   Name?

Soldier   Williams, sir. Leslie A.

Monsewer   Rank?

Soldier   Private.

Monsewer   Number?

Soldier   23774486.

Monsewer   That's the lot, carry on.

is that the end of the
mistake?
just goes on...

Soldier   Can I ask you a question, guv?

what what the problem?

not carrying on.
interruption. disruption.

Monsewer   Can he, Patrick?

Pat   Permission to ask a question, sir. One step forward. march.

Soldier   What are those pipes <u>actually</u> for?

Monsewer   Those pipes, my boy, are the instrument of the ancient Irish race. *different answer.*

Soldier   Permission to ask another question, sir.

Pat   One step forward, march.

Soldier   What actually is a race, guv?

Monsewer   A race occurs when a lot of people live in one place for a long period of time. *not an answer either.*

Soldier   I reckon our old sergeant-major must be a race; he's been stuck in that same depot for about forty years. *exactly ∼*

yup. not bad, the right def.

Monsewer (*in Irish*)   *Focail, Focaileile uait.*

Soldier   Smashing-looking old geezer, ain't he? Just like our old colonel back at the depot. <u>Same face, same voice.</u> Gorblimey, I reckon it is him. *→same "race" as Monsewer,*

Monsewer   *Sleachta – sleachta.*   *"race" is not fixed, rather chosen. choice to stay static is. Kw*

Soldier   Is he a free Hungarian, or something?

Monsewer   *Sleachta – sleachta.*

Soldier   Oh. That's Garlic, ain't it? *lol.*

Monsewer   That, my dear young man, is Gaelic. A language old before the days of the Greeks.

Soldier   Did he say Greeks?

Pat   Yes, Greeks.

Soldier   Excuse me, guv. I can't have you running down the Greeks. Mate of mine's a Greek, runs a caffee down the Edgware Road. Best Rosy Lee and Holy Ghost in London.

Order of magnitude confusion. personal & racial/ societal is conflated. pronoun = individual.

Monsewer   Rosy Lee and Holy Ghost . . . ? What abomination is this?

Soldier   C of E, guv.

Pat   Cockney humour, sir.

Monsewer   The language of Shakespeare and Milton.

Soldier   He can't make up his mind, can he? → what does he mean.
is B English an abomination or artful? both.

Monsewer   That's the trouble with the fighting forces today. No background, no tradition, no morale.

Soldier   We got background – we got tradition. They gave us all that at the Boys' Home. They gave us team spirit, fair play, cricket.
↳ not like race & culture inherited, some deep thing... You can always

Monsewer   Are you a cricketer, my boy?   assert & take on.

Soldier   Yes, sir. Do you like a game?

Monsewer   By Jove, yes.

Soldier   Mind you, I couldn't get on with it at the Boys' Home. They gave us two sets of stumps, you see, and I'd always been used to one, chalked up on the old wall at home.

Monsewer   That's not cricket, my boy.

Soldier   Now there you are, then. You're what I call a cricket person and I'm what I call a soccer person. That's where your race lark comes in.   any division is race.

Monsewer   Ah, cricket. By Jove, that takes me back. Strange how this uncouth youth has brought back memories of summers long past. Fetch the pianist, Patrick. A little light refreshment.

Ropeen *brings him tea.*

Monsewer   Thank you, my dear, two lumps.

As he sings of summers long forgotten, the genteel people of the house sip tea and listen – **Mulleady, Miss Gilchrist** *and* **Ropeen**.
↳ she too.
how are they categorized?

Monsewer (*sings*)

> I remember in September,
> When the final stumps were drawn,
> And the shouts of crowds now silent
> And the boys to tea were gone.
> Let us, O Lord above us,
> Still remember simple things,
> When all are dead who love us,
> Oh the Captains and the Kings,
> When all are dead who love us,
> Oh the Captains and the Kings.
>
> We have many goods for export,
> Christian ethics and old port,
> But our greatest boast is that
> The Anglo-Saxon is a sport.
> On the playing fields of Eton
> We still do thrilling things,
> Do not think we'll ever weaken,
> Up the Captains and the Kings!
> Do not think we'll ever weaken,
> Up the Captains and the Kings!
>
> Far away in dear old Cyprus, *same as banner.*
> Or in Kenya's dusty land,
> Where all bear the white man's burden
> In many a strange land,
> As we look across our shoulder
> In West Belfast the school bell rings,
> And we sigh for dear old England,
> And the Captains and the Kings.
> And we sigh for dear old England,
> And the Captains and the Kings.
>
> In our dreams we see old Harrow,
> And we hear the crow's loud caw,
> At the flower show our big marrow
> Takes the prize from Evelyn Waugh.
> Cups of tea or some dry sherry,
> Vintage cars, these simple things,

Monsewer's song: longest, complete imperialist & English.

So let's drink up and be merry
Oh, the Captains and the Kings.
So, let's drink up and be merry
Oh, the Captains and the Kings.

I wandered in a nightmare
All around Great Windsor Park,
And what do you think I found there
As I stumbled in the dark?
'Twas an apple half-bitten,
And sweetest of all things,
Five baby teeth had written
Of the Captain and the Kings.
Five baby teeth had written
Of the Captains and the Kings.

By the moon that shines above us
In the misty morn and night,
Let us cease to run ourselves down
But praise God that we are white.
And better still we're English,
Tea and toast and muffin rings,
Old ladies with stern faces,
And the Captains and the Kings.
Old ladies with stern faces,
And the Captains and the Kings.*

[handwritten margin notes: race. the days when he was a different race. Moreover has inside him two distinct identities. his English side is still here, wired, just need a trigger.]

A quavering bugle blows a staggering salute offstage.

Pat   Well, that's brought the show to a standstill.

Officer   Patrick, get that old idiot out of here.

The two IRA men have been listening horror-stricken to the last verse of the song.

Officer   Guard!

Volunteer   Sir.

* Actually, he never sings all of this song, as there isn't time. The usual order is to sing verses 1, 4 and 6, with one of the other verses optional.

[handwritten margin notes: author inserted, realistically within the play. both lack time.]

Officer   No one is to be allowed in here, do you understand? No one.

Volunteer   I understand, sir. Might I be relieved from my post?

Officer   Certainly not.

*The **Volunteer** is bursting.*

Volunteer   Two minutes, sir.

Officer   No, certainly not. Get back to your post. This place is like a rabbit warren with everyone skipping about.

*The **Volunteer** hobbles off.*

[handwritten: where/what HQ? TRA?]

Monsewer   Ah, the laddie from headquarters. There you are.

Officer   Yes, here I am. You being an old soldier will understand the need for discipline.

Monsewer   Quite right, too.

Officer   I must ask you what you were doing in here.

Monsewer   Inspecting the prisoner. *[handwritten: more like inspecting his "imprisoned" side]*

Officer   I'm afraid I must ask you to keep out of here in future.

Monsewer   Patrick, I know this young man has been working under a strain, but – there's no need to treat me like an Empire Loyalist. You know where to find me when you need me, Patrick. (*He sweeps off.*)

Pat   Yes, sir.   *[handwritten: how is this defined? he just sung an incredible loyalist song doesn't make him a loyal...]*

Monsewer (*as he goes*)   Chin up, sonny.

Soldier   Cheerio, sir.

Officer   I've had enough of this nonsense. I'll inspect the prisoner myself. *[handwritten: why do they have to inspect him constantly?]*

Teresa *is seen to be under the bed.*

Pat   Yes, sir. Stand by your bed.

Officer   One pace forward, march.

Soldier   Can I ask you what you intend to do with me, sir?

Officer   You keep your mouth shut and no harm will come to you. Have you got everything you want? *not need.*

→ does he know their plan?   *→ seems like he knows.*

Soldier   Oh yes, sir.

Officer   Right. Take over, Patrick. I'm going to inspect the outposts.   *Is that it?*

Pat   Have you got the place well covered, sir?

Officer   I have indeed. Why?

Pat   I think it's going to rain.

Officer   No more tomfoolery, please.

IRA Officer and **Patrick** *depart, leaving* **Teresa** *alone with* **Leslie**.

Soldier   You can come out now.

Teresa   No, he might see me.

Soldier   He's gone, he won't be back for a long time. Come on, sit down and tell me a story — the Irish are great at that, aren't they?

Teresa   Well, not all of them. I'm not. I don't know any stories.   *keeps escaping generalization.*

Soldier   Anything'll do. It doesn't have to be funny. It's just something to pass the time.

Teresa   Yes, you've a long night ahead of you, and so has he.

Soldier   Who?   *equivalents.*

Teresa   You know, the boy in Belfast.

Soldier   What do you have to mention him for?

Teresa   I'm sorry, Leslie.

Soldier   It's all right, it's just that everybody's been talking about the boy in the Belfast Jail.

Teresa   Will I tell you about when I was a girl in the convent?

Soldier   Yeah, that should be a bit of all right. Go on.

Teresa   Oh, it was the same as any other school, except you didn't go home. You played in a big yard which had a stone floor; you'd break your bones if you fell on it. But there was a big meadow outside the wall, we used to be let out there on our holidays. It was lovely. We were brought swimming a few times, too, that was really terrific, but the nuns were terrible strict, and if they saw a man come within a mile of us, well we . . .

Soldier   What? . . . Aw, go on, Teresa, we're grown-ups now, aren't we?

Teresa   We were not allowed to take off our clothes at all. You see, Leslie, even when we had our baths on Saturday nights they put shifts on all the girls.

Soldier   Put what on yer?

Teresa   A sort of sheet, you know.

Soldier   Oh yeah.

Teresa   Even the little ones four or five years of age.

Soldier   Oh, we never had anything like that.

Teresa   What did you have?

Soldier   Oh no, we never had anything like that. I mean, in our place we had all showers and we were sloshing water over each other – and blokes shouting and screeching and making a row – it was smashing! Best night of the week, it was.

Teresa   Our best time was the procession for the Blessed Virgin.

Soldier   Blessed who?

Teresa   Shame on you, the Blessed Virgin. Anyone would think you were a Protestant.

Soldier   I am, girl.   *protestant name*
makes everything fine.

Teresa   Oh, I'm sorry.

Soldier   That's all right. Never think about it myself.

Teresa   Anyway, we had this big feast.

Soldier   Was the scoff good?
same word as Pat.

Teresa   The – what?

Soldier   The grub. The food. You don't understand me half the time, do you?

Teresa   Well, we didn't have food. It was a feast day. We just used to walk around.   *kinda defeats the definition of a feast.*

Soldier   You mean they didn't give you nothing at all? Well, blow that for a lark.

Teresa   Well, are you going to listen to me story? Well, are you? Anyway, we had this procession, and I was looking after the mixed infants.

Soldier   What's a mixed infant?

Teresa   A little boy or girl under five years of age. Because up until that time they were mixed together.   *no distinction / definition of gender.*

Soldier   I wish I'd been a mixed infant.

Teresa   Do you want to hear my story? When the boys were six they were sent to the big boys' orphanage . . .   *really picking out elements.*

Soldier   You're one, too – an orphan? You didn't tell me that.   *same as his reading of the Bible, same as Gilchrist reading news.*

Teresa   Yes, I did.

Soldier   We're quits now.

Teresa   I didn't believe your story.

Soldier   Well, it's true. Anyway, never mind. Tell us about this mixed infant job.

Teresa   There was this little feller, his father was dead, and his mother had run away or something. All the other boys were laughing and shouting, but this one little boy was all on his own and he was crying like the rain. Nothing would stop him. So, do you know what I did, Leslie? I made a crown of daisies and a daisy chain to put round his neck and told him he was King of the May. Do you know, he forgot everything except that he was King of the May.

Soldier   Would you do that for me if I was a mixed infant?

They have forgotten all about Belfast Jail and the IRA.

Leslie takes **Teresa**'s hand and she moves away. She goes to the *window to cover her shyness.*

Teresa   There's a clock striking somewhere in the city.

Soldier   I wonder what time it is?

Teresa   I don't know.

Soldier   Will you give me a picture of yourself, Teresa?

Teresa   What for?

Soldier   Just to have. I mean, they might take me away in the middle of the night and I might never see you again.

Teresa   I'm not Marilyn Monroe or Jayne Mansfield.

Soldier   Who wants a picture of them? They're all old.

Teresa   I haven't got one anyway.

She pulls out a medal which she has round her neck.

Soldier   What's that?

Teresa   It's a medal. It's for you, Leslie.

Soldier   I'm doing all right, ain't I? In the army nine months and I get a medal already.

Teresa   It's not that kind of medal.

Soldier   Let's have a look . . . Looks a bit like you.

Teresa (*shocked*)   No, Leslie. → *why offence at that? heresy?*

Soldier   Oh, it's that lady of yours.

Teresa   It's God's mother.

Soldier   Yes, that one.   *→ resemblance btwn mother & daughter.*

Teresa   She's the <u>mother of everyone else in the world</u>, too. Will you wear it round your neck?   *all-encompassing.*
Teresa the mother,
Leslie the misled
infant

Soldier   I will if you put it on.

She puts it over his head and he tries to kiss her.

Teresa   Leslie. Don't. Why do you <u>have</u> to go and spoil everything? I'm going.

Soldier   Don't go! Let's pretend we're on the films, where all I have to say is 'Let me,' and all you have to say is 'Yes.'   *→ this is a new self.*

Teresa   Oh, all right.   *→ why the easy compliance?* *not Leslie, not Teresa.*

Soldier   Come on, Kate. *as if her*   *does Leslie ever call her*
error has been   *by name?*
They sing and dance.   *corrected.*   *doesn't even call the*
virgin Mary by name.

> I will give you a golden ball,
> To hop with the children in the hall,

Teresa

> If you'll marry, marry, marry, marry,
> If you'll marry me.

Soldier

> I will give you the keys of my chest,
> And all the money that I possess,

Teresa

> If you'll marry, marry, marry, marry,
> If you'll marry me.

Soldier

> I will give you a watch and chain,
> To show the kids in Angel Lane,

resa & Leslie's song: pretend we're in the films...

Teresa

> If you'll marry, marry, marry, marry,
> If you'll marry me.
>
> I will bake you a big pork pie,
> And hide you till the cops go by,

Both

> If you'll marry, marry, marry, marry,
> If you'll marry me.

Soldier

> But first I think that we should see,
> If we fit each other,

Teresa (*to the audience*)

> Shall we?

Soldier

> Yes, let's see.

They run to the bed. The lights black out. **Miss Gilchrist** *rushes on and a spotlight comes up on her.*

Miss Gilchrist (*horrified*)   They're away. (*To* **Kate**.) My music, please!

She sings.

> Only a box of matches
> 1 send, dear Mother, to thee.
> Only a box of matches,
> Across the Irish sea.
> I met with a Gaelic pawnbroker,
> From Killarney's waterfalls,
> With sobs he cried, 'I wish I had died,
> The Saxons have stolen my – '

Pat *rushes on to stop her saying 'balls' and drags her off, curtsying and singing again –*

Miss Gilchrist

> Only a box of matches –

Meg *enters the darkened passage.*

Meg   Teresa! Teresa!   *→ worries about Teresa, like a mother.*
Meg = mother Mary,

*The **Volunteer** enters in hot pursuit.*

Volunteer   Ey, you can't go in there. Sir! Sir!

*The **IRA Officer** enters and blocks **Meg**'s passage.*

Volunteer   Sir, there's another woman trying to get in to him.

Officer   You can't go in there. Security forbids it.

Volunteer   Common decency forbids it. He might not have his trousers on.

Meg   Auah, do you think I've never seen a man with his trousers off before?

Officer   I'd be very much surprised if you'd ever seen one with them on.

Meg   Thanks.

Volunteer   He's a decent boy, for all he's a British soldier.

Meg   Ah, there's many a good heart beats under a khaki tunic.

Volunteer   There's something in that. My own father was in the Royal Irish Rifles.

Officer   Mine was in the Inniskillings.   *} some legacy.*
} but they're all not soldiers
by profession
Meg   And mine was the parish priest.   *same joke.   worrying nonetheless.*

Officer (*horrified*)   God forbid you, woman. After saying that, I won't let you in at all.

Meg   I'm not that particular. I was going about my business till he stopped me.

Pat   You might as well let her go in – cheer him up a bit.

Officer   I don't think we should. He's in our care and we're morally responsible for his spiritual welfare.
= gotta make sure he doesn't have sex.
Volunteer   Well, only in a temporal way, sir.
what does that mean?
just temporary – word slip?

Meg I only wanted to see him in a temporal way.

Officer Jesus, Mary and Joseph, it would be a terrible thing for him to die with a sin of impurity on his –

The lights go up.

Soldier (*running downstage from the bed*) Die! What's all this talk about dying? Who's going to die?

Meg We're all going to die, but not before Christmas, we hope.

Pat Now look what you've done. You'll have to let her in now. You should have been more discreet, surely.

Officer Two minutes then.

*The **IRA Officer** and the **Volunteer** move away. **Teresa** stands by the bed. **Meg** goes into the room.*

Meg She's there, she's been there all the time.

Teresa I was just dusting, Meg.

Meg What's wrong with a bit of comfort on a dark night? Are you all right, lad?

Soldier Mum, what are they going to do with me?

Meg I don't know – I only wish I did.

Soldier Will you go and ask them, because I don't think they know themselves.

Meg Maybe they don't know, maybe a lot of people don't know, or maybe they've forgotten.

Soldier I don't know what you mean.

Meg There are some things you can't forget.

Soldier Forget?

Meg Like here in Russell Street, right next to the place where I was born, the British turned a tank and fired shells into people's homes.

Soldier   I suppose it was the war, missus.

Meg   Yes, it was war. Do you know who it was against?

Soldier   No.

Meg   Old men and women, the bedridden and the cripples, and mothers with their infants.

Soldier   Why them?

Meg   Everybody that was able to move had run away. In one room they found an old woman, her son's helmet and gas mask were still hanging on the wall. He had died fighting on the Somme.

Soldier   I don't know nothing about it, lady.

Meg   Would you like to hear some more? Then listen.

A military drum beats, the piano plays softly, and **Meg** *chants rather than sings:*

Who fears to speak of Easter Week,
That week of famed renown,
When the boys in green went out to fight
The forces of the Crown.

With Mausers bold, and hearts of gold,
The Red Countess dressed in green,
And high above the GPO
The rebel flag was seen.

Then came ten thousand khaki coats,
Our rebel boys to kill,
Before they reached O'Connell Street,
Of fight they got their fill.

As she sings everyone else in the house comes slowly on to listen to her.

They had machine-guns and artillery,
And cannon in galore,
But it wasn't our fault that e'er one
Got back to England's shore.

For six long days we held them off,
At odds of ten to one,
And through our lines they could not pass,
For all their heavy guns.

And deadly poison gas they used,
To try to crush Sinn Fein,
And burnt our Irish capital,
Like the Germans did Louvain.

They shot our leaders in a jail,
Without a trial, they say,
They murdered women and children,
Who in their cellars lay,

And dug their grave with gun and spade,
To hide them from our view.
Because they could neither kill nor catch,
The rebel so bold and true.

The author should have sung that one.

Pat   That's if the thing has an author.

Soldier   Brendan Behan, he's too anti-British.

Officer   Too anti-Irish, you mean. Bejasus, wait till we get him back home. We'll give him what-for for making fun of the Movement.

Soldier (*to audience*)   He doesn't mind coming over here and taking your money.

Pat   He'd sell his country for a pint.

What happens next is not very clear. There are a number of arguments all going on at once. Free-Staters against Republicans, Irish against English, homosexuals against heterosexuals, and in the confusion all the quarrels get mixed up and it looks as though everyone is fighting everyone else. In the centre of the mêlée, **Miss Gilchrist** *is standing on the table singing 'Land of Hope and Glory'. The* **IRA Officer** *has one chair and is waving a Free State flag and singing 'The Soldier's Song', while the* **Russian Sailor** *has the other and sings* *the Soviet National Anthem. The* **Negro** *parades through the room carrying a large banner inscribed* KEEP IRELAND BLACK. *The piano plays throughout. Suddenly the* **Volunteer** *attacks the* **Soldier** *and the* **Russian Sailor** *joins in the fight. The* **Volunteer** *knocks* **Mulleady**'s *bowler hat over his eyes and* **Ropeen** *flattens the* **Volunteer.** **Mulleady** *is now wandering around blind with his hat over his eyes, and holding* **Ropeen**'s *aspidistra. The* **Volunteer,** *somewhat dazed, sees the* **Russian Sailor**'s *red flag and thinks he has been promoted to guard. He blows his railway whistle and the fight breaks up into a wild dance in which they all join on the train behind the* **Volunteer** *and rush round the room in a circle. All this takes about a minute and a half and at the height, as they are all chugging round and round the* **Soldier,** **Pat** *interrupts.*

= imprisoned. like Leslie's entrance in end of Act 1.

Pat   Stop it a minute. Hey, Leslie, have you seen this?

> how does Pat know his name?

The train stops and the dancers are left in the position of forming a ring round **Leslie** *which resembles a prison cage.* **Pat** *hands* **Leslie** *a newspaper and everyone is quiet. The Irish, British, and Russian flags lie on the ground.*

Soldier   Let's have a look. 'The Government of Northern Ireland have issued a statement that they cannot find a reason for granting a reprieve in the case of the condemned youth. The IRA have announced that Private Leslie Alan Williams – ' Hey, that's me, I've got me name in the papers.

Pat   You want to read a bit further.

Miss Gilchrist   I'm afraid it's impossible – you're going to be shot.

↳ ?

Soldier   Who are you?

social workers > who are they really working for

Miss Gilchrist   I am a ~~sociable worker~~. I work for the St Vincent de Paul Society and I have one question to ask you: have you your testament?

IRA? country? people? when they must kill a young boy?

The **Soldier** *checks his trousers.*

Soldier   I hope so.

Miss Gilchrist   I feel for him like a mother.

She sings.

Only a box of matches –

Soldier   Shut up, this is serious. 'In a statement today delivered to all newspaper offices and press agencies . . . He has been taken as a hostage . . . If . . . executed . . . the IRA declare that Private Leslie Alan Williams will be shot as a reprisal.' Does it really mean they're going to shoot me?

Mulleady   I'm afraid so.   [handwritten: → name change.]

Soldier   Why?

Monsewer   You are the hostage.   [handwritten: just by definition]

Soldier   But I ain't done nothing.   [handwritten: he must die.]

Officer   This is war.   [handwritten: Just by definition we must fight.]

Soldier   Surely one of you would let me go?   [handwritten: even tho we could be danang.]

[handwritten left margin: names justify his death. with no other reason]

They all move backwards away from him, leaving him alone in the room. They disappear.

Well, you crowd of bleeding – Hey, Kate, give us some music.

He sings.

I am a happy English lad, I love my royal-ty,
And if they were short a penny of a packet of fags,
Now they'd only have to ask me.

I love old England in the east, I love her in the west,
From Jordan's streams to Derry's Walls,
I love old England best.

I love my dear old Notting Hill, wherever I may roam,
But I wish the Irish and the niggers and the wogs,
Were kicked out and sent back home.

A bugle sounds and he salutes.

Curtain.

[handwritten: → he ends Act 1,2,3.
Leslie's song: English patriotic song. hate for non-English..
= Monsewer's song.]

Act Three

Late the same night. The **Soldier** *sits alone in his room.* **Pat** *and* **Meg** *sit at the table down by the piano.* **Teresa**, **Colette**, **Rio Rita** *and* **Princess Grace** *are sitting or sprawling on the stairs or in the passage.* **Ropeen** *sits, knitting, on a beer barrel near* **Pat**, *and the* **Russian Sailor** *is fast asleep on the far side of the stage. Before the curtain rises there is the sound of keening as the women sit mourning for* **Leslie** *and the boy in Belfast Jail. The atmosphere is one of death and dying. The curtain rises and* **Pat** *seizes a bottle of stout from the crate beside him and bursts into wild song:*

[handwritten: doing nothing]
[handwritten: she's doing something. "graceful"? living, active.]
[handwritten: something that comes before the curtain rises.]

Pat
    On the eighteenth day of November,
    Just outside the town of Macroom –

Here, have a drink.

He gives **Leslie** *the stout.*

Soldier   What's the time? *[handwritten: he's counting. to others it does n't matter. he and the boy are already dead.]*

Pat   I don't know. Ask him.

Volunteer   My watch has stopped.

Pat (*sings*)
    The Tans in their big Crossley tenders,
    Came roaring along to their doom.

Meg   Shut up, will you, Pat!

[handwritten: anti-song.]

The keening stops. *[handwritten: → keening = part of the song.]*

Pat   What's the matter with you?

Meg   You'll have that Holy Joe down on us.

Pat   Who are you talking about?

Meg   That IRA general, or whatever he is.

Pat   Him a general? He's a messenger boy. He's not fit to be a batman.

[handwritten: everyone 13.]

[handwritten at bottom: Pat's song: from p.8, IRA defeating Tans → includes keening, mourning for death from war.]

Meg   I've heard they're all generals nowadays.

Pat   Like their <u>mothers</u> before them.

[handwritten: matrilineal..]

Miss Gilchrist *in her nightclothes attempts to sneak into* **Leslie**'s *room, but the* **Volunteer**, *who is mounting guard, sees her and challenges.*

Miss Gilchrist   Leslie – Leslie –

Volunteer   Hey, where are you going?

Pat   Come on, come and sit down.

Pat *drags a protesting* **Miss Gilchrist** *to sit at the table with them.*

Miss Gilchrist   Well, you must excuse the way I'm dressed.

[handwritten: deliberate]

Pat   You look lovely. Have a drink, Miss Gilchrist.

Miss Gilchrist   Oh no, thank you, Mr Pat.

Pat   Get it down you.

Miss Gilchrist   No really, Mr Pat. I never drink.

Meg   She doesn't want it.

Pat   Shut up, you. Are you going to drink?

Miss Gilchrist   No, Mr Pat.

[handwritten: why? must participate in mourning?]

Pat (*shouts*)   Drink. (*She drinks.*) Are you aware, Miss Gilchrist, that you are speaking to a <u>man who was a commandant at the times of the troubles</u>? *[handwritten: why evoke past authority? not quite like him.]*

Meg   Fine bloody commandant he was.

Pat   Commandant of 'E' Battalion, Second Division, Dublin Brigade. Monsewer was the Captain.

[handwritten: this is also a pronoun. "a" battalion.]

Meg   What the hell's 'E' Battalion?

Pat   You've heard of A B C D E, I suppose?

Meg   Certainly I have.

Pat   Well, it's as simple as that.

Miss Gilchrist   Wasn't that nice? It must be a lovely thing to be a captain.

Pat   Can I get on with my story or not?

Meg   I defy anyone to stop you.

Pat   Now, where was I?

Volunteer   Tell us about Mullingar, sir.

Pat   Shut up. Leslie, you want to listen to this. It was in Russell Street in Dublin –

Meg   That's my story and I've already told him.

Pat   Oh, then give us a drink.

Meg   Get it yourself.

Pat   Give us a drink!

Miss Gilchrist gives **Pat** a drink.

Miss Gilchrist   Please go on, Mr Pat.

Pat   I intend to. It was at Mullingar, at the time of the troubles, that I lost my leg . . .

Meg   You told me it was at Cork.

Pat   It doesn't matter what I told you, it was at Mullingar, in the Civil War.

Miss Gilchrist   Well if that's the kind of war you call a civil war, I wouldn't like to see an uncivil one.

Pat   The fightin', Miss Gilchrist, went on for three days without ceasing, three whole days . . .

Miss Gilchrist   And how did you lose your poor left foot, Mr Pat?

Pat   It wasn't me left foot, but me right foot. Don't you know your left from your right? Don't you know how to make the sign of the cross?

Miss Gilchrist   I do, thank you, but I don't make it with me feet.

Pat *retreats to join* **Leslie** *and the* **Volunteer** *inside the room.*

Pat   What the hell difference does it make, left or right? There were good men lost on both sides.

Volunteer   There's good and bad on all sides, sir.

The **IRA Officer** *crosses through the room and out again.*

Pat   It was a savage and barbarous battle. All we had was rifles and revolvers. They had Lewis guns, Thompsons, and landmines — bloody great landmines — the town was nothing but red fire and black smoke and the dead were piled high on the roads . . .

Meg   You told me there was only one man killed.

Pat   What?

Meg   And he was the County Surveyor out measuring the road and not interfering with politics one way or another.

Pat   You're a liar!

Meg   You told me that when the fighting was over both sides claimed him for their own.

Pat   Liar!

Meg   Haven't I seen the Celtic crosses on either side of the road where they both put up memorials to him?

Pat   It's all the same what I told you.

Meg   That's your story when you're drunk, anyway, and like any other man, that's the only time you tell the truth.

Pat   Have you finished?

Meg   No, begod, if whisky and beer were the pre-war prices, the father of lies would be out of a job.

[handwritten: = am I worthy or not?]

Pat   I lost my leg – <u>did I or did I not?</u> *[handwritten: why ask Meg?]*

[handwritten: I know he's trying to tell her the truth but it does nothing.]

Meg   You lost the use of it, I know that.

Miss Gilchrist   These little lovers' quarrels.

Pat   Shut up! I lost my leg. <u>Did I or did I not?</u> And these white-faced loons with their berets and trench coats and teetotal badges have <u>no right</u> to call themselves members of the IRA.   *[handwritten: → losing leg = prerequisite for IRA.]*

Miss Gilchrist   They're only lads, Mr Pat.

[handwritten: → about Pat as a boy Ought.]

Meg   He begrudges them their bit of sport now that he's old and beat himself.

Pat   What sport is there in that dreary loon out there?

Meg   They've as much <u>right</u> to their drilling and marching, their rifles and revolvers and crucifixes and last dying words and glory as ever you had.

Pat   I'm not saying they haven't, did I?

There is general disagreement.

Volunteer   Oh yes, you did, Pat.

Miss Gilchrist   I heard you distinctly.

Meg   Weren't you <u>young</u> yourself once?

[handwritten: Youth = vitality → Pat considers it a nuisance]

Pat   That's the way they talk to you, nowadays.

He sulks. The keening starts again. *[handwritten: → mourning of youth.]*

Miss Gilchrist   I always say that a general and a bit of shooting makes one forget one's troubles.

Meg   Sure, it takes your mind off the cost of living.

Miss Gilchrist   A poor heart it is that never rejoices.

[handwritten: → this is not smth the old IRA would have done.]

Pat   I'll tell you one thing, they've <u>no right to be going up to the</u> border and kidnapping young men like this and bringing them down here.   *[handwritten: true.]*

Meg   They've as much right to <u>leave their legs and feet up on the border</u> as ever you had at Mullingar or Cork or wherever it was.

Miss Gilchrist gets up to take a drink to **Leslie***. The* **Volunteer** *throws her out of the room.*

Volunteer   I've warned you before, you can't come in here.

Meg   Leave her alone.

Pat   She's coming on, you know, to be making smart remarks to a poor crippled man that never harmed anyone in his life.

Meg   Away with you.

Pat   Let alone the years I spent incarcerated in Mountjoy with the other Irish patriots, God help me.

Meg   Ah, Mountjoy and the Curragh Camp were universities for the like of you. But I'll tell you one thing, and that's not two, the day you <u>gave up work</u> to run this house for Monsewer and take in the likes of this lot, you became a <u>butler, a Republican butler, a half-red footman – a Sinn Fein skivvy.</u>

Miss Gilchrist   What a rough-tongued person.

Pat   Go on, abuse me, your own husband that took you off the streets on a Sunday morning, when there wasn't a pub open in the city.

Meg   Go and get a mass said for yourself. The only love you ever had you kept <u>for Mother Ireland and for leaving honest employment.</u>

Pat   Why did you stop with me so long?

Meg   God knows. I don't. God knows.

On the stairs and in the passage people are <u>dozing off.</u> **Pat** *and* **Meg** *are not speaking. The* **Soldier** *is thinking about tomorrow morning and to <u>cheer himself up,</u> sings. The* **IRA Officer** *passes on his rounds.*

Soldier
> Abide with me, fast falls the eventide,
> The darkness deepens, Lord with me abide.

Miss Gilchrist *places a black lace scarf on her head, lights a candle and starts walking slowly towards the* **Soldier**, *keening. The* **Volunteer** *is struck helpless.*

Meg   She's starting a wake for the poor lad and he's not dead yet.   *atemporal.*

As she passes **Pat**, *he blows out the candle and* **Miss Gilchrist** *suffers a great shock.*

Pat (*to* **Leslie**)   If you must sing, sing something cheerful.

Soldier   I don't know anything cheerful.   → Teresa: idle any stories

Volunteer   Then shut up!

Having got into the room, **Miss Gilchrist** *stays there.*

Miss Gilchrist   I know what it is to be in exile. Dublin is not my home.   = Teresa.

(≈ like my mum y esos's)

Meg   That's one thing in its favour.

Miss Gilchrist   I came here to work in a house, Mr Pat.

Meg   I told you what she was.   = Teresa.

Miss Gilchrist   It was in a very respectable district. We only took in clerical students. They were lovely boys, so much more satisfactory than the medical students.   ↔ Teresa, who left bc. clerical students.

Pat   Oh yes, the medicals is more for the beer.

Miss Gilchrist   Of course, my boys had renounced the demon drink. Being students of divinity they had more satisfactory things to do.

Meg   Such as?

Pat   You know what they go in for, reading all this stuff about 'Mat begat Pat' and 'This one lay with that one' and the old fellow that lay with his daughters – gen?

= sexual. Teresa fled to escape sexual harassment. but the movie pretense enables her to have sex?

Leslie's song: darkness song. "to cheer himself up"
→ he sings about what's happening to him atm.

Meg   And getting the best of eating and drinking, too. It's a wonder they're in any way controllable at all.

Miss Gilchrist   Sometimes they were not. Life has its bitter memories. Since then I've had recourse to doing good works, recalling the sinner, salvaging his soul. → having sex . as w. Mulleady.

Meg   Well, you can leave his soul alone, whatever about your own, or I'll set fire to you.

Miss Gilchrist (*standing on her dignity*)   Our Blessed Lord said, 'Every cripple has his own way of walking, so long as they don't cause strikes, rob, steal, or run down General Franco.' Those are my principles. ↳ weird attachment to authority

Meg   Your principal is nothing but a pimp.

Miss Gilchrist   To whom are you referring?

Meg   That creeping Jesus on the third floor back.

Miss Gilchrist   Oh, you mean Mr Mulleady.

Meg   I do.

Miss Gilchrist   But he is a fonctionnaire.

Meg   Is that what they call it nowadays?

Miss Gilchrist   I strove to save him, together we wrestled against the devil, but here I feel is a soul worth the saving.

She sings.

I love my fellow creatures –

Miss Gilchrist *chases* **Leslie** *round the table and the* **Volunteer** *chases* **Miss Gilchrist**.

Pat   Leave him alone, he's too young for you.

Miss Gilchrist   Mr Pat, I'm as pure as the driven snow.

The **Volunteer** *taps her on the backside with his rifle. She jumps.*

Meg   You weren't driven far enough.

Miss Gilchrist *returns to the table near the piano.*

Pat   Hey, Feargus, have a drink and take one up for Leslie. Hey, Leslie, don't be paying any attention to her. She's no use to you.

The **Volunteer** *takes* **Leslie** *a bottle of stout.*

Soldier   Here, it's all very well you coming the old acid, and giving me all this stuff about nothing going to happen to me, I'm not a complete bloody fool, you know.

Pat   Drink your beer and shut up.

Soldier   What have I ever done to you that you should shoot me?

→ it's not about "you"!

Pat   I'll tell you what you've done. Some time ago there was a famine in this country and people were dying all over the place. Well, your Queen Victoria, or whatever her bloody name was, sent five pounds to the famine fund and at the same time she sent five pounds to the Battersea Dogs' Home so no one could accuse her of having rebel sympathies.

doesn't *(Queen)*

equilibrium always balancing two sides.

Meg   Good God, Pat, that was when Moses was in the Fire Brigade.

Pat   Let him think about it.

Miss Gilchrist   They might have given us this little island that we live on for ourselves.

Soldier   Will you answer me one thing man to man? Why didn't they tell me why they took me?

Pat   Didn't they? Didn't they tell you?

Soldier   No.

Meg   There's a war on.

Leslie's been "told" more than once already. he just doesn't see it as his reason to die.

Pat   Exactly. There's a war going on in the north of Ireland. You're a soldier. You were captured.

sees it as past.

Soldier   All right, so I'm a soldier. I'm captured. I'm a prisoner of war.

Pat   Yes.

Soldier   Well, you can't shoot a prisoner of war. *you're a hostage.*

Pat   Who said anything about shooting?

Soldier   What about that announcement in the newspapers?

Pat   Bluff. Haven't you *every small dream* everything you could wish for? A bottle of stout, a new girlfriend bringing you every class of comfort? → *This is what Pat would wish for. youth.*

Soldier   Yeah, till that bloke in Belfast is topped in the morning; then it's curtains for poor old Williams. I'm due for a weekend's leave an' all.

Pat   It's bluff, propaganda! All they'll do is hold you for a few days.

Meg   Sure, they might give him a last-minute reprieve.

Soldier   Who, me? ← *gone tiny.*   *Leslie's got nothing to be forgiven for anyways.*

Meg   No. The boy in Belfast Jail.

Soldier   Some hopes of that.

Pat   The British Government might think twice about it now that they know we've got you.

why does Pat & Meg keep reassuring him Leslie will not die? — Volunteer unsure.

Volunteer   They know that if they hang the Belfast martyr, their own man here will be plugged.

Soldier   Plug you.

Pat   Be quiet, you idiot.

Volunteer + Pat need to keep him hoping?

They all turn on the **Volunteer**.

Soldier   You're as barmy as him if you think that what's happening to me is upsetting the British Government. I suppose you think they're all sitting around in the West End clubs with handkerchiefs over their eyes, dropping tears into their double whiskies. Yeah, I can just see the Secretary of State for War now waking up his missus in the night: 'Oh Isabel – Cynthia, love, I can hardly get a wink of sleep wondering what's happening to that poor bleeder Williams.'
↳ *another ambiguity.*

Miss Gilchrist   Poor boy! Do you know, I think they ought to <u>put his story in the *News of the World.*</u> Ah, we'll be seeing you on the telly yet. He'll be famous like that Diana Dors, or the one who cut up his victim and threw the bits out of an aeroplane. I think he has a serial running somewhere.

Soldier   I always heard the Irish were barmy, but that's going it, that is.

Pat   Eh, let's have a drink.

Meg   I want me bed, Pat. Never mind a drink.

Soldier   Here, mum, *listen* – (*Coming out of the room.*)

Pat (*to the* **Soldier**)   Where are you going?

Soldier   I'm just going to talk to . . .

Pat   I'm going to fix you . . . Leslie.

Meg (*starts to sing softly*)
I have no mother to break her heart,
I have no father to take my part.
I have one friend and a girl is she,
And she'd lay down her life for McCaffery.

Pat   Now, I'm going to draw a circle round you, with this piece of chalk. Now, you move outside that circle and you're a dead man. Watch him, Feargus.

He draws a circle round **Leslie** *and the* **Volunteer** *points his gun at him.*

Soldier   I bet that fellow in Belfast wouldn't want me plugged.

Pat   Certainly he wouldn't.

Soldier   What good's it going to do him?

Meg   When the boy's dead, what good would it be to croak this one? It wouldn't bring the other back to life now, would it?

The **Volunteer** *comes away from* **Leslie** *to sit near the piano.*

Soldier   What a caper! I'm just walking out of a dance hall –

[handwritten: reenactment. re "living"]

He tries to walk out of the circle and the **Volunteer** *grabs his gun.*

Pat   Walk in.

Soldier (*back inside*)   I was just walking out of a dance hall, when this geezer nabs me. 'What do you want?' I says. 'Information,' he says. 'I ain't got no information,' I says, 'apart from me name and the addresses of the girls in the NAAFI.' 'Right,' he says, 'we're taking you to Dublin. Our Intelligence want to speak to you.'

[handwritten left margin: why say this? seems like a very abrupt convo – assumes everything about Leslie]

[handwritten: only thing he can say about himself]

Pat   Intelligence! Holy Jesus, wait till you meet 'em. This fellow here's an Einstein compared to them.

[handwritten right margin: is there actual "intelligence"? just police?]

Soldier   Well, when will I be meeting them?

Pat   Maybe they'll come tomorrow morning to ask you a few questions.

Soldier   Yeah, me last bloody wishes, I suppose.

Miss Gilchrist (*sings*) *[handwritten: Meg's song]*
    I have no mother to break her heart,
    I have no father to take my part –

Meg   Pat, will you do something about that one?

Pat   Can you see that circle?

Miss Gilchrist   Yes.

Pat   Well, get in.

He rushes **Miss Gilchrist** *into the room.*

Miss Gilchrist *carries on singing.*

Miss Gilchrist
    I have one friend, and a girl is she,
    And she'd lay down her life for McCaffery.

[handwritten bottom: Gilchrist's song (= Meg's song) : no mother.]

Pat   Leslie, come down here. That old idiot would put years on you. I can't stand your bloody moaning.

Miss Gilchrist   I'll have you know, Mr Pat, I had my voice trained by an electrocutionist.

Meg   It sounds shocking.   *why suddenly? action within military*

Volunteer (*jumping to attention*)   Sir, it's neither this nor *premise vs.* that, sir, but if you're taking charge of the prisoner, I'll carry *non-* out me other duties and check the premises.   *premise is*   *different.*

Pat   Yes, you do that, Feargus.

Volunteer   It's only a thick would let the job slip between his fingers.

Pat   You may be blamed, Einstein, but you never will be shamed.

Volunteer   I hope not, sir. Of course, sir, God gives us the brains, it's no credit to ourselves.

Pat   Look – I don't wish to come the sergeant-major on you, but will you get about what you came for?

Volunteer   I will, sir, directly.

He salutes smartly and marches off into the growing dark, getting more and more <u>frightened</u> *as he goes.*

Miss Gilchrist   I have such a thirst on me, Mr Pat. (*She looks at the crate of empties.*) Oh, Mr Pat, you gave that twelve of stout a very quick death.   *same phrase as Meg. not so innocent desires.*

Pat   You could sing that if you had an air to it. Leslie, pop *deliberate?* out and get us twelve of stout. Go on – just out there and round the corner – Go on – you can't miss it. Tell 'em it's for me.   *→ able to free Leslie bc. Gilchrist is in the circle & Leslie is not. Just definition problems.*

Leslie *takes some persuading, but finally, seeing his chance to escape, leaves quietly. Everyone else is* <u>falling asleep</u>. *There is a long silence, then a terrific clatter.*   *↳ boredom?*

Volunteer   Hey, where do you think you're going?

Leslie   He told me I could . . .

Leslie *runs back, hotly pursued by the* **Volunteer**. *Everyone wakes up in alarm.* **Pat** *is furious.*

Volunteer   I caught the prisoner, sir, trying to escape.

Pat   You're a bloody genius, Einstein.

The **Volunteer** *beams.*

Pat   If you're so fond of that circle, you get in it.

He takes a swipe at the **Volunteer** *with his walking stick and drives him into the circle. The* **Volunteer** *is puzzled.*

Pat   Leslie, come and sit over here.

Leslie   Oh yeah, you're just leading me up the garden path, sending me out for beer. All of a sudden, I turn round and cop a bullet in my head. Anyway, I can tell you this, an Englishman can die as well as an Irishman any day.

Pat   Don't give me all that old stuff about dying. You won't die for another fifty years, barring you get a belt of an atom bomb, God bless you.

Leslie *comes down to sit with* **Pat** *and* **Meg**, *as* **Monsewer** *enters at the back of the room with the* **IRA Officer**. *The* **Volunteer** *reports to them about the disturbance.*

Monsewer   Have you checked his next-of-kin?

Volunteer   He hasn't got none, sir.

The **IRA Officer** *and* **Volunteer** *synchronise watches and the* **IRA Officer** *and* **Monsewer** *depart. The* **Volunteer** *sits at the table with his gun trained on* **Leslie**'s *back.*

Pat   Come and sit down here and don't pay any attention to them.

Meg   Ignore them. Come on, lad.

Soldier   You know, up till tonight I've enjoyed myself here. It's better than square bashing. You know what they say?

Sings:

> When Irish eyes are smiling,
> Sure, it's like a morn in spring,
> In the lilt of Irish laughter
> You can hear the angels sing.
> When Irish eyes are happy –

song of Irishness vs. actual Irishness.

None of the Irish know the words, but they all hum and whistle. **Miss Gilchrist** *starts keening and the singing stops.*

Pat   It's all right, it's one of ours.

Miss Gilchrist   Jesus, Mary and Joseph, I feel for this boy as if I were his mother.

who? → unclear

Meg   That's remarkable, that is.

Miss Gilchrist   It would be more remarkable if I were his father.

Meg   Were his father? How many of you are there? I never heard you were married.

Miss Gilchrist   You never heard the Virgin Mary was married.

Meg   That was done under the Special Powers Act by the Holy Ghost.

lol?

Miss Gilchrist   Oh, Miss Meg, I repulse your prognostications. It would answer you better to go and clean your carpet.

Meg   How dare you? When I was ill I lay prostituted on that carpet. Men of good taste have complicated me on it. Away, you scruff hound, and thump your craw with the other hippo-crites.

Miss Gilchrist   Pray do not insult my religiosity.

Meg   Away, you brass.

Miss Gilchrist   I stand fast by my Lord, and will sing my hymn now:

Leslie's song: Irish beauty → interrupted by keening.

I love my dear Redeemer,
My Creator, too, as well,
And, oh, that filthy Devil
Should stay below in Hell.
I cry to Mr Kruschev
Please grant me this great boon,
Don't muck about, don't muck about,
Don't muck about with the moon.

I am a little Christ-ian,
My feet are white as snow,
And every day, my prayers I say,
For Empire lamb I go.
I cry unto Macmillan,
That multi-racial coon,
I love him and those above him,
But don't muck about with the moon.

All
    Don't muck about, don't muck about,
    Don't muck about with the moon.

Meg   Get off the stage, you castle Catholic bitch.

Miss Gilchrist   She is a no-class person. Things haven't
been the same since the British went.

Soldier   They've not all gone yet – I'm still here. Perhaps
you can tell me what these people are going to do me in for?

Meg   Maybe you voted wrong.

Soldier   I'm too young to have a vote for another three
years.

Meg   Well, what are you doing poking your nose into our
affairs?

Soldier   In what affairs? What do I know about Ireland or
Cyprus, or Kenya or Jordan or any of those places?

Officer (*as he crosses the stage*)   You may learn very shortly
with a bullet in the back of your head.

Rio Rita   You'll put a bullet in the back of nobody's head, mate.

restoring some innocence/individuality to him.

Whores   Oh no, it's <u>not his fault</u>.

Mulleady   He should never have been brought here in the first place. It means trouble. I've been saying so all day. It's illegal.

→ also a technical category.

why → illegal.

→ this is the first he's spoken in a while

*The action takes a very sinister turn. At the mention of bullets there is a rush by everyone to blanket **Leslie** from the **Officer**, **Mulleady** appears as if by <u>magic</u> and summons **Rio Rita** and **Princess Grace** to him. They go into <u>a huddle</u>. The other inhabitants of the house are mystified. All that can be seen are three pairs of twitching hips, as they mutter and whisper to each other.* → why? how?

Meg   What are they up to?

Pat   I wouldn't trust them as far as I could fling them.

Colette   What are you up to?

Rio Rita   We've made a pact.

*There is much homosexual byplay between **Mulleady** and the two queers.*

Colette   What sort of a pact? Political or − ?

Mulleady   One might as well be <u>out of</u> the world as <u>out of the fashion</u>.

in fashion: pretense - catholic. ?

out-fashion: gay, but authentic life.

Miss Gilchrist *is horrified.*

Miss Gilchrist   Eustace, what are you doing with those persons?

Mulleady   Oh, we're speaking now, are we, Miss Gilchrist? That's a change. Ever since you've been interested in that young man's soul, a poor civil servant's soul means nothing to you.

Miss Gilchrist   Eustace, what has happened to you?

Mulleady   You can't do what you like with us, you know.

→ can't manipulate w sex & religion?

Rio Rita   Don't you know?

He comes down to the audience.

Do you? Well, for the benefit of those who don't understand we'll sing our ancient song, won't we, Uncle?

Mulleady *and* **Princess Grace** *join him.*

Rio Rita   Blanche? (*This to the* **Negro**.) Isn't he lovely? I met him at a whist drive. He trumped my ace. Give us a note, Kate. Will you try another one, please? We'll have the first one, I think.

[handwritten: ○ Grace's real name?]

[handwritten: this back & forth w. Kate is one of a kind. unforeseen]
[handwritten: first time we hear him.]

Rio Rita, **Mulleady** *and* **Princess Grace** (*sing*)
  When Socrates in Ancient Greece,
  Sat in his Turkish bath,
  He rubbed himself, and scrubbed himself,
  And steamed both fore and aft.

  He sang the songs the sirens sang,
  With Oscar and Shakespeare,
  We're here because we're queer,
  Because we're queer because we're here.

[handwritten:] lyrical. ∅ deferred meaning.]

Mulleady
  The highest people in the land
  Are for or they're against,
  It's all the same thing in the end,
  A piece of sentiment.

Princess Grace
  From Swedes so tall to Arabs small,
  They answer with a leer,

All Three
  We're here because we're queer
  Because we're queer because we're here.

Princess Grace   The trouble we had getting that past the nice Lord Chamberlain. This next bit's even worse.

[handwritten: ↗ anachronistic.]
[handwritten: Rio Rita, Princess Grace, Mulleady's song: queer = existence itself.]
[handwritten: outcast = life.]

The song ends and the three queers gyrate across the stage, twisting their bodies sinuously and making suggestive approaches to **Leslie**. **Leslie** *is about to join in when* **Miss Gilchrist** *throws herself at him.*

Miss Gilchrist   Leslie, come away, this is no fit company for an innocent boy. *) → they're playing into that role.*

Soldier   No, mum.

Miss Gilchrist   Leave off this boy. He's not used to prostitutes, male, female or *Whiston Mail.*

Meg   Get out, you dirty low things. A decent whore can't get a shilling with you around.

Rio Rita   Shut up, Meg Dillon, you're just bigoted.

Meg   Don't you use language like that to me.

Miss Gilchrist   Leave off this boy. He is not a ponce.

Soldier   No, I'm a builder's labourer. At least, I was.

Miss Gilchrist   Honest toil.

Soldier   It's a mug's game.

Miss Gilchrist   Oh, my boy!

They sing a duet, **Leslie** *speaking his lines. As the song goes on, the whores and queers sort themselves out into a dance for all the outcasts of this world. It is a slow, sad dance in which* **Ropeen** *dances with* **Colette** *and* **Princess Grace** *dances first with* **Mulleady** *and then with* **Rio Rita**. *There is jealousy and comfort in the dance.*

Miss Gilchrist
> Would you live on woman's earnings,
> Would you give up work for good?
> For a life of prostitution?

Soldier
> Yes, too bloody true, I would.

Miss Gilchrist
> Would you have a kip in Soho?
> Would you be a West End ponce?

*Gilchrist & Leslie's song : Immorality
(+ outcast dance)*

Soldier

> I'm fed up with pick and shovel,
> And I'd like to try it once.

Miss Gilchrist

> Did you read the Wolfenden Report
> On whores and queers?

Soldier

> Yeah, gorblimey, it was moving,
> I collapsed meself in tears.
>
> Well, at this poncing business,
> I think I'll have a try,
> And I'll drop the English coppers,
> They're the best money can buy.

Miss Gilchrist

> Goodbye, my son, God bless you,
> Say your prayers each morn and night,
> And send home your poor old mother
> A few quid – her widow's mite.

At the end of the dance the **Russian Sailor** *silently and smoothly removes* **Miss Gilchrist***. The whores and queers melt away, quietly cooing 'Leslie!' There is a moment of stillness and quiet, when* **Teresa** *comes down into the darkened room and calls.*

taking Colette's place.

Teresa   Leslie, Leslie!

The **Volunteer** *is asleep at* **Leslie***'s table. He wakes up and sees* **Teresa***.*

turn all the trouble!
he doesn't care, only cares about military.

Volunteer   You can call me Feargus! (*He leers lecherously.*)

Pat (*to* **Volunteer**)   Hey, you'll have us all in trouble. Attention! Quick march – left, right, left, right . . . Come on, leave 'em in peace.
this gets him to automatically listen -

Pat *throws out the* **Volunteer** *and takes* **Meg** *away, to leave* **Leslie** *alone with* **Teresa***.*

Teresa   That strict officer is coming back and I won't get a chance of a word with you.

Soldier   Well, what do you want?

Teresa   Don't be so narky. I just wanted to see you.

Soldier   Well, you'd better take a good look, hadn't you?

Teresa   What's eating you? I only wanted to talk to you.

Soldier   You'd better hurry up, I mightn't be able to talk so well with a hole right through me head.

Teresa   Don't be talking like that.

Soldier   Why not? Eh, why not?

Teresa   Maybe I could get you a cup of tea?

Soldier   No, thanks, I've just had a barrel of beer.

Teresa   Well, I'll go then.

Soldier   Eh, just before you go, don't think you've taken me for a complete bloody fool, will you? All this tea and beer lark: you even obliged with that. (*Indicating the bed.*)

Teresa   Leslie, for God's sake! Do you want the whole house to hear?

Leslie *takes her to the window.*

Soldier   Come here – I'll show you something. Can you see him over there, and that other one opposite? There are more than these two idiots guarding me. Look at those two, by the archway, pretending they're lovers. That should be right up your street, that, pretending they're lovers. That's a laugh.

Teresa   I wasn't pretending.

Soldier   How can I believe you, you and your blarney?

Teresa   The boys won't harm you. Pat told me himself; they only wanted to question you . . .

Soldier   Do you think he's going to tell you the truth, or me? After all – if you were really sorry for me, you might call the police. Well, would you, Teresa?

Teresa   I'm not an informer. →she's loyal to her first promise w. P[...]

Soldier   How long have I got? What time is it?

Teresa   It's not eleven yet. → how does she know? she "hears" the b[...] or just lies because who cares?

Soldier   Eleven o'clock. They'll just be waking up at   who know[...] home, fellows will be coming out of the dance halls.

Teresa (*still at the window*)   Look, there's an old fellow, half jarred, trying to sober up before he gets back home. → observation as[...]

Soldier   Back home, couple of hundred miles away, might just as well be on another bloody planet.

Teresa   Leslie, the chip shop is still open, maybe I could go out –

Soldier   I couldn't eat chips. Could you eat chips if you knew you were going to be done in? You're thinking of that poor bloke in Belfast. What about me, here now – Muggins?

Teresa   If I really thought they'd do anything to you –

Soldier   If you thought – I'm a hostage. You know what that means? What's the point of taking a hostage if you don't intend to do him in?

Teresa   Leslie, if they do come for you, shout to me.

Soldier   Shout! I wouldn't get a chance.   What help would she be?

Teresa   I can't be sure. uncertainty. → in a way, hope.

Soldier   Oh, go away and leave me in peace. At least that bloke in Belfast has peace, and tomorrow he'll have nuns and priest and the whole works to see him on his way.

Teresa   What do you want?

Soldier   Nothing – this bloke'll do the best he can on his own. Perhaps I'll meet that Belfast geezer on the other side. We can have a good laugh about it.

Teresa   Here's that officer coming. I'd better go.

She starts to leave him.

Leslie (*frightened*) Teresa! Don't go yet. I know I wasn't much good to you, but say goodbye properly, eh?

[handwritten: Act time]

Teresa *goes to him and they clasp in each other's arms.*

Soldier If I get away, will you come and see me in Armagh?

Teresa I will, Leslie.

Soldier I want all the blokes in the billet to see you. They all got pictures on the walls. Well, I never had any pictures, but now I've got you. Then we could have a bloody good time in Belfast together. *[handwritten: → Teresa = another representation.]*

Teresa It would be lovely, astore. *[handwritten: "proper Irish"]*

Soldier I'm due for a weekend's leave an' all . . .

Teresa I could pay my own way, too.

Soldier No, you needn't do that. I've got enough for both of us . . .

Teresa They're coming.

Pat *and the* **IRA Officer** *come down the stairs.*

Officer What's she doing here? Sleeping with him?

Pat Mind your own business. She's not interfering with you. You should be in bed now, girl. Where are you going?

Teresa I'm just going to the chip shop, to get some chips for him.

She starts to go, but the **IRA Officer** *stops her.*

Officer You can't go out there now.

Pat It's too late, girl.

Teresa It's only eleven.

Pat It's nearer one.

Teresa It's not the truth you're telling me.

[handwritten: how does she know? she had trusted his statement on Leslie being okay.]

Pat   Didn't you hear the clock strike?

Teresa   I did. *two different truths.*

Officer   Patrick, get her to her room or I will.

Teresa   You're lying to me. The chip shop is open till twelve.

Officer   Go to your room, girl.

Teresa   Do I have to go?

Pat   Yes, go to your room.

Leslie *is left alone in his room until* **Miss Gilchrist** *creeps from under the stairs to join him.*

Miss Gilchrist   Oh, Leslie, what's going to become of you?

Soldier   I don't know, mum, do I?

Miss Gilchrist   I've brought you a little gift.

She gives him a <u>*photograph*</u>. *again fed w. representations,*

Soldier   Oh, she's nice!

Miss Gilchrist   Oh, don't you recognise me, Leslie? It's me with me hair done nice.

Soldier   Oh, it's you. 'Ere, mum – I think you'd better go. Things might start warming up here.

Miss Gilchrist   God go with you, Leslie. God go with you.

She goes.

Soldier (*to the audience*)   Well, that's got rid of her. Now the thing is, will Teresa go to the cops? Even if old Einstein is half sozzled there's still the other two to get through. Will they shoot me? Yeah, I s'pose so. Will Teresa go to the cops? No.

There is an explosion which shakes the house, and smoke wreathes the stage. Sirens blow, whistles scream and all the lights go out. **Pat** *and*

Meg *rush into the room and they and the* **Soldier** *hide behind the table. Pandemonium breaks out. What is actually happening is that* **Mulleady** *has informed on* **Pat** *and* **Monsewer** *and has brought the police to rescue* **Leslie***. He has involved* **Rio Rita** *and* **Princess Grace** *in his schemes and they have corrupted his morals. The* **Russian** *has been a police spy all along. The police are now attacking the house and* **Mulleady** *and* **Rio Rita** *are guiding them in.*

Pat Take cover, there's a raid on.

Meg I want to see what's going on.

Pat Get your head down. They'll open fire any minute.

Mulleady (*from the roof*) Stand by. Two of you stay on the roof. The rest come down through the attic with me.

Rio Rita (*from the cellar*) Six round the front, six round the back, and you two fellers follow me.

Pat And take your partners for the eightsome reel.

The piano plays.

Mulleady O'Shaunessy!

O'Shaunessy (*from the rear of the house*) Sir!

Mulleady O'Shaunessy, shine a light for Jesus' sake.

O'Shaunessy (*off*) I will, sir.

Mulleady Shine a light, I can't see a bloody thing.

O'Shaunessy (*off*) I can't, sir, the battery's gone.

Mulleady To hell with the battery.

Rio Rita Charge!

His party go charging across the stage, but don't know where they're going or what they're doing. After confusion, they all charge back again.

Mulleady (*off*) Right, down you go, O'Shaunessy.

O'Shaunessy After you, sir.

Mulleady After you, man.

O'Shaunessy   After you, sir; I'm terrified of heights.

Mulleady   Then close your eyes, man. This is war.

→ "war" is enough to trigger response

*Pandemonium as the battle intensifies. Whistles and sirens blow,
drums beat, bombs explode, bugles sound the attack, bullets ricochet
and a confusion of orders are shouted all over the place. Bodies hurtle
from one side of the stage to the other and, in the midst of all the chaos,
the kilted figure of* **Monsewer** *slow marches, serene and stately,
across the stage, playing on his bagpipes a lament for the boy in Belfast
Jail.* **Pat** *screams at him in vain.*

→ but he comes out unharmed.

→ by this time this phrase has also become *utter oblivion.*

Pat   Sir! Sir! Get your head down. Get down, sir – there's
a raid on.

name.

He touches **Monsewer**.

Monsewer   What?

He stops playing and the din subsides.

Pat   There's a raid on.

Monsewer   Then why the devil didn't you tell me? Man
the barricades. Get the Mills bombs. Don't fire, laddie, till
you see the whites of their eyes.

Soldier   I've only got a bottle.

Monsewer   Up the Republic!

Pat   Get your head down, sir; they'll blow it off.

Rio Rita (*from under the stairs*)   Pat, do you want to buy a
rifle?

Pat   Get out, will you?

Rio Rita *goes. The din subsides and the battle dies down. Inside the
room are* **Monsewer**, *in command,* **Pat** *by the window, and* **Meg**,
Colette, **Ropeen** *and* **Leslie** *crawling round on the floor.
Around the room the shadowy shapes of the forces of law and order
flit in and out, darting across the stage and under the stairs.*

Monsewer   What's happening, Patrick?

Pat   I'll just find out, sir.

He looks out of the window and improvises a running commentary on the events outside.

They're just taking the field. The secret police is ready for the kick off, but the regulars is hanging back. Mr Mulleady has placed himself at the head of the <u>forces of law and order</u> and Miss Gilchrist is bringing up his rear. Princess Grace has joined the police . . .

A whistle blows.

The whistle's gone and they're off.

Mulleady *crawls past the window on the window sill.*

Pat   There's a man crawling along the gutter. He's going, he's going, he's gone!

Crash of falling body, and a quarrel below.

Soldier   Teresa! Teresa!

He thinks he's found her.

Meg   Shut up or I'll plug you, and your informer bitch when she comes in.

Soldier   Sorry, mum, I didn't know it was you.

There is an ominous silence. The piano is playing sinisterly.

Monsewer   Where's that officer chap?

Pat   I can't see him anywhere, sir.

Monsewer   Do you mean to say he's deserted in the face of fire?

Suddenly a bugle sounds the attack. Figures run to take up positions surrounding the room.

Pat   They're coming in.

Meg   Let's run for it.

Monsewer   Hold fast!

Pat   I'm running.

He runs.

Mulleady   Halt, or I fire.

Pat   I'm halting.

He stops with his hands up.

Monsewer   Up the Republic!

Soldier   Up the Arsenal! → fighting for smtn different still.

Mulleady   Hands up, we're coming in.

Monsewer   If you come in, we'll shoot the prisoner.

Teresa (*offstage*)   Run, Leslie, run.   → yes, he ends up being uro and it's by Monsewer.
→ why listen to teresa?

*The **Soldier** makes a break for it, zig-zagging across the stage, but the pl* *every door is blocked. The drum echoes his runs with short rolls. As he all no* *makes his last run there is a deafening blast of gunfire and he drops.*

Mulleady   Right, boys, over the top.

Mulleady*'s men storm into the room and round up the defenders.* **Mulleady** *is masked.* face /representation obscured.

Monsewer   Patrick, we're surrounded.

Meg (*to **Princess Grace***)   Drop that gun or I'll kick you up the backside.

Monsewer   Who are you?

Mulleady   I'm a secret policeman and I don't care who knows it. duality.

He reveals himself. Two nuns scurry across the room and up the stairs, praying softly.

Mulleady   Arrest those women.
← cowards

They are the two IRA men in disguise. **Teresa** *rushes into the room.*

Teresa   Leslie! Leslie! Where's Leslie?

They all look around. No one has seen him.

who they should be focusing on.
but not actually...
it was never about him.

Pat   He was here a minute ago.

He sees the body and goes down to it.

Teresa   Where is he? Leslie. (*She sees him.*)

Meg   There he is.

Pat   He's dead. Take his identification disc.

Rio Rita (*kneeling to do it*)   I'll do it, sir.

Finding the medal.

I didn't know he was a Catholic Boy.

[handwritten: Leslie's identity → given by Teresa. & misrepresented.]

Teresa   I gave it to him. Leave it with him.

Mulleady   Cover him up.

Rio Rita *covers the body with one of the nun's cloaks.* **Teresa** *kneels by the body. The others bare their heads.*

Teresa   Leslie, my love. A thousand blessings go with you.

Pat   Don't cry. Teresa. It's ~~no one's fault. Nobody meant to kill him.~~

[handwritten:) no intent, just results. like atemporality. doesn't matter when he dies. doesn't matter who killed.]

Teresa   But he's dead. ✓

Pat   So is the boy in Belfast Jail.

[handwritten: incredible sharpness.]

Teresa   It wasn't the Belfast Jail or the Six Counties that was troubling you, but ~~your lost youth and your crippled leg.~~ He died in a strange land, and at home he had no one. I'll never forget you, Leslie, till the end of time.

[handwritten: Teresa is the only one who can "see" him as is.]

She rises and everyone turns away from the body. A ghostly green light glows on the body as **Leslie Williams** *slowly gets up and sings:*

[handwritten: he's only "called" by name here. summoned by the author as his true self.]

The bells of hell,
Go ting-a-ling-a-ling,
For you but not for me,
Oh death, where is thy sting-a-ling-a-ling?
Or grave thy victory?
If you meet the undertaker,
Or the young man from the Pru,

Get a pint with what's left over,
Now I'll say goodbye to you.

The stage brightens, and everyone turns and comes down towards the audience, singing.

All

The bells of hell,
Go ting-a-ling-a-ling,   =leslie.
For you but not for him,
O death, where is thy sting-a-ling-a-ling!
Or grave thy victory.

Curtain.

Leslie's song: not dead.

Tom Murphy

Bailegangaire

*The story of Bailegangaire
and how it came by its appellation*

Bailegangaire was first performed by the Druid Theatre Company, Galway, on 5 December 1985 with the following cast:

Mommo   Siobhan McKenna
Mary   Marie Mullen
Dolly   Mary McEvoy

Directed by   Garry Hynes
Designed by   Frank Conroy
Lighting by   Roger Frith

Characters

Mommo
Mary
Dolly

Time and place

1984, the kitchen of a thatched house. The set should be
stylised to avoid cliché and to achieve best effect.

Note

'Notturno' in E Flat by Schubert introduces and closes the
play.

Mary's poem, which she misquotes, in Act One is 'Silences'
by Thomas Hardy.

Act One

Dusk is setting in on a room, a country kitchen. There are some modern conveniences: a cooker, a radio (which is switched on), electric light – a single pendant. Photographs on the walls, brown photographs. There is a double bed. It is the warmest room in the house (probably the central room of the traditional three-roomed thatched house). An old woman in the bed, **Mommo**, *is eating and drinking something out of a mug, occasionally rejecting pieces of food, spitting them on the floor. She is a good mimic. She interrupts her meal:*

Mommo   Shkoh cake! Shkoth!

Driving imagined hens from the house.

Dirty aul' things about the place . . . And for all they lay!

She is senile.

Mary, *her granddaughter, wears a wraparound apron draped tightly about her spinster frame; bare knees over half wellington boots; hair tight, perhaps in a bun. She is forty-one. A 'private' person, an intelligent, sensitive woman, a trier, but one who is near breaking point.* **Mommo** *has again interrupted her meal, this time to talk to imagined children at the foot of the bed.*

Mommo   Let ye be settling now, my fondlings, and I'll be giving ye a nice story again tonight when I finish this. For isn't it a good one?

The kettle is boiling. **Mary** *makes tea, lays the table. She produces the anomaly of a silver teapot.* **Mommo** *is now watching* **Mary** *and* **Mary***'s movements suspiciously.*

Mommo   . . . An' no one will stop me! Tellin' my nice story . . . (*Reverts to herself.*) Yis, how the place called Bochtán – and its *graund* (*grand*) inhabitants – came to its new appellation, Bailegangaire, the place without laughter. Now! What time is it?

Mary   Seven.

Mary *is taking off her apron.*

Mommo   Yis! Shkoth! – an' lock them in. Hah-haa! but I'll outdo the fox, I'll take the head of the every one of them hens tomorrow.

Mary   Mommo?

She has removed her apron and in her new image is smiling bravely against an increasing sense of loneliness and demoralisation.

I have a surprise for you.

Mommo   Pardon?

Mary   Look! (*She holds up an iced cake.*) We never knew your birthday but today is mine and I thought we might share the same birthday together in future. (*She has lit a candle.*)

Mommo (*eyes fixed on the candle*)   The cursèd paraffin.

Mary   Though someone once said – I may be wrong – yours was the first of May, a May child.

Mommo   The cursèd paraffin.

Mary   And you can get up for a while – if you wish.

Mommo   Birthday?

Mary   Yes! We'll have a party, the two of us.

Mommo   What's birthdays to do with us?

Mary   By candlelight.

Mommo   What's your business here?

Mary (*indicating the table*)   Isn't that nice?

Mommo   Do I know you?

Mary   Mary.

She bows her head, momentarily deflated, then smiles invitingly at **Mommo** *again.*

Mary   Hmm?

Mommo (*and there is defiance, hatred in the sound*)   Heh heh heh heh!

Mary   Mary. (*Deflated. And sits.*)

We get the end of the news in Irish on the radio, then Tommy O'Brien's
programme of light classics, Your Choice and Mine. *The candlelight,*
the table neatly laid, the silver teapot, the simple line of **Mary***'s dress*
becomes her, a book beside her, sipping tea, the grave intelligent face,
a picture of strange, elegant loneliness.

Mommo   Ooh! and to be sure and so as not to be putting
any over-enlargement on my narrative, the creatures left in
that place now can still *smile*, on occasion. And to be sure, the
childre, as is the wont of all childre in God's kingdom on
earth, are as clever at the laughing as they are at the crying,
until they arrive at the age of reason. That is well, my dears.
Now to tell my story. Here! You! Miss! Take this. Did you
manage to poison me? Ha-haa – No – ho-ho!

Mary *takes a cup of tea to* **Mommo** *and places it on the chair*
beside the bed, takes the mug and returns to the table.

A car passes by outside.

Mommo (*settles herself in the bed for her story*)   Now! It was a
bad year for the crops, a good one for mushrooms and the
contrary and adverse connection between these two is always
the case. So you can be sure the people were putting their
store in the poultry and the bonavs (*bonhams*) and the
creamery produce for the great maragadh mór (*big market*)
that is held every year on the last Saturday before Christmas
in Bailethuama (*the town of Tuam*) in the other county. And
some sold well and some sold middlin', and one couple was
in it – strangers, ye understand – sold not at all. And at day's
business concluded there was celebration, for some, and
fitting felicitations exchanged, though not of the usual
protraction, for all had an eye on the cold inclement weather
that boded. So, the people were departing Bailethuama in
the other county in diverse directions homewards. As were
the people of the place I'm talking about. And they were
only middlin' satisfied, if at all. The Bochtáns were never
entirely fortunate. An' devil mend them. An' scald them. No
matter. What time is it? . . . Miss!

Mary   Seven. (*The tips of her fingers to her forehead.*)

Mommo   I'm waiting for someone. Supa tea.

Mary   It's on the chair beside you.

Mommo   Oh, an' he will come yet. (*A warning to* **Mary**.) And he has a big stick.

Mary *remains seated: she knows from experience what the outcome of the conversation is going to be; she does not lift her eyes.*

Mary   And time to take your pills.

Mommo (*has no intention of taking them*)   The yellow ones?

Mary   Yes.

Mommo   They're good for me?

Mary   I'll give you a cigarette.

Mommo   They'll help me sleep?

Mary   Yes.

Mommo   Heh heh heh heh!

Mary (*to herself*)   And I'd like to read, Mommo.

Mommo   Now there was a decent man at that market and his decent wife the same. Strangers, strangers! Sure they could have come from the south of – Galway! – for all I know. And they had sold not at all. Well, if you call the one basket of pullets' eggs valiant trade. (*She takes a sip of the tea.*) Too hot. No. Their main cargo which consisted of eighteen snow-white geese still lay trussed in the floor of the cart, 'gus bhár ar an mi-ádh sin (*and to make matters worse*) the pitch on an incline of the road was proving an impossibility for the horse to surmount. But he was a decent man, and he took not belt – nor the buckle-end of it as another would – to the noble animal that is the horse. Put it down!

The last to **Mary**, *who is standing by having put a little more milk into* **Mommo**'s *tea.*

No. But spoke only in the gentlest of terms, encouraging the poor beast to try once more against the adversary. 'Try again, Pedlar.' For that was the horse's name. Is that a step?

Mary (*listening*)   . . . Dolly was to call last night.

The sound they have heard – if any – does not materialise further.

Nobody. She didn't call the night before either.

Mommo   What's this?

Mary *does not understand.*

Mommo   Taking down the good cup!

Mary   It tastes nicer out of a –

Mommo   Mug, a mug! – Oh leave it so now! Put it down!

Mary   And nicer to have your pills with.

Mommo   The yellow ones? – Try again, Pedlar, for-that-was-the-horse's name!

Mary *returns to the table.*

Mommo   And all the while his decent wife on the grass verge and she cráite (*crestfallen*). And a detail which you may contemplate fondly now but was only further testimonial to the misfortunes of that unhappy couple, each time she went to draw the shawl more tightly round her frailty, the hand peepin' out held three sticks of rock. Now! Yis, gifts for her care, three small waiting grandchildren. Like ye. Isn't it a good one? (*A sip of tea.*) Cold.

Mary (*to herself*)   I can't stand it.

But she is up again to add a little hot water to the tea.

Mommo   And she up to the fifty mark!

Mary (*to herself*)   And that bitch Dolly.

Mommo   Or was she maybe more?

Mary   In heat again.

Mommo   And what was her husband? Decorous efficiency in all he cared to turn his hand to, like all small men. Sure he had topped the sixty!

Mary   Taste that and see if it's alright for you.

Mommo   But he was unlucky. He was. He was. An' times, maybe, she was unkind to him. (*Childlike.*) Was she?

Mary   No. (*Returning to the table where she sits, her head back on her shoulders, looking up at the ceiling.*)

Mommo   And how many children had she bore herself?

Mary   Eight?

Mommo   And what happened to them?

Mary   Nine? Ten?

Mommo   Hah?

Mary   What happened us all?

Mommo   Them (*that*) weren't drowned or died they said she drove away.

Mary   Mommo? I'm Mary.

Mommo   Let them say what they like.

Mary   I'm very happy here.

Mommo   Oh, but she looked after her grandchildren. Tom is in Galway. He's afeared of the gander.

Mary   Mommo? Please stop.

Mommo   To continue. Now man and horse, though God knows they tried, could see the icy hill was not for yielding. So what was there for doing but to retrace the hard-won steps to the butt end of the road which, as matters would have it, was a fork. One road leading up the incline whence they came, the other to Bochtán.

Now that man knew that the road to Bochtán, though of circularity, was another means home. And it looked level

enough stretching out into the gathering duskess. And 'deed
he knew men from his own village (*who*) had travelled it and
got home safe and sound. Still he paused. Oh, not through
fear, for if he was a man to submit he would've threwn
himself into the river years ago. No. But in gentleness, sad
the searching eye on the road. And sadder still the same grey
eyes were growing in handsomeness as the years went by.
She had noted it. But she'd never comment on this becoming
aspect of his mien for, strange, it saddened her too. It did.
But the two little smiles appearing, one each side of his
mouth, before taking a step anywhere. Even when only to
go to the back door last thing at night an' call in the old dog
to the hearth.

Mary *hears the 'putt-putt' of a motorcycle approaching, stopping
outside.*

Mary   Right!

Suggesting she is going to have matters out with **Dolly***. She puts on her
apron, gets bucket, water, scrubbing brush, to scrub the part of the floor
that* **Mommo** *spat on.*

Mommo   Last thing at night . . . An' then the silence, save
the tick of the clock . . . An' why didn't she break it? She
knew how to use the weapon of silence. But why didn't he?
A woman isn't stick or stone. The gap in the bed, concern for
the morrow, how to keep the one foot in front of the other.
An' when would it all stop. What was the dog's name?
(*Childlike.*) D'ye know I can't remember.

Dolly   Mo Dhuine.

Dolly *has come in. Like her name, she is dolled up in gaudy, rural
fashion. She is thirty-nine. She has a handbag and she carries a crash
helmet.*

Mommo   Shep, was it?

Dolly   Mo Dhuine.

Mommo   Spot? Rover? Mo Dhuine! Mo Dhuine! Now!
Mo Dhuine.

Dolly   Jesus! (*To herself.*)

Mommo   He loved Mo Dhuine – Hona ho gus ha-haa! (*Laughing in celebration.*) An' the bother an' the care on him one time filling the eggshell with the hot ember an' leavin' it there by the door.

Dolly   Then the root in the arse –

Mommo   Then the root in the arse to poor Mo Dhuine, the twig 'cross his back, to get along with him an' the mouth burned in him! Oh but it did, *did*, cured him of thievin' the eggs.

Dolly *switches on the light.* **Mommo***'s eyes to the light bulb.*

Dolly   What're yeh doin' workin' in the dark?

Mommo   But they had to get home.

Dolly   Oh, she can't have everything her own way.

Mommo   Their inheritance, the three small waiting children, left unattended.

Dolly (*rooting in her bag, producing a bottle of vodka*)   How yeh!

Mary *merely nods, continues working.*

Mommo   And night fast closing around them.

Dolly   Stronger she's gettin'. A present.

Mary (*hopeful that the vodka is for her birthday*)   For what?

Dolly   'Cause I couldn't come up last night.

Mary   What do I (*want with a bottle of vodka*)!

Dolly   Yeh never know. She'll last for ever.

Mommo   Then, drawing a deep breath. (*She draws a deep breath.*) Oh but didn't give vent to it, for like the man he was I'm sayin', refusing to *sigh* or submit. An', 'On we go, Pedlar,' says he, an' man, horse, cart and the woman falling in 'tween the two hind shafts set off on the road to Bochtán which place did not come by its present appellation, Bailegangaire, till that very night. Now.

Dolly   Jesus, Bailegangaire – D'yeh want a fag? – night after night, can't you stop her? A fag?

Mary (*declines the cigarette*)   No.

Dolly   Night after night the same old story – (*Proffering cigarettes again.*) Ary you might as well.

Mary *ignores her.*

Dolly   By Jesus I'd stop her.

Mary   I wish you'd stop using that word, Dolly. I've been trying to stop her. (*Putting away bucket, etc.*)

Dolly   Michaeleen is sick. The tonsils again. So I couldn't come up last night. I'm worried about them tonsils. What d'yeh think? So I can't stay long tonight either.

Mary   Aren't you going to say hello to her?

Dolly   What's up with yeh? Home, I'm goin'.

Mary   Aren't you going to take off your coat?

Dolly   What do you mean?

Mary   What do you mean, what do I mean!

Dolly *turns stubbornly into the fire and sits.*

Mommo   But to come to Bochtán so ye'll have it all. Them from that place had been to the market were 'riving back home. One of them, a Seamus Costello by name. Oh, a fine strappin' man. Wherever he got it from. The size an' the breadth of him, you'd near have to step into the verge to give him sufficient right of way. 'Twould be no use him extending the civility 'cause you'd hardly get around him I'm saying. And he was liked. Rabbits he was interested in. This to his widowed mother's dismay, but that's another thing. And the kind of man that when people'd espy him approaching the gurgle'd be already startin' in their mouths – 'Och-haw.' For he was the exception, ye understand, with humour in him as big as himself. And I'm thinkin' he was the one an' only boast they ever had in that cursed place. What time is it?

Mary   Eight!

Dolly (*simultaneously*)   Nine!

They look at each other, laugh, and bygones are bygones.

Mary   Quarter past eight.

Mommo   Quarter past eight, an' sure that's not late. That's a rhyme. Now for ye! (*She takes a sip of tea.*) Too sweet.

Mary *rectifying the tea situation. A cajoling tone coming into* **Dolly**'s *voice — there's something on her mind, and she is watching and assessing* **Mary** *privately.*

Dolly   They say it's easier to do it for someone else's (*to take care of a stranger*). (*Declining tea which* **Mary** *offers.*) No thanks. And that old story is only upsetting her, Mary, isn't it?

Mary *is too intelligent to be taken in by* **Dolly**'s *tone or tactics — but this is not at issue here: she has other things on her mind. She sits by the fire with* **Dolly** *and now accepts the cigarette.* **Mommo** *is sipping tea.*

Dolly   Harping on misery, and only wearing herself out. And you. Amn't I right, Mary? And she never finishes it. Why doesn't she finish it and have done with it? For God's sake!

Mary *considers this* ('*Finish it and have done with it?*'), *then forgets it for the moment. She is just looking into the fire.*

Mary   I'd love to have a talk.

Dolly   About what?

Mary   Do you remember . . . (*She shakes her head: she does not know.*)

Dolly   What? . . . I know it affects you: like, her not reco'nisin' you ever – Why wouldn't it? But you were away a long time.

Mary *looks up: she has been only half listening.*

Dolly   That's the reason.

Mary   . . . I've often thought . . . (*She is just looking at the fire again.*)

Dolly   What?

Mary   I may have been too – bossy – at first.

Dolly   Well, well, there could be something in that, too.

Mary   But I wanted to . . . bring about change. Comfort, civilised.

Dolly   Yes, well, but. Though I don't know. You were away an awful long time. I was left holdin' the can. Like, when yeh think of it, you owe me a very big debt.

Mary (*looks up*)   Hmm? A very big?

Dolly   I mean, that's why she reco'nises me.

Mary *looking at the fire again;* **Dolly** *watching* **Mary**. *Something on* **Dolly**'s *mind; she coughs in preparation to speak –*

Mary   . . . We had a pony and trap once. The Sunday outings. You don't remember?

Dolly, *puzzled, shakes her head.*

Mary   Ribbons. Grandad would always bring ribbons home for our hair. You don't remember.

Dolly   . . . You work too hard.

Mary *laughs at* **Dolly**'s *explanation of it all.*

Dolly   What? (*Laughing because* **Mary** *has laughed.*)

Mary *shakes her head, 'It doesn't matter.'*

Dolly   And you're too serious.

Mary Do you remember Daddy?

Dolly Well, the photographs.

They look about at the photographs on the wall.

Aul' brown ghosts. (*Playful, but cajoling.*) Y'are, y'are, too serious.

Mary (*eyes back to the fire*) I suppose I am. I don't know what I'm trying to say. (*Sighs.*) Home!

Mommo (*puts down her cup*) And that, too, is well. And now with his old jiggler of a bicycle set again' the gable, Costello was goin' in to John Mah'ny's, the one and only shop for everything for miles around. 'Cold enough for ye, ladies!' Now! Cold enough for ye, ladies. And that was the first remark he was to utter that evening. And the two women he had thus accosted set to gurgling at once and together. 'Caw och-caw, Seamusheen a wockeen, God bless yeh, och-caw,' says the old crone that was in it buyin' the salt. And, 'Uck-uck-uck, uck-uck hunuka huckina-caw, Costello,' from the young buxom woman tendin' the shop end of the counter, and she turnin' one of the babes in her arms so that he too could behold the hero. 'Aren't they gettin' awful big, God bless them,' then saying Costello of the two twins an' they gogglin' at him. 'Jack Frost is coming with a vengeance for ye tonight,' says he, 'or the Bogey Man maybe bejingoes.' And to the four or five others now holding tight their mother's apron, 'Well, someone is comin' anyways,' says he, 'if ye all aren't good.' An' then off with him to the end where the drink was.

Dolly Good man Josie!

Mary No!

Mommo 'Good man, Josie!'

Mary (*overlapping*) Don't encourage her.

Mommo Now!

Mary (*overlapping*) I'm – (*going out of my mind*)!

Mommo   'Good man, Josie.'

Mary (*overlapping*)   I'm trying to stop it!

Mommo   And that was the second greeting he uttered that night.

Mary (*overlapping*)   Talk to her!

Dolly (*overlapping*)   That's what I try to do!

Mommo   He got no reply.

Dolly (*going to* **Mommo**, *under her breath*)   Good man, Josie, Jesus!

Mommo   Nor did he expect one.

Dolly (*calling back to* **Mary**)   And I'm going at quarter to nine! – Good man, Mommo, how's it cuttin'?

Mommo   Good man – ! Pardon?

Dolly   How's the adversary treatin' yeh?

Mommo (*to herself*)   Good man Mommo?

Dolly   I brought yeh sweets.

Mommo   There's nothing wrong with me.

Dolly   I didn't say there was.

Mommo   An' I never done nothin' wrong.

Dolly   Sweets!

Mary   Butterscotch, isn't it, Dolly?

Mommo (*to herself, puzzled again*)   Good man – *who*?

Dolly   Butterscotch, I've oceans of money.

Mary   Your favourites.

Dolly   You like them ones.

Mary   Try one. You (*Dolly*) give it to her.

Mommo   Do I like them ones?

Mary   Suck it slowly.

Dolly   Gobstoppers I should have brought her.

Mary   Shh!

Dolly   You're lookin' fantastic. (*Going back to the fire.*) It'd be a blessing if she went.

Mary (*placatory*)   Shh, don't say things like (*that*). Talk to her, come on.

Dolly   About what? It's like an oven in here – and I don't understand a word she's sayin'.

Mary   Take off your – (*coat*).

Dolly   I – don't – want – to – take – off – my – !

Mary   Tell her about the children.

Dolly   Seafóid, nonsense talk about forty years ago –

Mary   Come on –

Dolly   And I've enough problems of my own. Why don't you stick her in there? (*One of the other rooms.*)

Mary   It's damp. And she understands – recognises you a lot of the time.

Dolly *rolling her eyes, but following* **Mary** *back to the bed again.*

Mary   Where she can see you.

Dolly   Well, the children are all fine, Mommo. (*A slip.*) Well, Michaeleen is sick, the tonsils again. I've rubber-backed lino in all the bedrooms now, the Honda is going like a bomb and the lounge, my dear, is carpeted. I seen the lean and lanky May Glynn, who never comes near ye or this house, in her garden when I was motoring over but she went in without a salute. I must have distemper too or whatever. Conor, that other lean and lanky bastard, is now snaking his fence in another six inches, and my darlin' mother-in-law, old sharp-eyes-and-the-family rosary, sends her pers'nal blessings to ye both.

Mary   Is she babysitting for you?

Dolly   No. She is not babysitting for me. (I don't want her or any of the McGrath clan in my house.)

Mommo (*sucking the sweet*)   They're nice.

Dolly   An' the cat had kittens. (*To* **Mary**.) D'yeh want a kitten? Do you, Mommo? (*A touch of sour introversion.*) Does anyone? Before I drown them.

Mommo   Tom is in Galway.

Mary   Did you hear from Stephen?

Dolly   The 'wire' again on Friday, regular as clockwork.

Mary   Did you hear, Mommo?

Mommo   I did. But she told May Glynn not to be waitin', her own mother'd be needin' her, and that they'd be home before dark for sure.

Dolly   Eighty-five quid a week and never a line.

Mary   He's busy.

Dolly   Fuck him. I don't know what to do with the money! (*Sour introspection again.*) Or do I? I've started saving for a purpose. (*Then impetuously to* **Mary**.) Do you want some money? Well, do you, Mommo? To go dancin'.

Mary *is laughing at her sister's personality.*

Mary   Stephen will be home as usual for Christmas.

Dolly   For his goose.

Mary   Won't he, Mommo?

Mommo (*to herself*)   Stephen, yes, fugum.

They laugh. Then, **Dolly**, *grimly:*

Dolly   Well, maybe it'd be better if the bold Stephen skipped his visit home this Christmas. (*Rises and turns her back on them.*) Jesus, misfortunes.

Mary *now wondering, her eyes on* **Dolly***'s back, the stout figure.*

Mommo (*to herself*)   Yes. Misfortunes.

Mary   Dolly?

Dolly   Ooh, a cake, a candle – candles! what's the occasion? (*She gives a kiss to* **Mommo**.) Well, I'm off now, darlin', an' God an' all His holy saints protect an' bless yeh.

Mommo (*buried in her own thoughts until now*)   When did you arrive?

Dolly   What?

Mommo   When did you arrive?

Dolly   I arrived –

Mommo   Sure you're welcome, when did you arrive?

Dolly   I arrived –

Mommo   Well, did yeh?

Dolly   I did.

Mommo   From where?

Dolly   From –

Mommo   Now. And is that where y'are now?

Dolly   The very location.

Mommo   Now! I never knew that. Where?

Dolly   Ahm . . . Aw Jesus, Mommo, you have us all as confused as yourself! Ballindine! Ball-in-dine.

Mommo   Hah? Oh yes, yeh told me. Now. Who are you?

Dolly   Dolly, I think.

Mommo (*considering this, sucking her sweet*)   Now. Dolly.

Dolly   Dolly!

Mommo   Yes.

Dolly   Look, I have to be − (*going*). I'm Dolly, your granddaughter, and that's Mary, your other granddaughter, and your grandson Tom, Tom is dead.

Mary   Shh!

Dolly   Ah, shh! (*To* **Mommo**.) Now do you know?

Mommo   I do. I'm waiting for someone.

Dolly   Who're yeh waiting for?

Mommo   I'm not tellin' yeh.

Dolly   A man, is it?

Mommo (*laughing*)   'Tis.

Dolly   Ahona ho gus hah-haa, an' what'll he have for yeh!

Mommo (*laughing*)   A big stick.

Dolly   M-m-m-m! − A big stick, the bata! Mmmah! (*Sexual innuendo.*) Now! Try that subject on her if you want to stop her.

Mommo   Oh, but they were always after me.

Dolly   An' did they ketch yeh?

Mommo   The ones I wanted to.

Dolly   An' are they still after yeh?

Mommo   But I bolt the door − on some of them. (*Laughing.*)

Dolly (*to* **Mary**)   That's what all the aul ones like to talk about. I think you're goin' soft in the head.

Mommo (*recognising her*)   Is it Dolly? Aw, is it my Dolly! Well, d'yeh know I didn't rec'nise yeh. Sure you were always the joker. Aw, my Dolly, Dolly, Dolly, come 'ere to me!

Dolly *hesitates, is reluctant, then succumbs to the embrace; indeed, after a moment she is clinging tightly to the old woman.*

Mary *stands by, isolated, watching the scene. She would love to be included. The smallest gesture of affection or recognition would help greatly.*

Mommo   Ah, lovee. Lovee, lovee, lovee. Sure if I knew you were comin' – (*Aside to* **Mary**.) Will you put on the kettle, will you? Standing there! – I'd've baked a cake. That's an old one. Oh, mo pheata (*my pet*). Why didn't you send word? An' you got fat. You did! On me oath! Will you put on the kettle, Miss, will you! (*Whispering.*) Who is that woman?

Dolly (*tearfully, but trying to joke*)   She's the sly one.

Mommo   She is. (*Loudly, hypocritically.*) Isn't she nice?

Dolly   Watch her.

Mary *goes off to another room.*

Mommo   Why is she interfering?

Dolly   Shh, Mommo.

Mommo   Be careful of that one.

Dolly   Shh, Mommo, I'm in terrible trouble.

Mommo   Yes, watch her.

Dolly (*extricating herself from the embrace, brushing away a tear*) Leave her to me. I'll deal with her. (*Calls.*) Miss! Will you come out, will you, an' make a brew! An' put something in it! Sure you should know about all kinds of potions.

Mary *has returned with a suitcase. She places it somewhere.*

Dolly   . . . Someone going on a voyage?

Mary   I have to come to a decision, Dolly.

Dolly   Again?

Mary   She's your responsibility too.

Dolly   I know you think I inveigled you back here so that Stephen and I could escape.

Mary   No one inveigled me anywhere. You're not pulling your weight.

Dolly (*shrugs*)   There's always the County Home.

Mary   You –

Dolly   Wouldn't I? Why should I stick myself again back in here?

Mary   Why should I?

Dolly   In a place like this.

Mary   Why do I? In a place like this.

Dolly (*shrugs*)   That's your business. Well, I have to be going.

Mary   I'd like to go out sometimes too.

Dolly   *Home*, I'm going.

Mary   You look it.

Dolly   Alright, I'll tell you, so that you can go, where the man is waiting.

Mary   Man? *Men!*

Dolly *shrugs, is moving off.*

Mary   I need to talk to – *someone!*

Dolly (*her back to* **Mary**, *quietly*)   I need to talk to someone too.

Mary (*an insinuation*)   Why don't you take off your coat?

Dolly (*faces* **Mary**; *a single solemn nod of her head; then*) Because, now, I am about to leave. I'll figure out something. I might even call back in a while, 'cause it doesn't take long, does it? Just a few minutes; that's all it takes.

Mary   You're disgusting.

Dolly   Am I?

Mary (*going to one of the other rooms*)   I've come to a decision. (*Off.*) County Home! You won't blackmail me!

Dolly (*to herself*)   I hate this house. (*To* **Mommo**.) Good man, Josie! (*Going out; an undertone.*) Ah, fuck it all.

Mommo   Oh yes. 'Good man, Josie!' Now! Good man, Josie. And that was the second greeting Costello was to utter that evening.

Mary (*coming in*)   I'll leave everything here for you spick and span, of course.

She has not heard **Dolly** *go out; now she stands there looking at the door, the motorcycle outside driving away, her hands clapping together some of her wardrobe (as if demonstrating the possibility that she is leaving rather than confirming it).*

Mommo   He got no reply. Nor did he expect one. For Josie was a Greaney and none was ever right in that fambly.

Mary   It's not fair. (*To herself.*)

Mommo   Though some say he had the knack of mendin' clocks, if he had.

Mary (*angrily: still to the door*)   Your husband wined, dined and bedded me! Stephen? *Your* Stephen?! It was *me* he wanted! But I told him: 'Keep off! Stop following me!' That's why he took you!

Mommo (*she has had a sip of tea*)   What's in this? Miss!

Mary   The County Home!

Gesturing, meaning did **Mommo** *hear what* **Dolly** *said.*

Mommo   Hot drink, decent sup a tea!

Mary (*automatically sets about making fresh tea, then she stops*) I have come to a decision, I said! Do you understand? So if you could wait a moment –

She starts to discard some of the clothes, packing others; talking to herself again.

Just to see who is in earnest this time.

Mommo   Me mouth is dry, d'ye know.

Mary   And I was doing well – I was the success! Now I'm talking to myself.

Mommo   Howandever. 'How the boys!' was Costello's third greeting. This time to two old men with their heads in the fire. The one of them givin' out the odd aul' sigh, smoking his pipe with assiduity and beating the slow obsequies of a death roll with his boot. An' the other, a Brian by name, replying in sagacity, 'Oh yis,' sharing the silent mysteries of the world between them. Me mouth is (*dry*), d'ye know.

Mary   Just a moment! (*Going to other room.*) Dependent on a pension and that bitch.

Mommo   Where is she? Miss!

Mary (*off*)   And you know very well who I am!

Mommo   Miss!

Mary (*off*)   Miss! Miss! Miss is coming! (*Entering with more clothes.*) Miss: as if I didn't exist. That's the thanks I get, that's the – (*Winces to herself.*) It's – not – thanks I'm looking for. (*Absently.*) What am I looking for? I had to come home. No one inveigled me. I wanted to come home.

She comes out of her reverie, in the realisation that **Mommo** *has got out of bed. And she is hurrying to* **Mommo**'s *assistance.*

Mommo   Shhtaap!

Mary *is stopped by the ferocity.* **Mommo** *squats, hidden behind the headboard of the bed (perhaps on a commode).*

Mary   . . . And to change your nightdress . . . I was a nurse, Mommo . . . And offers of marriage.

Then, quickly, efficiently, she takes the opportunity of remaking the bed. She replaces the sheets with clean ones, removes the bed-warmer – which is a cast-iron lid of a pot in a knitted woollen cover; she puts the lid into the fire to reheat it. She appears almost happy when she is working constructively, and she starts to sing:

'Once I loved with fond affection,
All my thoughts they were in thee,
Till a dark-haired girl deceived me,
And no more he thought of me.

Too-ralloo-ralloo-ralladdy,
Too-ralloo-ralloo-rallee,
Till a dark-haired girl deceived me,
And no more he thought of me.'

And sure you have lots of poems, lots of stories, nice stories, instead of that old one. 'Mick Delaney' – do you remember that one? We loved that one. How did it begin? Or ghost stories. People used to come miles to hear you tell stories. Oh! And do you remember: the gramophone? Yes, we had a gramophone too. 'The banshee is out tonight go down (*on*) your knees and say your prayers – wooooo!' Or would you like me to read you a story?

Mommo (*reappearing from behind the bed*)   Heh heh heh heh!

Mary   Why can't you be civil to me? At least tonight. There was happiness here too, Mommo. Harmony?

Mommo (*straight back, neck craned*)   You can be going now, Miss.

Mary   . . . Alright.

She collects the chamber pot from behind the headboard of the bed and goes out.

Mommo   She knows too much about our business entirely. (*She calls hypocritically.*) And thank you! (*Giggles getting back into the bed.*) Now amn't I able for them?

But now that Costello was in it the aspect was transforming. 'An',' says old Brian, taking his head out of the fire, 'what's the news from the Big World?' 'The Dutch has taken Holland!' says Costello with such a rumble out of him near had the whole house shook asunder and all in it in ululation so infectious was the sound. Save Josie who was heedless, but rapping with severity on the counter for more libation. And

'John!' says the young buxom woman, calling to her husband
– 'John!' – to come out and tend his end of the counter, an'
she now putting questions on bold Costello.

'You wor in Tuam?' says she, 'I was in Tuam,' says he, 'Yeh
wor?' says she, 'I was,' says he, 'An' how was it?' says she.

'Well, not tellin' you a word of a lie now,' says he, 'but 'twas
deadly.'

And 'Ory!' says the crone that was in it buyin' the salt.

'Did yeh hear?' says the young buxom woman to her
husband, John, to be sure. He had 'rived from the kitchen
an' was frownin' pullin' pints. Merchants d'ye know: good
market or bad, the arithmetic in the ledger has to come out
correct.

'Well do yeh tell me so?' says the young buxom woman.

'I do tell yeh so,' says Costello. 'Talkin' about a Maragadh
Mór? – I never in all me born days seen light or likes of it!'

Now they were listening.

Mary *comes in. She selects her 'going-away' suit. She tries the waist
against herself. She puts the suit on a chair beside the fire to air it.
Through the following she goes out/comes in with turf for the night.*

Mommo 'Firkins of butter,' says he, 'an' cheese be the
hundredweight. Ducks, geese, chickens, bonavs and – geese!'
says he, 'geese! There was hundreds of them! There was
hundreds upon hundreds of thousands of them! The ground
I tell ye was white with them!'

And 'White with them,' says the crone.

'They went ch-cheap then?' says John, still bowed frownin'
over the tricks of pullin' porter.

'Cheap then?' says Costello. 'Sure yeh couldn't give them
away sure. Sure the sight of so many chickens an' geese an'
sure all the people could do was stand and stare.'

'They were puzzled,' says the crone.

'I'm tellin' ye,' says Costello, 'Napoleon Bonaparte wouldn't have said no to all the provisions goin' a-beggin' in that town of Tuam today.'

An' 'Hah?' says John, squintin', the head-work interrupted.

'On his retreat from Moscow, sure,' says Costello. 'Or Josephine – Wuw! – neither.'

Now! Wuw. Them were his ways, an' he having the others equivalently pursuant: 'Wo ho ho, wo ho ho!'

'But you sis-sold your rabbits, did yeh, Costello?' says John. An' wasn't there a gap. Oh, only for the second. 'Oh I sold them,' then sayin' Costello. 'Oh I did, did,' saying he, 'Oh on me solemn 'n dyin' oath! Every man-jack-rabbit of them.' Like a man not to be believed, his bona fides in question.

'Yeh-yeh codjer yeh-yeh,' says John. Whatever he meant. But he was not at all yet feeling cordial.

But thus was the night faring into its progression, others 'riving back home an' how did they do an' who else was in it, did they buy e'er a thing, Costello settin' them laughin', John frownin' an' squintin', an' the thief of a Christmas they wor all goin' t'have. What're ye doin' there?

Mary *is putting the dirty bed linen into a bucket to soak. She holds up a sheet and bucket to show* **Mommo**.

Mommo   Hah? . . . There's nothing here for people to be prying in corners for. Bring in the brishen of turf for the night an' then you may go home to your own house.

Mary   Alright.

She moves as if going out the door, then silently to the comparative dark of the far corner where she remains motionless.

Mommo   You couldn't be up to them. (*She yawns:*) Oh ho huneo! An' twas round about now the rattlin' of the horse an' cart was heard abroad on the road an' had them in the shop peepin' at the windy. 'Twas the decent man an' his decent wife the same was in it. And 'Stand, Pedlar,' says the

man in (*a*) class of awesome whisper. And his decent wife
from the heel of the cart to his side to view the spectre was
now before them. The aspect silver of moon an' stars
reflecting off the new impossibility. Loughran's Hill.
Creature. She now clutching more tightly the sweets to her
breast. (*She yawns again; her eyes close.*)

Mary (*whispers*)   Sleep.

Mommo (*eyes open*)   Hah? *Now* what was there for doing?
Which way to cast the hopeful eye? No-no, not yet, in
deliberate caution, would he acknowledge the shop, John
Mah'ny's, forninst them, but looked behind him the road
they came, forward again, but to what avail? There was only
John Mah'ny's now for his contemplation, nature all around
them serenely waiting, and didn't the two little smiles come
appearing again.

Mary (*whispers*)   Sleep.

Mommo   Hah?

Mary   Sleep, sleep, peace, peace.

Mommo   An' the strangers, that decent man an' his
decent wife the same, rounded the gable into the merchant's
yard, an' sorry the night that was the decision. What time
is it? . . . She's gone. An' she can stay gone. But them are the
details, c'rrect to the particular. And they can be vouched
for. For there was to be many's the inquisition by c'roner,
civic guard and civilian on all that transpired in John
Mah'ny's that night. Now. (*She yawns.*) Wasn't that a nice
story? An' we'll all be goin' to sleep.

She is asleep.

Mary (*looking at* **Mommo**)   Sleep? For how long? . . .
(*Testing* **Mommo**.) 'Now as all do know the world over'?

*She switches off the radio. She switches off the light. She goes to the
table and idly starts lighting candles on the cake, using a new match to
light each one. A car passes by outside. She blows out the candles, tires
of them.*

Now what to do? . . . (*Idly at first.*) Now as all do know the
world over . . . Now as all do know . . . Now as all do know
the world over the custom when entering the house of
another is to invoke our Maker's benediction on all present.
(*Adds a piece of sardonic humour:*) Save the cat. Well, as the
Bochtáns would have it later, no mention of our Maker, or
His Blessed Son, was mentioned by the strangers as they
came 'cross John Mahoney's threshel (*threshold*) that night.
But no, no, no, no, no. No now! They were wrongin' that
couple. (*To the sleeping* **Mommo**.) Weren't they? They were.
They wor. (*To* **Mommo**.) And when you. And when that
decent woman gave the whole story to her father, what did
he say? (*A touch of mimicry of* **Mommo**.) An' believe you me
he knew all about them. That them Bochtáns were a
venomous pack of jolter-headed gobshites. Didn't he? He
did. An ill-bred band of amadáns an' oinseachs, untutored in
science, philosophy or the fundamental rudimentaries of
elementary husbandry itself. A low crew of illiterate plebs,
drunkards and incestuous bastards, and would ever continue
as such, improper and despicable in their incorrigibility.
Them were his words. Weren't they? They wor. They're not
nice, he said. Supa tea. (*She pours a glass of vodka for herself.*)
And he was the man to give the tongue-lashin'. An' 'twas
from him I got my learnin'. That's who I'm waitin' for. (*She
has a sip of the vodka.*) Too sweet. (*She dilutes the vodka with water.*)
Me father. He has a big stick. (*She has a drink: then, whimpering
as* **Mommo** *might.*) I wanta go home, I wanta go home. (*New
tone, her own, frustrated.*) So do I, so do I. Home. (*Anger.*) Where
is it, Mommo?

*The silence is now being punctuated by another car passing outside,
again leaving a vacuum in its wake, making the place lonelier.*

A lot of activity tonight. And all weekend.

*She picks up her book and does not open it. She starts to pace the
periphery of the room.*

'There is the silence of copse or croft
When the wind sinks dumb.

And of belfry loft
When the tenor after tolling stops its hum.

And there's the silence of a lonely pond
Where a man was drowned . . . '

She stops for a moment or two, looking at one of the sepia-coloured photographs.

Where a man, and his brother who went to save him were drowned. Bury them in pairs, it's cheaper.

Continues pacing.

'Nor nigh nor yond
No newt, toad, frog to make the smallest sound.
But the silence of an empty house
Where oneself was born,
Dwelt, held carouse . . . '

Did we? Hold carouse.

'With friends
Is of all silence most forlorn.
It seems no power can waken it – '

Another car passes by. **Mary***'s reaction to the car:*

Come in! . . .

'It seems no power can waken it,
Or rouse its rooms,
Or the past permit
The present to stir a torpor like a tomb's.'

Bla bla bla bla bla like a tomb's. (*To the book, and dumping it.*) Is that so? Well, I don't agree with you . . . Going crazy. (*Then, on reflection.*) No, I'm not. (*Then suddenly to* **Mommo**.) Wake up now, Mommo. Mommo! Because I don't want to wait till midnight, or one or two or three o'clock in the morning, for more of your – unfinished symphony. I'm ready now.

She switches on the light. She switches on the radio.

On with the story! But that decent man and his decent wife the same did as was proper on entering John Mahoney's that

night – Mommo! The customary salutation was given – 'God
bless all here!' – though quietly, for they were shy people,
and confused in their quandry. Mommo? And then, without
fuss, the man indicated a seat in the most private corner.

Mommo   An' they were wrongin' them there again! So
they wor.

Mary   They were.

Mommo   The whispers bein' exchanged were not of
malevolent disposition. Yis! – to be sure! – that woman!
Maybe! – had a distracted look to her. Hadn't she reason?

Mary   The Bochtán gawpin' at them.

Mommo   They knew no better.

Mary   Where would they learn it?

Mommo (*absently asking*)   Cigarette. 'An' I caught Tom
playin' with the mangler the other evenin', his feet dancin'
in the cup.' That's what she was whisperin'. And he lookin'
round, 'Not at all, not at all,' tryin' to look pleasant in the
house of another. 'An' won't they have to light the lamp?'
that's what she was whisperin'. 'Not at all, not at all,' still
lookin' for the place to put his eyes. 'Isn't Mary a big girl
now an' well able to look after them?' That's what he was
whisperin'. 'And won't May Glynn be lookin' in on them.'
That's what he was whisperin'. But she'd told May Glynn
that mornin' not to be waitin', her mother'd be needin'
her to look after her young brothers, an' they'd be home
before dark for sure. And-sure-she-was-gettin'-on-his-nerves!
Till he had to go an' leave her there to a quiet spot at the
counter . . . Sure she should've known better. An' she's sorry
now. She is. She is.

She's beginning to whimper, puffing on the cigarette **Mary** *has given
her.*

Mommo   I wanta go home, I wanta see mah father.

Mary *coming to comfort her.*

Mommo   Shtap! (*Warning* **Mary**.) And he has a big stick. And he won't try to stop me telling my nice story.

Mary (*a realisation: thoughtfully, to herself*)   . . . No, I'm not trying to stop you, 'Why doesn't she finish it and have done with it.' (*A* **Dolly** *line from earlier.*) Yes.

Mommo (*becomes conscious of the cigarette*)   What's this? An' who asked for this?

Mary (*taking cigarette from her*)   I'm not stopping you!

Mommo   Me mouth is burned.

Mary   We'll finish it – we'll do it together!

Mommo   Rubbishy cigarettes – spendin' money on rubbishy cigarettes –

Mary   I'm not stopping you.

Mommo (*singing: her defiance to* **Mary**)
    'Once I loved with fond affection – '

Mary   And if we finish it, that will be something, won't it?

Mommo
    'All my thoughts they were in thee – '

Mary   Won't it? –

Mommo
    'Till a dark-haired girl deceived me,
    And no more he thought of me.'

She lapses into silence; she grows drowsy, or feigns drowsiness.

Mary   Don't go to sleep, and don't be pretending to sleep either. Mommo? 'And what'll you be havin'?' says John Mahony the proprietor. But the stranger now was taking in the laughter and Costello's great bellow dominating over all.

'A lotta noise an' little wool, as the devil says shearin' the pig!' sayin' Costello. 'Wo ho ho!' 'An' what'll you be havin', Mister?' says John Mahony again. 'A little drop of whiskey an' a small port wine.' And readying the drinks, says John: 'The f-frost is determined to make a night of it?'

'Behell I don't know,' says old Brian, like the nestor long ago, 'comin' on duskess there was a fine roll of cloud over in the west and if you got the bit of a breeze at all I'm thinkin' you'd soon see a thaw.' And the stranger had produced his purse and was suspended-paused, takin' in the forecast. But the two little smiles appearing again: such good fortune as a thaw was not to be. Then – and with a deft enough flick – he pitched the coin on the counter, like a man rejecting all fortune. Good enough.

He took the drink to his decent wife and was for sitting next to her again but wasn't her head now in and out of the corner and she startin' the cryin'.

Mommo   She should have known better.

Mary   So what could he do but leave her there again?

Mommo   An' the church owed him money.

Mary   Did it?

Mommo (*growls*)   The-church-owed-him-money. Oh, the church is slow to pay out, but if you're givin', there's nothin' like money to make the clergy fervent.

Mary   Yes?

Mommo (*drowsily*)   And I'm thinkin' that decent man of late was given to reviewin' the transpirations since his birth . . . But if he was itself, wasn't his decent wife the same? . . . At the end of her tether . . . They were acquainted with grief. They wor . . . Switch off that aul' thing, there's nothing on it. (*The radio.*) . . . They wor.

Mary (*has turned the volume down*)   Mommo? I know you're pretending.

Mommo *is asleep. The silence again.*

Mary   They were acquainted with grief . . . Alright, I won't just help you, I'll do it for you. (*Progressively she begins to dramatise*

the story.) Now John Mahony – (*She corrects her pronunciation.*)
Now John *Mah'ny* – was noticing the goings-on between the
two and being the proprietor he was possessed of the licence
for interrogating newses. And 'You have a d-distance teh-teh
go, Mister?' says he at the stranger. An' says Grandad. An'
says the stranger, class of frownin': 'Would that big man down
there be a man by the name of Costello?' And, 'Th-that's
who he is,' says John, 'd'yeh know him?' 'No,' says the
stranger, in curious introspection, an' 'No' says he again,
still puzzled in the head. 'But that's a fine laugh.' 'Oh 'tis a
f-fine laugh right enough,' says John, 'hah?' Knowin' more
was comin' but hadn't yet reached the senses. And the
stranger now drawin' curlicues with his glass upon the
counter! Then says he, 'I heard that laugh a wintry day two
years ago across the market square in Ballindine an' I had
t'ask a man who he was.' 'Yeh had,' says John. 'I had,' says
the stranger. An' John was in suspense. And then of a
suddenness didn't the frown go disappearin' up the stranger's
cap. He had it at last. 'Well,' says he – oh, lookin' the
merchant between the two eyes – 'Well,' says he, 'I'm a
better laugher than your Costello.'

What time is it? Half-nine. Someone will come yet. *'Nother*
supa milk. (*Short laugh to herself as she gets another glass of vodka.*)
Well, I'm a better laugher than your Costello. (*She swallows
the drink.*) Now the merchant betrayed nothing. He was well
versed in meeting company, an' all he did was nod the once –
(*She nods.*) – and then, quick enough of him, referred the
matter. And 'Sh-Sheamus!' says he, 'Sh-Sh-Sheamus!' callin'
Costello to come down.

She is now listening to the 'putt-putt' of the motorcycle approaching.

A mortal laughing competition there would be.

Mary *now into action, putting away her glass, switching off the radio,
getting needle, thread, scissors and the skirt of her 'going-away' suit to
take in the waist.*

I knew someone would call. Dolly. Again! I wonder why.
(*Cynically.*) Bringing tidings of great joy.

Dolly *comes in. She stretches herself. (She has had sex in ditch, doorway, old shed or wherever.) She takes in the packed suitcase, but as usual leaves such baiting topics until it suits her.*

Dolly　I have it all figured out.

Mary　The County Home?

Dolly　Well, maybe nothing as drastic as that. That's a nice suit.

Mary *(does not lift her head from her work)*　Kill her?

Dolly *(a sideways twist of the head – 'Kill her?' – a more feasible suggestion)*　Can I have a drop of this? *(Vodka.)*

Mary　You brought it.

Dolly *(produces two bottles of mixers)*　I forgot the mixers earlier. In my haste. *(She pours two drinks.)* We might as well have a wake, an American wake for yeh.

Mary　Not for me. I had a little one earlier, thank you.

Dolly　You had *two* little ones, *(Puts drink beside **Mary**.)* vodka and white. It's a long time since I seen you wearing that.

Mary　Saw.

Dolly　What?

Mary　I wore it coming home.

Dolly　Did you have to let out the waist?

Mary　I have to take *in* my things. *(A gesture of invitation.)* You need to talk to someone.

Dolly　Go on: cheers! Since you're off. Are yeh?

Mary *(does not drink, does not look up, but lifts her glass and puts it down again)*　Cheers!

Dolly　And it often crossed my mind the years Stephen and I were here with herself. Kill her. And it wouldn't be none of your fancy nurses' potions either. Get them out of bed, the auld reliable, start them walkin'. Walk the heart out of them. No clues left for coroner or Dr Paddy. And that's how manys the one met their Waterloo. What's the matter?

Mary *shakes her head; just when she does not want to, she is about to break into tears.*

Dolly   . . . What? . . . Joking! . . . I have it all figured out.

Mary *is crying.*

Dolly   What's the matter?

Mary   Stop it, Dolly.

Dolly   Mary?

Mary   Leave me alone.

To get away from **Dolly** *she goes to the radio and switches it on.*

Dolly   What's the − Why are you − ? (*She emits a few whimpers.*) Mary?

Mommo (*has woken up*)   What's the plottin' an' whisperin' for?

Dolly   Good man, Josie! (*And immediately back to* **Mary** *again.*) What? (*Crying.*) What? . . . Don't. Please. (*Her arms around* **Mary**.)

They are all speaking at once. **Mary** *and* **Dolly** *crying.*

Mommo   Oh yes, 'Good man, Josie.' Now! Good man, Josie. And that was the second greeting he uttered that night.

Dolly   What's the matter? . . . Shh! . . . What?

Mary   I don't know, I don't know.

Mommo   He got no reply. Nor did he expect one. For Josie was a Greaney, an' none was ever right in that fambly.

Mary   I wanted to come home.

Dolly   What?

Mary   I had to come home.

Mommo   Though some say he had the knack of mendin'
clocks, if he had.

Dolly   What?

Mary   This is our home.

Dolly   I know, I know.

Mary   This is *home*?

Dolly   I know, I know.

Mary (*pulling away from* **Dolly** *to shout at* **Mommo**)   Finish it,
finish it, that much at least –

Mommo   Heh-heh-heh-heh! (*Defiantly.*)

Mary   Have done with it! – that much at least! (*To* **Dolly**,
who is following her.) Why don't you take off your coat! (*To*
Mommo.) What was waiting for them at dawn when they
got home in the morning?

Mommo   Hona ho gus hahaa!

A defiant shout. And, looped back in time, she picks up the story:

Howandewer. 'How the boys!' was Costello's third greeting.
This time to two old men with . . . (*Etc.*)

And, again, **Dolly** *is coming to* **Mary** *to offer comfort, to be comforted,
both of them crying while the lights are fading and a car passes by
outside.*

Act Two

An announcement for the Sunday concert on the radio together with
Mommo*'s voice continuing her story.* **Mommo** *has arrived at and*
is repeating the last section of the story where **Mary** *left off in Act One.*

A sniff from **Mary***, her tears are all but finished. Both she and* **Dolly**
have their 'vodkas and white' and a slice of the birthday cake on plates
beside them.

Mommo   . . . 'Yeh had,' says John, 'I had,' says the stranger.
An' John was in suspense. An' then of a suddenness didn't
the frown go disappearing up the stranger's cap. He had it
at last. 'Well,' says he – oh, lookin' the merchant between
the two eyes – 'Well,' says he, 'I'm a better laugher than your
Costello.'

A car passes by outside.

What time is it? Miss!

Mary   Seven. (*Then, to* **Dolly***.*) I'm sorry for (*crying*).

Dolly   Ar – phhh – don't be silly. Did yeh see the helicopter
on Friday? The plant, they say, is for closure. The Chinese
are over.

Mary   Japanese. (*Her attention now returning to* **Mommo***.*)

Dolly   I prefer to call them Chinese.

Dolly*'s mind beginning to tick over on how to present her 'proposition'*
to **Mary***.* **Mary***'s nervous energy, after the lull, setting her to work*
again, removing the bed-warmer from the fire and slipping it into the
bed at **Mommo***'s feet, wrapping up the cake in tinfoil and putting*
it away . . . but, predominantly, her eyes, concentration, returning to
Mommo*; a resoluteness increasing to have* **Mommo***'s story finished.*

Mommo   Now the merchant has betrayed nothing. He
was well-versed at meeting company. And all he did was nod
the once. (*She nods solemnly.*)

Mary   I must get a set of decent glasses for you the next time I'm in town.

Mommo   Then, quick enough of him, referred the matter.

Dolly   And I'm sure there's rats in that thatch.

Mommo   An' 'Sh-Sheamus!' says he.

Dolly   I could see Hallilan the contractor about slatin' it.

Mommo   'Sh-Sh-Sheamus!' Calling Costello to come down.

Dolly   What d'yeh think?

Mary   Shhh!

Mommo   A laughing competition there would be.

Dolly (*puzzled by* **Mary**'s *behaviour*)   And I was thinking of getting her a doll.

Mary   Let's see if she'll continue.

Dolly   What?

Mary   Good enough. Then down steps the bold Costello.

Mommo (*instead of continuing she starts singing*)
    'Once I loved with fond affection,
    All my thoughts they were in thee,
    Till a dark-haired girl deceived me,
    And no more he thought of me.'

Mary (*through* **Mommo**'s *song, returning to the fire, all the time looking at* **Mommo**)   Down steps the bold Costello – You have a suggestion, something figured out.

Dolly   What?

Mary   She's going to finish it.

Dolly   Finish it? Why?

Mary   I don't know. I can't do anything the way things are.

Mommo   Now. Ye like that one.

Dolly   Sit down. I thought you were trying to stop her.

Mary   She's going to finish it.

Dolly   You're always on your feet –

Mary   *Tonight!*

Dolly   Another drink?

Mary   No. A laughing competition there will be! (*And goes to* **Mommo**.) Then down steps the bold Costello –

Mommo   Pardon?

Mary   Then down steps the bold Costello –

Mommo   Oh yes.

Dolly   Well, as a matter of fact, I do have a proposition.

Mary   Shhh!

Mommo   Then down steps the bold Costello. And 'Hah?' says he, seeing the gravity on the proprietor's mien. But the proprietor – John, to be sure – referred him like that. (*She nods in one direction.*) An' 'Hah?' says Costello, lookin' at the stranger. But weren't the eyes of the stranger still mildly fixed on John, an' 'Hah?' says Costello, lookin' back at John. But there was no countin' John's cuteness. He takes the two steps backwards, then the one to the sidewards, slidin' his arse along the shelf to 'scape the stranger's line of vision an' demonstrate for all his neutrality in the matter. 'Hah?' poor Costello goin'. 'Hah?' to the one, 'Hah?' to the other. 'Hah?' 'Hah?' The head near swung off his neck, an' now wonderin' I'm sure what on earth he'd done wrong.

Dolly   Mary? (*Topping up the drinks.*)

Mommo   An' no help from John. Puffing a tuneless whistle at the ceiling! 'Phuh-phuh-phuh-phuh.' (*John's tuneless whistle.*)

Mary (*absently accepting drink*)   Phuh-phuh-phuh-phuh.

Dolly (*to herself*)   Jesus! She's gone loopy too.

Mommo   Then says the stranger, lookin' straight ahead at
nothing, 'How d'yeh do, Mr Costello, I'm Seamus O'Toole.'
Costello: 'Hah?! I'm very well, thanking you!' His face was a
study. An' 'Oh,' says John of Costello, 'he's a Sh-Sheamus
too, phuh-phuh-phuh-phuh.' 'I know that,' says the stranger,
'but I'm a better laugher than 'm.' 'Quawk awk-awk-awk?'
in Costello's throat. In response didn't the stranger make
serious chuckle. And in response didn't Costello roar out
a laugh.

A silent 'Jesus' from **Dolly**. *She decides to take off her coat and see
what effect flaunting her pregnancy will have.*

Mary (*encouraging* **Mommo**)   Good girl! (*Silently with*
Mommo.) Then loud as you please . . .

Mommo   Then loud as you please, says Costello: 'He says,
he says, he says,' says he, 'he's a better.' (*She claps her mouth
shut.*) An' that was far as he got. For in the suddenness of a
discovery he found out that he was cross.

'Ara phat?' says he. – He was nimble? – The full size of him
skippin' backwards, the dancing antics of a boxing man. An'
lookin' 'bout at his supporters, now hushed an' on their
marks, 'He says, he says, he says,' says he, 'he's a better
laugher than me!'

What! Sure they never heard the likes. Nor how on earth
to deal with it. An' the upset on their own man's face! Oh,
they wor greatly taken 'back. Oh they wor. An' not up to
disseration things wor lookin' dangerous.

Dolly   She's getting tired – the creature.

Mary   Shhh!

Dolly   Cheers!

Mary   Cheers – Things were looking dangerous.

Mommo   Oh, they wor.

Mary   'Ary give me (*a*) pint outa that.'

Mommo   Costello?

Mary *nods.*

Mommo   Swivellin' an' near knockin' them wor behind
him, but then in retraction comes wheelin' back 'round,
the head like a donkey's flung up at the ceilin', eyes like a
bullfrog's near out their sockets an' the big mouth threwn
open. But God bless us an' save us, all the emission was (*a*)
class of a rattle'd put shame to a magpie.

Mary (*silently, excited*)   Shame to a magpie.

Mommo   Now he was humbled, the big head on him
hangin', went back to his corner, turned his back on all
present. The hump that was on him! Oh, his feelin's wor
hurted. (*She yawns.*) Oh ho hun-neo!

Mary   Aa no!

Mommo (*insistent*)   Oh ho hun-neo!

Mary   Don't be pretendin', you had a little nap a while
ago.

Mommo   Put the sup of milk there for me now for the
night.

Mary   I'll get the milk later. And the others, Mommo?

Mommo   Lookin' wildly, one to the other, from their giant
to the stranger, none knowin' what to do.

Dolly (*getting the milk*)   Let her settle down.

Mary   But they were vexed.

Mommo   An' they knew it?

Mary *nods agreement and encouragement.*

Mommo   Oh, they knew they were cross. An' strainin'
towards the stranger like mastiffs on chains, fit to tear him
asunder.

Dolly   And I don't know if you've noticed, Mary, but the
turf out there won't last the winter. (*Approaching with the milk.*)
Here we are! I'll see to the turf.

Mary (*takes the milk from* **Dolly**)   No milk.

Dolly   What are you at?

Mary   No milk! (*She puts it away.*)

Mommo   And even Josie! – the odd one –

Dolly (*to herself*)   Jesus, Josie! –

Mommo   That always stood aloof! Even he was infected with the venom (*that*) had entered, an' all of the floor was 'vailable round him he began to walk circles screechin' 'Hackah!' at the stranger.

Dolly   I want to have a talk!

Mary   Later.

Dolly   A plan, a proposition.

Mary   Later!

Mommo   Pardon?

Dolly   I've a little problem of my own.

Mary   I think I've noticed. Go on, Mommo, no one is stopping you.

Mommo   Where's the milk for the night, Miss?

Mary   Then striding to the stranger – Costello: 'Excuse me there now a minute, Mister – '

Dolly   Mary –

Mary   No! No! 'Excuse me there now a minute now – '

Mommo   Pardon?

Mary   'But what did you say to me there a minute ago?'

Waits for a beat to see if **Mommo** *will continue.*

. . . 'That you're a better laugher than me, is it?' . . . 'Well, would you care to put a small bet on it?'

Mommo (*suspiciously, but childlike*)   How do you know that?

Mary   Oh, I was told. But I never heard all of the story.

Mommo   Hah? . . . At shurrup (*shut up*) outa that.

Mary   'Well, would you care to put a small bet on it?' And 'No,' saying the stranger going back to his wife. 'But you're challenging me, challenging me, challenging me, y'are!'

Mommo   'No,' saying the stranger, ''twas only a notion,' his eyes on the floor. For why? Foreseeing fatalistic danger. Then joined the two little smiles cross the width of his mouth which he gave up to the hero as evidence sincere that he was for abnegating. Can yeh go on?

Mary   No. (*Cajoling.*) Can you?

Mommo   Well, Costello was for agreein'? An' for understandin'? But th' others wor all circlin', jostlin', an' pushin' – 'He is, he is, challe-gin' yeh, he is!' 'Up Bochtán, up Bochtán, Bochtán for ever!' Putting confusion in the head of Costello again. But the stranger – a cute man – headin' for the door, gives (*the*) nod an' wink to Costello so he'd comprehend the better the excitation (*that*) is produced by the abberation of a notion. Then in the fullness of magistrature, 'Attention!' roaring Costello, 'Attention!' roaring he, to declare his verdict was dismissal, an' decree that 'twas all over.

Mary   Yes?

Mommo   An' 'twas.

Mary   Aa, you have more for me?

Mommo (*childlike*)   Have I?

Mary *nods.* **Mommo** *thinking her own thoughts, then she shakes her head.*

Mary   A laughing competition there would be.

Mommo (*absently*)   A what?

Dolly   She's exhausted.

Mary   She's not!

Mommo   Where was I? . . . In the jostlin' an' pushin' . . .

Then her eyes searching the floor, in half-memory, lamenting trampled sweets.

The sweets.

Mary   Here they are. (*The ones that* **Dolly** *brought.*)

Mommo   No. The sweets. (*Her eyes still searching the floor.*) In the jostlin' an' pushin' . . . The sweets for her children trampled under their boots.

Dolly   Can't you see she's –

Mary   She's not!

Mommo   Phuh: dust.

Mary   But if Costello decreed 'twas all over, how did it start up again?

Mommo   How did? The small stranger, I told yeh, goin' out to check the weather for as had been forecasted the thaw was setting in.

Mary   I see!

Mommo   An' sure they could have got home.

Mary   I see!

Mommo   They could have got home. (*Brooding, growls; then.*) Costello could decree. All others could decree. But what about the things had been vexin' *her* for years? No, a woman isn't stick or stone. The forty years an' more in the one bed together (*and*) he to rise in the mornin' (*and*) not to give her a glance. An' so long it had been he had called her by first name, she'd near forgot it herself . . . Brigit . . . Hah? . . . An' so she thought he hated her . . . An' maybe he did, like everything else . . . An' – (*Her head comes up, eyes fierce.*) 'Yis, yis-yis, he's challe'gin' ye, he is!' She gave it to the Bochtáns. And to her husband returning? – maybe he would recant, but she'd renege matters no longer. 'Hona ho gus hah-haa!' – she hated him too.

Mary *and* **Dolly** *are silenced: they have not heard this part of the story before.*

Mary   . . . And what happened then?

Mommo   An' what happened then. Tried to pacify her. (*Growls.*) But there-was-none-would-assuage-her. An' what happened then, an' what happened then. 'Stand up then,' says Costello. They already standin'. 'Scath siar uaim,' to the rest to clear back off the floor. The arena was ready.

Mary   And what happened then?

Mommo   An' what happened then? . . . Tired, tired.

Mary   Mommo?

Mommo (*savagely*)   Shthap! Tired! What's your business here? There are no newses here for anyone about anything.

Dolly   It's ten to ten, so your father'll hardly come now, so off with yeh to sleep. There's the good girl, and we'll hear your confession again tomorrow night. There, there now. (*To* **Mary**.) That was a new bit. There, there now . . . She's in bye-byes.

Mary   She's not.

Dolly   She's asleep! Mommo? . . . Ten to ten, 1984, and I read it – how long ago was it? – that by 1984 we'd all be going on our holidays to the moon in *Woman's Own*.

Mary   She's not asleep.

Dolly   I'm not arg'in' about it. She's – resting.

Mary   And I'm going to rouse her again in a minute. You were saying?

Dolly   And a telly would fit nicely over there.

Mary   A plan, a proposition, you have it all figured out?

Dolly   And I'm sorry now I spent the money on the video. No one uses it. You'd make more use of it. It has a remote. (*In answer to* **Mary**'s *query 'Remote?'*) Yeh know? One of them things yeh – (*hold in your hand*) – and – (*further demonstrates*) – control.

Mary   I have a video here already (*Mommo*). What's your plan?

Dolly   Wait'll we have a drink. She's guilty.

Mary   Guilty of what?

Dolly   I don't know.

Mary   Then why –

Dolly   I'm not arg'in' with yeh! (*Offering to top up* **Mary***'s drink.*)

Mary   Why can't you ever finish a subject or talk straight? I don't want another drink.

Dolly   I'm talking straight.

Mary   What's on your mind, Dolly? I'm up to you.

Dolly   There's no one up to Dolly.

Mary   Tck!

Dolly   I'm talkin' straight!

Another car passes by outside.

Traffic. The weekend-long meeting at the computer plant place. And all the men, busy, locked outside the fence.

Mary (*abrupt movement to the table*)   On second thoughts. (*And pours lemonade into her glass.*)

Dolly (*a bit drunk and getting drunker*)   No, wait a minute.

Mary   What-are-you-saying, Dolly?

Dolly   An' that's why she goes on like a gramophone: guilty.

Mary   This is nonsense.

Dolly   And so are you.

Mary   So am I!

Dolly   An' you owe me a debt.

Mary   What do I owe you?

Dolly   *And* she *had* to get married.

Mary (*to herself*)   Impossible.

Dolly   No! No! – Mary? Wait a minute

Mary (*fingers to her forehead*)   Dolly, I'm –

Dolly   I'm talkin' straight.

Mary   Trying to get a grip of – ahmm – I'm trying to find ahmm – get control of – ahmm – my life, Dolly.

Dolly   Yes. You're trying to say make head and tail of it all, talk straight, like myself. No, Mary, hold on! You told me one thing, I'll tell you another. D'yeh remember the pony-and-trap-Sunday-outings? I don't. But I remember – now try to contradict this – the day we buried Grandad. Now I was his favourite so I'll never forget it. And whereas – No, Mary! – whereas! She stood there over that hole in the ground like a rock – like a duck, like a duck, her chest stickin' out. Not a tear.

Mary   What good would tears have been?

Dolly   Not a tear. And – *and!* – Tom buried in that same hole in the ground a couple of days before. Not a tear, then or since. Oh, I gathered a few 'newses' about our Mommo.

Mary   Maybe she's crying now.

Dolly   *All* of them had to get married except myself and my darling mother-in-law, Old Sharp Eyes. But she bore a bastard all the same. Her Stephen. (*She switches off the radio.*)

Mary   Leave it on.

Dolly   I've a proposition.

Mary   It's the Sunday concert, switch it on.

Dolly (*switches on the radio*)   So what d'yeh think?

Mary   About *what*?

Dolly   The slated – (*gestures 'roof'*), the other things I mentioned.

Mary   It would stop the place falling down for someone alright.

Dolly   An' half of this place is mine, I'll sign it over.

Mary   To whom?

Dolly   To *whom*. To Jack-Paddy-Andy, to Kitty-the-Hare, to you. And there might be – other things – you might need.

Mary   What else could anyone possibly need?

Dolly *now looking a bit hopeless, pathetic, offering a cigarette to* **Mary***, lighting it for her.*

Dolly   An' would you like another? (*Drink.*)

Mary *shakes her head.*

Dolly   Lemonade?

Mary   No. What are you trying to say?

Dolly   An' the turf out there won't last the winter.

Mary   You said that.

Dolly   And one of the children.

She looks at **Mary** *for a reaction. But all this time* **Mary***'s mind, or half of it, is on* **Mommo***.*

Dolly   Yeh. Company for yeh.

Mary   I get all this if I stay.

Dolly   Or go.

Mary (*becoming alert*)   What? . . . You want me to go? With one of the children? . . . *Which* one of the children?

Dolly (*continues with closed eyes through the following*)   Jesus, I'm tired. A brand new one.

Mary *laughs incredulously, high-pitched.*

Dolly   Would you? Would you? Would you?

Mary   What?

Dolly   Take him. It.

Mary   With me?

Dolly *(nods)*   An' no one need be any the wiser.

Mary   And if I stay?

Dolly   Say it's yours. It'll all blow over in a month.

Mary   You're crazy.

Dolly   That makes three of us. I'm not crazy, I'm – as you can see.

Mary   Yes, I've wondered for some time, but I thought you couldn't – you couldn't! – be that stupid.

A car passes by outside.

Dolly   More takeaways for the lads. *(She starts wearily for her coat.)* My, but they're busy.

Mary   No one is asking you to leave.

Dolly *(stops; eyes closed again)*   You'll be paid.

Mary   I've heard you come up with a few things before, but!

Dolly   Stephen'll kill me.

Mary   What about me?

Dolly   Or he'll cripple me.

Mary   Do you ever think of others!

Dolly   Or I'll fix him.

Mary   And you'll be out – gallivanting – again tomorrow night.

Dolly *(blows her top)*   And the night after, and the night after! And you can be sure of that. *(And regrets blowing her top.)*

Mary   . . . How long are you gone?

Dolly   Five, six months.

Mary   Five, six months.

Dolly   Trying to conceal it.

Mary   Who's the father?

Dolly   I have my suspicions.

Mary   But he's busy perhaps tonight, picketing?

Dolly   Yes, very busy. Travelling at the sound of speed. But the Chinese'll get them.

Mary   And this is the help? This is what you've been figuring out?

Dolly   You can return the child after, say, a year. If you want to.

Mary   I thought your figuring things out were about − ?

She indicates **Mommo**. *Then she goes to* **Mommo**.

Mary   Mommo, open your eyes, time to continue.

Dolly   After a year it'll be easy to make up a story.

Mary   Another story! (*She laughs, high-pitched − there's hysteria in it.*)

Dolly   You're a nurse, you could help me if you wanted to.

Mary   Trying all my life to get out of this situation and now you want to present me with the muddle of your stupid life to make sure the saga goes on.

Dolly   Oh, the saga will go on.

Mary   Mommo!

Dolly   I'll see to that, one way or the other.

Mary (*to herself*)   I go away with a brand new baby. Mommo! (*To* **Dolly**.) Where! Where do I go?

Dolly *nods.*

Mary   You have that figured out too?

Dolly   We can discuss that.

Mary *laughs.*

Dolly   You're its aunt.

Mary   Its! (*She laughs.*)

Dolly   Aunt! – Aunt! – Aunt!

Mary   Mommo! I know you're not asleep.

Dolly (*shrugs*)   Okay. (*Now talking to herself.*) And if it's a boy you can call it Tom, and if it's a girl you can call it Tom.

Continues through the following, **Dolly***'s speech, though to herself, dominating.*

Mommo   Supa milk, where's the milk?

Mary   Later. To continue. Where had you got to?

Mommo   But in the jostlin' an' pushin'. (*Eyes searching the floor.*) The sweets . . . the sweets . . .

Dolly (*through the above*)   But I've discussed something with someone. 'Cause if I don't get Stephen, Stephen'll get me. But I know now how to get him and that's what got me saving, of late. I've made the preliminary enquiries. That little service of fixing someone is available – 'cause it's in demand – even round here. I've discussed the fee with someone.

Mommo   Phuh: dust.

Mary (*to* **Dolly**)   Have you finished?

Dolly (*intensely*)   You had it easy!

Mary   I had it easy? No one who came out of this – house – had it easy. (*To herself.*) I had it easy.

Dolly   You-had-it-easy. The bright one, top of your class!

Mary (*to herself*)　What would you know about it?

Dolly　Top marks! Hardly had your Leaving Cert and you couldn't wait to be gone.

Mary　I won't deny that.

Dolly　You can't! State Registered Nurse before you were twenty –

Mary　Twenty-one –

Dolly　A Sister before you were twenty-five, Assistant Matron at the age of thirty.

Mary　And a midwife?

Dolly　Yes, SRN, CMB, DDT!

Mary　All very easy.

Dolly　Couldn't get away fast enough.

Mary　But I came back, Dolly.

Dolly　Aren't you great?

Mary　I failed, it all failed. I'm as big a failure as you, and that's some failure.

Dolly *is stopped for a moment by* **Mary**'*s admission.*

Mary　You hadn't considered that?

Mommo *has started rambling again, repeating the last section of the story which she told earlier, down to 'The arena was ready.'*

Mommo　An' sure they could have got home. They could have got home. Costello could decree . . . (*Etc.*)

Dolly (*her voice over* **Mommo**'*s*)　No! No! You had it easy! – You had it – You had – I had – I had ten! – I had a lifetime! – A lifetime! – here with herself, doin' her every bidding, listenin' to her seafóid (*rambling*) gettin' worse till I didn't know where I was! Pissin' in the bed beside me – I had a lifetime! Then the great Stephen – the surprise of it! – comes coortin'! Never once felt any – real – warmth from him –

what's wrong with him? – but he's my rescuer, my saviour.
But then, no rhyme or reason to it – he could've got a job at
that plant – but he couldn't wait to be gone either! Then
waitin' for the hero, my rescuer, the sun shining out of his
eighty-five-pounds-a-week arse, to come home at Christmas.
No interest in me – oh, he used me! – or in children, or the
rotten thatch or the broken window, or Conor above moving
in his fence from this side. I'm fightin' all the battles. Still
fightin' the battles. And what d'yeh think he's doin' now
this minute? Sittin' by the hearth in Coventry, is he? Last
Christmas an' he was hardly off the bus, Old Sharp Eyes
whisperin' into his ear about me. Oooo, but he waited. Jesus,
how I hate him! Jesus, how I hate them! Men! Had his fun
and games with me that night, *and* first thing in the morning.
Even sat down to eat the hearty breakfast I made. Me thinkin',
still no warmth, but maybe it's goin' to be okay. Oooo, but
I should've known from *experience* about-the-great-up-standin'-
Steph-en-evrabody's-fav-our-ite. Because, next thing he has
me by the hair of the head, fistin' me down in the mouth.
Old Sharp Eyes there, noddin' her head every time he struck
an' struck an' kicked an' kicked an' pulled me round the
house by the hair of the head. Jesus, men! (*Indicating the
outdoors where she had sex.*) You-think-I-enjoy? I-use-*them*! Jesus,
hypocrisy! An' then, me left with my face like a balloon – you
saw a lot of me last Christmas, didn't yeh? – my body black
and blue, the street angel an' his religious mother – 'As true
as Our Lady is in Heaven now, darlin's' – over the road to
visit you an' Mommo with a little present an' a happy an' a
holy Christmas now darlin's an' blessed St-fuckin'-Jude an'
all the rest of them flyin' about for themselves up there.

Mommo   The arena was ready. A laughing competition
there would be. (*She coughs in preparation.*) 'Wuff-a-wuff.'

Dolly   Jesus, how I *hate*! I hate her (*Mommo*) – I hate this
house – She hates you – I hate my own new liquorice-allsorts-
coloured house –

Mary (*ashen-face, shaking her head*)   No . . . No.

Dolly   She! – She! – She hates you!

Mary   No.

Dolly   And I hate you!

Mary   Why?

Dolly   Why? You don't know terror, you don't know hatred, you don't know desperation! No one came out of this house had it easy but you had it easy.

Mommo *has unwrapped a sweet and is sucking it.*

Mary   Dolly, stop it at once!

Dolly   'Dolly, stop it at once.' Look, go away an' stay away.

Mary   Dolly!

Dolly   'This is our home' – You'll need a few bob. I'll give it to you, and my grand plan: I'll look after things here, all fronts, including lovee lovee Mommo, an' Stephen'll never raise a finger to me again.

Mary   You're –

Dolly   Am I?

Mary   You're –

Dolly   Am I? We'll see – hah! – if I'm bluffing.

Mary   Have you finished ranting?

Dolly   Ooh, 'ranting'!

Mary   You're spoilt, you're unhappy, you're running round in circles.

Dolly   *I'm* running round in circles? Suitcase packed – how many times? Puttin' on airs – look at the boots, look at the lady! You're stayin', you're goin', 'I need to talk to someone' – Fuck off! 'I wanted to come home, I had to come home' – Fuck off!

Mary   Stop it this moment, I won't have it! You're frightening her.

In reply to 'frightening her', **Dolly** *indicates* **Mommo***, who is sucking a sweet, lost in her own thoughts. Then* **Dolly** *turns her back to* **Mary***; she continues in quieter tone.*

Dolly   The countryside produced a few sensations in the last couple of years, but my grand plan: I'll show them what can happen at the dark of night in a field. I'll come to grips with my life.

Short silence.

Mommo*'s eyes fixed on* **Mary***.*

Mommo   Miss? . . . Do I know you?

Mary *shakes her head, 'No'; she is afraid to speak; if she does she will cry.*

Mommo   . . . Pardon?

Mary *shakes her head.*

Dolly (*to the fire*)   I'll finish another part of this family's history in grander style than any of the others.

Mary   . . . The arena was ready.

Mommo   'Twas.

Mary   But Costello's laugh wasn't right at all.

Mommo   Then ''Scuse me a minute,' says he lickin' his big mouth, puts a spit in the one hand, then one in the other, an' ponders the third that he sent to the floor. (*Coughs.*) 'A wuff.'

Dolly   A wuff, wuff!

Mommo   'A wuha wuha wuha wuha, a wuha huha huha hoo, quawk awk-awk-awk a ho ho ho, a wo ho ho ho ho ho ho!' An' 'twasn't bad at all. Was it? An' Costello knew it. An' by way of exper'ment, though 'twasn't his turn, had a go at it again, his ear cocked to himself.

Dolly   We filled half that graveyard. Well, I'll fill the other half.

Mommo   Then, ''Scuse me too,' says the stranger makin' Costello stiffen, an' 'Heh heh heh, heh heh heh, heh heh heh,' chuckled he.

Dolly   Heh heh heh, heh heh heh, heh heh heh –

Mary (*ferociously at* **Dolly**)   Shhhtaaaap!

Mommo   . . . Miss?

Mary (*to* **Mommo**)   . . . No, you don't know me. But I was here once, and I ran away to try and blot out here. I didn't have it easy. Then I tried bad things, for a time, with someone. So then I came back, thinking I'd find something – here, or, if I didn't, I'd put everything right. And tonight I thought I'd make a last try. Mommo? Live out the – story – finish it, move on to a place where perhaps, we could make some kind of new start. Mommo?

Mommo   Where's the milk for the night?

Mary *nods that she will get it.*

Mommo   Tck!

Mary (*to* **Dolly**)   She may hate me, you may hate me. But I don't hate her. I love her for what she's been through, and she's all that I have. So she has to be my only consideration. She doesn't understand. Do you understand, Dolly? Please . . . And I'm sorry.

Dolly (*drunkenly*)   For what?

Mary (*turns away tearfully*)   I'm not the saint you think I am.

Dolly   The what? Saint? That'd be an awful thing to be. 'Wo ho ho, ho ho ho!'

Mommo   Yis. Did ye hear? The full style was returnin' 'Wo ho ho, wo ho ho!' An' like a great archbishop turnin' on his axis, nods an' winks to his minions that he knew all along. The cheers that went up in John Mah'ny's that night! Now

what did they start doin', the two gladiators, circlin' the
floor, eyes riveted together, silent in quietude to find the
advantage, save the odd whoop from Costello, his fist through
the ceilin', an' the small little stranger'd bate the odd little
dance.

Now. Then. And.

'Yeh sold all your cargo?' Costello roarin' it like a master to
friken a scholar. The laugh from his attendants, but then so
did the stranger.

'Where (*are*) yeh bound for?' – stern Costello – 'Your
destination, a Mhico?'

'Ballindineside, your worship.'

'Ballindineside, a Thighearna!'

Dolly   Oh ho ho, wo ho ho.

Mommo   'Cunn ether iss syha soory.' (*Coinn iotair is saidhthe
suaraighe.*)

Dolly   Hounds of rage and bitches of wickedness!

Mommo   An' the description despicable more fitting their
own place.

Dolly (*to the fire, almost dreamily*)   Why the fuck did he marry
me?

Mommo   'A farmer?' says Costello. 'A goose one,' says the
stranger. An' t'be fair to the Bochtáns they plauded the self-
denigration.

Dolly   I don't hate anyone.

Mommo   'An' yourself?' says the stranger. 'Oh now you're
questionin' me,' says Costello. 'An' rabbits,' screeches Josie,
'Hull-hull-hull, hull-hull-hull!'

Dolly (*stands*)   What did I get up for?

Mommo   An' 'Rabbits!' says the stranger. 'Rabbits?!'
saying he. 'Well, heh heh heh, heh heh heh, heh heh heh,

heh heh heh!' 'What's the cause of your laughter?' Costello frownin' moroya (*mar dhea: pretending seriousness*). 'Bunny rabbits!' says the stranger – 'Is that what you're in!'

'Not at all, me little man,' says Costello, 'I've a herd of trinamanooses in Closh back the road.'

'Tame ones?' says the stranger.

'Tame ones, what else, of a certainty,' says Costello, 'an' the finest breed for 'atin' sure!'

'But for the Townies though for 'atin',' says the stranger, most sincerely. An' not able to keep the straight face, Costello roared out a laughter, an' gave beck to his attendants to plaud the stranger's cleverality.

Now wasn't he able for them?

Dolly Where's the flashlamp?

Mommo An' the contrariety an' venom was in it while ago!

Dolly I want to go out the back.

Mary It's on top of the dresser.

Mommo But now they couldn't do enough for that decent man an' woman, all vying with each other – an' sure they didn't have it – to buy treats for the strangers, tumblers of whiskey an' bumpers of port wine. A strange auld world right enough. But in some wisdom of his own He made it this way. 'Twas like the nicest night ever.

Dolly (*a plea for help*) Mary?

Mary 'Twas like the nicest night ever.

Mommo But they'd yet to find the topic would keep them laughin' near for ever.

Dolly Mary?

Mary Topic?

Mommo   Then one'd laugh solo, the other'd return it, then Costello'd go winkin' an' they'd both laugh together, a nod from the stranger (*and*) they'd stop that same moment to urge riotous chorus, give the others a chance.

Dolly   Don't want the fuggin' flashlamp.

Then, as if driving cattle out of the house, she goes out the door.

How! – How! – Hup! – Skelong! – Bleddy cows! Howa-that-how! Hup! Hup! . . .

Mary   What topic did they find?

Mommo   But there can be no gainsayin' it, Costello clear had the quality laugh. 'Wo ho ho, ho ho ho': (*in*) the barrel of his chest would great rumbles start risin', rich rolls of round sound out of his mouth, to explode in the air an' echo back rev'berations. An' next time demonstratin' the range of his skill, go flyin' aloft (*to*) the heights of registration – 'Hickle-ickle-ickle-ickle!' – like a hen runnin' demented from the ardent attentions of a cock in the yard after his business. Now!

Mary   And what about Grandad?

Mommo   Who?

Mary   The stranger.

Mommo   Not much by way of big sound?

Mary   No.

Mommo   Or rebounding modulation?

Mary   No.

Mommo   But was that a stipulation?

Mary   No.

Mommo   He knew the tricks of providence and was cunning of exertion. Scorn for his style betimes?

Mary *nods.*

Mommo   But them wor his tactics.

Mary   And he was the one most in control.

Mommo   He was. (*She yawns.*) Tired.

Mary   No, Mommo – It *is* a nice story – And you've nearly told it all tonight. Except for the last piece that you never tell.

Mommo   Who was that woman?

Mary   What woman?

Mommo   Tck! – The woman just went out of the door there. (*Mimicking* **Dolly**.) 'Hup-hup-howa that!'

Mary   That was Dolly . . . Dolly.

Mommo   An' does she always behave that way?

Mary   Sometimes.

Mommo *thinking about this; it does not make sense to her. Then eyes scrutinising* **Mary***: in this moment she is possibly close to recognising her.*

Mommo   Who are (*you*)?

Mary   Try a guess. Yes, Mommo? – Yes, Mommo? – Please – who am I?

Mommo   Here she is again!

Dolly *comes in. She looks bloated and tired. She wolfs down the slice of cake which she deliberately resisted earlier. Then looking for her bag, putting on her overcoat, etc.*

Dolly   And I've been starving myself.

Mommo (*whispering*)   She'd eat yeh out of house an' home . . . Is there something you require, Miss, that you're rummaging for over there?

Dolly   Your pension.

Mommo   Oh, it's time for ye both to be going – ten to ten. He doesn't like calling when there's strangers in the house.

Mary   We're off now in a minute. What was that topic again that kept them on laughing?

Mommo   Misfortunes. (*She yawns.*)

Mary   Mommo?

Mommo's *eyes are closed.*

Dolly (*to herself, looking at the door*)   I hate going home.

Mary   Mommo?

Mommo (*very tired*)   Tom is in Galway. I bet him with nettles. Mitchin' from school. D'yeh think he remembers?

Mary (*gently*)   No.

Mommo   Well, I don't remember . . . I don't remember any more of it . . . (*She's asleep.*)

Mary *is defeated.*

Dolly   . . . What were you trying to do with her?

Mary   'Twas only a notion. She's asleep.

Dolly   Maybe she'd wake up again?

Mary (*slight shake of her head, 'No'*)   Sit down.

Dolly   What're yeh goin' to do?

Mary (*slight shake of her head, a tremulous sigh*)   Ahmm.

Dolly   Back to the nursing?

Mary   No. That wasn't me at all. And no confidence now anyway.

She collects up a few odds and ends and puts them in the suitcase.

Who's looking after the children?

Dolly   Maisie Kelly. They're stayin' the night in her house.

Mary (*absently*)   The nicest night ever.

Dolly   . . . What were we doin' that night?

Mary Ahmm. The shade on that light: do you mind if I – ?

She switches off the light and lights a candle.

We let the fire go out. The cursèd paraffin.

Mary *has collected up a silver-backed hairbrush and a clothes brush.*

Dolly . . . But if you're not going back to the nursing?

Mary There must be *some* future for me, somewhere.

She is brushing the back of **Dolly***'s coat.*

Mary I can certainly scrub floors.

Dolly (*a little irritably*) What're you doin'?

Mary Just a little – dust – here.

Dolly Who cares?

Mary It's just that people talk at the slightest.

Dolly Do you care what people say?

Mary I'm afraid I do. There.

Coat brushed; she now brushes **Dolly***'s hair.*

Mary When I was a nurse there was a patient, terminal, an elderly woman, and we became very close. I don't know why she used to watch me or why she chose to make friends with me.

Dolly What are you doin' now?

Mary But one day she said, in the middle of – whatever – conversation we were having, 'You're going to be alright, Mary.' Simple remark. But it took me by surprise. It was like, a *promised* blessing. And why I should have – (*Shrugs.*) – believed in it for, oh, twenty years? until recently, I don't know. There.

Dolly*'s hair is brushed.*

Mary She left me these (*the brushes*), and this (*the teapot*) and the book. (*She dumps the lot into the suitcase.*)

Dolly If I sat down to write a book.

Mary Though the book has always depressed me a bit. *Winter Words.* I can't do a thing for you, Dolly. Can you lend me a hundred quid?

Dolly *nods.* **Mary** *switches off the radio.*

Mary Well, that's it then.

Dolly *is just sitting there and* **Mary** *is standing: two figures frozen in time. Then a cortège of cars approaching, passing the house (at comparatively slow speed).*

Dolly The funeral. The weekend-long meeting at the plant is over. Now are they travelling at the sound of speed?

Mary *laughs – titters.*

Dolly I told you the Chinese'd get them!

Mary *laughs.* **Dolly** *joins in the laughter.* **Dolly** *now flaunting herself, clowning, addressing her stomach, the bulge.*

Dolly Good man 'Josie'! . . . And you're 'Josie's' aunt!

They laugh louder, the laughter getting out of hand . . . until they collapse together on the floor.

Good man, Josie! . . . (*Uproariously.*) Jesus, misfortunes!

Then the unexpected: **Mommo** *is awake. She is laughing to herself.*

Mary (*in a whisper*)   Shh, Dolly, shhh! (*And waits, frozen.*)

Mommo Yis. Did ye hear? Explosions of laughter an' shouts of hurrahs! For excess of joy.

Dolly Jesus, I'm tired. (*And titters.*)

Mary Shh, Dolly, shhh! (*And waits, frozen.*)

Mommo An' didn't he ferret out her eyes to see how she was farin', an' wasn't she titherin' with the best of them an' weltin' her thighs. No heed on her now to be gettin' on home. No. But offerin' to herself her own congratulations at hearin' herself laughin'. An' then, like a girl, smiled at her husband, an' his smile back so shy, like the boy he was in youth. An' the moment was for them alone. Unaware of all cares, unaware of all the others. An' how long before since their eyes had met, mar gheal dhá gréine, glowing love for each other? Not since long and long ago.

Dolly 'S alright, 's alright, Mommo: I'm Dolly, I'm like a film star. (*She lies on the bed perhaps.*)

Mommo But now Costello's big hand was up for to call a recession. 'But how,' says he, 'is it to be indisputably decided who is the winner?' And a great silence followed. None was forgettin' this was a contest. An' the eyes that wor dancin', now pending the answer, glazed an' grave in dilation: 'Twas a difficult question. (*Quietly.*) Och-caw! Tired of waiting male intelligence, 'He who laughs last,' says she.

An' 'cause 'twas a woman that spoke it, I think Costello was frikened, darts class of a glance at her an' – (*She gulps.*) 'That's what I thought,' says he.

But wasn't that his mistake? Ever callin' the recession an' he in full flight. 'Cause now, ready himself as he would, with his coughin' an' spittin', the sound emanating from a man of his talent, so forced and ungracious, he'd stop it himself.

(*Whispering.*) 'He's lost it,' says someone. (*Her derisory shout on the night.*) Hona ho gus hah-haa! (*Whispering.*) 'He should never have stopped.' Their faces like mice.

An' he'd 'tempt it an' 'tempt it an' 'tempt it again. Ach an fear mór as Bochtán (*but the big man from Bochtán*) in respiratory disaster is i ngreas casachtaí (*and in bouts of coughing*). (*She coughs . . .*) The contest was over.

Mary The contest was over?

Mommo Oh the strangers'd won.

Mary But what about the topic?

Mommo Hah?

Mary Would keep them laughing near for ever.

Mommo (*whispers*)   Misfortunes . . . She supplied them
with the topic. And it started up again with the subject of
potatoes, the damnedable crop was in that year.

'Wet an' wat'rey?' says the stranger.

'Wet an' wat'rey,' laughing Costello. 'Heh heh heh, but not
blighted?'

'No ho ho, ho ho ho, but scabby an' small.'

'Sour an' soapy – Heh heh heh.'

'Yis – ho ho,' says the hero. 'Hard to wash, ladies, hard to
boil, ladies?'

'An' the divil t'ate – Heh heh heh!'

But they were only getting into their stride. 'An' the hay?'
says old Brian, 'behell.'

'Rotted!' says the contestants, roarin' it together.

'The bita oats,' shouts young Kemple, 'Jasus!' Lodged in the
field.' An' the turf says another. Still in the bog, laughed the
answer, an' the chickens the pip, pipes up the old crone.

An' the sheep, the staggers, an' the cow that just died, an' the
man that was in it lost both arms to the thresher, an' the dead.

Mary   . . . And the dead, Mommo? Who were the dead?

Mommo   Skitherin' an' laughin' – ih-hih-ih – at their nearest
an' dearest. Her Pat was her eldest, died of consumption,
had his pick of the girls an' married the widdy again' all her
wishes. The decline in that fambly, she knew the widdy'd
outlast him. She told them the story – an' many another. An'
how Pat had come back for the two sheep (*that*) wor his –
An' they wor – an' he was her firstborn – but you'll not have
them she told him. Shy Willie inside, quiet by the hearth,
but she knew he'd be able, the spawgs of hands he had on
him. 'Is it goin' fightin' me own brother?' But she told him
a brother was one thing, but she was his mother, an' them
were her orders to give Pat the high road, and no sheep, one,

two or three wor leavin' the yard. They hurted each other.
An' how Pat went back empty to his strap of a widdy, an'
was dead within a six months. Ih-hih-ih. (*The 'ih-hih-ih' which
punctuate her story sound more like ingrown sobs rather than laughter.*)
She made great contributions, rollcalling the dead. Was she
what or 'toxicated? An' for the sake of an auld ewe stuck in
the flood was how she lost two of the others, Jimmy and
Michael. Great gales of laughter following each name of the
departed. Ih-hih-ih. An' the nice wife was near her time,
which one of them left behind him?

Mary Daddy.

Mommo Died tryin' to give birth to the fourth was to be
in it. An' she herself left with the care of three small childre
waitin'. All contributions receiving volleys of cheers . . .
Nothin' was sacred an' nothing a secret. The unbaptised an'
stillborn in shoeboxes planted, at the dead hour of night
treading softly the Lisheen to make the regulation hole. Not
more, not less than two feet deep. And too fearful of the field,
haunted by infants, to speak or to pray. They were fearful for
their ankles – ih-hih-ih. An' tryin' not to hasten, steal away
again, leaving their pagan parcels in isolation for ever. Ih-
hih-ih. And Willie too, her pet, went foreign after the others.
An' *did* she drive them all away? Never ever to be heard of,
ever again. Save shy Willie, aged thirty-four, in Louisaville
Kentucky, died, peritonites. The nicest night they ever had,
that's what I'm sayin'. And all of them present, their heads
thrown back abandoned in festivities of guffaws: the wretched
and neglected, dilapidated an' forlorn, the forgotten an'
despairing, ragged an' dirty, eyes big as saucers ridiculing an'
defying of their lot on earth below – Glintin' their defiance
of Him – their defiance an' rejection, inviting of what else
might come or *care* to come! – driving bellows of refusal at
the sky through the roof. Hona ho gus hah-haa! . . . 'Twas
an insolence at Heaven. But they'd soon get their answer.

Mary Who would?

Mommo The Bochtáns, the Bochtáns sure! Tck! Mauleogs
drunk?

Mary *nods.*

Mommo   Them all packed together?

Mary *nods.*

Mommo   The foul odour that was in it, you'd hardly get your breath. The two contestants sweating, the big man most profusely – Sure they'd been contending the title now five or six hours. An' Costello, openin' down his shirts an' loosenin' his buckle, was doublin' up an' staggerin' an' holdin' his sides. 'Aw Jasus, lads, ye have me killed – hickle-ickle-ickle,' an' the laughing lines upon his mien wor more like lines of pain. An' the stranger, 'Heh heh heh heh, heh heh heh heh,' aisy an' gentle. Then beholding his 'ponent, his complexion changin' colours the frown came to his brow bringin' stillness upon him an' the two little smiles to the sides of his mouth. Suddenly he shouts, 'Costello's the winner!' But sure they wouldn't have it – nor herself in the corner. 'He's nat (*not*), he's nat, he's nat, he's nat!' 'On, on-on, Bochtán for ever!'

'No-no! – heh-heh – he has me bet!'

'He's nat, he's nat, he's nat, he's nat!'

The others, 'Up Bochtán! Bochtán for ever!'

An' Costello now all the while in upper registration – 'hickle-ickle-ickle-ickle' – longin' to put stop to it, his own cacklin' wouldn't let him. An' 'deed, when he'd 'tempt to rise an arm – an' sure he wasn't able – in gesture of cessation, th' others mistakin' of his purpose would go thinkin' t' do it for'm (*for him*) puncturin' holes in the ceilin', batin' stomps on the floor.

An' the stranger now could only stand and watch. An' late it was herself realised the Great Adversary had entered.

'Hickle-ickle-ickle-ickle – Aw Jasus, lads, I'm dyin'.' Then slow in a swoon he went down to the floor. For the last moments were left him 'twas the stranger that held him, for there was nothing now in the world to save him or able to save him.

Mary   And what's the rest of it? Only a little bit left.

Mommo (*musing*)   For there was nothing now in the world to save him –

Dolly   Mary?

Mary   You're going to be alright, Dolly. Roll in under the blanket.

She helps **Dolly** *get under the blankets.*

Mommo   – or able to save him. Did I not say that bit? Oh yis. 'An' the rabbits, lads,' says Cost'llo, 'I didn't sell e'er the one of them, but threwn them comin' home for fun again' Patch Curran's door.' And that was the last he was to utter that night or any other.

Mary   They don't laugh there any more.

Mommo   Save the childre, until they arrive at the age of reason. Now! Bochtán for ever is Bailegangaire.

Through the following **Mary** *puts away her suitcase, tidies some things away, undresses behind the headboard, puts on a simple nightdress and gets the cup of milk for* **Mommo**.

Mary   To conclude.

Mommo   Yes. They wor for lettin' them home, d'yeh know? Home without hinder. Till the thief, Josie, started cryin' at death, and was demanding the boots be took of the stranger to affirm 'twas feet or no was in them. An' from trying to quieten his excitation someone of them got hit. Then he struck back. Till they forgot what they wor doin' sure, or how it had started, but all drawin' kicks an' blows, one upon the other, till the venom went rampant. They pulled the stranger down off the cart an' gave him the kickin'. Oh they gave him such a doin', till John Mah'ny an' the curate (*that*) was called prevailed again' the Bolsheviks.

'Twas dawn when they got home. Not without trepidation? But the three small childre, like ye, their care, wor safe an' sound fast asleep on the settle. Now, my fondlings, settle down an' be sayin' yer prayers. I forget what happened the three

sticks of rock. Hail Holy Queen – Yes? Mother of Mercy –
Yes? Hail our lives? – Yes? Our sweetness and our hope.

Mary   It was a bad year for the crops, a good one for
mushrooms, and the three small children were waiting for
their gran and their grandad to come home. Mommo? My
bit. Mary was the eldest. She was the clever one, and she
was seven. Dolly, the second, was like a film star and she was
Grandad's favourite. And they were in and out of the road
watching for the horse and cart. Waiting for ribbons. And
Tom, who was the youngest, when he got excited would go
pacing o'er and o'er the boundary of the yard. He had
confided in Mary his expectation. They would be bringing
him his dearest wish – Grandad told him secretly – a mouth
organ for Christmas. That was alright. But in the excitation –
of their waiting they forgot to pay attention to the fire. Then
Mary and Dolly heard – 'twas like an explosion. Tom had
got the paraffin and, not the careful way Grandad did it,
shhtiolled it on to the embers, and the sudden blaze came
out on top of him. And when they ran in and . . . saw him,
Mary got . . . hysterical. Then Mary sent Dolly across the
fields for May Glynn. And sure May was only . . . eleven?
Then Mary covered . . . the wounds . . . from the bag of flour
in the corner. She'd be better now, and quicker now, at
knowing what to do. And then May Glynn's mother came
and they took Tom away to Galway, where he died . . . Two
mornings later, and he had only just put the kettle on the
hook, didn't Grandad, the stranger, go down too, slow in a
swoon . . . Mommo?

Mommo   It got him at last.

Mary   Will you take your pills now?

Mommo   The yellow ones.

Mary   Yes.

Mommo   Poor Seamus.

She takes the pills with a sup of milk.

Mary   Is there anything else you need?

Mommo   To thee do we cry – Yes? Poor banished children of Eve.

Mary   Is there anything you have to say to me?

Mommo   Be sayin' yer prayers now an' ye'll be goin' to sleep. To thee do we send up our sighs – yes? For yer Mammy an' Daddy an' Grandad is (*who are*) in Heaven.

Mary   And Tom.

Mommo   Yes. An' he only a ladeen was afeared of the gander. An' tell them ye're all good. Mourning and weeping in this valley of tears.

She is handing the cup back to **Mary**.

Mommo   And sure a tear isn't such a bad thing, Mary, and haven't we everything we need here, the two of us. (*And she settles down to sleep.*)

Mary (*tears of gratitude brim to her eyes*)   Oh we have, Mommo.

She gets into the bed beside **Mommo**. **Dolly** *is on the other side of* **Mommo**.

Mary   . . . To conclude. It's a strange old place alright, in whatever wisdom He has to have made it this way. But in whatever wisdom there is, in the year 1984, it was decided to give that – fambly . . . of strangers another chance, and a brand new baby to gladden their home.

Schubert's 'Notturno' comes in under **Mary**'s *final speech.*

Christina Reid

The Belle of the Belfast City

The Belle of the Belfast City was first produced by the Lyric Players Theatre, Belfast, in May 1989, with the following cast:

Dolly Dunbar Horner	Sheila McGibbon
Vi	Stella McCuskar
Rose	Fay Howard
Belle	Suzette Llewellyn
Janet	Lindy Whiteford
Jack	John Hewitt
Davy Watson, **Tom Bailey**, **Isaac Standaloft**, **Customs Man**, **Peter**	Richard Howard

Directed by Tim Luscombe
Designed by James Helps
Lighting Designer Patrick Dalgety
Production Manager Rose Morris

'The Ballad of William Bloat' was written by Raymond Calvert and 'Ballad to a Traditional Refrain' ('May the Lord in His Mercy be kind to Belfast') by Maurice James Craig. My thanks to both authors and also to Irene Calvert, Agnes Bernelle, the Blackstaff Press, the Linen Hall Library, Belfast Leisure Kids, the Kingham Mission for the Deaf and the Council for the Advancement of Communication Skills with Deaf People, Belfast. And a very special 'thank you' to John and Agnes Carberry for teaching and translating their language of signing during rehearsals.

Characters

Dolly Dunbar Horner
Vi, *Dolly's daughter*
Rose, *Dolly's daughter*
Belle, *Dolly's granddaughter*
Janet, *Dolly's niece*
Jack, *Dolly's nephew*
Davy Watson
Tom Bailey
Isaac Standaloft
Customs Man
Peter

Act One

Scene One

Belfast, November 1986.

Dolly *(aged seventy-seven) sits looking at a photo album. She wears a dressing gown. Her walking stick is propped against a dressing-up box alongside her chair. The room has many framed photographs, old and new. The largest and most dominant image is of the young* **Dolly** *on a concert poster, circa 1925, when she topped the bill in the halls as 'The Belle of the Belfast City'.*

Dolly *(sings)*
  I'll tell me ma when I go home
  The boys won't leave the girls alone
  They pulled my hair, they stole my comb
  Well that's all right till I go home
  She is handsome, she is pretty
  She is the Belle of the Belfast City
  She is courtin' One Two Three
  Please won't you tell me who is she.

Davy *taps out the rhythm of the song on the spoons,* **Dolly** *listens, and in the distance, as if she is conjuring it, we hear her family singing. It is 1958.* **Dolly**'s *daughters* **Vi** *(aged twenty-nine) and* **Rose** *(eight), and her niece* **Janet** *(eight) come running to her from the past. They dress up with clothes from the box and perform the song.* **Dolly**'s *nephew (* **Janet**'s *brother* **Jack**, *aged twelve) beats out a drum rhythm with his hands.* **Jack** *does not dress up nor join in the love and laughter that envelops the girls. During the singing and dancing,* **Dolly** *joins in and becomes an agile woman of forty-nine. Her eighteen-year-old granddaughter* **Belle** *watches with delight.* **Belle** *is in the present time and watches as if seeing an often-heard story re-created.*

Vi, **Rose** *and* **Janet** *sing.* **Dolly** *joins in.*

  Joe Horner says he loves her
  All the boys are fightin' for her
  They knock at the door and they ring the bell

Saying 'Oh my true love are you well'
Out she comes as white as snow
Rings on her fingers bells on her toes
Oul Dolly Dunbar says she'll die
If she doesn't get the fella with the rovin' eye

I'll tell me ma when I go home
The boys won't leave the girls alone
They pulled my hair, they stole my comb
Well that's all right till I go home
She is handsome, she is pretty
She is the Belle of the Belfast City
She is courtin' One Two Three
Please won't you tell me who is she.

Back to the present time. **Jack** *and* **Janet** *exit.* **Dolly** *looks at the photo album.* **Vi** *is in the family shop with* **Davy**. **Belle** *and* **Rose** *are in Aldergrove airport, Belfast, waiting for transport to the family home.*

Belle   She is my grandmother. Dolly Dunbar. Child star of the twenties. Songs, recitations and tap dancing. She won a talent competition when she was ten and was top of the bill before she was thirteen. I'm called after her. Not Dolly, but Belle. That was her stage name and my grandfather Joe never called her anything else.

Rose   My mother, the Belle of the Belfast City, happened to be performing in an Orange Hall in Belfast one night when my father Joe Horner was at a Lodge meeting in an upstairs room. They say he heard her singing and walked out of the meeting and into the concert like a man under a spell. And that was it. They eloped a fortnight later, and from then on she gave up the stage and did all her dressing-up and singing and dancing just for him.

Vi   Our Rose is nuthin' if not romantic. The truth is that my mother's family were still dressin' her up as if she was thirteen instead of goin' on nineteen, an' trailin' her round draughty oul halls to sing to audiences of twenty or thirty. My father took her away from all that, and waited on her hand and foot for the rest of his life. Still, as they say, it's a poor family can't afford to support one lady.

Dolly   An' a poor story that doesn't improve with the tellin'.

Rose   When I was very small I used to lie in bed with my big sister Vi and listen to our parents gossiping and giggling like a couple of kids in the room next door. When the bed-springs started to creak, our Vi used to stuff cotton wool in my ears.

Vi   Forty-one mother was when she had our Rose, and me already over the age of consent. It was the talk of the neighbourhood.

Rose   Bad enough to be still doing it at their age, but even worse to be enjoying it so much that she was careless enough to get caught. Our Vi was that mortified she wouldn't go out of the house. My mother and father were over the moon.

Dolly (*looking at the album or pointing to one of the framed photos*) He was as proud as a peacock. My Joe. The cock of the North.

Vi   Mother! That'll do!

Dolly   She always calls me Mother when she's bein' prim an' proper. She must of got that from your side of the family, Joe. But you see our Rose? She's like *my* ones. Fulla life an' rarin' to go. She's travelled the world you know, takin' pictures. Imagine that!

Rose *walks to* **Belle**.

Rose   No sign of the airport bus yet?

Belle   It's been delayed indefinitely. There was a demonstration earlier today near Belfast city centre and some of the roads are still blocked.

Rose   What sort of a demonstration?

Belle   A Loyalist protest against the Anglo-Irish Agreement. The speakers were the Reverend Ian Paisley and your cousin Jack.

Rose   Welcome to the land of your forefathers, Belle.
Come on, let's see if we can get a taxi.

Dolly (*sings*)
    Let the wind and the rain and the hail blow high
    And the snow come tumblin' from the sky
    She's as nice as apple pie
    And she'll get her own man by and by
    When she gets a man of her own
    She won't tell her ma when she comes home
    Let them all come as they will
    For it's Joe Horner she loves still.

Scene Two

Dolly *sits in the room off the family shop. The shop is small and sells
crisps, sweets, cigarettes, newspapers, magazines and a few groceries
and carry-out snacks (sandwiches, pies etc). There is a small table and
chairs for the occasional customer to eat on the premises.*

Vi *is setting out the local magazines which have been delivered by*
Davy, *who is deaf and mute.* **Vi** *and* **Davy** *communicate through
lip-reading and/or hand signals. If* **Vi** *has her back to* **Davy**, *he
attracts her attention by clapping his hands.*

*The shop is in East Belfast in a side street that the Army has closed to
traffic.*

Jack *walks into the street. He is very neatly and expensively dressed
and wears slightly tinted glasses. He moves silently. All* **Jack**'s
movements are very careful and controlled.

Vi *takes two bars of chocolate from a shelf.*

Vi   Thanks for bringin' the magazines round, Davy. Here,
that's for you and one for your mother. Don't you be eatin'
both of them, mind.

Davy *shakes his head and signals thanks.* **Jack** *has come into the
shop quietly without* **Vi** *and* **Davy** *being aware of him. He deliberately
moves one of the chairs to make a noise.*

Vi   God, Jack, you made me jump!

Jack   They say that's the sign of a bad conscience, Vi.

Vi   A bad conscience? Me? Huh! Chance would be a fine thing!

Dolly (*sings*)
    There was an oul woman down Donegall Street
    Who went to the doctor 'cause she couldn't . . .

Vi   Mother!

Jack   Aunt Dolly sounds in fine form the day.

Vi   Did you ever know a day when she wasn't?

Davy *becomes aware of* **Jack** *and talks rapidly in sign language to* **Vi**. *He is very excited that* **Jack** *is there.*

Vi   He says, can he get you anything, Mr Horner? A cup of tea, a sandwich, a hot pie . . .

Jack   Tell him no . . . thanks. I have to go to a meeting.

Vi *signals to* **Davy** *who looks crestfallen.*

Jack   I just called to ask you if you're still thinking of selling the shop.

Vi (*glancing nervously towards the room where* **Dolly** *sits*)   It's not something I've thought out, Jack, nor mentioned to nobody else . . . Why do you ask?

Jack   I have a friend who's looking for a shop and dwelling around here.

Vi   What friend?

Jack   Nobody you know. A business acquaintance. An Englishman. He's in Belfast for a few days, looking at property. I mentioned this place to him and he's very interested. It's the right size and in the right area. He's got the money to make you a good offer.

Davy *signals to* **Vi** *again.*

Vi   Have a quick cup. Just to please him, Jack. The kettle's already boiled, it won't take a minute, and you can have a wee word with Dolly.

She signals to **Davy** *that* **Jack** *will have a cup of tea.* **Davy** *is delighted and almost runs behind the counter.* **Vi** *moves quickly towards the other room, anxious that* **Jack** *won't pursue the subject of selling the shop.* **Jack** *follows her.*

Vi   Here's Jack to see you, Mother.

Dolly   Jack who?

Vi   Our Jack.

Dolly   The one with the haircut that's never off the television?

Vi   You know right well who he is, now stop actin' the eejit.

Dolly *points out a photo to* **Jack**.

Dolly   That's you, with a face like a Lurgan spade as usual. An' that's me, and Rose and Vi and your wee sister Janet, God love her. My Joe took that photo the week after we brought the two of you here to live with us. *(Pause.)* Janet's stoppin' here again, ye know. Left her man. Don't know what's goin' on there at all. *(At* **Vi**.*)* Nobody never tells me nuthin' these days.

Jack *looks sharply at* **Vi**. **Vi** *looks away.* **Dolly** *reaches out as if to take off* **Jack**'s *glasses.* **Jack** *recoils.*

Dolly   I only wanted to have a look at your sore eye.

Jack *(off guard)*   I haven't got a sore . . .

He stops, realising that **Dolly** *is making fun of him.*

Vi   Mother! Behave yourself!

Jack *walks angrily back to the shop.* **Vi** *gives* **Dolly** *an exasperated look.* **Dolly** *smiles innocently.* **Vi** *follows* **Jack**. **Davy** *rushes forward eagerly with a cup of tea for* **Jack** *and sets it on the table.* **Davy** *signals to* **Vi**.

Vi He says, God bless you, John Horner, and God bless Ian Paisley. He says you're the boys'll see Ulster right.

Jack What's all this about Janet?

Vi She's left Peter. She's been here about a week.

Jack Why wasn't I told?

Vi She didn't want –

Jack You should have phoned me immediately.

Vi It wasn't my place.

Jack What's happened?

Vi I don't know. She won't say.

Jack She'll say to me. Where is she?

Vi She's out.

Jack You tell her I'll be back and I want to see her. Has *he* been here?

Vi Just the once. Peter hasn't a lot of free time. The RUC are on full standby, what with one thing and another . . .

Jack I knew no good would come of that marriage. Sneaking off to a registry office instead of standing up and declaring themselves without shame in the eyes of the Lord. I suppose he's got himself another woman. Catholic licentiousness. It never leaves them.

Vi Peter's a good man.

Jack A Catholic policeman! It's the like of him who've infiltrated the Royal Ulster Constabulary. Corrupted the force into fighting against us instead of standing alongside us as they've always done.

Dolly (*recites loudly*)
  Holy Mary Mother of God
  Pray for me and Tommy Todd

For he's a Fenian and I'm a Prod
Holy Mary Mother of God.

Jack   That old woman should be in a home!

Vi   If that old woman hadn't taken you and Janet in when
your mother died, that's where you'd have ended up, in a
home! And don't you ever forget that, Jack!

Jack   I'm sorry if I offended you, Vi. I –

Vi   You offended *her*. This family never badmouths its own.

Jack   I apologise. I said it without thinking. Not like me.
One of the first things you learn in politics. Never speak
without knowing exactly what you're going to say . . . I was
angry with Janet. That marriage has always been a thorn in
my side.

He becomes aware of **Davy** *watching them.*

Jack   Does he understand what we've been talking about?

Vi   No. He needs to be close up and facing you to lip-read.

Jack   I don't want family business gossiped about.

Vi   I don't think you need worry about Davy doin' much
gossipin', Jack.

She signals and talks to **Davy**.

Vi   Away in and sit with Dolly for a while and look at the
photos. Here. (*Putting some sweets in a bag.*) Share these with her.

Davy *goes to* **Dolly**. *Holds out the bag of sweets.* **Dolly** *takes one.
Turns up her nose and calls to* **Vi**.

Dolly   Brandy balls! Are they not makin' it in bottles any
more?

She turns the pages in the photo album. **Davy** *gets excited and points
when he sees* **Jack** *as a boy.*

Dolly   Aye, that's Jack when he was a wee lad, wearin' the
National Health specs. Suited him better than them *Miami
Vice* jobs he wears these days.

In the shop, **Jack** *stands hesitantly as* **Vi**, *still angry at what he has said, tidies up the magazines.*

Jack   You wouldn't fall out with me, would you, Vi? We've always been friends, haven't we?

Vi   Yes, of course we have.

Jack   I've always appreciated what your parents did for me and Janet. I'm not ungrateful. But I . . .

Vi   It's all right, Jack.

Jack   I just want you to know that I've not forgotten how *you* looked after *me* . . . Dolly always sided with Janet and Rose . . . You're the only person in the world I've ever enjoyed singing with . . . do you know that?

They are both awkward about this declaration.

Do you still sing?

Vi   There's no children here to sing for any more, and she does enough singin' for both of us.

Jack   You had a good voice.

Vi   You weren't so bad yourself.

Dolly (*sings*)
    In the county Tyrone near the town of Dungannon
    Where many's the ruction myself had a hand in
    Bob Williamson lived there, a weaver by trade
    And all of us thought him a stout Orange blade

    On the Twelfth of July as it yearly did come
    Bob played on the flute to the sound of the drum
    You may talk of your harp, your piano or lute
    But nothing could sound like the oul Orange flute.

Vi (*to* **Jack**)   We used to sing it better than that. When you were a wee lad.

Sings:

    But Bob the deceiver, he took us all in
    And married a Papish called Brigid McGinn

    Turned Papish himself and forsook the oul cause
    That gave us our freedom, religion and laws

Jack

    Now the boys in the townland made comment upon it
    And Bob had to flee to the province of Connaught
    He flew with his wife and his fixins to boot
    And along with the latter the oul Orange flute

Vi

    At the chapel on Sundays to atone for past deeds
    Bob said Paters and Aves and counted his beads
    Till after some time at the priest's own desire
    Bob went with his oul flute to play in the choir

Jack

    And all he could whistle and finger and blow
    To play Papish music he found it no go
    'Kick the Pope' and 'Boyne Water' and such like it
      would sound
    But one Papish squeak in it couldn't be found

Vi

    At the council of priests that was held the next day
    They decided to banish the oul flute away
    For they couldn't knock heresy out of its head
    And they bought Bob another to play in its stead

Jack

    So the oul flute was doomed and its fate was pathetic
    It was fastened and burned at the stake as heretic
    As the flames licked around it they heard a strange noise
    'Twas the oul flute still playin' 'The Protestant Boys'!

Dolly *points to the album and cackles with laughter.* **Jack***'s rare moment of pleasure is broken.*

Jack   And then Rose came sneaking in and took a photo of us.

Vi   She meant no harm. I never could understand why you were in such a state about it.

Jack   I don't like being caught off guard like that. Rose always was a sly one. (*Hurriedly, in case* **Vi** *objects to him slighting one of the family.*) When's she arriving?

Vi   Now how did you know about that?

Jack   You must have told me.

Vi   I haven't seen you since Rose phoned to tell me that her and Belle were coming.

Jack   She's bringing her daughter here?

Vi   She is indeed. And about time too. That child's over eighteen and been all over the world with our Rose and never in her own home town. It's a disgrace, so it is. I told Rose, now that Dolly's not able to travel to London no more you'll have to bring Belle here to see us. She must have took it to heart, for the pair of them are arrivin' the day . . . and would you look at the state of this place.

She fusses about, tidying the shop.

Don't mind me gettin' on, Jack, I don't want Belle thinkin' we run this shop like a midden. I want her to think well of Belfast and have a holiday she'll never forget.

Jack   Oh, Rose is on holiday, is she?

Vi (*slightly puzzled at his tone of voice*)   Aye, and Belle's on half term from her college.

Jack   What's she like, this daughter of Rose's?

Vi   Like you. Clever. She's studying Drama and Irish History at university. I suppose she gets the drama from Dolly. And she's beautiful lookin' too. Mind you, it's over a year since I've seen her, but Rose keeps us up to date with photos. Great they are, but then they would be, wouldn't they, it's Rose's job. Janet brought some lovely photos back from London. Would you like to see –

Jack   Nobody told me that Janet had been in London.

Vi   You're not around much these days to be told anything, Jack.

Davy *comes back into the shop. He takes a crumpled newspaper cutting out of his pocket. Signals to* **Vi**.

Vi   He says, would you autograph this for him? It's you and Ian Paisley the day of the last strike on the platform at the City Hall.

Jack (*to* **Davy**)   A great day. Were you there?

Vi   Yes, he was there, Jack, and that's something I want to talk to you about. Davy's mother asked me if I would ask you to tell him that he's not to go to the big demonstration next Saturday.

Jack   I can't do that.

Vi   He's deaf. His sight's poor. He shouldn't be in a crowd like that. It's dangerous. His mother is worried sick about him. He won't heed her, but he'll do anything you say. He worships the ground you walk on.

Jack   He has faith in me because of what I believe in. I can't weaken that loyalty by telling him not to go to the rally. Every good Protestant must go.

Vi   Look at him, Jack. In God's name, do you need the like of him on the streets of Belfast in order to win? He has a mental age of ten.

Jack   Saturday is the first anniversary of the signing of the accursed Anglo-Irish Agreement. Every loyal man, woman and child must take to the streets to show the British government they will never defeat us. Never! Never! Never!

Vi   He can't hear the grand speeches, Jack. He goes because the flags and the banners and the crowds excite him. The violence excites him.

Jack   There will be no violence. It will be a peaceful protest.

Vi   You said that last time, and look what happened.

Jack   It was not our doing. The police created the violence.

Vi   There was a riot, Jack. I was there. I saw it.

Jack   The Catholics riot. We do not. We are a respectable people.

Davy *points proudly to the newspaper cutting. Signals.*

Vi   He says that's him there, in the crowd directly in front of the platform.

Jack   He must have been there early to get so near the front. You know it's said that simple people like him are truly the Children of God?

Vi   Try tellin' that to his mother.

Jack   God works in mysterious ways. Ours not to reason why. Don't you consider it miraculous that he can neither hear nor speak, but he knows instinctively what we're fighting for?

Vi   He knows because he lip-reads the television and reads the papers. He had partial hearing until he was about ten, and before it left him entirely, his mother taught him to read. That's the miracle her love and faith worked when all them clever doctors said it was impossible. He's all she has, Jack. Please tell him not to go.

Jack   God will look after him.

Dolly (*sings*)
 I don't care if it rains or freezes
 I am safe in the arms of Jesus
 I am Jesus' little lamb
 Yes by Jesus Christ I am.

Jack *takes the newspaper cutting from* **Davy** *and signs it.* **Rose** *and* **Belle** *come into the shop.*

Rose   Shop!

Vi   Oh Rose, you're here! And Belle – look at you, all grown up! You're not a child any more. You're a young woman. Not too big to give your oul aunt a hug, are you?

A lot of hugging and kissing between the women. **Rose** *becomes aware of* **Jack***.*

Rose   Hello, Jack.

Jack   Hello, Rose. How are you?

Rose   I'm very well. And you?

Jack   I'm well too, thanks be to God.

Rose   This is my daughter, Belle. Belle, this is my cousin John Horner. Jack to the family.

Belle   Hello, Jack.

She half moves to shake his hand but doesn't, as he just nods his head slightly to acknowledge the introduction.

Vi   And this is Davy Watson, lives round the corner, gives me a hand in the shop nigh an' again.

Belle   Hello, Davy.

She holds out her hand to **Davy** *who has been staring at her since she came in. He hesitantly touches her hand then, shyly, almost touches her face. Stops and signals to* **Vi***.*

Vi (*laughs*)   He's all of a dither because he's never seen nobody with dark skin before, except on the television.

Belle   Is this a joke?

Rose   There aren't many like you in Belfast, Belle. And those that are, are well-to-do. Restaurant owners, doctors, university lecturers, overseas students. They don't live round here.

Belle   No working-class black ghettos?

Rose   None.

Belle (*looking directly at* **Jack**)   No prejudice?

Davy *signals to* **Vi** *again.* **Vi** *shakes her head at him and looks sideways at* **Belle***, who grins, and surprises* **Vi** *by signalling to* **Davy** *as she talks.*

Belle   No Davy, I'm not from Africa. I'm from England.
And my mother is from Belfast and my father is from
America. I think that makes me an Anglo-Irish Yank.

Vi   Now, where did you learn to do that?

Belle   I have a friend who's deaf.

Vi   Isn't that great? Now Davy'll have three people to talk
to. You, me an' his mother. It was *her* taught *me*. (*She looks at*
Jack.) She's a nice wee woman.

Davy *signals self-consciously to* **Belle**.

Belle   Thank you, Davy. I may take you up on that.

He signals goodbye to everyone, then shakes **Belle**'s *hand and leaves
very quickly. He passes* **Janet** *in the street and signals to her excitedly
and runs off.* **Janet** *stands for a moment outside.*

Rose   What did he say?

Belle   He offered to be my escort if I want to see Belfast.

Vi   Hey girl, I think you've clicked there.

Jack   I must go.

Rose   Affairs of state, Jack?

Jack   Think over what I mentioned, Vi. And don't forget
to tell Janet I want to talk to her.

Rose *and* **Vi** *exchange looks.*

Jack   I see *you* know about it.

Rose   I know she's here. She phoned me.

Jack   She tells everybody but not her own brother.

Rose   Some things are easier discussed between women.

Jack   Women! That's always been the trouble with this
house. Women having secrets, whispering, gossiping.

Vi   I told you, Jack, I don't know anything to gossip about.

Jack   But *you* do. Don't you, Rose?

Janet *comes in. There is a strained silence.*

Jack   I'm late for a meeting. I'll talk to you later, madam.

He walks out.

Belle   God, he's a bundle of laughs, isn't he?

Vi   He's under a lot of strain at the moment. He's all right when you get to know him.

Rose *and* **Janet** *exchange looks.*

Vi   And we'll have less of the looks between you two if you don't mind. It's a long time since this family were all together under one roof, and I want it to be happy. Like the old days. No troubles.

Janet   I'm sorry. This is all my fault.

Rose (*sharply*)   No it's not, Janet! (*More gently.*) You have got to stop always blaming yourself when it's Jack who's at fault.

Dolly (*sings*)
In and out go the dusty bluebells
In and out go the dusty bluebells
In and out go the dusty bluebells
I'll be your master
Tapper-rapper-rapper on her left-hand shoulder
Tapper-rapper-rapper on her left-hand shoulder
Tapper-rapper-rapper on her left-hand shoulder
I'll be your master.

Scene Three

Dolly *and* **Belle** *sit turning the pages in the photo album.*

Belle   Not so fast. I want you to tell me about every one of them. What age everybody is. Where you were at the time. What you were doing. I want to know all about my family. I want to know all about Ireland.

Dolly   Well, I can tell you all about the family. But as for Ireland, I've lived here all my life and I still can't make head nor tail of it. Better leave that to them clever professors at your university.

Belle   So many photographs.

Dolly   Aye, my Joe was a dab hand with a camera. That was one of the last photos he ever took, God rest him. That's me and your mammy and Janet and Vi settin' off one August mornin' for the Dublin train. I give your mammy Joe's oul camera after he died, an' she took to it like a duck to water. Then me an' Vi bought her a good camera when she was older an' she's never looked back since.

Belle   You all look so happy.

Dolly   We had good times. Outin's an' parties an' sing-songs an' dressin' up, you don't know the half of it.

Belle   It must be lovely being part of a big family.

Dolly   You *are* part of a big family.

Belle   I mean, having a big family around you all the time. A granny who lives nearby. I miss you not coming to London.

Dolly   I've missed you too. You'll have to come here now and see me. I'm sure Rose misses you now you're at the university.

Belle   She's all right. She has lots of friends.

Dolly   Friends are not the same as family. Does she have a man?

Belle   Sort of.

Dolly   Oh aye. Does that mean he's married?

Belle   No. It means that *he* has *his* flat and *she* has *hers*. She's an independent woman, my mother.

Dolly   She always was. She takes that after me.

Belle   But you ran off and got married before you were nineteen.

Dolly   But I was never a housewife. My Joe never wanted that. He was a rare bird. An Ulsterman who could cook.

Pause.

Belle   Did you ever meet *my* father?

Dolly   Not at all. We knew nothin' about any of it till you were born, an' he was back in America by then.

Belle   I met him last Christmas, when Mum and I were in New York. I told her I wanted to see him and she got in touch with him through some mutual friends. He arranged to meet us in a very expensive restaurant. Bought us lunch. Kept looking over his shoulder in case someone he knew might see us. He's a very respectable married man now. A pillar of a Baptist church. He made a great point of telling me that he hadn't left my mother. I already knew all that. Rose has never lied to me about anything. I told him that now that I'd met him I could understand why she'd thrown him out. He's a sanctimonious American Bible-belt prig. I bet he votes for Ronald Reagan. I asked him what he told his God about me, and he got up and walked away.

Dolly   I'm sorry, child.

Belle   I'm not. Now that I know what he's like, I can get on with my life knowing I haven't missed much. I didn't like him. I don't like your nephew Jack either. Does he always talk to Janet like that?

Dolly   Has that skittery ghost been gettin' at Janet again? I should never have told him that she was here. I only said it to annoy him. To let him know that when Janet was in trouble it was us she come to an' not him.

Belle   Why is she afraid of him?

Dolly   I thought I'd put a stop to all that years ago. But maybe it was too deep ingrained by the time me and Joe got them. God knows what went on before that. Their father was a Presbyterian minister, you know. Joe's only brother, Martin. Martin died young an' the mother took the two childer back to Scotland where she come from. An oul targe of a schoolteacher she was. You know the sort. Goes to church on Sunday, an' prays to God to give her strength to beat the kids on Monday.

Belle   She beat them?

Dolly   Into the ground. Not with a big stick. With words. Words like sin, the world and the devil. And the worst sins were the sinful lusts of the flesh. Jack's job as the man of the house was to protect his sister from temptation. I used to wonder how his mother and Martin ever had kids. I mean, it's not as if they were Catholic an' he could dip it in the Holy Water first. May God forgive her an' Jack for the way they scared that wee girl, for I know I never will. Do you know, the day me an' Joe arrived in Scotland to get them, I picked Janet up an' she stiffened like a ramrod. An' then she sort of crumpled up an' she cried, an' she fell asleep in my arms. Eight years old an' nobody had ever cuddled her. That's what I call a sin.

Belle   And what about Jack?

Dolly   Jack doesn't like bein' touched. Did ye not notice? I suppose that's why he never married.

Belle   I thought perhaps it was just me he didn't want to touch.

Dolly   Do ye come in for much of that? I mean, is it a bother to ye, bein' neither one thing nor the other?

Belle   Only when it bothers other people.

Dolly   Well, you needn't worry about round here, love. All they're interested in is what religion ye are.

Belle   Do you believe in God, Gran?

Dolly   I believe I'll be with my Joe someday, an' I hope it'll be soon.

Belle   Oh no, Gran!

Dolly   Ach, I don't mean right this minute, love. I'm all right for the time bein'. But I don't want to outlive my time. End up bein' kep' goin' by machines in a hospital. I have a horror of that. I can cope with not bein' able to dance with my feet no more. But I couldn't cope with not bein' able to dance in my head. I want to go under my own steam when my time comes. If you're around, will you see to that?

Very slight pause.

Belle   Yes, I will.

Dolly   I knew you'd say that, without a moral debate. You think straight. You see clear. Like me. Vi's too responsible, an' Rose is too romantic, an' Janet . . . Janet's fallin' to bits an' I think I know why, but I can't say till I know for sure. The rest of them think I'm a daft oul woman who can't be told certain things. But I know more about life than they'll ever know. It's got nuthin' to do with age. I was born knowin'. Like you. (*Pause.*) Will you tell me what happened to Janet in London?

Belle   Yes, I will.

*She takes **Dolly**'s hands and talks quietly to her about **Janet**. In the shop **Rose** is helping **Vi** to clean and tidy.*

Vi   Man, that's great. It's weeks since I had the time to give the place a proper reddin' out.

Rose   Do you do much business, Vi?

Vi   Not the way we used to. Since the Army closed the street to traffic, we don't get the passin' trade. An' apart from that we can't compete with the prices in the new supermarket. I've cut out most of the groceries. But we get by on the snacks, an' people comin' in for the cigarettes an' the papers an' the magazines.

Rose has been looking at some of the magazines as she tidies the rack.

Rose   Why do you sell this stuff, Vi?

Vi   It's what all the shops round here sell. It's a good local paper for local people.

Rose (*holding out a copy of* Ulster)   And what about this load of racist propaganda?

Vi   What are ye talkin' about? The UDA aren't against the blacks.

Rose   Racism is not necessarily to do with colour, Vi.

Vi   Don't you be startin' on one of your grand political speeches, Rose. You're only back five minutes. Give your tongue a rest. An' put that magazine back in its place. An' don't be creasin' them, or they won't sell, an' I'll have to pay for them.

Rose   What else do you have to pay them for, Vi?

Vi   What do you mean?

Rose   I mean the man in the black leather jacket, who came in late last night for a sandwich. Does everybody who buys a sandwich here get a sealed envelope with it?

Vi   We've always given to the Loyalist Prisoners Fund.

Rose   That was no voluntary contribution in a collecting tin. That was notes by prior arrangement. How much do they make you pay, Vi?

Vi   They protect the shop.

Rose   From what?

Vi   From vandals.

Rose   You give them money and in return, they tell their vandals not to break your windows. Is that it? Or are you afraid they'll publish your name in their 'Did You Know' column? (*She reads from the* Ulster Magazine.) 'Did you know that Paul Reilly & Sons, building contractors in Newry, employ workmen from the Irish Republic? Are these IRA spies working in your area? . . . Did you know that the new canteen manageress in the Protestant-owned firm of Spencer Brothers is a Catholic and has a brother with known terrorist links in the town? Staff and customers who have any links with the security forces – beware!' Do you never worry,Vi, that you might sell this distorted information to a customer who'll go out of this shop and shoot an innocent canteen manageress?

Vi   Don't you lecture me, Rose! It's all very fine and easy livin' in London and makin' noble decisions about what's right and what's wrong about how we live here. I'm the one who has to live here. You've been on your travels since you were seventeen. You don't even talk like us any more. Talk's cheap. And it's easy to be brave when you've somewhere safe to run.

Rose   So you admit that you pay them because you're afraid.

Vi   I admit nuthin'! (*Slight pause.*) I talked to the police about it. They said there was nuthin' they could do. Advised me to pay. The sergeant said, 'Think of it as doin' your bit to keep the peace, Miss Horner. It's cheap at the price.'

Rose   What's the going rate for intimidation? Do they give you a discount because John Horner was raised in this house?

Vi   Jack has no connection with them. He's a politician.

Rose   Jack's a gangster. He's well connected with the Protestant paramilitaries here, and other right-wing organisations in the United Kingdom.

Pause.

Vi   Why are you here, Rose? It's not just a holiday, is it? Jack knew you were comin' before I told him.

Rose   Did he now? That's interesting. But not surprising. Jack's English allies are very well informed.

Vi   About what?

Short pause. **Janet** *comes into the shop from the street.*

Janet   Look what I've got. Dulse and yellowman for Belle. (*Pause.*) What's the matter?

Rose   Nothing that dulse and yellowman won't cure.
Come on. Let's introduce my daughter to the gastronomic
delights of her homeland.

They go to **Dolly** *and* **Belle**.

Rose   Hey Belle, Janet's bought you a present.

Belle (*peering into the two small paper bags*)   What is it?

Janet   The sticky stuff is called yellowman. It's a sort of
toffee.

Belle   And the black stuff?

Janet   It's called dulse. You'll love it. Try a bit.

Belle *eats some dulse. Splutters and coughs.*

Belle   What is it?

Janet   Dried seaweed.

Belle   Dried seaweed!

Rose   It's very good for you.

Vi   Puts hairs on your chest.

Belle   It's revolting!

Dolly   It's an acquired taste, love. You have to start on it
young. This lot were weaned on it.

Vi   Have a bit of the yellowman. It'll take the taste of the
salt out of your mouth.

Dolly   Remember that wee shop in Dublin sold the great
yellowman? We always bought some for the train journey
home. Look, there's a photo of us all in the station. Laden
with pruck.

Belle   Pruck?

Vi   Pruck. Pickin's. Smuggled goods. Did your mother
never tell you that you come from a long line of customs
dodgers?

Sound of a train. A British **Customs Man** *walks on.* **Belle**
watches as **Dolly**, **Vi**, **Rose** *and* **Janet** *dress up from the box.*
They assume position as if on a train. They eat the dulse and yellowman.
The year is 1959. **Dolly** *is fifty;* **Vi** *thirty;* **Rose** *nine;* **Janet**
nine.

Dolly (*sings*)
    At the Oul Lammas Fair boys
    Were you ever there
    Were you ever at the fair at Ballycastleo
    Did you treat your Mary Ann
    To some dulse and yellowman
    At the oul Lammas Fair at Ballycastleo.

Customs Man   Anything to declare, ladies?

Dolly   Ach no, son. Sure me and the wee childer have just
been visitin' a sick oul aunt in Dublin. All I've got's the wee
drop of whiskey she give me for my man an' a few sweets for
the wains. We're allowed that without payin' the duty,
aren't we?

Customs Man (*to* **Rose** *and* **Janet**)   And did your poor
old aunt put the sweets in those pretty little handbags?

They open the bags which contain only sweets.

Dolly (*aside to* **Vi**)   The oul get. Searchin' innocent childer.

She smiles sweetly at the **Customs Man** *as he turns to her and* **Vi**.

Customs Man   And now you two.

*They hold out their bags. He looks inside. Removes a half-bottle of
whiskey from* **Dolly**'s *bag.*

Dolly   Like I said, son. Just the half-bottle.

Customs Man   What about your pockets?

They turn out their pocket linings. They are empty.

Are you telling me that you've been to the south and haven't
bought anything?

Dolly   No money, son. It was as much as we could do to scrape up the spondulics for the train fares. The oul aunt wanted to see the wains before God took her.

The **Customs Man** *looks totally unconvinced.*

Rose *(quickly, to distract him)*   Janet bought an ornament for our bedroom. Show him, Janet.

Janet *takes the 'ornament' out of her pocket. It is a religious statue of the Virgin Mary.*

Vi   Mother of God!

Dolly *(aside to* **Vi***)*   She didn't know what it was, an' I hadn't the heart to tell her she couldn't have it, she was that taken by it.

Vi   Jack'll go mad.

Dolly   Ach, he'll never see it in the girls' bedroom.

Janet   It's a pretty lady. Isn't she lovely?

The **Customs Man** *is completely distracted from his suspicions by* **Janet***'s sweet, innocent face. He smiles at her.*

Customs Man   It's very nice, dear. Have a pleasant journey.

He exists. **Dolly** *laughs delightedly.*

Dolly   God. You're great, Rose, distractin' him like that. For a minute I thought he was considerin' takin' us off the train for a body search. They took my cousin Annie off the train one time. Made her take all her clothes off. Every stitch. Mortified she was. Particularly when they found the two bottles of whiskey an' the hundred John Players she'd hid in her knickers.

Vi   Mother!

Janet *and* **Rose** *go to get up.*

Dolly   Sit down, the pair of ye! Yer not to move one inch till we're well clear of the border. Sometimes the oul buggers start the train an' stop it again just to catch ye on.

The train noise starts up again. They all sit very still for a minute.

Right! All clear!

Janet *and* **Rose** *jump to their feet and hand* **Vi** *the smuggled goods they've been sitting on.*

Rose   Two bags of sugar, and a carton of cigarettes for Daddy.

Janet   Two bags of tea and a bottle of gin for Auntie Dolly.

Vi *gets up.*

Vi   Pair of shoes for me an' two bottles of whiskey for my father.

Dolly   Never mind all that. Will yous get this curtain material off me before I suffocate!

She gets to her feet and removes her dressing gown. There are layers and layers of lace curtain material wrapped round her body. **Rose** *and* **Janet** *unwind the material by dancing round* **Dolly** *as if she's a Maypole.* **Dolly** *dances and sings.*

Dolly
> Our Queen can birl her leg
> Birl her leg, birl her leg
> Our Queen can birl her leg
> Birl her leg leg leg.

All (*sing*)
> Our Queen can ate a hard bap
> Ate a hard bap, ate a hard bap
> Our Queen can ate a hard bap
> Ate a hard bap bap bap.

Dolly *puts her dressing gown on again and falls exhausted back into her seat.*

Dolly   Now I know how a swaddled child feels. I thought I was gonna expire with the heat. Oh dear God, I forgot about the sausages. They must be half-cooked in the perspiration.

She removes a package from her brassiere.

Rose   What's that, Mammy?

Dolly   Two poun' of Haffner's sausages. Best sausages in Ireland. They're for Jack's Church Brigade Supper the marra night.

Rose   Jack won't eat anything that was made in the South of Ireland.

Dolly   Jack won't know where they come from. Nor how they were smuggled over the border. With any luck, they'll choke the Church Lads' Brigade.

Rose   Can we tell Jack after they've eaten them, Mammy?

Dolly   I don't see why not, darlin'.

Vi   You're a wicked woman, Mother, an' stop encouragin' them wee ones to be the same.

Dolly   Our Rose doesn't need any encouragin', do ye love?

The group freezes with the exception of **Janet***, who lifts the statue and dances into the shop. She sings quietly.*

Janet
    Our Queen can birl her leg
    Birl her leg, birl her leg
    Our Queen . . .

She stops singing as **Jack** *as a boy of thirteen walks towards her.*

Jack   What's that you've got?

Janet   She's my pretty lady. I bought her in Dublin.

Jack *grabs the statue. Shouts at* **Janet***.*

Jack   That's no pretty lady. It's a blasphemous Popish statue. A heathen image of Christ's mother. 'Thou shalt not make unto thee any graven image, or any likeness of any thing that is in Heaven above, or that is in the Earth beneath, or that is in the water under the Earth. Thou shalt not bow down thyself to them, nor serve them; for I the Lord thy God am a jealous God, visiting the iniquity of the fathers upon the children unto the third and fourth generation of them that hate me.' You have sinned, Janet. You have broken the fourth commandment. You must be punished.

Janet   Leave me alone. I'll tell Aunt Dolly.

Jack   No you won't, or God will punish you. You must repent, you must atone. You have broken His commandment. Now you must break this.

He holds out the statue.

Janet   No!

Jack   Then I must break it for you. I am the guardian of your faith.

He raises the statue above his head.

Janet   If you hurt her I'll tell the Church Brigade about the sausages!

Jack   What!

Janet   Nothing.

Jack   What did you say! What about the sausages?

Janet   Nothing.

Jack *grabs her. Twists her arm.*

Jack   Tell me! Tell me!

Janet   They were from Dublin. Dolly bought them. It wasn't me! It wasn't me!

Jack   Women! Women! Temptation! Deception! You're the instruments of the Devil! The root of all evil!

He smashes the statue on the shop counter and scatters the pieces.
Turns furiously towards **Janet**.

Janet   Leave me alone! Leave me alone!

Jack *exits.* **Janet** *continues shouting. The frozen group look up. It*
is 1986 again.

Dolly   In the name of God, what was that! Where's Janet?

Rose   I'll go.

Vi *moves to follow* **Rose** *into the shop.*

Dolly   No, Vi. Sit down. I want to talk to you about Janet.
(*To* **Belle**.) She has to be told, Belle. This family always
looks after its own, no matter what. And maybe it's Vi's
common sense that's needed here as much as anything else.

Rose *finds* **Janet** *kneeling on the floor in the shop, sobbing and*
picking up little pieces of the broken statue.

Janet   Shattered . . . Shattered . . . Not just seven . . .
twenty-seven . . . twenty-seven years' bad luck . . . the luck
of the Irish. . . the luck of the Devil . . .

Rose   Janet.

Janet   Too many little pieces. It can never be put right.

Rose *picks up a piece of broken china.*

Rose   It's only a plate. One of the cheap ones Vi uses in
the shop.

Janet   Cheap . . . damaged goods . . . like me . . .

Rose   No.

Janet   Every morning I waken filled with the knowledge
of him. And I think maybe I dreamt it. Maybe I made it up.
But I didn't. And I don't know what to do. Tell me what to
do, Rose.

Rose   I don't know what you want.

Janet   I want it never to have happened.

Rose   Why?

Janet   Sin.

Rose   No. Sex.

Janet   And shame.

Rose   What are you ashamed of?

Janet   I don't feel guilty, and I should feel guilty. I need to feel guilty.

Rose   Why?

Janet   There is no forgiveness without repentance. And I'm not sorry.

Rose   Good.

Janet   Good? I go to a party in London. I spend all that night and most of the next day in bed with a . . . a boy . . .

Rose   Martin should be so flattered. He's twenty-six if he's a day.

Janet   And I am thirty-six and married.

Rose   To Peter Pan. You can't be worried about *him* forgiving you. He forgives everybody.

Janet   I never give Peter a thought. All I think about is Martin. His face, his hair, his hands, his smell. Maybe I'm possessed. Maybe Martin is the Devil my mother said was always there. Waiting at your shoulder. Fornication. Adultery. Adultery. Adultery . . .

Rose   Stop it! Stop it! That's Jack talking. Not you.

Janet   'Ashes to ashes. Dust to dust. If the Lord don't get you, the Devil must.' Jack won't rest till he knows.

Rose   There's no need for Jack to know.

Janet   He'll make me tell him.

Rose   You don't have to tell Jack anything. It's none of his business. He's only your brother. Not your keeper. Not your God. You don't need Jack's permission to do anything. You're a grown woman.

Janet   I've been avoiding Vi. Can't look her straight in the face. What am I going to tell her?

Rose   Whatever you want to tell her.

Janet   I want to tell her the truth. She'll despise me.

Rose   Don't be daft. She'll be a bit shocked, and then she'll get over it, and then she'll be on your side regardless of what she thinks, because you're family and the family always comes first with Vi. You know that. Remember when Belle was born? Vi was on the next plane to London. I didn't ask her to do that. She just came. Before they brought Belle in from the nursery, I said to her, 'Vi, so that it doesn't come as a bit of a shock, I think you should know that although the father's Protestant, he's not exactly what you'd call a white Anglo-Saxon.' And Vi just gave me one of her long looks and she said, 'See you, Rose? If there's an awkward way of doin' a thing, you'll find it.'

The telling of this story has relaxed **Janet**. *She manages a smile.*

Janet   Does Martin care about me at all?

Rose (*carefully*)   Martin, like Peter, fell in love with your innocence.

Janet   And now that's gone. And so has Martin.

Rose   He's married.

Janet   I know. He told me. Before we went to bed. So I can't even claim I was tricked. Or seduced. I don't even feel guilty about that. It wasn't true when I said I wish it had never happened. It was everything I ever dreamt it might be. Did you love Belle's father like that?

Rose   I suppose I did. At first. Don't remember it clearly any more. It's a romantic notion that first love is always an unforgettable, special, never-to-be-equalled experience. I've had better love since. What I remember most clearly about Belle's father is how inadequate and dependent he made me feel. How outraged he was when I turned down his noble offer to make an honest women of me. Admitting that it was a fucking shambles made an honest woman of me.

Janet   Peter wants me to come home. I had a letter from him this morning.

Rose   What do you want?

Janet   Remember the little girl in the *Just William* stories who wanted to scream and scream and scream?

She walks away from **Rose**. *Talks to herself as if in a dream.*

Janet   I want what I can't have. I want it to be like it was. Like the old days in the photo album. I want Dolly to put her arms around me and sing me to sleep. And when I waken, I want Jack to have gone away for ever. And Peter too. I'm tired being the sister of a devil and the wife of a saint.

Jack *walks on stage.* **Peter**, *in RUC uniform, walks on from the other side.* **Janet** *is situated centre stage between them. She looks from one to the other.*

Peter (*sings*)
　　Green gravel, green gravel
　　Your grass is so green
　　You're the fairest young damsel
　　That ever I've seen

　　Green gravel, green gravel
　　Your true lover's dead
　　So I've sent you a letter
　　To turn round your head

　　I washed her and I dressed her
　　And I robed her in silk
　　And I wrote down her name
　　With a glass pen and ink

　　Green gravel, green gravel
　　Your grass is so green
　　You're the fairest young damsel
　　That ever I've seen.

Jack (*quoting from St Paul*)   It is good for a man not to marry. But since there is so much immorality each man should have his own wife and each woman her own husband. The husband should fulfil his marital duty to his wife, and likewise the wife to her husband. The wife's body does not belong to her alone, but also to the husband. In the same way, the husband's body does not belong to him alone but also to his wife. Do not deprive each other except by mutual consent. Then come together again so that Satan will not tempt you because of your lack of self-control. I say this as a concession, not as a command. I wish that all men were as I am.

Peter   I love you. Come back to me.

Jack   I love you. Come back to me.

Janet   Out of the frying pan into the fire. A devil and a saint are the same thing. Afraid of women. Afraid we'll tempt you. Afraid we won't. They say there are no women in Ireland. Only mothers and sisters and wives. I'm a sister and a wife. But I'll never be a mother. Will I, Peter? Why did you marry me? Why did I marry you? (*To* **Jack**.) Because he was everything you were not. Quiet. Gentle. Kind. After the ceremony we went to Dublin for a week. It was the one city I could be sure you wouldn't be in. But you were with me, all the way there on the train. (*To* **Peter**.) It was very late when we got to the hotel. I wanted you to take me . . . to teach me . . . I wanted to exorcise him . . . to find out that it wasn't an act of sin and shame and pain and guilt. But as soon as you touched me I turned away. And then I turned back to you and you said, 'It's been a long day. Let's go to sleep.' The next day we hired a car and drove around Dublin. When we got back to the hotel we were both very tired. You told me that there was nothing to worry about. You said lots of newly married couples didn't . . . for a while. You said there was no hurry. I felt grateful because you were so patient, so kind. It was years before I realised that you were relieved, that you didn't want . . . had never wanted . . . that you were content with things that way. (*To* **Jack**.) And

I suppose I was content too. Knowing that I would never have to contend with you and Peter's mother fighting over the religion of the children of this unholy union. Peter's very fond of children. He's a community policeman. Does a lot of work with teenagers. One of them asked him once, 'Why does an Irish Catholic join a sectarian force like the Royal Ulster Constabulary?' And Peter said, 'It will always be a sectarian force if Catholics never join.' He was such a good little boy that his mother expected him to become a priest, but Peter sees his mission in life as doing something more positive towards peace and reconciliation. (*To* **Peter**.) Was marrying me part of that mission?

Peter   I love you.

Janet   I am not your mother! I am not your sister!

Jack   I love you.

Janet   I am not your virgin mother, nor your virgin wife!

Peter   I love you. Come back to me.

Jack   I love you. Come back to me.

Janet *throws back her head and screams.* **Rose** *runs to her. The two men exit.* **Janet** *runs past* **Rose** *to* **Dolly**. **Vi** *storms into the shop and shouts at* **Rose**.

Vi   What have you and your loose-livin' English friends done to that child? Look at the state of her!

Rose   She's not a child!

Vi (*indicating where* **Dolly** *and* **Belle** *are comforting* **Janet**) You call that bein' grown-up?

Rose   It's a damn sight more grown-up than living in Never-Never Land!

Vi   By God, you have a lot to answer for.

Rose   When in doubt, always find a woman to blame. If it's answers you want, ask Peter, ask Jack!

Vi And what about this Martin? This so-called friend of yours! I suppose he has nuthin' to answer for either! A married man in no position to stand by her. The road to nowhere. And you set her on it. May God forgive you.

Dolly *sits cradling* **Janet***'s head in her lap. She strokes* **Janet***'s hair and sings.*

Dolly
I know where I'm goin'
And I know who's goin' with me
I know who I love
But the dear knows who I'll marry

I'll wear gowns of silk
And shoes of fine green leather
Ribbons for my hair
And a ring for every finger

I know who is sick
And I know who is sorry
I know who I've kissed
But God knows who I'll marry.

Act Two

Scene One

Janet *sits at* **Dolly***'s feet, looking through the photo album.* **Belle** *walks on and watches* **Dolly** *and* **Janet** *from the other side of the stage.* **Dolly** *recites.*

Dolly

In a mean abode on the Shankill Road
Lived a man called William Bloat
He had a wife, the curse of his life
Who continually got his goat
So one day at dawn, with her nightdress on
He cut her bloody throat

With a razor gash he settled her hash
Oh never was crime so quick
But the steady drip on the pillow slip
Of her lifeblood made him sick
And the pool of gore on the bedroom floor
Grew clotted, cold and thick

And yet he was glad that he'd done what he had
When she lay there stiff and still
But a sudden awe of the angry law
Struck his soul with an icy chill
So to finish the fun so well begun
He resolved himself to kill

Then he took the sheet off his wife's cold feet
And twisted it into a rope
And he hanged himself from the pantry shelf
'Twas an easy end, let's hope
In the face of death with his latest breath
He solemnly cursed the Pope

But the strangest turn to the whole concern
Is only just beginnin'
He went to Hell but his wife got well

And she's still alive and sinnin'
For the razor blade was German-made
But the sheet was Irish linen.

Belle   Before I came here, I had two images of Belfast.
A magical one conjured by my grandmother's songs and
stories and recitations, and a disturbing one of the marches
and banners and bands on the six o'clock news . . . They
are both true, but not the whole truth of this bizarre and
beautiful city. Belfast is surrounded by soft green hills. All its
inhabitants live within walking distance of the countryside,
and like village people they are inquisitive, friendly, hospitable.

Belfast must be the best kept social secret in the British Isles
. . . There was a bomb scare in Marks & Spencer's today.
A voice from a loudspeaker asked the customers to evacuate
the building. Nobody panicked. Nobody ran. The general
feeling was one of annoyance that the shopping had been
interrupted. One woman was very cross because the girl at
the checkout wouldn't finish ringing through her purchases.
'It'll be another one of them hoax calls,' she said. And it
was.

I wasn't frightened by the bomb scare, but I was frightened
by their complacency, by their irritated acceptance that it's
a normal part of everyday life, like being searched before
entering the shops. The situation has existed for so long now
that the people have come to accept the abnormal as normal.
Armed soldiers in suburban streets. Armed police in armoured
cars. An acceptable level of violence. There's a new generation
of citizens who've never known it to be any other way.

I accepted Davy's offer to show me around but discovered
that he has only ever been round here and the city centre.
That's not peculiar to him. Belfast is not so much a city as
a group of villages forming an uneasy alliance. My Aunt
Vi has lived here all her life and has never set foot in West
Belfast. Injun Country. The Badlands. Her images of the
Falls Road are conjured by Nationalist songs and stories
and recitations. And the news bulletins and the rhetoric of

the Reverend Ian Paisley confirm everything she fears to be true. She votes for the Unionist Party to keep the Republican Party out.

Dolly (*sings*)
>Will you come to our wee party, will you come?
>Bring your own bread and butter and a bun
>You can bring a cup of tea
>You can come along with me
>Will you come to our wee party, will you come?
>
>Will you come to Abyssinia, will you come?
>Bring your own ammunition and a gun
>Mussolini will be there, firing bullets in the air
>Will you come to Abyssinia, will you come?

Belle *walks into the shop, where* **Vi** *and* **Rose** *are making sandwiches and heating sausage rolls.*

Belle   I've got party poppers and paper hats.

Vi   What's a party popper when it's at home?

Belle   It's a sort of friendly hand grenade.

She pulls one of the poppers and covers **Vi** *with streamers.*

Vi   Sometimes I wonder if we're all mad or mental in this family.

Belle   Why?

Vi   Havin' a party in the middle of all these terrible goin's on with Janet.

Belle   Janet's looking forward to it.

Rose   Mum always has a party on Dad's birthday.

Vi   Dolly has had a party every day of her life.

Belle   I think it's a wonderful idea. What good does it do him or any of us making a mournful pilgrimage to a graveside on a cold November day? Much better to be here, reminiscing and singing and celebrating his life.

Vi It's well seein' who you take after. I tell ye, Dolly'll never be dead as long as you're alive. Come the three-minute warnin' an' no doubt the pair of ye'll be organisin' a wee sing-song to pass the time till the bomb goes off. I hope you have your party piece ready. Everybody has to do a turn, you know.

Rose Except Jack. Jack only ever did a party piece once because Dolly made him, and he refused ever to do one again.

Belle Jack's been invited?

Vi Of course he has. He's one of the family, whether your mother likes it or not.

Rose He'll only be calling briefly. He has a prior engagement.

Belle Does Janet know he's coming?

Vi She has to face him sooner or later. And I told her, better sooner while the family's all here gathered round her. And I've told Jack he's not to be gettin' at her. She has to work things out for herself.

Rose You didn't tell him about . . .

Vi I did not. And I don't intend to. Least said soonest mended. He'd never understand it. *I* don't understand it. I always thought her and Peter were the happiest couple in the land. Never a cross word between them, and neither of them lookin' a day older than the day they were wed. And as for this man in London . . .

Belle Sexy Martin? What a way to lose your virginity after fifteen years of celibate marriage.

She grins at **Vi**'s *outraged expression.*

Belle Aren't you glad she enjoyed it? Wouldn't it have been awful if she hadn't, after waiting all that time?

Vi   I have never heard such talk from a youngster in all my life. When I was your age . . .

Belle   I'm the age now that my mother was when she had me.

Vi   Maybe my trouble is, I never was that age. I never remember a time when I was really young, the way children are. As soon as I was tall enough to see over the counter, Dolly kept me off school to work in the shop. I tell you, Davy can read and write better than I can.

Dolly (*sings*)
   Our wee school's a good wee school
   It's made of bricks and mortar
   And all that's wrong with our wee school's
   The baldy-headed master
   He doesn't care, he pulls our hair
   He goes to church on Sunday
   And prays to God to give him strength
   To beat the kids on Monday.

Janet (*as a child*)   Auntie Dolly?

Dolly   What darlin'?

Janet   Can I stay off school tomorrow and help in the shop?

Dolly   Now you know what Vi's like about you wee ones missin' your schoolin' unless you're really sick. Not that she was ever all that keen on goin' to school when she was your age. Any excuse to get stayin' at home.

Janet *coughs exaggeratedly.*

Dolly   An' there's no point in tryin' it on. It might work with me but it'll never fool Vi.

Vi *and* **Rose** *as a child come in with plates of sandwiches and sausage rolls.* **Jack** *as a boy stands sulking in the street.*

Dolly   Where's the Prophet Isaiah?

Rose   He's out in the street sulkin'.

Janet   He says we should be thanking God for taking Uncle Joe to Heaven and not having a sinful party.

Dolly   Oh, does he indeed? I'll decide how we mourn my Joe. And Jack'll do as he's bid as long as he lives in Joe's house. Vi! Away an' tell him to come in this minute and join the party.

Vi   Ach, leave him alone, Mother.

Rose   I'll tell him.

She runs gleefully to the street to fetch **Jack**.

Vi   He doesn't like parties.

Dolly   He'll sing for Joe along with the rest of the family.

Rose *returns, followed very reluctantly by* **Jack**.

Dolly   Right. Now that we're all assembled, how's about 'Soldier, Soldier'? My Joe loved 'Soldier, Soldier'. You can play the man, Jack.

Jack   I don't know the words.

Dolly   Course you do. You've watched the girls often enough.

Jack   I don't.

Rose   I'll help you.

She smiles sweetly at him. **Jack** *gives her a murderous look.*

Dolly   We'll all help you. Where's the dressin'-up box, Vi?

Vi   It's here.

Dolly   Right. Away ye go, Janet. You be the girl.

Belle *watches the performance of the song with the photo album on her knee.* **Janet** *sings the girl's part and fetches the clothes for the soldier from the box.* **Jack***, assisted by* **Rose***, sullenly sings the man's part.* **Dolly** *puts the clothes on him when he looks as if he is about to refuse.* **Dolly** *and* **Vi** *and* **Rose** *sing the chorus.* **Jack** *becomes increasingly angry and humiliated as the song progresses.*

Janet

Oh soldier, soldier, won't you marry me?
With your musket, fife and drum

Jack

Oh no sweet maid I cannot marry you
For I have no coat to put on

Chorus

So, off she went to her grandfather's tent
And got him a coat of the very very best
She got him a coat of the very very best
And the soldier put it on

Janet

Oh soldier, soldier, won't you marry me?
With your musket, fife and drum

Jack

Oh no sweet maid I cannot marry you
For I have no boots to put on

Chorus

So, off she went to her grandfather's tent
And got him some boots of the very very best
She got him some boots of the very very best
And the soldier put them on

Janet

Oh soldier, soldier won't you marry me
With your musket, fife and drum

Jack

Oh no sweet maid I cannot marry you
For I have no hat to put on

Chorus

So, off she went to her grandfather's tent
And got him a hat of the very very best
She got him a hat of the very very best
And the soldier put it on.

By this stage **Jack** *looks utterly ridiculous.* **Rose** *is making faces at him behind his back.* **Vi** *is trying hard not to laugh aloud.* **Dolly** *makes no attempt to conceal her mirth.*

Janet
Oh soldier, soldier won't you marry me . . .

She dissolves into laughter. **Jack** *is almost in tears with anger and humiliation. He grabs hold of* **Janet**, *shakes her, shouts.*

Jack
Oh no sweet maid I cannot marry you!
For I have a wife of my own!

He runs out.

Back to the present time. **Dolly**, **Rose**, **Janet** *and* **Belle** *are laughing at the memory.* **Vi** *looks uncomfortable.*

Belle   Oh, I wish I could have seen that. Isn't there a photograph of Jack dressed up?

Dolly   You must be jokin'. He run out of here like a scalded cat. Wouldn't speak to any of us for days after.

Vi   It wasn't really funny.

Dolly   Away on with ye. Ye were laughin' as much as the rest of us. Did him the world of good. He's always been full of his own importance.

Vi   It wasn't easy for him, livin' in a household of women, with no man to . . .

Dolly   My Joe was around for a year after he come here to live. I never noticed Jack makin' any effort to enjoy Joe's company. Jack likes to be the *only* man. The one in charge. Thought he'd be the man of the house when Joe died. I soon put him right on that score.

Vi   It's gettin' dark. I'll put up the shutters on the shop.

Rose   I'll give you a hand.

Dolly An' we'll open a bottle. With any luck Jack'll not turn up an' we can all get bluttered without him sittin' there like Moses makin' the tribe feel guilty.

Vi *and* **Rose** *go to put the steel-mesh shutters over the shop windows for the night.*

Rose Why do you always defend him, Vi?

Vi Somebody has to defend him. Everybody needs a friend on their side.

Rose Even when they've done what he's done to Janet?

Vi Have you ever stopped to wonder what their mother and father done to Jack?

Rose They were Janet's parents too, but she's not cruel and vindictive.

Vi You're pretty good at bein' vindictive when it comes to Jack. You never give him a chance. You never liked him from the day and hour he come here.

Rose Do *you* really like him?

Vi He was that lost and lonely, I felt heart sorry for him. Nobody liked him . . . I didn't like him either and I felt bad havin' such feelin's about a child. It's a terrible thing not to like a child. Terrible. I always tried to make it up to him.

Rose By agreeing with his mad religious politics?

Vi I've never been strong on religion, I'm all for people worshippin' as they please. But I've never had to pretend to agree with Jack's politics. I'm with him all the way on that.

Rose No you're not, Vi.

Vi We need somebody strong to speak up for us. To tell the British government that we won't be handed over to a foreign country without a fight. That we won't be patted on the head and complimented on our loyalty and patriotism through two world wars, but now it's all over, thank you very much, and your loyalty and your patriotism are an embarrassment to us and our American and European allies. We are bein' sold down the river because England doesn't need us no more. An' what we need now is somebody to shout our cause an' our rights from the rooftops. We are as much a part of Great Britain as Liverpool or Manchester or Birmingham. How would they feel if they were suddenly told that the Dublin government was to have a say in the runnin' of their country?

Rose   A third of the population of Northern Ireland were denied a say in how their country should be run.

Vi   I've never been opposed to the Catholics havin' their say. Doin' their part. As long as they are prepared to do it with us and not against us. But they've made their position very clear. They don't want to share power. They want to take it.

Rose   And the Unionists want to hold on to it. Absolutely. They have to. They will never agree to power-sharing because they can't. Northern Ireland was created as a Protestant state for a Protestant people, and if they agree to power-sharing, they'll have agreed to do away with the very reason for the state's existence. Don't you see that?

Vi   And isn't the South a Catholic state for a Catholic people?! You only see what suits you, Rose. And don't try to tell me it would suit you to live in a country where priests make the laws and tell you how to vote from the altar. Where things like contraception and divorce are a legal and a mortal sin. It's written into their Catholic constitution. You're a great one for women's rights. We wouldn't have many rights in a United Ireland!

Rose   We won't have many rights here either, if Jack and his gang get the independent Ulster they want. Their right-wing Protestant church is in total agreement with the right-wing Catholic church on issues like divorce and abortion, on a woman's right to be anything other than a mother or a daughter or a sister or a wife. Any woman outside that set of rules is the Great Whore of Babylon. One of the first things they'll do if they get their independent state of Ulster is vote that into their Protestant constitution.

Vi   So, the choice is the devil or the deep blue sea, is that what you're sayin'? Well, in that case I'll stay with the devil I know . . . I don't see why we have to change anything. We were all gettin' on all right before the Civil Rights started the violence. We never had no quarrel with our Catholic neighbours.

Rose   There was one Catholic family in this street, and they were intimidated out in 1972.

Vi   By strangers. Fly-by-nights from God knows where. Not by the neighbours. Not by us. The Dohertys lived next door for twenty years an' we all got on great. I nursed two of them kids through the measles when their mother was in the hospital havin' her veins done. And she used to come in here regular on the twelfth of July and help my father put on his Orange sash for the parade.

Rose   No! That's not true, Vi. Bridie Doherty came in here *once* on the twelfth of July. It was the morning that Granny Dunbar had the stroke, and instead of you and Dolly being here as usual to dress Father up for the parade, the two of you were at the hospital. Bridie came in to enquire about Granny, and there Father was blundering and bellowing like a bull because he couldn't find his sash.

Vi   And Bridie found it behind the sofa and put it round his neck.

Rose   She lifted it up and she held it out to him. And suddenly there was a terrible awkwardness between them. She hesitated, and then she placed the sash around his neck.

Vi   Like I said.

Rose   There was nothing neighbourly or affectionate about it. He was afraid that if he took it out of her hands it would look as if he didn't want a Catholic handling it. And she was afraid that if she set it down again it would look like an insult. That's why she put it round his neck. And then both of them were so uncomfortable and embarrassed that Bridie left without saying a word. That's the truth of what happened. I know, because I was there. I told you that story, Vi. And over the years, you and Dolly have romanticised it into something it wasn't.

Vi   Better than demeanin' it the way you're now doin'.

Rose   Oh, Vi. Belfast abounds with half-baked sentimental stories like that. About the good old days and how well we all got on with our Uncle Tom Catholic neighbours. Sure we did. As long as they stayed indoors on the twelfth of July and didn't kick up a fuss when the Kick-the-Pope bands marched past their houses, beating big drums to remind them of their place here. The stories are myths. Fables. Distortions of the truth. Bridie Doherty was the best neighbour we ever had. And what did this family do when the bully boys daubed red paint on her windows and stuffed petrol-soaked rags through her letter box?

Vi   We put out the fire! We brought them in here! We . . .

Rose   We helped them pack and move out.

Vi   Now you're distortin' the truth. We didn't want them to go. We wanted them to stay. All the neighbours did.

Rose *raises her eyebrows.*

Vi   Well, all except that Sinclair clan up the street. But I soon give them a piece of my mind when they started mouthin' about the Dohertys bein' in the IRA. Molly Sinclair never said nuthin' like that within earshot of me again, I can tell ye.

Rose   Yet you voted for Molly Sinclair's son in the council elections. Head-the-Ball Harry. Don't be vague. Burn a Tague.

Vi   I had no choice. He was the only Unionist candidate.

Rose   You could have voted for one of the more moderate parties.

Vi   What! Split the vote and let the Sinn Feiners in? The mouthpiece of bombers and murderers. Sinn Fein. Ourselves Alone. Not much hint of power-sharin' in that! Maybe you'd like to see the IRA in control of Belfast City Council.

Rose   I'd like to see the people here voting for, and not against, in every election. Sooner or later, Protestant or Catholic, we have all got to take that risk.

Vi   We? That's easy to say, when you don't live in the middle of it. When there's no risk of losin' your nationality, your religion, everything you've lived your life by, and believed in.

Dolly (*sings*)
> In and out the windows
> In and out the windows
> In and out the windows
> As you have done before
>
> Stand and face your partner
> Stand and face your partner
> Stand and face your partner
> As you have done before.

She pulls a party popper. **Belle** *hands her a drink.*

Dolly (*sings*)
> Vote vote vote for Maggie Thatcher
> In comes Belle at the door, io
> For Belle is the one that'll have a bit of fun
> And we don't want Maggie any more, io.

As she sings, **Jack** *walks into the street with* **Tom Bailey**. **Tom** *is middle-aged, elegantly dressed, and has a soft, cultured British accent. He has the calm self-assurance that comes from a life of wealth and privilege. The two men stand for a moment looking at the street and the shop before entering.*

Jack   Vi, this is Tom Bailey, the English businessman I mentioned to you last time I was here.

Tom   How do you do, Miss Horner. It's a pleasure to meet you.

Vi   How do you do, Mr Bailey.

Jack   We had hoped to have a quiet word with you . . . alone.

Vi   This is my sister Rose.

There is a pause as **Rose** *looks steadily at* **Tom Bailey**. *He smiles and acknowledges the introduction with a slight nod of his head.*

Jack   I just called to let you know that I can't come to Dolly's party. I'm taking Tom to the airport after the meeting.

Tom   My apologies for this intrusion on a family occasion. I had hoped for the opportunity of an informal private chat, Miss Horner, but it's obviously inconvenient. Perhaps we could arrange to meet later. I'll be back in Belfast in a couple of days.

Rose   In time for the Anglo-Irish Protest Rally?

Tom   Of course.

Rose   What business have you with my sister?

Jack   Private business. None of your concern.

Vi   Now you just hold on a minute, Jack. I don't know what's goin' on here, but anything to do with this house is not goin' to be a dark secret between you and me. It'll be discussed properly by the whole family before any decisions are made. You're rushin' me into somethin' and I don't like it. I never intended to consider this so soon.

Rose   Consider what?

Vi   I mentioned to Jack one time that I had a mind to move away from here. Take Dolly to end her days somewhere nice and quiet. By the sea, maybe. You know she always loved the seaside. Not right now, but maybe in a couple of years or so when I get the pension. I didn't intend so soon . . . so quick . . .

Jack   We don't have to discuss this now, Vi. We'll call again next week.

Rose   Oh no you won't. There is nothing to discuss. This house is not for sale to Tom Bailey as long as I have any say in the matter.

Vi   You know this man, Rose?

Rose   Let me introduce you properly, Vi, to the Reverend Thomas Bailey. Formerly of the Anglican Church, until his Bishop ordered him to sever his connections with the National Front. So Thomas took a leaf from the book of another reverend, Dr Ian Paisley, and formed his own Free Church where no one had the authority to tell him that all God's children are not necessarily blue-eyed, blonde-haired and white.

Jack   This is outrageous. We don't have to listen to this.

Rose   No. But Vi must.

Jack   My apologies, Tom. I did warn you this would happen if she was here.

Rose (*to* **Tom**)   He knew I would be here. Conceit. Arrogance. You couldn't resist letting me know personally.

Vi   How do you know him, Rose?

Rose   We met in court when he was prosecuted under the Race Relations Act.

Unlike **Jack**, **Tom Bailey** *has remained urbane and calm throughout* **Rose**'s *outburst.*

Tom   Unsuccessfully prosecuted.

Rose   His wife, the Lady Elizabeth Montgomery Bailey, QC, got him acquitted on a legal technicality. When Mrs Bailey isn't in court defending the British right to racism she advises the Ulster Unionists at Westminster on how to break the law within the law in order to keep Northern Ireland Protestant, Orange and White. I wonder, Vi, what a well-heeled, upper-crust couple like the Baileys would be wanting with a huxtery shop and dwelling in a small street in East Belfast? It's a far cry from their luxury flat in Westminster and their rolling acres in Surrey.

Tom   A purely rhetorical question, Miss Horner. Your sister and her associates are well informed about my every move.

Rose   Not as well as we thought, it would seem. I knew your associates were looking for premises. I didn't know it would be *you*. I didn't know it would be *my home*. Was that *your* idea? Does the notion of operating from my family home appeal to your bizarre sense of humour? Or is it just simple vindictive revenge?

Tom   You flatter yourself, Ms Horner. You are not that important. You made a minor, misguided incursion into my life once. It scarcely caused a ripple.

Vi   Would somebody mind tellin' me what's goin' on here? Jack?

Jack   Tom, we must be going. We'll be late.

Tom   There is no hurry. The meeting cannot begin without me. And I have nothing to hide from Miss Horner. Can her sister say the same?

Rose   I have never tried to hide my part in bringing the activities of you and your family to the attention of the public. In fact I'm rather proud of those photographs. Some of the best I ever took, considering the circumstances.

Tom   Blurred images from a concealed camera.

Rose   Not so blurred that you and those other wealthy aristocratic Fascists in Nazi uniforms couldn't be identified.

Tom   A man may dress as he pleases in the privacy of his own home.

Rose   But not in the privacy of mine!

Vi   What has all this to do with my shop?

Rose   Mr Bailey doesn't parade publicly through the streets with the National Front. He's much too refined for that. But he does provide them with advice, legal assistance, money, meeting places. They're planning to open an HQ in Belfast. A twenty-four hour service for the faithful. A shop outlet for their propaganda. Back rooms for meetings. They've been here quietly for years. Observing. Participating. One of their leaders recently described Northern Ireland as the perfect springboard for their activities in the United Kingdom. They're now confident enough to crawl out of the woodwork, and go public.

Tom   I have always had confidence in the loyalty of the Protestant people of Ulster.

Rose   The type of loyalty you're talking about is of *some* of the Protestant people. Not *all* of the Protestant people. And not nearly as many as Paisley claims.

Tom   You are mistaken, Ms Horner. You represent a very small minority. Without support. Without power.

Jack   She is also, as ever, a deceiver. Even as a child you delighted in knowing and telling other people's secrets while being close about your own. Vi asked a question and you answer it with exaggerated gossip about why Tom Bailey is here, but carefully avoid mentioning why you are here.

Vi   Rose?

Rose   This week I am here for the pure pleasure of being with my family. Next week I won't be going back to England with Belle. I'll be moving into the Europa Hotel to work with two colleagues, journalists, who are here investigating the links between the National Front, the British Friends of Ulster, and the Democratic Unionist Party.

Vi   You were plottin' to stay on in Belfast and not say?

Rose   There was no plot, Vi. I happened to have a free week when Belle was on half-term holiday, and it was a perfect opportunity to come home with her. The fact that I have a job here next week is coincidental.

Vi   Oh, I see. If you hadn't happened to be free this week, you would have sneaked into a Belfast hotel next week, without even lettin' the family know you were in the city?

Rose   Yes. I would. Partly because it's business and it's confidential. But mainly, because it would be too risky to work from home. John Horner may be safe in the arms of Tom Bailey, but John Horner's cousins are not safe from abusive phone calls and threatening letters and other tactics of the violence Tom Bailey funds. I couldn't risk exposing you and Dolly to the possibility of that.

Tom   I would commend your concern about your family, Ms Horner, if I didn't know how willingly you have already exposed them to possible risk in your determination to discredit your cousin John Horner. However, I suppose the betrayal of one's family is a minor consideration in one so ready to betray one's country.

Rose   What country would that be, Mr Bailey?

Tom   England. Ulster.

Rose   You are as ill-informed as most of the English about this country. This is Northern Ireland, not Ulster. Not Donegal, Cavan and Monaghan. The so-called Ulster Unionists gave those areas with a Catholic majority to the South in 1920 in order to create and maintain their own false majority.

Tom   I see you've been reading your daughter's history books. I hear she's quite an intelligent student, despite her antecedents . . . and despite a rather dangerous tendency to support somewhat suspect left-wing causes . . .

Vi (*very quietly*)   Get out of this house.

Jack   Vi . . .

Vi   Makin' threats about Belle . . .

Jack   Tom didn't intend . . .

Vi   I know a threat when I hear one. Even when it's made by a well-spoken gentleman. And nobody threatens our Belle, nobody! She's my sister's child with the same ancestors as me. She's my niece and your cousin. She's family, and by the looks of things, the only grandchild this family's likely to have.

Jack   She's not family! She's . . .

Rose   A black bastard?

Jack   If the cap fits . . .

Rose   She's a blood relation of yours whether you like it or not, Jack. Or maybe first cousins once removed don't count with your chums in the National Front?

Jack   Why should I be considered responsible for your ungodly fornications?

He walks out.

Rose   If you're going to join the war here, Thomas Bailey, never forget that loyalty to one's immediate family will always take precedence over loyalty to the Unionist family.

Tom   I'll bear that in mind.

Rose   You do that. Ireland has been the death of better Englishmen than you.

He smiles and leaves unhurriedly.

Pause. **Vi** *and* **Rose** *just look at each other.*

Rose   Thanks, Vi.

Vi   For what! For defendin' Belle? Or for havin' the fall-out with Jack that you've been engineerin' ever since you were a child! You never could leave well alone, could you? You were an indulged brat when you were wee and you haven't changed one whit. Still stirrin' it. Always gettin' away with it. A pretty face. A clever tongue. Father always said you could charm the birds off the trees. 'Look after Rose, Vi. She's our wee flower.' He never had a pet name

for me. Good old Vi. Martha to your Mary. Vi'll make the
dinner while Rose is makin' daydreams. No matter what I
did for him he always took it for granted. No more than was
his due. God, he had it made. A wife to play-act for him. A
little daughter to pet and indulge. And a dutiful dependable
grown-up daughter to cook his meals and starch his shirts.

Rose   Don't, Vi. Don't. You always loved him so. He
loved you.

Vi   Aye. Because I deserved it. But he adored you regardless.
He adored you. *Dolly* adored you. *Everybody* adored you.

Pause. **Rose** *is very shaken that* **Vi** *might be about to say she hated
her.* **Vi** *continues more quietly.*

Vi   *I* adored you. Silly oul maid. Pushing you round the
park in that great Silver Cross pram they bought when you
were born. 'Nothing's too good for our Rose.' Strangers
used to stop and compliment me on my beautiful baby.
And I let them assume you were mine. I expect they also
assumed you got your good looks from my husband. Not
from a plain lump like me. I used to get into these terrible
panics in case one of them would happen to come into the
shop and discover that you were really my sister, and tell
Dolly about my foolishness. And then she would have told
Father and they would have laughed together in that close
way of theirs as if they were the only two people in the
world.

A long pause.

Rose   I'm sorry, Vi. I don't know what else to say. Except
that, if you and I had never been born, they would still have
been totally happy, just the two of them.

Vi   I know. (*Pause.*) Why have you never got married, Rose?

Rose   Why haven't you? And don't say you were never
asked, because I know you were.

Vi   Nosy wee bitch. I knew you were listenin' at the door.
He's an assistant manager in the Ulster Bank now. If I'd

played my cards right, I could be livin' in a split-level bungalow in Holywood, Co. Down.

Rose   And I could be singing hymns in a Baptist church in America.

Vi   Maybe it's just as well that growin' up with the real thing made us both too choosy, eh?

Belle *comes in.*

Belle   Gran says if you two don't come in this minute, she's starting the party without you.

Vi   Since when did Dolly ever need the go-ahead to start a party? You go in and monitor her drink allowance, Rose. Belle, you give me a hand with the shutters.

Belle *carries the shutters outside.*

Vi   Don't let her go to the rally.

Rose   Don't worry. I'll talk to her later. (*Pause.*) I love you, Vi.

Vi   I love you too. Even if you are the most thrawn child this family has ever known.

Vi *goes outside.*

Rose *goes to* **Dolly** *and* **Janet**.

Dolly   One down. Two to go.

Rose   They're putting up the shutters. They won't be a minute.

Dolly   You and Vi have had enough time to put shutters round the Great Wall of China. What's been goin' on out there?

Rose   Jack's been and gone. He won't be back for the party.

Dolly   That's the best bit of news there's been since the Relief of Derry.

Janet   Do you want a drink, Rose?

Rose   Yes, please.

Dolly   Here, top mine up while you're at it.

Rose   Take it easy. You know what the doctor said.

Dolly   You're a long time dead. Here. (*Holding out the photo album.*) Remember this one? It was the time you an' Janet got saved down in the mission hall by that buck eejit Issac Standaloft and his sister Naomi.

Janet (*to* **Rose**)   Remember? We only went down in the first place because we'd heard about Naomi crossing her hands when she played the piano.

Dolly   God, the way that woman murdered a good tune wasn't ordinary.

Dolly *sings* (*badly*) *and mimes* **Naomi Standaloft** *playing the piano with exaggerated gestures. Sound of a piano. As* **Dolly** *sings, she becomes* **Naomi**. **Janet** *and* **Rose** *join in as ten-year-olds. They are torn between giggling and fascination at* **Naomi***'s elaborate playing.*

Dolly/Naomi (*sings*)
    Climb climb up Sunshine Mountain
    Singing as we go
    Climb climb up Sunshine Mountain
    Faces all aglow
    Turn turn your back on Satan
    Look up to the sky
    Climb climb up Sunshine Mountain
    You and I.

She shouts 'All together now!' and **Rose** *and* **Janet** *sing the song and march around the room. As they finish, the preacher* **Isaac Standaloft** *walks on. He is a plump, perspiring man in an ill-fitting suit. He has a north of England accent.* **Naomi** *heralds his arrival with a fanfare on the piano.* **Isaac** *stands for a moment, eyes shut, a tortured expression on his face.* **Dolly/Naomi** *goes to him and comforts him.*

244 244 The Belle of the Belfast City

Isaac   Behold a pearl among women. My dear devoted
sister Naomi. But for her faith and goodness, I, Isaac
Standaloft, would still be sliding down the slippery slopes,
towards the fires of Hell! I was a bad child, corrupted by the
unholy passions of Satan's cinemas. I became a dissipated
youth who forsook his Christian home for the drinking dens
of the Devil and the dreadful desires of women who dance!
Be not like them. The Devil's voluptuous temptresses with
painted faces and lacquered nails and hair dyed red with
sin. Beware of the Devil who lurks in the dark dance halls
and hostelries and picture palaces. He wants your youth.
He wants your bodies. He wants your souls. Be as Naomi.
Be unadorned. Be modest. Be chaste. Be not the foul
instrument of the downfall of men. Your souls belong to
God. Your bodies are his temple. Only your lawful wedded
husband may worship and enter therein, not for pleasure,
but purely for the procreation of God's children. But first,
you must cleanse that temple of the original sin of your
worldly birth. Ye must be saved. Ye must be born again.
You must, or you will surely face the fiery furnace and burn
for ever. Come on to me. Come on to me, before it is too
late.

Naomi, *who has been gazing at* **Isaac** *with ecstatic passion, brings
the two children forward.* **Isaac** *embraces* **Naomi**, **Janet** *and*
Rose. *There are sexual overtones in how he touches them.*

Isaac   Sing, Naomi! Sing!

Dolly/Naomi (*sings*)
    There is one thing I will not do
    I will not stand in a cinema queue

Isaac *and* **Dolly/Naomi**
    There is one thing I will not do
    I will not stand in a cinema queue
    I ain't a gonna grieve my Lord no more

Dolly/Naomi All together now!

All
    I ain't a gonna grieve my Lord

I ain't a gonna grieve my Lord
I ain't a gonna grieve my Lord no more

Isaac
There are two things

Dolly/Naomi
There are two things

Isaac
I do detest

Dolly/Naomi
I do detest

Isaac
A painted face

Dolly/Naomi
A painted face

Isaac
And a low-backed dress

Dolly/Naomi
And a low-backed dress

All
There are two things I do detest
A painted face and a low-backed dress
I ain't a gonna grieve my Lord no more
I ain't a gonna grieve my Lord
I ain't a gonna grieve my Lord
I ain't a gonna grieve my Lord no more

Isaac
There are three things

All
There are three things

Isaac
I will not do

All

I will not do

Isaac

I will not gamble, smoke nor chew

All

There are three things I will not do
I will not gamble, smoke nor chew
I ain't a gonna grieve my Lord no more
I ain't a gonna grieve my Lord
I ain't a gonna grieve my Lord
I ain't a gonna grieve my Lord no more.

During the singing of the last chorus, **Isaac** *and* **Dolly/Naomi**
dance off. **Rose** *and* **Janet** *sit down and look pious. They sing a
few bars of 'Sunshine Mountain' without much enthusiasm.* **Dolly**
*returns (as herself). She takes a photo of them. She shakes her head
in exasperation.*

Dolly   Tell me this an' tell me no more! How long are
the pair of ye plannin' to keep up this daft carry-on? I mean,
I can cope with a couple of ten-year-olds not boozin' nor
gamblin' nor smokin' nor frequentin' the Plaza Ballroom.
But I declare to God if I hear one more chorus about
climbin' up that friggin' Sunshine Mountain, it's the friggin'
Sunshine Home for Wayward Girls for you two before this
day's over. Now away out to the street and play with the
other kids an' give my head peace.

Janet   There's nobody to play with. They're all away to
the pictures.

Rose (*wistfully*)   It's Lassie, so it is. An' Bugs Bunny.

Dolly   What time does it start?

Janet   Two o'clock.

Dolly   I think I'll go an' see that. He's great crack, that oul
Bugs Bunny.

Janet *and* **Rose** *watch with mounting anguish as* **Dolly** *prepares to go.*

Dolly   If I rush I'll see the comin' attractions as well. I hear *A Hundred and One Dalmatians* is on next week. Now how much money do I have on me . . . (*She looks in her purse.*) Enough for three an' a bit over for choc ices . . . Pity ye can't come with me. Still, yiz can say a wee prayer for me while I'm away sinnin'.

She moves towards the door. **Janet** *and* **Rose** *look at each other.*

Rose   That oul Isaac Standaloft's a smelly pervert, so he is.

She runs after **Dolly**.

Janet   Wait for me! Wait for me!

She runs to **Dolly** *and* **Rose**. **Dolly** *links a child on each arm. They exit with* **Dolly** *singing 'Onward Christian Soldiers'.*

Scene Two

The morning of the protest rally.

Vi *carries the steel shutters from outside into the shop.*

Rose *comes in from the house.*

Rose   What are you doing?

Vi   What does it look like I'm doin'?

Rose   You're opening the shop?

Vi   No. I'm takin' up weight-liftin' in my old age. Here, prop that behind the counter instead of stand in' there with both your arms the same length.

Rose   I thought you were supporting the strike.

Vi   Well, you thought wrong. I'm in support of the protest, but I'm gettin' out of the corner they've boxed us into. 'Close your shop, an' take to the streets if you don't support the agreement.' I will never support that agreement, never. But neither will I be a part of what they've got us involved in. Civil disobedience aided and abetted by thugs. Them's IRA tactics, an' I'll have no part of it. I've paid my rates, despite their orders not to. I've never been in debt in my life, an' I won't start now.

Rose   Vi, I never intended this . . .

Vi   I'm not doin' it for you. I'm doin' it for me. And well dare anybody round here suggest I'm not as loyal as the next one. I'm British, an' that's what I'll fight to stay as long as there's breath in my body. But I'll do it respectably and with dignity. I won't be associated with the dictates of criminals.

Rose   I should be at home today.

Vi   No. Your place is with the rest of the media who've congregated here, hopin' there's goin' to be a riot this day.

Rose   I don't hope that.

Vi   Maybe not. But the rest of them surely do. A peaceful protest is no news.

Belle *comes in.*

Vi   What are you doin' up at this hour of the mornin'?

Belle   I want to get into town early. Get near the front. See the speakers.

Rose   You are not going to the rally.

Belle   I am going to the rally. It's a historical happening. When I get back to college, I can tell those dusty old history lecturers that while they've been reading about it, I've been there.

Vi   You can watch it on the six o'clock news. You'll get a better view. And a safer one.

Belle   I'll be all right. Davy has promised to hold my hand.

Vi   The blind leadin' the blind. You said you would talk to her, Rose.

Rose   I did talk to her. (*To* **Belle**.) Weren't you listening to a word I said?!

Belle   I listened. And I've thought about it. And I want to go to the rally. I'm not afraid of the National Front.

Rose   Well, I am. And I'm telling you to stay indoors today.

Belle   You can't tell me what to do. I'm eighteen. And I don't live at home any more. I can fight my own battles.

Rose   I have worked day and night since you were born to make sure that you've never had to fight this battle. You've never known what it's like to be hated because you are black. I have kept you safe, well clear of poor, violent streets and schools, and . . .

Belle   And now you want to live my life for me?

Rose   I didn't give you a life to see it destroyed on the streets of Belfast. Now, stop being silly.

Belle   And you stop being so melodramatic!

Vi   Hey, hey, calm down the pair of you.

Rose   It's always the same. I talk to her. I'm reasonable. She's not. She just goes off quietly and does whatever it was she decided to do in the first place.

Vi   I wonder who she takes that after? (*To* **Belle**.) Listen, love. We're both worried. Nobody's tryin' to lead your life for you. We just don't want you to come to no harm.

Pause.

Belle   The National Front are recent arrivals here. Like me. Why have I never been in Belfast before now?

Vi   It was always easier for Dolly and me to visit you than for Rose to bring a baby across the water. Dolly loved them trips.

Belle   I haven't been a baby for a long time.

Rose   I couldn't afford the fare. You don't remember our early days in London. The rotten rooms we lived in before I began to earn decent money.

Belle   You've had a well-paid job for as long as I *can* remember, and you've taken me all over the world with you. But never to Belfast. One hour away by plane. So if it wasn't the time and it wasn't the money, what was the reason?

Rose   Belle, love, what is all this about?

Belle   You haven't protected me from racism, you know. No amount of money can buy immunity from that. But I've always dealt with it in my own way. Quietly. Never told you because you're always too anxious to fight on my behalf.

Rose   You're my daughter.

Belle   You're not black. I am. You can decide not to be a Protestant. I can't decide not to be black. I have no problem about being black. Is it a problem to you?

Rose   What are you saying?

Belle   I don't know. (*Pause.*) I'm saying that I'm not as concerned about political issues like the National Front as I am by the thought that you . . . this family . . . might have been embarrassed by me. Maybe still are.

Rose   How could you think such a thing?

Belle   I don't know. Didn't realise it was in my head until I said it. Don't look at me like that. I feel bad enough already.

Rose   And so you should.

Vi   Better sayin' it than harbourin' it. And she has a right to know.

Rose   There's nothing to know.

Vi   Oh, come on, Rose. You know as well as I do that although we never sat down and discussed it, we came to an unspoken agreement that it would be easier all round if me and Dolly visited you and Belle instead of you comin' here and copin' with the waggin' tongues. (*To* **Belle**.) Bein' an unmarried mother was scandal enough here all them years ago, but havin' a black child was unheard of. We may say we meant it for the best, but it's not to our credit that we took the easy way out at first, and then over the years just let it go on that way. If I'm ashamed of anything, it's us. Not you. The very idea! I couldn't love you more if you were my own.

Belle (*after a small pause, smiles*)   Me too.

A longer pause, as **Vi** *gestures/signals with her eyes that* **Belle** *is to make her peace with her mother.*

Belle   Sorry, Mum.

Rose   Me too.

But there is still a small awkwardness between **Belle** *and* **Rose**.

Vi (*deadpan*)   Don't strain yourselves. (*To* **Rose**.) Away you to your warm work. (*To* **Belle**.) And you can give me a hand in the shop the day.

Belle   Janet's here. I could go in with *you*, Mum. Then you wouldn't need to worry about me.

Rose   No. This is not an outing. This is work. And I'm late. But I'm not going in until I have your promise that you won't go in on your own.

Belle   It's not fair!

Rose   Please, Belle. This is one crowd I don't want you standing out in.

Belle (*reluctantly*)   All right.

Rose   Promise?

Belle   I promise. Okay?

Rose   Thank you. I'll get back as soon as I can. Take care, Vi.

Vi   You too.

Rose *leaves.*

Belle   Do you want me to make the sandwiches?

Vi   No point. Nobody'll be in to buy them.

Belle   Then why bother opening? We could go in to Belfast together. I only promised Mum I wouldn't go in alone.

Vi   Your mother did not say, don't go in alone. She said, don't go in on your own. Meanin' off your own bat. Under your own steam. With or without company.

Belle   That's not how I understood it.

Vi   Oh, is it not, clever clogs? Well, the answer is still no. I've made up my mind to open the day, an' I won't be deterred. Not even by the big brown eyes of the Belle of the Belfast City. Now you just content yourself and keep an eye on the shop while I get Dolly up and dressed. I'll send Janet down to keep you company and out of mischief.

Vi *moves towards the house.*

Belle   Vi?

Vi   What?

Belle   Are you opening the shop, making a stand, just because of me? I mean . . . would you feel so strongly about the National Front being here if I were white?

Vi   After the Second World War, your grandfather sent me and Dolly to the pictures to see the newsreels of what had been goin' on in them camps in Germany. He was there, when they were liberated, you see, an' he said everybody should see what he'd seen, an' never forget it, so that it could never happen again. He was a good man. A decent man. I wish you could have known him. He would have spoilt you rotten. He would never have condoned the followers of them butchers marchin' on the streets of Belfast. And neither will I.

She goes upstairs. There is the sound of bands in the road near the street. **Belle** *goes out to look.* **Davy** *comes into the street. He is wearing even more red, white and blue badges and Loyalist slogans than usual. He has an 'Ulster Says No' poster taped to the back of his coat. He signals excitedly to* **Belle***, miming the bands and telling her to come with him.*

Belle   I can't, Davy . . . I promised . . . (*She hesitates, then signals.*) Hold on a minute. I'll get my coat.

She puts on a coat. Scribbles a note to **Vi***. Leaves it on the counter. She holds out her hand to* **Davy***. He smiles shyly and takes it. The noise of the bands increases. As* **Belle** *and* **Davy** *leave the street,* **Janet** *comes into the shop. She reads the note, grabs her coat and runs after them.*

Scene Three

Late afternoon the same day. A room in Unionist Party headquarters. **Jack** *stands rehearsing a speech. At first he refers occasionally to his notes but by the end of the speech he is in a state of masturbatory ecstasy.*

Jack   Today, the internal feuding within the Unionist family is ended. No longer divided, we shall not fall. Strong and reunited we stand. Unafraid in the face of our common enemy. We are at war with the British government, and our ranks will never be broken again. We will never submit to the conspiracy of the Anglo-Irish Agreement. Fight the Good Fight. Rejoice in your strength. But beware of complacency. For therein lies weakness. And weakness may be seduced by that other great conspiracy – the corruption and perfidy of Rome.

Be constantly on your guard against the satanic smells and heathen incantations that pervade the Roman Catholic Church. The descendant Church of the Semitic God Baal.

Baal the Sun God. Baal the Master. Baal the Possessor. Baal the Seducer.

Guard our women. Guard our children. Lest they succumb to the insidious evil that festers and grows in our land. The phallic worship of priests in scarlet and gold. The pagan rites of black nuns. Sisters of Satan. Sisters of sin. Defilers of man's innocence.

Guard your mothers. Guard your daughters. Guard your sisters and your wives.

And may God guard us lest we weaken and yield to Unholy Desire.

Janet *comes in. There is a long pause.*

Janet   They said I would find you here.

Jack   I gave instructions that I was not to be disturbed.

Janet   I told them I was your sister. I have to talk to you.

Jack   You'll have to wait. I'm about to address a meeting.

Janet   This can't wait. I need your help.

Jack   So. You've come to your senses at last.

Janet   It's not for me. It's for Davy.

Jack   Who?

Janet   Davy Watson. You've met him in the shop. He's deaf and dumb.

Jack   What about him?

Janet   He's been arrested and I can't find out where they've taken him.

Jack   Ask your policeman.

Janet   Peter's on duty. I don't know where.

Jack   I've more important things to do than wander round the police stations looking for a halfwit.

Janet   I'll tell Vi I asked for your help and that's what you said.

Jack   Wait. Tell me what happened.

Janet   He went to the rally with Belle. She was told not to go, but she was determined to see it for herself. I went after them, but there was no stopping her.

Jack   Every inch her mother's daughter. Disobedient and defiant.

Janet   I couldn't talk her out of it, so I went with them. On the way home, we were stopped by a crowd of kids wearing National Front T-shirts. Five boys and two girls. The girls were wearing Union Jacks around their shoulders. Like cloaks. They couldn't have been more than fourteen years old.

Jack   Will you get on with it? I haven't got all night.

Janet   They made a circle round Belle. Started taunting her, pushing her about, pulling her hair. Davy went berserk. Dived on them like a madman. A police patrol came along and the kids ran away. All that was left was me and Belle trying to calm Davy down. The police assumed he was attacking us, and dragged him into the Land Rover. We tried to explain to them, but they weren't interested. One of them kept shouting about a colleague who'd been injured earlier on at the City Hall. I suppose they were determined to get somebody. Anybody. Then something came through on the radio and they drove off. Belle and me have been everywhere, Jack, and nobody will give us any information. So we came here.

Jack   You've brought her here?

Janet   She's outside. In a taxi.

Jack   Go home! I'll make some phone calls.

Janet   Belle says she's not going home without him.

Jack   Tell her to clear off from here, or I'll leave him to rot!

Janet   Can you get him out?

Jack   We still have some friends in the RUC. Influential men. Not community do-gooders like your husband.

Janet   I no longer have a husband.

Pause.

Jack   You will always have a brother.

Janet   Goodbye, Jack.

She turns to leave.

Jack   You need me!

Janet   I never needed you. I was only ever afraid of your need of me. And now I'm not afraid any more.

Jack   What are you going to do? Live out your days with that mad old woman? She's already got one foot in the grave. She won't last for ever. And Vi's not getting any younger. What'll you do when they're both gone? You'll never manage alone. You never could. You've always needed somebody to take care of you.

Janet   It's time I took care of myself. I'm going to London.

Jack   You met a man there, didn't you? Didn't you?!

Janet   Yes, I did. But I'm not running back to him. I want a life of my own. My own! Nobody else's! Not his, not Peter's. Not yours. Most of all not yours. I am walking away from this violence.

Jack   I am not a violent man. I abhor violence.

Janet   You love it, Jack. You need it. It excites you. Violence is the woman you never had.

Jack   I need no woman.

Janet   Then you don't need me.

She walks away.

Jack (*shouts after her*)   I have never needed you! Harlot! Whore!

Dolly (*sings*)
　　Let him go, let him tarry
　　Let him sink or let him swim
　　He doesn't care for me
　　And I don't care for him
　　He can go and get another
　　That I hope he will enjoy
　　For I'm goin' to marry a far nicer boy.

Janet *walks away into Scene Four.*

Scene Four

Evening. The same day.

Dolly, **Vi**, **Rose**, **Janet** *and* **Belle** *in the house.*

Vi　There were two of them. A young lad of about fifteen and a middle-aged man. The boy was loud-mouthed, abusive, every other word a swear word. The man was quiet spoken. Quite reasonable I suppose. In his own way. He sent the boy outside and then he talked to me about the agreement and how we all had to oppose it. When I pointed out that the organisers had promised there would be no intimidation, he said there would be no damage done to the shop, but that it would be boycotted if I didn't close. After he left I put the shutters back on the windows. Just as well, as it turned out. They started comin' back from the rally in the late afternoon. A gang of them. Singin'. Shoutin'. I thought it was stones they were throwin'. It was golf balls.

Janet　They smashed in the windows of a sports shop near the city hall. They used the golf balls to attack the police. The owner of that shop is a Protestant businessman. He'd closed his premises. But that didn't deter them.

Rose　They wrecked and looted about a dozen shops. They were very selective in what they stole. Alcohol. Leather jackets. Ski anoraks. I got a great photograph of one young boy walking around with a bottle of champagne in each hand and a pair of ski boots round his neck.

Dolly   Maybe the UDA are plannin' to open a ski resort in the Mourne Mountains.

Belle   Was that a car?

Jack *walks into the street with* **Davy**. *He brings him into the house.* **Davy** *is in a distressed, confused state.*

Jack   I don't know where he lives, and he couldn't tell me, so I brought him here.

Belle *and* **Vi** *try to comfort* **Davy**. *But he cowers and whimpers and won't let them touch him.*

Vi   In the name of God, what have they done to him?

Belle   It's all right Davy, it's all right.

Davy *signals that she is not to come near.*

Belle   I won't touch you. I won't come near. I promise. Just talk to me. Tell me.

After a pause, **Davy** *signals to* **Belle**.

Belle (*interpreting*)   They put me in a room. No windows. Bright light. No toilet. They laughed. They made me take my clothes off. All of them. Cold. Cold. They gave me an old blanket. Pushing. Shouting. Shoving. Bright light. Stop. Don't. Cry-baby. Cry . . . I couldn't help it. It wouldn't stop. Dirty. All over the blanket. Don't laugh . . . don't laugh . . . don't . . . They put the blanket over my head.

Davy *touches his hair, looks at his hands with disgust.*

Belle (*interpreting*)   Don't touch. Don't touch . . .

Davy *rocks back and forward, weeping.*

Vi   Come on, son. Come with me. It doesn't matter. It'll wash off. I'll fill a bath for you. Come on now. You don't want to be going home to your mother in that state. Don't worry. It'll all wash away, and nobody need ever know. We won't tell it. Come on, now.

She leads **Davy** *off.* **Dolly** *and* **Janet** *have been watching and listening to the story with horror.* **Rose** *has been watching* **Jack***.*

Rose   But you'll tell it, won't you, Jack? What a godsend to distract attention from the violence of your gangsters today. I can just see the headline. 'Brutal RUC interrogation of innocent, retarded Loyalist.' A heaven-sent piece of propaganda in your favour.

Jack   You think they should be allowed to get away with it?

Rose   No I don't. No more than I thought they should have been allowed to get away with it when they did that and worse during the interrogation of suspected IRA terrorists. But that never bothered the Unionists at all, did it? In fact you were all for it, as long as it was being done to the Catholics, innocent or guilty.

Jack   They're all guilty. Potential traitors every one.

Belle   Regardless of what your motives are, I'm grateful to you for getting Davy out of there.

Jack   I did it for Vi, because she cares for him and I care about her. But as for the rest of this family, you can all go to hell!

Dolly   I doubt there'll be much room left down there. It must be packed out with the clergy by now.

She grins as **Jack** *turns angrily to leave. She chants:*

Dolly   Two little sausages frying in the pan. One went pop and the other went bang.

She starts to laugh and then falls forward out of the chair. **Belle** *runs to* **Dolly***, cradles her in her arms.*

Rose   Janet! Phone for an ambulance!

Dolly   No ambulance . . . no hospital . . . my own time . . .

Jack *pushes* **Belle** *aside as* **Dolly** *stops breathing. He very expertly begins to resuscitate her.*

Belle   Leave her alone! Leave her alone!

Rose   Belle!

She restrains **Belle** *from pulling* **Jack** *away.*

Belle   Make him stop! She doesn't want this! Let her go!
Let her go!

Jack   She's breathing again. Put a blanket over her, keep
her warm.

Belle   Who taught you to do that? The Church Lads
Brigade? Why couldn't you leave her alone? I promised her!
I promised her! People have the right to die when they want
to. When their time has come.

Jack   That is for the Lord God to decide.

Belle   And you're the Lord God, are you?

Jack   I am the instrument of His will.

Belle   So were the thumbscrews and the rack.

Janet   The ambulance is on its way.

Belle   I'm sorry, Gran . . . I'm sorry . . .

Scene Five

A few months later. A 'Sold' sign on the shop.

Dolly *sits in the wheelchair. She looks very old. Vacant. Her mouth
is slightly twisted. Some knitting lies in her lap.* **Vi** *is packing things
in cardboard boxes.* **Belle** *sits on a suitcase at one side of the stage.*
Rose *and* **Janet** *stand a little way off.* **Janet** *is looking at a
newspaper.*

Vi   We got a fair price for the shop. Better than I expected.
I suppose I should have guessed. It sold so quick. She
seemed a nice young woman. Paid cash. Transpired Tom
Bailey put up the money, and as soon as it was all signed,
sealed and delivered, she transferred the deeds into his
name. Rose says he's buyin' up property all over the town.
It's one of the ways he makes his money. Buyin' cheap an'

waitin' an' sellin' dear. I suppose in the end that's what it all boils down to. Property. Land, who owns what. God, would you listen to me. Next thing, I'll be votin' for the Workers' Party.

She gives **Dolly** *a drink out of a child's plastic cup with a lid and spout.*

Vi   You'll love the wee house in Donaghadee. You can see the sea and the Copeland Islands and the lighthouse. And the girls are comin' over from London to help us pack up and move. It'll be just like the old days, only better and you'll get better. It'll take time . . . but you will . . . (*She picks up the knitting.*) Encourage her to knit, the doctor said. It'll help to get those hands working again. You never knit nor sewed nuthin' in your life, did you, Mother? I suppose it's a bit late in the day to expect you to learn new tricks.

She puts the photo album on **Dolly**'*s lap.*

Vi   Here, look at the pictures. Turn the pages. That'll do your hands and your heart more good.

Dolly *stares at the album. Slowly turns the pages.* **Davy** *comes running in. He is wearing an expensive ski anorak and waving a local magazine. He signals to* **Vi** *to look, points to a photograph, points to himself.*

Vi   Calm down. Calm down. I can see it's you. I'd know that ugly mug anywhere. (*She reads.*) 'British barrister to represent Loyalist victim of RUC brutality.' I hope the Lady Elizabeth has been forewarned to advise you not to appear in court in that jacket. Fell off the back of a protest lorry, did it? How much did they sting ye for it?

Davy *signals.*

Vi   A tenner? Was that with or without golf balls?

Janet *reads to* **Rose** *from the newspaper.*

Janet   'Mr David Watson has a mental age of ten. He is deaf and mute. Mr Jack Horner announced today that he would be Mr Watson's voice in court. Mr Horner said that he had learned sign language specially to communicate with Mr Watson, who is an old family friend.'

Rose   Suffer the little children to come unto me . . . for of such is the Kingdom of Heaven . . .

Davy *shows the magazine to* **Dolly**.

Vi   He's got his photo in the magazine, and there's a write-up . . . She's not herself the day, Davy. Come back the marra and see her, eh? Maybe she'll be a bit brighter.

Davy *signals goodbye. As he leaves he makes a victory sign and then signals again.*

Vi (*to* **Dolly**)   He says 'No Pope Here'.

She shakes her head as **Davy** *exits.*

Vi   No bloody wonder, son. No bloody wonder.

Dolly *stares at the concert hall poster.* **Belle** *sings.*

Belle
   Red brick in the suburbs, white horse on the wall
   Eyetalian marble in the City Hall
   O stranger from England, why stand so aghast?
   May the Lord in His mercy be kind to Belfast

   This jewel that houses our hopes and our fears
   Was knocked up from the swamp in the last hundred years
   But the last shall be first and the first shall last
   May the Lord in His mercy be kind to Belfast

   We swore by King William there'd never be seen
   An all-Irish Parliament at College Green
   So to Stormont we're nailing the flag to the mast
   May the Lord in His mercy be kind to Belfast

   O the bricks they will bleed and the rain it will weep
   And the damp Lagan fog lull the city to sleep
   It's to hell with the future and live on the past
   May the Lord in His mercy be kind to Belfast.

Sebastian Barry

The Steward of Christendom

The Steward of Christendom was first performed in the Royal
Court Theatre Upstairs, London, on 30 March 1995, with
the following cast:

Thomas	Donal McCann
Smith	Kieran Ahern
Mrs O'Dea	Maggie McCarthy
Recruit	Rory Murray
Willie	Jonathan Newman
Annie	Tina Kellegher
Maud	Cara Kelly
Dolly	Aislín McGuckin
Matt	Rory Murray

Director   Max Stafford-Clark
Designer   Julian McGowan
Lighting Designer   Johanna Town
Music   Shaun Davey
Sound Designer   Paul Arditti

Characters

Thomas Dunne, *early to mid-seventies at the time of the play, 1932*
Smith, *fiftyish*
Mrs O'Dea, *likewise or older*
Recruit, *eighteen*
Willie Dunne, *Thomas's son, born late 1890s, died in the First World War, thirteen or so as he appears in the play to Thomas, his voice not yet broken*
Annie Dunne, *Thomas's middle daughter, bowed back, about twenty in 1922, thirtyish 1932*
Maud Dunne, *Thomas's eldest daughter, early twenties in 1922*
Dolly Dunne, *Thomas's youngest daughter, about seventeen in 1922*
Matt Kirwin, *Maud's suitor and husband, mid to late twenties in 1922, mid to late thirties in 1932*

Setting

The play is set in the county home in Baltinglass, County Wicklow, in about 1932.

Act One

Circa 1932. **Thomas***'s bare room in the county home in Baltinglass. A toiling music-hall music distantly. A poor table, an iron bed with a thin mattress and yellowing sheets. A grey blanket, a three-legged stool. A poor patch of morning light across* **Thomas***, a solitary man of seventy-five, in the bed. His accent is south-west Wicklow, with his words clear.*

Thomas Da Da, Ma Ma, Ba Ba, Ba Ba. Clover, clover in my mouth, clover honey-smelling, clover smelling of Ma Ma's neck, and Ma Ma's soft breast when she opens her floating blouse, and Da Da's bright boots in the grasses, amid the wild clover, and the clover again, and me the Ba Ba set in the waving grasses, and the smell of honey, and the farmhands going away like an army of redcoats but without the coats, up away up the headland with their scythes, and every bit of the sun likes to run along the scythes and laugh along the blades, now there are a score of shining scythes, dipping and signalling from the backs of the men.

A sharp banging on the door.

Smith Wakey, wakey!

Thomas Who is there?

Smith Black Jim. Black Jim in the morning.

Thomas Oh, don't come in, Black Jim, with your blackthorn stick raised high.

Smith It's Black Jim.

Thomas But don't you come in. There's no need. Is it Da Da?

Smith It's Black Jim, and he must come in.

Thomas There's no need. Thomas sleepy sleepy, beddy bye. Is it Da Da?

No answer. More distantly on other doors there's a banging and the same 'Wakey, wakey' receding.

Da Da comes in, Da Da comes in, Tom no sleepy, Tom no sleepy. Tom you sleep, says Da Da, or you get big stick. And when little Tom no sleepy sleep, big stick comes in and hitting Tom Tommy, but now the polished boots are gone, and the dark has closed over the fields, and the smell of the clover is damped down now by summer cold, and the dress of Ma Ma hangs on the chair, and her face is pressed into the goosey pillow, and all is silence in the wooden world of the house, except the tread of the Da Da, a-worrying, a-worrying, except the fall of the big stick, cut from the blackthorn tree in the hushed deeps of winter. Da Da is golden, golden, golden, nothing that Da Da do takes away the sheen and the swoon of gold.

He bestirs himself, wipes his big hands on his face vigorously, gets out of bed with good strength. He is big-framed but diminished by age, in a not-too-clean set of long johns.

You bloody mad old man. Gabbling and affrighting yourself in the dark. Baltinglass, Baltinglass, that's where you are. For your own good, safe from harm. Like the milking cow taken down from the sloping field when the frost begins to sit on her tail. When her shit is frosty. Snug in the byre.

He sits on the stool and leans in to the table as if pressing his face against the cow.

Come to it, Daisy now, give your milk. Go on. (*Slaps a leg.*) Ah, Daisy, Daisy, sweet, give it up, for Thomas. Oh. (*As if getting a jet into the bucket.*) Oh, oh. (*Happily.*) Aye. (*Catching himself, stopping.*) The county home in Baltinglass, that's where you're situated. Seventy-five summers on your head and mad as a stonemason. Safe, safe, safety, safe, safe, safety, mad as a barking stonemason. Because you were not civil to your daughter, no, you were not. You were ranting, you were raving, and so they put you where you were safe. Like a dog that won't work without using his teeth, like a dog under sentence. But please do not you talk to Black Jim, Thomas, please do not, there's the manny. Because he is not there. (*Singing.*) There was an old woman that lived in the wood, willa, willa, wallya.

His own silence.

Da Da?

Mrs O'Dea, *the seamstress, a small plump woman in an ill-made dress and a white apron with big pockets full of tape and needles and oddments of black cloth, opens the door with her key and comes in.*

Mrs O'Dea (*a local accent*)   Will you let me measure you today, Mr Dunne?

Thomas   What for indeed?

Mrs O'Dea   You can't wear those drawers for ever.

Thomas   I won't need to, Mrs O'Dea, I won't live for ever.

Mrs O'Dea   And what will you do when summer's gone? How can you bear to wear rags?

Thomas   I rarely go out, you see.

Mrs O'Dea   Look at the state of yourself. You're like something in a music hall. Mrs Forbes, the Boneless Wonder, or some such.

Thomas   This is a madhouse, it suits me to look like a madman while I'm here.

Mrs O'Dea   If you allow me measure you, I'll make up a fine suit for you, as good as my own attire.

Thomas   With that black cloth you use for all the poor men?

Mrs O'Dea   Yes and indeed, it must be black, by regulation of the board.

Thomas   If you had a bit of gold or suchlike for the thread, something to perk the suit up, why then, Mrs O'Dea, I would let you measure me.

Mrs O'Dea   Gold thread? I have none of that, Mr Dunne.

Thomas   That's my bargain. Take it or leave it.

Mrs O'Dea   Would a yellow do?

Thomas   Yes, yes.

Mrs O'Dea   You're not afraid of looking like a big goose?

Thomas   I go out but rarely. If I look like a goose, few will see me. (*As an inspiration.*) I won't venture out at Christmas!

Mrs O'Dea (*taking out her measuring tape*)   Have you fleas?

Thomas   No, madam.

Mrs O'Dea (*calling out the door*)   Mr Smith! (*To* **Thomas**.) You won't mind Mr Smith washing you, just a little.

Thomas (*anxiously*)   Don't let Black Jim in here. Don't let him, for I've no sugar lumps. It's only sugar lumps appeases him.

Mrs O'Dea   He must wash you, Mr Dunne. It's just Mr Smith. You smell like a piece of pork left out of the dripping press, man dear.

Smith*, about fifty, balding, with the cheerfulness about him of the powerful orderly, comes in with a basin.*

Smith   Raise 'em.

Thomas (*backing away*)   The blackthorn stick hurts Tommy Tom. Sugar lumps, sugar lumps!

Mrs O'Dea   Take off your old long johns, and be easy in yourself. It's only a sponging.

Thomas (*trying to hold his clothes fast*)   Tum tum tum, bum bum bum.

Smith *roughly unbuttons the long johns and pulls them off,* **Thomas** *miserably covering himself.*

Smith   I'd a mind once to join my brother on the Hudson river. He has a whale flensing business there, flourishing. Would that I had joined Jack, I say, when I have to wash down an old bugger like you. I would rather flense whales, and that's a stinking task, I'm told.

Thomas (*smiling red-faced at* **Mrs O'Dea**)   Da Da.

Mrs O'Dea (*as* **Smith** *begins to sponge*)   Good man yourself, Mr Dunne.

Thomas (*weeping*)   Da Da, Ma Ma, Ba Ba.

Mrs O'Dea   My, my, that's a fine chest you have on you, Mr Dunne. What was your work formerly? I know you've told me often enough.

Thomas (*proudly enough*)   I was a policeman.

Mrs O'Dea   You had the chest for it.

Thomas   I had, madam.

Smith (*sponging*)   Dublin Metropolitan Police, weren't you, boyo? In your braid. The DMP, that are no more. Oh, la-di-da. Look at you.

Thomas (*smiling oddly*)   La-di-da.

Smith (*sponging*)   Castle Catholic bugger that you were. But you're just an old bastard in here with no one to sponge you but Smith.

Thomas   Black Jim no like Tommy Tom. No like Tommy Tom.

Smith   Chief Superintendent, this big gobshite was, Mrs O'Dea, that killed four good men and true in O'Connell Street in the days of the lock-out. Larkin. Hah? His men it was struck down the strikers. (*A gentle hit with the drying cloth.*) Baton-charging. A big loyal Catholic gobshite killing poor hungry Irishmen. If you weren't an old madman we'd flay you.

Mrs O'Dea   That's fine, Mr Smith, leave him be. Can't you see you terrorise him? That's him scrubbed.

Smith (*going off with the basin*)   Excusing my language.

Mrs O'Dea   Can you put on your own clothes, Mr Dunne?

Thomas   I can, madam.

Mrs O'Dea   Is it true you gave your previous suit to a man in the walking meadow?

Thomas   It is. (*Dressing.*)

Mrs O'Dea   Why would you do a thing like that, and go in those rags yourself? Was the man you gave it to cold?

Thomas   No. He was hungry.

Mrs O'Dea   There's no eating in a suit, man dear.

Thomas   I was out a-walking in the lunatics' meadow, and Patrick O'Brien asked me for the suit. He was in former times the finest thrower of the bullet in Kiltegan. Do you know what a bullet is? It is a ball of granite whittled down in an evening by a boy. I could tell you tales of Patrick O'Brien and the bullet, on the roads there round about. All the men of the village milling there, raging to win fame at the bulleting if God shone the light of luck on them, the thrower slowly slowly raising the bullet, slowly dipping it, then away, with a great fling of the arm, down the road with it, and well beyond the next corner if he could. And if the bullet touched the grassy marge, a terrible groan would issue from the man and his supporters. And the young boys red in the face from ambition and desire. Patrick O'Brien, a tall yellow streak of a man now, that thinks he is a dog. A dog, Mrs O'Dea. When he asked for the suit, I couldn't refuse him, for memory of his great skill. They were evenings any human person would remember.

Mrs O'Dea (*measuring him now with the tape, putting up his arms and so on as necessary*)   What did he want with your suit?

Thomas   To eat, he said. To bury it and eat it, piecemeal, as the spirit took him.

Mrs O'Dea   You gave your good suit to a poor madman to be eaten?

Thomas   I was glad to give it to him. Though indeed truly, it was one of Harrison's suits, and the last of my finery from the old days. A nice civilian suit, made by Harrison, in North Great George's Street, years ago.

Mrs O'Dea   I can't believe that you gave away a suit like that. A lovely bespoke suit.

Thomas   Why not? Amn't I a lunatic myself?

Mrs O'Dea (*sensibly*)   Well, there must be a year's eating in a man's suit. You won't need to give him the new one.

Thomas   No, but it won't be much to me all the same, if it has no gold in it. The boy that sings to me betimes wears gold, and I have a hankering now for a suit with a touch of gold. There was never enough gold in that uniform. If I had made Commissioner I might have had gold, but that wasn't a task for a Catholic, you understand, in the way of things in those days.

Mrs O'Dea   You must have been a fine policeman, if they made you all of a Chief Superintendent.

Thomas   Maybe so. But, to tell you the truth, I was forty-five years in the DMP when they did so, and promotion was really a matter of service. Not that they would put a fool to such a task, when you think of the terrible responsibility of it. I had three hundred men in B Division, and kept all the great streets and squares of Dublin orderly and safe, and was proud, proud to do it well.

Mrs O'Dea   I am sure you did, Mr Dunne, because you carry yourself well yet. You mustn't mind Mr Smith. He's younger than yourself and one of his brothers was shot in the twenties, so he tells me.

Thomas   The DMP was never armed, not like the Royal Irish Constabulary. The RIC could go to war. That's why we were taken off the streets during that rebellion at Easter time, that they make so much of now. We were mostly country men, and Catholics to boot, and we loved our king and we loved our country. They never put those Black and Tans among us, because we were a force that belonged to Dublin and her streets. We did our best and followed our orders. Go out to Mount Jerome some day, in the city of Dublin, and see the old monument to the DMP men killed in the line of duty. Just ordinary country men keen to do well. And when the new government came in, they treated us badly. Our pensions were in disarray. Some said we had been traitors to Ireland. Though we sat in Dublin Castle all through twenty-two and tried to protect the city while the whole world was at each other's throats. While the most dreadful and heinous murders took place in the fields of Ireland. With nothing but our batons and our pride. Maybe we weren't much. You're thinking, of course he would speak well for his crowd. Yes, I'll speak well for them. We were part of a vanished world, and I don't know what's been put in our place. I'd like to see them clear Sackville Street of an illegal gathering without breaking a few heads. There was a proclamation posted the week before that meeting. It was my proper duty to clear the thoroughfare. There was no one killed that day that I know of, there were scores of my men in Jervis Street and the like, with head wounds. I'm sorry Smith's brother was killed. I'm sorry for all the poor souls killed these last years. Let them come and kill me if they wish. But I know my own story of what happened, and I am content with it.

Mrs O'Dea   Mercy, Mr Dunne, I didn't mean to prompt a declaration. You're all in a sweat, man. The sooner you have a new suit, the better.

Thomas   But I tell you, there's other things I regret, and I regret them sorely, things of my own doing, and damn history.

Mrs O'Dea   We all have our regrets, man dear. Do calm yourself.

Thomas   I regret that day with my daughter Annie and the sword, when we were home and snug in Kiltegan at last.

Mrs O'Dea   There, there, man dear. We'll see if we can't keep the next suit on you, when you go a-walking in the lunatics' meadow, as you call it. It's just the exercise field, you know, the walking meadow. It will have plenty of yellow in it.

Thomas (*differently, head down*)   I suppose it is very sad about Patrick O'Brien. I suppose.

Mrs O'Dea   I have all your measurements now, Mr Dunne. And a fine big-boned gentleman you are. (*Looking at his bare feet.*) What became of your shoes, but?

Mrs O'Dea *and* **Thomas** (*after a moment, as one*)   Patrick O'Brien!

Mrs O'Dea   Maybe there's a pair of decent shoes about in the cupboards, that someone has left.

Thomas   Coffin shoes, you mean, I expect. Oh, I don't mind a dead man's shoes. And a nice suit, yes, that I can wear in my own coffin, to match, with yellow thread.

Mrs O'Dea   Not yet, Mr Dunne, not by a long chalk. (*Going out.*) I'll do my best for you. (*Locking the door.*)

Thomas (*alone, in an old summer light*)   When the rain of autumn started that year, my mother and me went down into the valley by the green road. Myself trotting beside her in my boyish joy. We passed the witch's farm, where the witch crossed the fields in her dirty dress to milk her bloodied cow, that gave her bloodied milk, a thing to fear because she used the same well as ourselves, and washed her bucket there before drawing water. My father was the steward of Humewood and she should have feared to hurt our well, but you cannot withstand the mad. Well, we passed the nodding bell-flowers that I delighted to burst, and ventured out on to the Baltinglass road, to beg a perch for our bums on a cart. (*Sitting up on the bedstead.*) For my father would not let my mother take the pony and trap, because he said the high lamps made too great a show of pride, and we were proud people enough without having to show it. Not that he didn't drive the trap himself when he needed. But we were soon in the old metropolis of Baltinglass, a place of size and wonder to a boy. (*Pulling out his ragged socks from under the mattress.*) There we purchased a pair of lace-up boots. A pair of lace-up boots which banished bare feet, which I was soon able to lace and tighten for myself of a morning, when the air in the bedroom was chill as a well, and the icy cock crowed in the frosty yard, and Thomas Dunne was young and mightily shod. (*Looking down at his feet.*) And Dolly my daughter later polished my policeman's boots, and Annie and Maud brought me my clothes brushed and starched in the mornings, as the castle of soldiers and constables woke. When my poor wife was dead those many years, and Little Ship Street stirred with the milkman's cart. And the sun herself brought gold to the river's back. (*He looks at the locked door.*) If they lock that door, how can my daughters come to rescue me? (*He holds out a hand and takes it with his other hand, and shakes.*) How do you do? How do you do? (*Very pleased.*) How do you do? (*Holds out his arms, embraces someone.*) How do you do? (*Gently.*) How do you do? Oh, how do you do?

Music. After a little, **Smith** *enters with a cracked bowl with a steam of stew off it. He hands* **Thomas** *a big spoon which* **Thomas** *holds obediently.*

Smith   You look just like an old saint there, Mr Dunne, an old saint there, with your spoon. You may think me a rough sort of man but I know my saints. I seen a picture of St Jerome with a spoon like that and a bowl like that.

Thomas *sits to eat.*

Smith   Eat away, man. You should see the cauldron of that stuff the cooks have made. The kitchens are in a fog. Seven lambs went into it, they say. Isn't it good stuff? (*Friendly.*) What's it your name is again, your first name? I've so many to remember.

Thomas   Thomas. They named me Thomas long ago for my great-great-grandfather, the first steward of Humewood, the big place in Kiltegan, the main concern. Though all his own days they called him White Meg on account of his fierce white beard. He'd stride up the old street from his house to the great gates and say nothing to no one. White Meg. But Thomas it was, was his name.

Smith   With your spoon. St Thomas! When I brought Mrs O'Dea her cocoa in at five, she had you all cut out and hung up on a hook with the other inhabitants, and the breeze was blowing you softly from the crack in the pane. She's a keen seamstress. St Thomas. Do you like the stew?

Thomas (*expansively*)   Of all the dishes in the world I may say I relish mostly a stew.

Smith   You, St Thomas, that knew kings and broke Larkin. Stew.

Thomas (*alerted*)   Put a piece of lamb in it at the bottom, for the men that are working, and let the child eat off the top of it. The child's spoon is a shallow spoon. Parsnips. The secret of stew on our hillside was just a scrape of crab apple in it – just a scrape. But then we'd fierce crab apples. And not to curse while it was cooking. And not to spit while it was cooling.

Smith   What was the name of the patriot was killed years past in Thomas Street outside the church of St Thomas, in the city of Dublin?

Thomas (*thinking, innocently*)   Thomas Street wasn't in my division. But Emmet, was it, you mean? Robert Emmet?

Smith   That's the one. They hung him there and the people cried out against the soldiers and the peelers, and after they dragged his body over the parade ground till it was bleeding and broken in its bones, and then they got a loyal butcher to cut him into four pieces. He was dead then.

Thomas   I should think.

Smith   That's what they did to him, those official men, and a fine Protestant gentleman at that.

Thomas (*pleasantly*)   It's as well to throw a bit of rosemary across it too, if you have rosemary. Rosemary smells good when the land gets hot. Across the stew. Rosemary. Thyme would do either, if you've none. When you put in the spuds. Or lavender maybe. Did you ever try clover? A child will eat clover when he is set down on the meadow to sit. The bee's favourite. A cow makes fine milk from a field of clover. So put in rosemary, if you have it. Ah, fresh spuds, turned out

of the blessed earth like – for all the world like newborn pups.
(*Laughing*.)

Smith   I suppose you held the day of Emmet's death as
a festive day. A victory day. I suppose you did. I suppose
you were all very queer indeed up there in the Castle. I'm
thinking too of the days when they used to put the pitch
caps on the priests when they catched them, like they were
only dogs, and behind the thick walls of the city hall all the
English fellas would be laughing at the screams of the priests,
while their brains boiled. I'm thinking of all that. I suppose
you never put a pitch cap on anyone. They weren't in
fashion in your time. A pity. It must have been a great sight,
all the same.

Thomas (*eating rapidly*)   Good stew, good stew. Wicklow
lambs.

Smith (*looking at him*)   St Thomas, isn't it?

Thomas (*smiling*)   St Thomas.

Smith *goes off with the empty bowl.*

Thomas   I loved her for as long as she lived, I loved her
as much as I loved Cissy my wife, and maybe more, or
differently. When she died it was difficult to go from her
to the men that came after her, Edward and George, they
were good men but it was not the same. When I was a
young recruit it used to frighten me how much I loved her.
Because she had built everything up and made it strong,
and made it shipshape. The great world that she owned was
shipshape as a ship. All the harbours of the earth were trim
with their granite piers, the ships were shining and strong.
The trains went sleekly through the fields, and her mark was
everywhere, Ireland, Africa, the Canadas, every blessed
place. And men like me were there to make everything
peaceable, to keep order in her kingdoms. She was our pride.
Among her emblems was the gold harp, the same harp we
wore on our helmets. We were secure, as if for eternity the
orderly milk-drays would come up the streets in the morning,
and her influence would reach everywhere, like the salt sea

pouring up into the fresh waters of the Liffey. Ireland was hers for eternity, order was everywhere, if we could but honour her example. She loved her prince. I loved my wife. The world was a wedding of loyalty, of steward to Queen, she was the very flower and perfecter of Christendom. Even as the simple man I was I could love her fiercely. Victoria.

The **Recruit**, *a young man of eighteen or so, comes on. He has obviously made a great effort to smarten himself for this meeting. He is tall and broad, and stoops a little as he takes off his hat.*

Thomas   Good morning, son. How are you?

Recruit   Oh, most pleasant, sir, most pleasant.

Thomas   You had a good journey up from your home place?

Recruit   It didn't take a feather out of me, sir.

Thomas   Good man. What age are you?

Recruit   Eighteen, sir, this November past.

Thomas   Height?

Recruit   Six foot three, sir, in my winter socks.

Thomas   Well, you look a very fine man indeed. You were never in trouble yourself, son?

Recruit   Oh, no, sir.

Thomas   And did you serve in the Great War? I don't suppose you could have.

Recruit   No, sir. I was too young.

Thomas   Of course. A soldier doesn't always make a good policeman. There's too much – sorrow – in a soldier. You're a drinking man?

Recruit   I'll drink a glass of porter, with my father.

Thomas   Very good. I've read your father's letter. And I want to tell you, we are going to give you a go at it. I have a big book in my office within, bound in gold, that has the name of every DMP man that has ever served the crown. Do you wish for your own name to be added in due course?

Recruit   Oh – indeed and I do, sir. Most fervently.

Thomas   I hope you will do well, son. These are troubled times, and men like yourself are sorely needed. I will be watching your progress – watching, you understand, in a fatherly way. Do your best.

Recruit   I will, sir. Thank you, sir!

Thomas (*taking his hand*)   I was a young recruit myself once. I know what this means to you.

Recruit   The world, sir, it means the world.

Thomas   Good man. I'll write to your father in Longford. Take this now as a token of our good faith. (*Handing him the spoon.*)

Recruit   Thank you, sir, thank you.

The **Recruit** *shadows away.* **Thomas** *kneels at the end of his bed and grips the metal tightly.*

Thomas   I must not speak to shadows. When you see the shadows, Thomas, you must not speak. Sleep in the afternoon, that's the ticket. How did I get myself into this pickle, is it age just? I know I did what Annie said I did, but was it really me, and not some old disreputable creature that isn't me? When it was over, I knew suddenly in the car coming here what had happened, but at the time, at the time, I knew nothing, or I knew something else. And it was the gap between the two things that caused me to cry out in the car, the pain of it, the pain of it, the fright of it, and no one in the world to look at me again in a manner that would suggest that Thomas Dunne is still human, still himself. Everything is as clear as a glass. I can remember how lovely Cissy was the day we married, and that smile she gave me when the priest was finished, how she looked up at me in front of all our people, her face shining, astonishing me. You don't expect to see love like that. And that's a long time ago. And I can remember, now, the last day with Annie, and how I was feeling that day, and I can see myself there in the kitchen, and I know how mad I was. And I am ashamed. I am ashamed. I am ashamed. (*After a while of breathing like a runner.*) Hail Mary, full of Grace, the Lord is with thee, blessed art thou amongst women, and blessed is the fruit of thy womb. (*He gets stuck, bangs his head with his right palm.*) – Jesus. Holy Mary, mother of. Holy Mary, mother of. I remember, I do remember. Hail Mary full of grace the Lord is with me blessed art thou amongst women and blessed is the fruit of thy womb Jesus holy Mary Mother of . . . of . . . of God! Of God! (*Climbs into bed.*) Robert Emmet. (*Pulls the sheet over his face.*) Robert Emmet. (*Spits the t's so the sheet blows up from his lips.*) Robert Emmet. (*After a moment.*) Sleep, sleep, that's the ticket.

His son, **Willie**, *neat and round, comes in and sits on the end of his bed and sings to him Schubert's* Ave Maria. *At the end,* **Thomas** *looks over the sheet.* **Willie** *wears his army uniform.*

Thomas   Hello, child. Are you warm?

Willie   It's cold in the mud, Father.

Thomas   I know, child. I'm so sorry.

Sunlight grows slowly over the scene, banishing **Willie**. *The imagined stir and calling of the Castle below.* **Thomas** *is at ease suddenly. His middle daughter,* **Annie**, *in a light cotton dress of the early twenties, a bow in her spine, carries on a white shirt, which illumines like a lantern when she crosses the windowlight. There's an old music.*

Annie   Now, Papa – there's the best-ironed shirt in Christendom.

Thomas   Thank you, dear.

Annie   It took the best part of an hour to heat the hearth, to heat the iron. There's enough starch in the breast to bolster Jericho.

Thomas   Thank you, dear.

Annie   If Dolly had ironed it, you'd look at it more intently.

Thomas   I am looking at it, Annie. Or I would, if it weren't so blinding white.

Annie   And it isn't that white, Papa. And you've things on your mind today, I know. A black day.

Thomas   I expect it is.

Annie   Why Collins of all people to give the Castle to? Couldn't they find a gentleman?

Thomas   He is the head of the new government, Annie.

Annie   Government! We know what sort of men they are. Coming in here to the likes of you. Whose son gave his life for Ireland.

Thomas (*coming over to her, kindly*)   Will gave his life to save Europe, Annie, which isn't the same thing.

Annie   I miss Willie, Papa. I miss him. We need him today.

Thomas   I blame myself. There was no need for him to go off, except, he hadn't the height to be a policeman. The army were glad to take him. I blame myself.

Annie   Will was proud, Papa, proud to be in the Rifles. It was his life.

Thomas   It was the death of him. You cannot lose a son without blaming yourself. But that's all history now, Annie.

Maud, *his eldest, a very plain woman with black hair, dressed heavily for the bright day, carries on his dress uniform, struggling to balance the ceremonial sword.*

Thomas   Let me help you.

Maud   It's all right, Papa, I'll plonk it on the bed.

Thomas   Where's Dolly?

Maud   Polishing the boots. I hate to see a woman spit. Lord, Lord, she's a spitter, when it's Papa's old shoes. And she was away out this morning, I know not why, all secretive.

Annie   Away out this morning? She didn't touch her bed all night. Up at that dance at the Rotunda. She should be whipped.

Maud   And did you say she could go to that dance?

Annie   I didn't say she could take all night to walk home.

Thomas   Thoughtful daughters you are, to be helping me so. How did you get the creases so firm?

Maud   I slept on them. In as much as I slept. I cannot sleep these times.

Thomas   I could meet the emperor of the world with those creases.

Annie   You'll have to make do with Michael Collins.

Maud   Oh, don't start that old story, Annie. We've had enough of it now, God knows.

Annie   I was only saying.

Maud   Well, don't be only saying. Go and stir the teapot, can't you, and give over the politics.

Annie   I was only saying.

Maud   You're only always only saying, and you have me stark wide-eyed in the bed all night, worrying and turning and fretting, and a great headache pounding away, because you can leave nothing alone, Annie, till you have us all miserable and mad with concern.

Thomas   Now, girls, think of your mother. Would she want you to be talking like this?

Maud   No, Papa, of course not. She would not.

Annie   Mam? What do you know about Mam, if I may ask?

Maud   Don't I see her often when I sleep? Don't I see her blue polka-dot dress, yes, and her bending down to me and making me laugh?

Annie   That's only ould stuff Willie told us.

Maud   Oh, Annie, Annie, I was four years old, you were only two!

Thomas   Daughters, daughters – what a terrible thing to be arguing about!

Annie   Oh, a thing indeed.

Maud (*after a little*)   I'm sorry, Annie.

Annie   That's all right, girl. It's not your fault Collins is a criminal.

Maud   I'll be dead, that's it! I'll be dead by day's end. I can't take everything in! My head's bursting with Papa and Michael Collins and I don't know what . . .

Dolly, *holding out the polished boots carefully from her dress, starts across to* **Thomas**, *smiling.* **Thomas***'s face lights like a lamp.*

Thomas   Oh, Dolly, Dolly, Dolly!

Before she reaches him, an intrusion of darkness, the scattering of his daughters. **Thomas** *roars, with pain and confusion. He lifts his arms and roars. He beats the bed. He hits the table. He roars.* **Smith** *unlocks the door and hurries in, brandishing a pacifier. It looks like a baton.*

Smith   What the hell is all the shouting? You have the pauper lunatics in a swelter! Crying and banging their heads, and laughing like fairground mechanicals, and spitting, and cutting themselves with items. (*Looking back out.*) Mrs O'Dea, Mrs O'Dea – try and sort those screamers!

Mrs O'Dea (*off*)   I will, I will!

Smith   Even the long ward of old dames with their dead brains, have some of them opened their eyes and are weeping to be woken, with your bloody shouting. Do you want to go in with them, old man? After I beat you!

Thomas (*hurrying back into his bed*)   I only shouted the one time. It must have been the moon woke them. (*Drawing the sheet high.*) My daughter Annie gives you the shillings for the room, Black Jim.

Smith   She can give all the shillings she likes. She won't
know where we throw you.

Thomas   Don't put Thomas with the poor dribblers.
I've seen them. I've seen that terrible long ward of women,
belonging to no one at all, no one to pay shillings for them.
Don't put me there.

Smith   Then show me silence. (*Striking the end of the bed.*)

Thomas   Don't strike there. My son sits there.

Smith   You are a violent, stupid man, Mr Dunne, and
I want silence out of you!

Thomas (*a finger to his lips*)   Silence.

Smith *goes, banging the door, locking it harshly.*

Thomas (*pulling up the sheet*) Robert Emmet.

Annie *has slipped over to his bed.*

Annie   Papa.

Thomas (*looking out again*)   I must be silent, child.

Annie   Papa, please will you tell me.

Thomas   What, child?

Annie   Why is my back bowed, Papa?

Thomas   Why, child, because of your polio.

Annie   Why, Papa?

Thomas   I don't know, Annie. Because it afflicts some
and leaves others clear. I don't know.

Annie   Will I ever have a husband, Papa?

Thomas   I do hope so.

Annie   I think a woman with such a back will not find a
husband.

Thomas   She might.

Annie   I see the prams going by in Stephen's Green, glistening big prams, and I look in when the nannies are polite, and I look in, and I see the babies, with their round faces, and their smells of milk and clean linen, and their heat, and, Papa –

Thomas   Yes, child?

Annie   They all look like my babies.

Annie *goes.* **Thomas** *looks after her, then covers his face again. A country music. He sleeps, he sleeps. The moon, the emblem of lunacy, appears overhead, pauses, then faintly fades again. It is a very delicate, strange sleep. The calling of a cock distantly, birdsong, the cock louder. An arm of sunlight creeps into the room and across* **Thomas**'s *covered face. His hand creeps out and his fingers wave in the light. He pulls down the sheet and the noises cease. He listens. Imitates the cock softly.*

Thomas   The cock crows in the morning yard, banishing all night fears. No person, that has not woken to the crowing of a familiar cock can know how tender that cry is evermore, stirring the child out into the fresh fingers of sunlight, into the ever-widening armfuls of sunlight. How stray the child looks in the yard, bare feet on the old pack-stones in the clay, all his people have come out in their own vanished times, as small as him, surrounded by the quiet byres just wakening now, the noses of the calves wet in the closed dark, the sitting hens in the coop anxious to be released, out away from the night fear of foxes, so they may lay their eggs beyond finding in the hayshed and the hawthorn bushes. Only the boy knows their terrible tricks. He inserts an arm into the known places and feels the warm eggs, smells them happily in his brown palms, and searches out the newest places of the hens in the deepest bowers of the straw. He carries them back in to his Ma Ma, folded in his gansey, with the glow of pride about him as big as the sun. Then he goes back out into the yard while the eggs are boiling, or put aside carefully for the cake, and tries to read the story of the day in the huge pages of the clouds. And he sees the milking cow driven up on to the top field where the summer grass is rich and moist, and how well he knows the wild garden there of meadowsweet, where the dragonfly is hard as pencil. And the boy's Ma Ma is calling him, and he goes, and there is no greater morning, no morning in his life of greater importance.

Smith *enters with a newspaper. He fetches out* **Thomas***'s po. It's empty.*

Smith   I hope you're not blocking up like some of the old fellows.

Thomas   A deserted house needs no gutter. Is that my newspaper?

Smith   It is.

Throws it to him. **Thomas** *opens it.*

Smith   Can you not order a decent newspaper?

Thomas   *Irish Times* suits me.

Smith   It's all fools on horseback.

Thomas   Not so much. I'm trying to keep up on the activities, if I may call them that, of a certain Hinky Dink Kenna, who runs the first ward in Chicago. I tell you, you'd have to call him a criminal here. Himself and Bath-house John Coughlan. Villains. If they had never left Ireland, I'd have had to lock them up in Mountjoy. But you can do what you like in America, or so it seems.

Smith   Is that right? And what do they get up to, those two?

Thomas   Oh, they're in the liquor trade, you might say. It makes powerful reading.

Mrs O'Dea *comes in with big flaps of black cloth* – **Thomas***'s suit in its unsewn parts.*

Smith   He hasn't washed himself.

Mrs O'Dea   Didn't you wash him yesterday? Do you want to rub him out? Come on up, Mr Dunne, and let me pin these to you for a look at it.

Smith   Can't you see he's reading?

Thomas (*getting out of bed*)   Oh, I've time for reading. In my retirement.

He stands for the fitting. **Mrs O'Dea** *begins to pin the sections of the suit to his long johns.*

Mrs O'Dea   You're the cleanest man in Baltinglass.

Thomas *seems agitated, looking down at the sections.*

Mrs O'Dea   What's the matter, Mr Dunne?

Thomas   That's just the old black stuff.

Mrs O'Dea   And what if it is?

Thomas (*so* **Smith** *won't hear*)   Didn't we discuss yellow?

Mrs O'Dea   Yellow thread, Mr Dunne. I can only stitch the sections together with yellow. The trustees buy us in the black cloth from Antrim.

Thomas   But it's fierce, foul stuff, isn't it?

Smith   I'll leave you to it, Mrs O'Dea. I'll be over in the Monkey Ward, sluicing them out, if you need me. Be good, Mr Dunne. (*Goes.*)

Mrs O'Dea (*taking a bobbin from her apron*)   Look it, isn't that the bee's knees? That's from my own sewing box, that Mr O'Dea gave me in the old days. I can't do fairer than that.

Thomas   Oh, it's very sunny.

Mrs O'Dea   Now. (*Pinning again.*) It'll do beautifully. Can't your daughter bring you in clothes, if you don't like mine?

Thomas   I wouldn't go bothering her. All my daughters are good, considerate women. We looked after each other, in that fled time, when their mother was dead.

Mrs O'Dea   I'm sorry, Mr Dunne. And how did she die?

Thomas   They never failed their father, their papa, in that fled time. You should have seen them when they were little. Three little terrors going round with the knicks to their knees.

Mrs O'Dea (*pricking him by mistake*)   Oh, sorry. And where are your other daughters, Mr Dunne, these days?

Thomas   We stood under the hawthorn, while the bees broke their hearts at the bell-flowers, because the fringes of darkness had closed them.

Mrs O'Dea   Who did, Mr Dunne?

Thomas   My wife Cissy and myself. Cecilia. In courting days. Old courting days.

Mrs O'Dea   And what did she die of, did you say? (*Pricking.*)

Thomas   Nothing at all. Her farm was Lathaleer, her father's farm. The most beautiful piece of land. He was woodsman and keeper at Humewood, but he was a most dexterous farmer. The Cullens of Lathaleer. What a match she was for me! A strong, straight-backed, sensible person that loved old steps and tunes. She'd rather learn a new step than boil turnips, old Cullen said to me – but it wasn't so. What does a father know? King Edward himself praised her hair, when we were presented in nineteen-three. A thorough mole-black devious hair she had.

Mrs O'Dea   I'm sure. And didn't you do well by her, rising so high, and everything?

Thomas   Our happiest days were when I was only an inspector in Dalkey village. We lived there in a house called Polly Villa. There was precious little villainy in Dalkey. Three girls she bore there, three girls. And the boy already, before we came.

Mrs O'Dea   You have a son too? You have a lot.

Thomas   No. No, he didn't come back from France that time. He wrote me a lovely letter.

Mrs O'Dea (*after a little*)   And King Edward praised your wife's hair. Fancy.

Thomas   Aye – all the ladies loved him. Of course, he was old in that time. But a true king.

Mrs O'Dea (*finished with the fitting, unpinning him again*) What would you say about King De Valera?

Thomas   I would say very little about him, in that I wouldn't know much to say. Of course, I see a bit about him in the papers.

Mrs O'Dea   As much a foreigner as the king of England ever was, Mr O'Dea used to say, when he was overground. Mr O'Dea was a pundit, I'm afraid.

Thomas   He wants to buy the Irish ports back from Mr Churchill. I think that's a great pity. A man that loves his king might still have gone to live in Crosshaven or Cobh, and called himself loyal and true. But soon there'll be nowhere in Ireland where such hearts may rest.

Mrs O'Dea   You're as well to keep up with the news, Mr Dunne.

Thomas   I had an admiration for the other man though, the general that was shot, I forget his name.

Mrs O'Dea (*ready to go*)   Who was that?

Thomas   I forget. I remember the shock of sorrow when he was killed. I remember Annie and me crying in the old parlour of our quarters in the Castle. A curiosity. I met him, you see, the one time. He was very courteous and praised Wicklow and said a few things to me that rather eased my heart, at the time. But they shot him.

Mrs O'Dea (*going*)   They shot a lot of people. Was it Collins?

Thomas   I don't know, I forget. I remember the sorrow but not the name. Maybe that was the name.

Mrs O'Dea   I may have left a few pins in you, Mr Dunne, so don't go dancing about unduly.

Thomas   Dancing? I never danced in my life. I was a tree at a dance.

Mrs O'Dea *goes off.* **Thomas** *discovers a pin and holds it up.*

Thomas   Where are your other daughters, Mr Dunne, these days? (*After a little, moving the pin about like a tiny sword.*) The barracks of Ireland filled with new faces. And all the proud regiments gone, the Dublin Rifles and the Dublin Fusiliers. All the lovely uniforms. All the long traditions, broken up and flung out, like so many morning eggs onto the dung heap. Where are your other daughters, Mr Dunne, these days? Dolly of the hats. Annie told me the name of the place. Somewhere in America. What was the name?

The light of their parlour in the Castle. **Annie** *comes on with a big bundle of socks to sort. She sits on the three-legged stool. The socks are all the same. She looks in the socks for holes by thrusting her right hand into each of them, sorts the good from the bad.*

Annie   There's a terrible queer sort of a quietness settled over this Castle. How Papa expects to hang on here now till September. The city will be rubble, rubble by September.

Maud *follows on, looking pale and alarmed.*

Maud   Have you seen that Dolly?

Annie   No.

Maud   I can't keep a hoult on her at all these days.

Annie   She'll be down the town, as usual.

Maud   How can she go shopping in times like these?

Annie   What's civil unrest to Dolly and her shopping?

Maud (*feeling the back of her head*)   Oh, dear.

Annie   What is it, Maud?

Maud   Nothing, nothing at all.

Annie   Maud, what is it now?

Maud   I have an ache here, Annie, at the base of the skull, do you think it might be something deadly?

Annie   I never knew a one to worry like you do, girl.

Maud   Do you want to feel it? Is there a lump?

Annie   Don't come near me with your head! It's nothing. It's called a headache. Any normal person would accept that it's a headache. Girl, sometimes I don't wonder if you mightn't be seriously astray in your wits, girl.

Maud   Oh, don't say that, Annie.

Annie   Am I not allowed sort the darning in peace?

Dolly *comes in to them, wearing a neat outfit. She looks subdued.*

Annie   What's happened you, Dolly?

Maud   I was all over the yards looking for you, Dolly, where on earth do you get to, these days?

Dolly   I was down at the North Wall with the Galligan sisters.

Maud   At the North Wall?

Annie   What were you doing there, Dolly?

Dolly   Mary Galligan was going out with one of the Tommies, and he and his troop were heading off home today, so we went down to see them off.

Annie (*sorting away*)   Well, well, I don't know, Dolly, if you aren't the biggest fool in Christendom.

Dolly   No, I'm no fool. They were nice lads. There was a good crowd down there, and the Tommies were in high spirits, singing and so on. It was very joyful.

Maud   You've to keep your skirts long these times, Dolly. You're not to be seen waving to soldiers.

Dolly   They're going from Ireland and they'll never be back, why shouldn't we say goodbye? Do you know every barracks in Ireland has lost its officers and men? Regiments that protected us in the war, who went out and left thousands behind in France. Willie's own regiment is to be disbanded, and that's almost entirely Dublin lads.

Annie   Dolly, why are you so surprised? Haven't we known for the last six months that Ireland is to be destroyed? I don't know why it's such news to you. Haven't you listened? Haven't you seen your father's face? Haven't you felt for him, Dolly?

Dolly   It's different when you see it.

Annie   You're a fool, Dolly.

Dolly   I'm no fool.

Annie *picks up in one hand the good socks and in the other the ones needing mending – they look like two woolly hands themselves.*

Dolly   And I'll tell you. Coming home in the tram, up the docks road, Mary Galligan was crying, and we were talking kindly to her, and trying to comfort her, and I don't know what we said exactly, but this woman, a middle-aged woman, quite well-to-do, she rises up and stands beside us like a long streak of misery, staring at us. And she struck Mary Galligan on the cheek, so as she left the marks of her hand there. And she would have attacked me too, but that the conductor came down and spoke to the woman. And she said we were Jezebels and should have our heads shaved and be whipped, for following the Tommies. And the conductor looked at her, and hadn't he served in France himself, as one of the Volunteers, oh, it was painful, the way she looked back at him, as if he were a viper, or a traitor. The depth of foolishness in her. A man that had risked himself, like Willie, but that had reached home at last.

Dolly *crying.* **Annie** *gets up and puts her arms around her, still holding the socks.*

Annie   Things will sort themselves out, Dolly dear.

Dolly   If she had shot us it wouldn't have been so bad.

Annie   Things will sort themselves out.

Maud *feeling the back of her head again, confused.*

Annie   We'll put on our aprons and get the tea. We'll go on ourselves as if we were living in paradise.

The three go out.

Thomas   Their father's face. Their father's face.

He puts his hands over his face. **Matt**, *a youngish man in a hat, his shirt sleeves held by metal circlets, sets up his easel centrestage. Sunlight gathers about him, clearing the sense of* **Thomas**'s *room. Rooks. A suggestion of meadow grass.* **Matt** *holds a square of cut-out cardboard to the view, deciding on a composition. He wipes at his face.*

Matt   Midges! The artist's bane!

Thomas *approaches him, a little wildly.*

Thomas   Patrick O'Brien, Patrick O'Brien, wherever did you bury my suit, man dear? They are tormenting me with dark cloth, and I hope you will give it back to me, despite your great prowess and fame, as a bulleter.

Matt   It isn't who you think, Thomas. It is Matt Kirwin that married your daughter Maud.

Thomas (*astonished*)   Oh – is it? (*After a moment.*) You have a strong look of Patrick about you. Except I see now, you are not on all fours, as I would expect. Are you a hero too?

Matt (*kindly*)   How are you getting on, Thomas?

Thomas   How does it come that you are here in the walking meadow? I only ask, as I am used to seeing people hither and thither and yon. (*Feeling his arms for solidity.*) Have you lost your wits also?

Matt   Maybe so, but I have brought Annie over in the Ford. We're over there in Kiltegan for a week or two with the little boys. I thought I might capture a water-colour while I waited.

Thomas   You might, like a man might capture a butterfly. You haven't started your capturing.

Matt   In a minute, when I decide the view I want. The painting itself will only take a moment.

Thomas   They're all choice views. Where's Maud then?

Matt   She stayed in Dublin this time.

Thomas   It isn't the melancholy?

Matt   I don't know what it is. She has certainly kept to her bed of recent months. Has she been right since the second boy came? I don't know.

Thomas   Her mother was always very jolly. I don't know where she gets it from.

Matt   The sea air of Howth will cure all that, in time, the sea air, the quieter nature of life there in Howth, and the boys. She does love to see the boys, and they are most dignified and splendid boys.

Thomas   You say? (*Warmly.*) Well, Matt, (*Taking* **Matt**'s *hand.*) how are you? (*Oddly.*) How do you do?

Matt   We're going along fine. I'm teaching in the technical school in Irishtown – for my sins. And painting for myself when I can. I have done a great deal of work on the Great South Wall, in my lunchtimes. The Poolbeg Lighthouse? But we couldn't get by at all without Annie. She keeps everything going.

Thomas   Yes, yes, she told me you had one of your drawings printed up in a book, didn't you, yes, of the Bailey Lighthouse I think she said. You will be a great expert soon on lighthouses.

Matt (*pleased*)   It was little enough.

Thomas   Ah, Matthew, it is good to see you. You're
looking so well. I forget, you know, I forget how much I like
you. And the boys, the two grand boys, will I see them
today? Are they in the Ford?

Matt   No, Thomas. They're so little still, and this is such
a strange spot, for children, and, you know, they were a bit
upset the last time. The elder boy has read his *Oliver Twist*
and you were all mixed up in his mind with Fagin. Do you
remember, at the end of the book, when the child is brought
in to see Fagin before Fagin is hanged?

Thomas   Hanged? No.

Matt   Maud was worried that . . .

Thomas   Certainly, certainly. You must excuse my long
johns. I lost my suit only recently. As a matter of fact, it
must be buried around here somewhere. Well, no matter,
they'll make me another, and then maybe you will bring my
grandsons again to see me? Or you could fetch me over to
Kiltegan in the Ford if they were afraid of this place. I'd be
very quiet for you in the Ford.

Matt   Of course, Thomas.

Thomas   I know I look a sight. And that won't do for
such fine boys. I only saw them those few times, but, I think,
it is the smell of children that gets in upon you. You long for
it then. And the roundness of them, and the love they show
you. It could be anywhere about here, my suit. But I'm
having a touch of gold put into the new one – well, yellow,
anyhow.

Matt   You'll find Annie in your room if you go up, I'll be
bound. She thought you were inside, you know.

Thomas   Yellow thread, you know?

Matt   All right.

Thomas   Matt, I don't like to ask Annie, to bother her,
but do you think there's any great likelihood of my getting
away from here at all in the coming times?

Matt   I don't know rightly, Thomas.

Thomas   Of course, of course. It is quite a pleasant station. You see all the country air we have. Not like the city. The city would ruin a man's health. Though it has its beauties. Do you know, I used at one time to be a policeman? Do you know I used at one time be Chief Superintendent of B Division? With responsibility for the Castle herself? It was I cleared all the vermin out of Yorke Street, that time, the fancy men from the Curragh and all their girls – it *was* me, wasn't it, Matt? I held that post? You must bring the boys to Kiltegan as often as you can.

Matt   Well, we do, Thomas. You have a fine vista here, look. (*Having him look into the cardboard framer.*) You do, what with those oaks, and the field of wheat beyond.

Thomas (*peering, after a moment*)   It's only grass just.

Matt   Oh, is it grass?

Thomas   Paint away, Matthew.

Matt   Thank you.

The light of **Thomas***'s room again finds* **Annie***, more spinsterish now, strong, bony, simply dressed, with her handbag and a brown paper bag. She looks anxious.* **Thomas** *goes to her with a great smile, raising his arms.*

Thomas (*searching in his mind for her name*)   Dolly – Maud – Annie!

Annie   Papa.

Thomas (*his arms collapsing slowly*)   What has happened to you, Annie? You look very different to how you were just this morning.

Annie   What happened to your clothes, Papa?

Thomas   I don't know, Dolly.

Annie   Annie, it is.

Thomas   Annie. I don't know. I think I heard there was a bit of thievery going on, but I don't think there's any truth in it. Nothing for the magistrate. I'll deal with it. You know Mr Collins is to take over the Castle in January. I'll need all my clothes done over like new.

Annie   No, Papa. That was all years ago. In bygone times. You are in Baltinglass County Home, Papa.

Thomas   I know. And I tell myself, so I won't forget. I had it written down somewhere, but I lost the bit of paper. What is it about the old head? Give me the name of any street in Dublin and I'll name every lane, alleyway, road, terrace and street around it. I could knit you the whole thing with names, and if you forgot a few places, and found a hole there in your memory, I could darn it for you. I am in effect a sort of Dublin street directory. But when it comes to the brass tacks of things, everyday matters, as, for instance, where in the name of God I am, well, daughter dear, I'm not so quick then. But look, girl, what Annie gave me. (*Going to his mattress and fetching a book out.*) A wonderful strange story about a boy on the Mississippi. And his friend. They are lost in a cave together, the two boys, and the poor bit of a greasy candle they have is burning lower and lower, and the demons of the dark are surely approaching . . . I feel I know that cave. Do you see, Dolly? I can see it when I put my hands over my face. Like this. Yes, there she is, the mighty Mississippi, going along like Godly pewter. And those poor boys, Huckleberry and Tom, and the yellow walls of the cave, and the big drips of water. Oh, Dolly, and the old granite bathing place at Vico Rock. And there's the terrible suck-up of water when Davy Barnes the newspaper vendor takes his dive, the fattest man in Ireland, and there's Annie, all decked out in her first communion regalia like a princess, oh, mercy, and there's the moon over a bay that reputable people have compared to Naples – Sorrento, Vico, beautiful Italian names living the life of Reilly in old Killiney and Dalkey. On a summer's night, you were born, Dolly, deep in the fresh dark, just when the need for candles failed. Oh, Dolly.

Annie (*trying to calm him*)   I gave you the book about the Mississippi, Papa. It's a book you loved in your youth, so you always said.

Thomas (*gripping her arm a bit roughly*)   Where is Maud, where is she, that she doesn't come in to me?

Annie   She's taken refuge, taken refuge you might say, in her own difficulties.

Thomas   Is that right? And Dolly, where is Dolly?

Annie   Gone out into the wide world, Papa. Would you blame her?

Thomas   Blame her? (*Formal again.*) How do you do? How is Maud? How are the boys? No, no, I know all that. Don't tell me. I won't waste your time, never you fear. How are you? That's the important thing to establish. That's how people go on among themselves, family people. Is there any word from Dolly in America? Annie, Annie, where is she in America?

Annie   Ohio, Papa?

Thomas   Ohio, Ohio! That's the place. Ah, I was tormented trying to think of the word. Ohio. Dolly in Ohio. I must write it down. Do you have a dragonfly – a pencil?

Annie   No, Papa, I don't. This room is so bare and dark, for all the shillings I give them. I hope they give you your paper. It's all I can manage, Papa, out of your pension. It is a very miserly pension. Matt makes up the rest of it for us. And he has a pittance.

Thomas   Don't I have a beautiful pension for my forty-five years of service?

Annie   No, Papa, you don't.

Thomas   I think I should have.

Annie   Look, Papa, what I brought for you. (*She pulls a bunch of heather from the bag.*)

Thomas   Oh, Lord, Lord. (*Smelling it in his hands tenderly.*) From the hills above Kiltegan. How the heat of the day makes the heather raise its smell to the grateful native. The peace, the deep peace in the evening as we stared, you and me, into the last lingering flames running across the ashen turf, and the ghostly tiredness in us after slaving about the place all day.

Annie   When was that, Papa?

Thomas   Those three years in Kiltegan, Annie, when you and me were left to amuse ourselves as we could, Annie. You remember?

Annie   I do, Papa, I remember the three years well enough. With you sinking lower and lower in your chair beside that fire, and muttering about this and that, and the way you had been abandoned, you wouldn't treat a dog like that, you said, muttering, muttering, till I was driven mad. And all the work of the dairy and the byre and the hens to do. It was like living with Hannibal in Abyssinia, when Hannibal was a leader no more.

Thomas   Who? Where? But didn't the Cullens of Lathaleer come visiting like royalty in their high trap, and the Dunnes of Feddin, and the Cullens of Kelsha?

Annie   No, Papa, they did not, not after you drove them away with insult and passing remarks.

Thomas   I never did. We lived there like, like . . .

Annie   Like, like the dead, Papa.

Thomas (*angry*)   All right. So there were demons in the high wood, and the screams of the lost from the byres, and the foul eggs in the rotting hay, and every pitchfork in the barn was sharp, glinting sharp, for you to thrust into my breast.

Annie   Papa, Papa, calm and ease, calm and ease.

Thomas   Oh, fearsome, fearsome, fearsome. Can I see my grandsons?

Annie (*holding on to her father*)   Papa, Papa. Your grandsons are afraid of you.

Thomas   Afraid? Filthy, filthy.

Annie   Papa, Papa. How many miles to Babylon?

Thomas (*smiling*)   Babylon.

Annie   Three score and ten. Remember, Papa, remember?

Thomas   Will I be there by candlelight?

Annie   Sure, and back again.

Thomas   Candlelight. Oh, yes, yes. (*Weeping.*) Yes. (*Smiling.*) Yes.

Annie   How many times in that last year in Kiltegan did I have to sing you the songs to calm your fears?

Thomas   Was it so many?

Annie   Many, many, many. Three score and ten, Papa.

Thomas (*after a long breath*)   My father was the steward of Humewood, and I was the steward of Christendom. Look at me.

Annie   Papa, we've all to grow old.

Thomas (*patting her back with his right hand, like a child*)   Oh, yes. Oh, yes.

Annie *goes quietly.* **Thomas** *sits on the stool slowly. The door ajar.*

Thomas   Candlelight. (*After a little.*) A bit of starch for a new shirt, a bit of spit for my shoes, I could set out for Kiltegan as an ordinary man and see those shining boys. (*After a little.*) No. (*After a little.*) And take them up and smell their hair and kiss their noses and make them do that laughter they have in them. (*After a little.*) No. (*After a little.*) Dear Lord, put the recruits back in their barracks in Fitzgibbon Street, put the stout hearts back into Christendom's Castle, and troop the colours once more for princess and prince, for queen and for king, for Chief

Secretary and Lord Lieutenant, for Viceroy and Commander-in-Chief. (*After a little.*) But you cannot. (*After a little.*) Put the song back in the mouth of the beggar, the tune back in the pennywhistle, the rat-tat-tat of the tattoo back in the parade ground, stirring up our hearts. (*After a little.*) But you cannot. (*After a little.*) – Gone. The hearth of Kiltegan. How many miles to Kiltegan, Nineveh and Babylon? The sun amiable in the yard and the moon in the oaks after darkness. The rabbitman stepping out of the woods at dusk with a stick of dangling snags and a dark greeting. – Gone. (*After a little, quietly.*) Candlelight. I walked out through the grounds of Loreto College as far as the sea. The midwife had bade me go. I was a man of fifty. Rhododendrons. All night she had strained in the bed, she was like a person pinned by a fallen rock, waving her arms and legs and groaning, and shouting. Her shouts escaped from Polly Villa and ran up the road to the station and down the road to the village in darkness. I was becoming distressed myself, so the midwife bade me go. Willie, Maud and Annie had been difficult for her too, because she was small, small and thin and hard-working. Cullen's daughter. And she was like a sort of dancer in the bed, but stuck in the dance. King Edward himself praised her hair, it was mole-black, though there are no moles in Ireland. Out at sea, the lighthouse was hard at work too, warning the mail-packet and the night fishermen. I thought of all the nuns asleep up in the college, asleep in their quiet rooms, the sea asleep herself at the foot of the cliff. And I thought, I would do anything for that woman of mine behind me in the house, where we had done all our talking and laughing and our quarrelling. But my mind was in a peculiar state. I thought of all the Sunday roasts she had made, all piled up somewhere in eternity, a measure of her expertise. And I thought of how much her daughters and her son loved her, and depended on her for every sort of information, and how stupid and silent I was with my son. How she made the world possible and hopeful for him and the two girls. (*Sits on bed.*) I started to tremble, it was a moment in your life when daily things pass away from you, when all your concerns seem to vanish, and you are allowed

by God a little space of clarity and grace. When you see that
God himself is in your wife and in your children, and they
hold in trust for you your own measure of goodness. And
in the manner of your treatment of them lies your own
salvation. I went back to the house with a lighter heart, a
simpler man than the one who had set out. And the house
was quiet. It was as if it were itself asleep, the very bricks,
living and asleep with a quiet heartbeat. (*Holding the pillow.*)
Suddenly I was terribly afeared that my new child was dead,
I don't know why. You expect its cries, you long for its cries.
I pushed open my front door and hurried down into the
back room. The midwife was over by the window, with a
little bundle. And Cissy was lying quiet, still, at ease. The
midwife came over immediately and placed her bundle in
my arms. It was like holding a three-pound bag of loose
corn. (*The pillow.*) And there was a little face in the midst of
the linen, a little wrinkled face, with red skin, and two big
round eyes seeming to look up at me. I pledged all my heart
and life to that face, all my blood and strength to that face,
all the usefulness of my days to that face. And that was
Dolly. And that was just as the need for candlelight fails,
and the early riser needs no candle for his task.

Music. Dark after a few moments.

Act Two

Thomas's room as before, **Maud** *holding his sword in readiness.*
Annie *near.* **Dolly** *looking at* **Thomas** *with the polished shoes
just on. He wears his dress uniform, the helmet as yet on the table.*

Thomas   Oh, Dolly, Dolly, Dolly.

Dolly   Will they do, Papa?

Thomas   They're beautiful shoes now.

Dolly   This whole day reminds me of when I was twelve,
and there were snipers on the roofs above the music hall, and
me and Annie and Maud would be crawling along the
sandbags outside the gates, trying to get in home from the
shops. And laughing. And the soldiers at the gates laughing
too.

Annie   That poor lieutenant didn't laugh when they put
a bullet in his head.

Maud   And you were only ten then, Miss Dolly, and as
wild as a tenement cat.

Dolly   Will it be like that today?

Thomas   No, sweet, that's all done with now. This is an
act of peace.

Annie   My foot.

Thomas (*putting an arm about* **Dolly**)   Mr Collins and a
small staff will come in, and we'll all meet like gentlemen.

Annie   Ha.

Thomas   And he will take command of the place, in
effect. Don't you worry, Dolly, don't you worry.

Dolly   And what time is the meeting, Papa?

Thomas   Shortly. The Chief Secretary wanted to meet at
six but Collins sent in a note to say he wasn't a blackbird.

Annie   Blackguard more like.

Dolly   You are sure no one will try to shoot you?

Thomas   Why would they want to shoot me?

Annie   They would hardly have offered Papa a position in their new police force if they wanted to shoot him.

Dolly   Did they, Papa? Oh, and will you take up that offer, Papa? It would be exciting.

Thomas   We'll be Wicklow people again by year's end. Look at your father, Dolly. I am sixty-six years old! I am too old for new things. Indeed, I wish I were a younger man again, and I could kiss your noses, like when you were babies, and make you scream with delight.

Maud   Papa! Come along, Papa, and we'll get your sword on you.

Maud *and* **Annie** *attach the sword to its belt.*

Thomas   A man with three such daughters, three beautiful daughters, will never be entirely worthless. This January morning is the start of peace, and we may enjoy that peace till September, and then be gone – gone like shadows of an old dispensation.

Dolly   A girl of eighteen is never a shadow, Papa.

Thomas   Today is – what do you call it – symbolical.

Maud *doing the last buttons on the jacket.*

Thomas   Like those banners in the Chapel Royal for every Lord Lieutenant that has ruled Ireland. It's a mighty symbolical sort of a day, after all these dark years. I'll be worn out. I'll be practising now. (*Taking* **Dolly***'s hand.*) Good man, Joe, good man, Harry – that's the constables, because they're young too, Dolly, and will be greatly affected. Oh, big country hands, with rural grips! I'll have crushed fingers, like a visiting king.

Annie   And well, Papa, you are a king, more than some of those other scallywags.

Thomas   That is the whole crux of the matter. I am not a king. I am the servant of a king. I am only one of the stewards of his Irish city.

Annie   Collins is no king either, begging your pardon. With a tally of carnage, intrigue and disloyalty that would shame a tinker. And that king, for all his moustaches and skill on horseback, has betrayed us.

Maud   Annie, Annie, be quiet while Papa goes out. It isn't Papa's fault.

Thomas   I served that king, Annie, and that will suffice me. I hope I guarded his possession well, and helped the people through a terrible time. And now that story is over and I am over with it, and content. I don't grieve.

Maud   Of course you don't. Won't we have the great days soon in Kiltegan?

Thomas   But won't Dolly miss the fashions and the shops and the to-do of the town?

Annie (*before* **Dolly** *can answer*)   I'll miss nothing. If they want to destroy everything, let them do so without us. It will be whins and waste everywhere, with bits of stones sticking up that were once Parliament, Castle and Cathedral. And people going round like scarecrows and worse. And Cuckoo Lane and Red Cow Lane and all those places just gaps with rubbish in them.

Maud   Annie, you're giving me a powerful headache.

Annie   The like of Collins and his murdering men won't hold this place together. They haven't the grace or the style for it. So you needn't mourn your shops and hats and haircuts, Dolly Dunne – they won't be there.

Thomas   Will I tell Mr Collins you said so, Annie?

Maud   You'll miss the show if you don't go now, Papa. You don't want to be running over the square to them and sweating in your finery.

Thomas   Am I shipshape?

Maud   Shipshape as a ship.

Dolly   Wait, don't let the King go! (*Hurrying out for something.*)

Thomas   Where's she off to now?

Annie   Who can say where Dolly goes?

Maud   Poor Dolly – I do feel sorry for her.

Annie   Why for Dolly? Feel sorry for yourself, woman.

Dolly (*coming back with a buttonhole*)   I got this for you last night, Papa.

Annie   On that dangerous trek back from the dance at the Rotunda . . .

Dolly (*looking at* **Annie**)   Fresh up from the country.

Annie   I hope you can wear a buttonhole today? It seems frivolous.

Thomas   Put it in for me, Dolly. A white rose! Now I'm ready for them.

Dolly (*catching sight of the heather on the table*)   Oh, but, Papa, you'd flowers already – maybe you meant to wear a bit of this?

Annie   It isn't there at all yet. Just mere hints of flowers. That heather was born in the snow.

Maud (*smelling it*)   That heather was born in the snow, right enough, Annie.

Annie (*drawn to the heather, as are* **Thomas** *and* **Dolly**) It came up on the Wicklow train. Sometimes you find you need a hint of home.

Dolly   Born in the snow, like a lamb.

Thomas   That's from the hill beside the sloping field. I know that colour. (*Smelling, all of them smelling.*) It smells like God's breath, it does.

Maud   We won't mind going home to such riches.

Thomas   It is the very honeyed lord of a smell, so it is.

He goes out of the door happily. The daughters scatter. Then the noise of a ruckus in the corridor.

Smith (*off*)   Where are you wandering to? (*After a little.*) Where are you heading, old man?

Thomas (*off*)   What are you saying to me, constable? – Get back from me!

Smith (*off*)   Mrs O'Dea, Mrs O'Dea! Lie in there against the wall, you scarecrow, you. Mrs O'Dea! Come up, come up!

Mrs O'Dea (*off*)   Oh, I'm hurrying, I'm hurrying . . .

Mrs O'Dea *steps into the room.*

Thomas (*off*)   But I have to go and meet Collins!

Smith (*off*)   Collins is stone dead.

Thomas, *in his long johns again, propelled in by* **Smith**.

Thomas   Where are you putting me? This isn't our quarters!

Smith   Who was it left his door open? He might have gone raving up the main street of Baltinglass.

Mrs O'Dea   I don't know. It must have been his daughter.

Thomas   What have you done with my daughters? (*Pushing* **Smith**.) Get back from me, you blackguard. By Christ, assaulting a policeman. That's the joy for you, you scoundrel.

Smith (*drawing out the pacifier*)   Right, boy, I did warn you. Now you'll get it. (*Raising the implement.*) Mrs O'Dea, fetch the jacket off the hook in the corridor.

Mrs O'Dea *goes out.*

Smith   You'll see the suit she has for you now, Thomas Dunne.

Thomas   You'll see the suit, Tomassy Tom. You'll see the suit.

He escapes from **Smith***, leaps the bed like a youth.*

Smith   Jesus of Nazareth.

Smith *goes after him,* **Thomas** *ducks around to the stool,* **Mrs O'Dea** *brings in the straitjacket.*

Thomas   Nicks, nicks.

Smith   He's claiming nicks off the three-legged stool.

He strides to **Thomas** *and strikes him with the pacifier, expertly enough.*

Smith   Why couldn't I go with my brother flensing whales?

Thomas (*wriggling*)   You think I haven't had worse? See this thumb? See the purple scar there? My own Da Da did that, with a sheath knife. What do you think of that?

Smith *struggles to place the jacket on him.*

Thomas   Do you want to see my back? I've a mark there was done with a cooper's band, and on a Sunday too. But he loved me.

Mrs O'Dea   Lie up on your bed, Mr Dunne. (*To* **Smith**.) He'll be worn out in a minute. I have your suit ready, Mr Dunne, will I bring it up to you? He'll be good now, Mr Smith.

Thomas (*lying on the bed awkwardly, bound*)   Give it to Patrick O'Brien that excelled mightily at the bulleting. He'll eat it piecemeal like a dog.

Mrs O'Dea *and* **Smith** *go out, and lock the door.*

Thomas   We're all here, the gang of us, all the heroes of my youth, in these rooms, crying and imagining, or strung out like poor paste pearls of people along the rows of the graveyard. Lizzie Moran and Dorothy Cullen I saw there, two beauties of Lathaleer, and Hannigan that killed his mother, under a whinbush. And the five daughters of Joseph Quinn, the five of them, much to my amazement, side by side in five short graves. All of them lost their wits and died, Black Jim. If I could lead those poor souls back across the meadows and the white lanes to the hearths and niches of their youth, and fill the farms with them again, with their hopes and dreams, by God . . . I am a tired old man and I'll have terrible aches forthwith. Let him hit. What else has he, but hitting? Does he know why the calf is stupid? No. There he is in his ignorance, hitting. Let him hit. (*After a little.*) My two bonny grandsons would cure me. (*After a little.*) It's a cold wind that blows without forgiveness, as the song says.

There's a sort of darkness in the room now, with a seep of lights. **Willie** *stands in the corner, quietly, singing softly.*

Thomas   My poor son . . . When I was a small child, smaller than yourself, my Ma Ma brought me home a red fire engine from Baltinglass. It was wrapped in the newspaper and hid in the hayshed for the Christmas. But I knew every nook and cranny of the hayshed, and I soon had it found, and the paper of it. And quite shortly I had invented a grand game, where I stood one foot on the engine and propelled myself across the yard. I kept falling and falling, tearing and scumming my clothes, but no matter, the game was a splendid game. And my mother she came out for something, maybe to fling the grains at the hens in that evening time, and she saw me skating on the engine and she looked at me. She looked with a terrible long face, and I looked down and there was the lovely engine all scratched and bent, and the wheel half-rubbed off it. So she took the toy quietly from under my foot, and marched over to the dunghill and shoved it in deep with her bare hands, tearing at the rubbish there and the layers of dung. So I sought out her favourite laying hen and put a yard-bucket over it, and it wasn't found for a week, by which time the Christmas was over and the poor hen's wits had gone astray from hunger and darkness and inertia. Nor did it ever lay eggs again that quickened with chicks. And that was a black time between my Ma Ma and me. (*After a little.*) You were six when your

Mam died, Willie. Hardly enough time to be at war with her, the way a son might. She was very attached to you. Her son. She had a special way of talking about you, a special music in her voice. And she was proud of your singing, and knew you could make a go of it, in the halls, if you wished. I wanted to kill her when she said that. But at six you sang like a linnet, true enough. (*After a little.*) I didn't do as well as she did, with you. I was sorry you never reached six feet. I was a fool. What big loud talking fools are fathers sometimes. Why do we not love our sons simply and be done with it? She did. I would kill, or I would do a great thing, just to see you once more, in the flesh. All I got back was your uniform, with the mud only half-washed out of it. Why do they send the uniforms to the fathers and the mothers? I put it over my head and cried for a night, like an owl in a tree. I cried for a night with your uniform over my head, and no one saw me.

Mrs O'Dea *unlocks the door and comes in with the new suit, a rough black suit that she has joined with her yellow thread. She brings it to his bedside, dispelling* **Willie**.

Mrs O'Dea   Look at the lovely thread I used in it, just like you asked. Do you think you are quiet now?

Thomas   Yes.

Mrs O'Dea *starts to untie him,* **Smith** *comes in with a bowl of food, puts it on the table.*

Mrs O'Dea (*to* **Smith**)   Help me get him into bed. He'll lie quiet. (*To* **Thomas**.) Take off the long johns too, I'll wash them for you.

Smith *pulls down the top. The two wounds from the beating are revealed on* **Thomas***'s chest.*

Mrs O'Dea   We should put something on those weals.

Smith   He's only scratched. Let the sleep heal him. He'll spring up in the morning, gabbling as always, crazy as ever. God knows I can't deal with him now, I have a fancy dress to go to in the town.

Mrs O'Dea   Well, I can't wash a man, Mr Smith.

Smith   He doesn't need washing. He's barely marked.

Mrs O'Dea   Won't you at least wash his hands, they're all black from the floor. And I suppose his feet are as bad.

Smith   He may be St Thomas, Mrs O'Dea, but I'm not Jesus Christ, to be washing his hands and feet.

Mrs O'Dea   What is he talking about, Mr Dunne?

Smith   I have to collect my costume at six, Mrs O'Dea, off the Dublin train.

Mrs O'Dea   Tuck yourself up, Mr Dunne, and have a rest.

They go out. **Annie** *and* **Dolly** *come on in mid-conversation.*

Dolly   Where is my husband to come from, if we're to go back to Wicklow? I'm not marrying a farmer.

Annie   Oh, are you not, Dolly? Isn't it pleasant to pick and choose? What farmer would take a woman like me, and I might have had a sailor once for a husband if I'd been let. So you're not the only one with difficulties, though you always think you are. That's the way of the pretty.

Dolly   You couldn't go marrying a sailor, Annie. You never see a sailor. They're always away – sailing.

Annie   And our father humiliated by renegades. Collins!

Dolly   They didn't humiliate him, Annie, indeed, not at all. I'm sure it was all very polite. I think the truth is, Papa is delighted to be going back to Kiltegan, where he can have us all about him, slaving for him, and being his good girls, and never never marrying.

Annie   Dolly, that's poor wickedness.

Dolly   I know.

Annie   He's desolated to be going back.

Dolly   I don't believe he is. Or he'd have taken the new post in the whatever you call them. The Civic Guard.

Annie   You don't think they were offering him Chief Superintendent?

Dolly   So. Let him be a superintendent again, and stay in Dublin, where a person can buy a decent hat. There's nothing in Baltinglass but soda bread and eggs.

Annie   There's your father struggling to put a brave face on this day, which is no doubt the death of all good things for this country, and you're worrying about hats.

Dolly   Hats are more dependable than countries.

Annie   You're a nonsensical girl, Dolly. Why don't you go away somewhere with yourself, if you don't want to go back to Wicklow?

Dolly   I might!

Annie   You will not!

Dolly   Aren't you just after telling me to?

Annie   Dolly, don't dream of going and leaving me alone in Wicklow!

Dolly   For you to be giving out to me, like I was a little girl, and telling me I mustn't think of hats?

Annie (*seriously*)   Dolly, Dolly, you wouldn't go?

Dolly   Why not?

Annie (*almost shaking her*)   Dolly, I'm serious, say you wouldn't. (*After a little.*) Say you wouldn't.

Dolly   All right, all right, I wouldn't! I wouldn't. I wouldn't, Annie, dear.

Annie *nods at her fiercely. They go off.*

Thomas (*from the bed*)   I could scarce get over the sight of him. He was a black-haired handsome man, but with the

big face and body of a boxer. He would have made a
tremendous policeman in other days. He looked to me like
Jack Dempsey, one of those prize-fighting men we admired.
I would have been proud to have him as my son. When he
walked he was sort of dancing, light on his pins, like a good
bulleter. Like Patrick O'Brien himself. He looked like he
might give Patrick O'Brien a good challenge for his money
on some evening road somewhere, hoisting that ball of
granite. He had glamour about him, like a man that goes
about with the fit-ups, or one of those picture stars that
came on the big ship from New York, to visit us, and there'd
be crowds in the streets like for royalty, and it would be a
fierce job to keep them held back. Big American men and
women, twice the size of any Irish person. And some of
them Irish too, but fed those many years on beef and wild
turkeys. He was like that, Mr Collins. I felt rough near him,
that cold morning, rough, secretly. There never was enough
gold in that uniform, never. I thought too as I looked at
him of my father, as if Collins could have been my son and
could have been my father. I had risen as high as a Catholic
could go, and there wasn't enough braid, in the upshot.
I remembered my father's anger when I failed at my schooling,
and how he said he'd put me into the police, with the other
fools of Ireland. I knew that by then most of the men in
my division were for Collins, that they would have followed
him wherever he wished, if he had called them. And for an
instant, as the Castle was signed over to him, I felt a shadow
of that loyalty pass across my heart. But I closed my heart
instantly against it. We were to have peace. On behalf of
the Crown the Chief Secretary wished him well. And indeed
it was peaceful, that moment. The savagery and ruin that
soon followed broke my heart again and again and again.
My streets and squares became places for murder and fire.
All that spring and summer, as now and then some brave
boy spat at me in the streets, I could not hold back the tide of
ruin. It was a personal matter. We had restored order in the
days of Larkin. One morning I met a man in St Stephen's
Green. He was looking at a youngster thrown half-in under

a bush. No more than eighteen. The man himself was one of that army of ordinary, middle-class Irishmen with firm views and moustaches. He was apoplectic. We looked at each other. The birds were singing pleasantly, the early sun was up. 'My grandsons,' he said, 'will be feral in this garden – mark my words.'

Dolly, **Maud** *and* **Annie** *come on and move* **Thomas***'s table out a little and start to half-set it. There's a knock, and* **Matt** *appears.*

Annie   Who are you? What do you want?

Dolly   Who is that, Annie?

Annie   What do you want here?

Matt   My name's Matthew Kirwin, ma'am. I was asked to supper by Maud Dunne.

Annie   By Maud Dunne?

Maud (*coming over*)   Oh, hello, Mr Kirwin. How kind of you to come.

Annie   How kind of him to come?

Maud   Come in, Mr Kirwin, and meet my sisters. This is Dolly.

Dolly   How do you do?

Maud   And this is Annie.

Annie   Yes, this is Annie. And who is this, Maud?

Maud   My friend, Annie, Mr Matthew Kirwin.

Annie   Since when do you have friends, Maud, coming to supper?

Maud   I suppose I can have friends just as soon as Dolly? I suppose I can.

Annie   And have you known Mr Kirwin long, Maud?

Maud   We have an acquaintance. Mr Kirwin was painting in Stephen's Green last Saturday, and I happened to look over his shoulder at what he was doing, and as a matter of fact he was quite cross with me, weren't you, Mr Kirwin, for doing so, and we fell to talking then, and I explained my interest in the old masters . . .

Annie   Your interest in the old masters?

Maud   Yes, Annie. And we both agreed that the newer type of painters were all mad, and I invited him to supper.

Annie (*almost pushing him back*)   I'm sorry, Mr Kirwin, but you'll have to go.

Maud   Annie Dunne!

Annie   I don't know how you got past the gates, but there are to be no strangers coming in here. (*Pushing him elegantly.*)

Matt   If it isn't convenient . . .

Annie   It isn't even desirable, Mr Kirwin.

Maud   Annie, lay your hands off that man, he is my artist that I found in Stephen's Green.

Annie   And do you go out into the street, these times, Maud, and shake hands with everyone you see, and ask them to supper, if they are not doing anything better that night?

Maud   I do not, Annie Dunne.

Annie   What do you know about a man like this, with the leisure to be painting in daylight . . .

Matt   It was my day off, Miss Dunne . . .

Annie   And with a foreign accent . . .

Matt   I'm from Cork city . . .

Annie   And who may be the greatest rogue or the greatest saint that ever came out of – Cork city . . .

Maud   You are not my mother, Annie, in fact I am older and wiser than you . . .

Dolly   Let him stay till Papa comes, Annie, and if Papa says he is all right, we can have him to supper. It would be lovely to have friends to supper again. Let's, Annie.

Annie   And if he is an assassin?

Dolly   He's just a young man like any other young man.

Annie   So are assassins. No, it cannot be. (*Pushing him more vigorously.*) Out with you, Mr Kirwin.

Maud   Leave him be, oh, Annie, leave him be! (*She seems faint now, her legs buckling under her.*) Leave my artist be . . .

Dolly *tries to hold her up.*

Dolly   Help me, please.

Matt *holds her too.*

Annie   Let go of her, let go of her!

Maud *falls to the ground.*

Dolly   Oh, Annie, look what you've done now. Now we're the assassins, and Maud is killed.

The banging of a door below.

Annie   That's Papa. Papa always bangs the lower door for us, Mr Kirwin, because he has a house of girls. Now you'll get your supper!

Matt   I assure you, Miss Dunne . . .

Thomas *comes from the bed and stops by them. He doesn't speak.* **Maud** *opens her eyes, looks at him, gets up.* **Dolly** *goes and kisses her father.*

Dolly   What is it, Papa? You look so pale.

Maud   Do you have a chill, Papa?

Matt (*to* **Annie**)   I'll go, I'll go . . .

Annie (*not hearing him*)   Are you all right, Papa?

Thomas (*after a little*)   The city is full of death. (*After a little, crying.*) The city is full of death.

Annie (*hissing, to* **Maud**)   Look at the state Papa is in – it's no night for a visitor.

Thomas   How do you do, how do you do.

Maud (*to* **Matt**)   By the pillar, Saturday noon.

Matt *nods and goes.*

Thomas   Do I smell a stew, a real stew? Is that the aroma of lamb, bless me?

Annie   It is, Papa.

Thomas   Where did you get lamb, Annie?

Annie   The Dunnes of Feddin sent it up. It's Wicklow lamb.

Thomas   Wicklow. It is – Elysium. It is paradise . . . We'll be happy there, girls . . .

Annie   We will, Papa. We'll fetch the supper, Papa.

But they go out taking the things from the table with them. The door unlocks behind **Thomas**, *and* **Smith** *enters with a basin and a bottle of ointment. He is dressed like a cowboy complete with six-shooters.* **Thomas** *stares at him.*

Thomas   Black Jim!

Smith   Ah, never let it be said I left you alone with those cuts. Come here and sit, if you will.

Thomas *obediently goes to the stool.* **Smith** *puts down the bowl and begins to tend to* **Thomas**.

Smith   What's got into me? There's a lovely party going on in the town.

Thomas   I could be a man war-wounded.

Smith   You could. Or the outcome of a punch-up in a western saloon.

Thomas (*laughing*)   You think so?

Smith (*posing with the ointment*)   Do I not remind you of anyone in this get-up?

Thomas (*trying*)   No.

Smith   Maybe you never fancied the pictures, did you?

Thomas   I went the odd time to the magic lanthorn show.

Smith   You couldn't guess then who I am, besides being Mr Smith, I mean?

Thomas   Black Jim?

Smith   Gary Cooper, Gary Cooper. Ah, you're no use.

Thomas   Gary Cooper? Is that the Coopers of Rathdangan?

Smith (*putting on the ointment*)   *Lilac Time*. Did you never catch that? You haven't lived. Of course, it wasn't a cowboy as such. *Redemption* was a hell of a good cowboy.

Thomas   No man is beyond redemption, my Ma Ma said, when he let the dog live.

Smith   Who, Thomas? If men were beyond redemption, Thomas, what would we do in Ireland for presidents?

Thomas   That's a fair question. (*Laughing.*)

Smith (*doing a cowboy*)   You dirty dog, you dirty dog. (*After a little.*) Did you go to the war, Thomas?

Thomas   Me? No – I was too old. My son was with the Dublin Rifles.

Smith   Oh, I think I knew that. He was the boy that was killed.

Thomas   He was that boy.

Smith   I had a first cousin in it. A lot of men went out.

Thomas   Did he come home?

Smith   Not at all. They sent the uniform.

Thomas   That's right, they do. I've only a letter from him, that's all I have in the world of him.

Smith   Written from the battlefield?

Thomas   Oh, aye, from the trenches themselves.

Smith   I'd be very interested to see that letter.

Thomas   Would you, Mr Smith? Of course. I have it somewhere, stuck in Annie's book. Will I get it?

Smith   Do, get it, man, and we'll have a read of it. Why not?

Thomas (*fetching the letter*)   Do you not want to get to your fancy dress?

Smith   The party can wait. (*Taking the old letter.*) It looks old enough.

Thomas   Well, it's coming up to twenty year ago now.

Smith (*opening it carefully*)   It's an historical document.

Thomas (*laughing*)   Oh, aye. Historical.

Smith (*reading*)   He has a good hand at the writing, anyhow.

Thomas (*nudging his knee*)   Would you not . . .

Smith   Read it aloud? You want me to?

Thomas   I do. I would greatly like that.

Smith   Fair enough. Okay. (*Settling himself to read it, clearing his voice, a little self-conscious.*) Of course, I don't read aloud much, so . . .

Thomas *smiles.*

Smith   Right. – 'My dearest Papa, here I am writing to you in the midst of all these troubles. We are three weeks

now in the one spot and we all feel we are dug in here for an
eternity. The shells going over have become familiar to us,
and my friend the first lieutenant from Leitrim, Barney
Miles, has given our regular rats names. Our first idea was
to thump them with spades because they eat the corpses
up on the field but surely there has been enough death.
We have not got it as bad as some companies, because our
position is raised, and we get drainage, but all the same we
know what real mud is by now. We have had some miracles,
in that last week deep in the night one of our men was
thrown back over the rampart wounded, by what hands we
do not know. Another man was sent out with a dispatch and
on his way back found a big sow thrashing in the mud. He
would have taken her on with him for chops except she was
twice his weight and not keen. It made us remember that all
hereabout was once farms, houses and farms and grass
and stock, and surely the farmer in you would weep, Papa,
to see the changes. I hope you don't mind my letter going
on. It gives me great comfort to write to my father. You will
probably think I am raving a bit, and ranting, but nevertheless,
since I am so far distant, I tell myself you will be interested
to get news of me here. I wish I could tell you that I am a
hero, but truth to tell, there are few opportunities for valour,
in the way we all imagined when we set out. I have not seen
the enemy. Sometimes in the dark and still of the night
times I see lights over where their position is, and on the
stillest evenings you can just hear their voices. Sometimes
they sing! Sometimes we sing, low and quiet, we have quite
a repertoire now of risky songs, that you wouldn't approve
at all. But it is a grand thing that we can still use our voices,
and when I sing I think of home, and my sisters, and my
father, and hope and know that my mother is watching over
me here. God keep you all safe, because we have been told
of the ruckus at home, and some of the country men are
as much upset by that as they would be by their present
emergency. I know you are in the front line there, Papa, so
keep yourself safe for my return, when Maud will cook the
fatted calf! The plain truth is, Papa, this is a strange war and

a strange time, and my whole wish is to be home with you all in Dublin, and to abide by your wishes, whatever they be. I wish to be a more dutiful son because, Papa, in the mire of this wasteland, you stand before my eyes as the finest man I know, and in my dreams you comfort me, and keep my spirits lifted. Your son, Willie.'

Thomas (*after a little, while* **Smith** *folds the letter and gives it back to him*)   In my dreams you comfort me . . .

Smith   That's a beautiful letter, Mr Dunne. A memento. A keepsake.

Thomas *nods his head, thinking.*

Smith (*getting up to go*)   Good man, good man. (*Goes, locks the door.*)

Thomas *puts away his letter and climbs into bed. After a little,* **Dolly** *enters and goes to his bedside, with a big ticket in her hand.* **Thomas** *looks at her, takes the ticket, reads it, looks at her.*

Dolly   You aren't angry, Papa? It took all my courage to buy it, every ounce I had, you can't imagine. (*After a little.*) You are wondering how I could afford it? It was quite expensive, but it's only steerage. I had to sell Mam's bracelet that I was given, the ruby one you gave me, and I've to work for an agency the first two years, as a domestic, in Cleveland, Ohio.

Thomas (*after a little*)   Is it because she died on us? She was mortally sorry to die. She died as the need for candlelight failed. She would have adored you, even as she gave her life for you.

Dolly   Papa, don't be angry with me, please, I could not bear it, it took all my courage.

Thomas   Why would you go, Dolly, that is loved by us all, and young men going crazy over you here, and queuing up to marry you?

Dolly   They're not, Papa. I want to be liked and loved, but people are cold towards me, Papa.

Thomas   Why would they be, Dolly?

Dolly   Because – because of you, Papa, I suppose.

Thomas   It will pass, Dolly. In Wicklow we will be among our own people.

Dolly   I don't want to be like the Dunnes of Feddin, three wild women with unkept hair and slits on the backs of their hands from ploughing. You're old, Papa, it's not the same for you.

Thomas (*smiling, giving back the ticket*)   Yes, I am old.

Dolly   I didn't mean to say that, Papa. I knew you would be angry with me, I prayed you wouldn't be.

Thomas   Come here to me. (*He embraces her.*) How could I be angry with you? It's a poor look-out if I am angry with my own baby because she is afraid.

Dolly   I didn't want to hurt you, Papa.

Thomas   Papa is strong enough for all these things.

Dolly   You'll take care, Papa, and write to me, about all the goings on in Kiltegan?

Thomas   I will of course.

The lock turns in the door, **Dolly** *breaks from him, goes.*

Thomas   I will of course!

Mrs O'Dea *pops in and places a pair of black shoes by his bed.*

Mrs O'Dea   I'm just putting these here for you. I found you shoes at last, to go with the beautiful suit. I didn't mean to disturb you. You're the neatest sleeper I ever did meet, Mr Dunne. Never a ruffle in the sheets, just a long warm nest where your body lies.

Thomas   That's about the height of it.

Mrs O'Dea   Oh, you're a man for a bit of philosophy, I know.

Thomas   Whose shoes were they, Mrs O'Dea?

Mrs O'Dea   Let's see now. They were Patrick O'Brien's, Mr Dunne.

Thomas (*after a moment*)   You must take them for another man. I'd never fill them.

Mrs O'Dea   But what if your grandsons come to see you and you've nothing to put on your feet?

Thomas   There's no chance of that now.

Mrs O'Dea (*taking up the bowl of food*)   It's stone cold and you ate nothing. (*Going.*) Didn't I make you a beautiful suit?

She goes, locks the door. **Annie** *comes on with one of his big socks to darn, sits on the stool and works on the darning.* **Thomas** *dons* **Mrs O'Dea**'*s suit.*

Annie   Three days now, Papa.

Thomas   Three days, Annie. And we'll be set up in the old house again. We'll get that dairy going again first thing, a good scrub-down with the carbolic.

Annie   Yes.

Thomas   And I'll have our milking cow fetched over from Feddin, and the Dunnes of Feddin can hire someone else's fields, because we'll need them presently.

Annie   We will.

Thomas   And we'll be dog tired every night from the wealth of work, and be proud. And we have eight Rhode Island Reds and a crowing cock, that they are keeping for me in Lathaleer. And they're looking out for a pony, they say they know a fair-minded tinker will sell us something apt, and two hours at the most with a pot of polish will have those high lamps on the old trap gleaming. And we will cut a fine figure, you and I, Annie, Thomas Dunne and his daughter, throughout Kiltegan, Feddin and Kelsha.

Annie   We'll enjoy ourselves.

Thomas   And I'll lime the whole place. The house will be blinding white. We'll have red geraniums on the sills like the very dark conscience of summer or we're not Christians at all.

Annie   And Maud to visit, and we'll be peering at her, you know? (*Winking.*)

Thomas   And letters from Dolly, in the meantime, till she wishes to come home.

A knocking. The Recruit, now a **Constable***, comes on.* **Annie** *goes to him. The* **Constable** *whispers in her ear.* **Annie** *comes back to* **Thomas***.*

Annie   It's one of the constables, Papa. He wants a word with you privately.

Thomas *goes over to him. The* **Constable** *whispers to him.* **Thomas** *at length pats the man briefly on the arm. The* **Constable** *goes.* **Thomas** *returns slowly to* **Annie***.*

Annie   What, Papa?

Thomas   They have killed Collins in Cork.

Annie (*after a little*)   We'll be doubly glad to be going home now, and free of it all, Papa.

Thomas *can say nothing.*

Annie   Doubly glad.

A country music, and the wide ash-glow of a fire in the grate.

Thomas (*to himself*)   She died as many persons do, at the death of candlelight, as the birds begin to sing. She was a child again at the end, as if she was back again years ago in Lathaleer, and talking to her father, Cullen the coppicer. I stood by her bed, holding Dolly in my arms like a three-pound bag of loose corn, and Cissy spoke to me as if I were her own father. But our account was clear. (*Calling.*) Annie! When I went out that day to stop Larkin in Sackville Street, all the world of my youth, the world of Ireland that I knew, was still in place, loyal, united and true. I had three lovely daughters, and a little son as glad as a rose. And I had risen as high as Catholic could in the Dublin Metropolitan Police. And we were drawn up, ready to dispel them. (*Sits in near fire.*) Annie!

Annie Yes, Papa?

Thomas Bring my sword, would you?

Annie No, Papa, I'm not bringing your sword.

Thomas There's fellas roaming the countryside seeking out the maiming of this man and the death of that man, old scores must be settled, they're whispering and conspiring in the dark.

Annie There's nothing and no one out there, Papa.

Thomas But there is. I can smell them. Dark boys in black suits bought off the back of carts in county fairs, with old guns that might as soon blow off their own fingers when they fire. They won't get us. You must bring the sword.

Annie There's nothing but your own fears. Go in to your bed and pull the blankets over your face and get a sleep, Papa.

Thomas And lose my last daughter to ruffians and murderers?

Annie You have the respect of the district, Papa.

Thomas And what about that filthy mass of men that came up the yard last week and rattled our latch, and shouted in at me, while you were away at the well?

Annie It was only a crowd of tinkers, Papa, that thought you were a woman alone, and wanted to frighten you. They took two churns from the shed and a length of rope because you wouldn't go out to them.

Thomas I didn't dare breathe, I didn't dare breathe. I held fast to the fire.

Annie Papa, you know country life better than me, but you are not suited to it, I think.

A soughing in the maples outside.

Thomas   There's them breathing now. Fetch the sword!

The soughing. **Thomas** *bolts from the stool and gets the sword, comes back and stands in the middle of the room, holding it high.*

Come in now to us, and see what you'll get!

Annie   Papa, Papa, please. (*She tries to hold him and take the sword.*) If you'll be quiet, I'll make us another pot of tea and then we can go to our rest.

Thomas (*breaking from her*)   I must strike, I must strike.

He goes about hitting at whatever he can, table and stool and such.

Look at them running about like rats! Annie, there's rats come in, down the chimney! (*Striking the floor.*) Look at them, they're too quick for me!

Annie   There's no rats in my house! (*She covers her face with her hands.*) It's a clean house.

Thomas (*raving*)   What a to-do and a turmoil it is, with all their heroes lying in state about the city! They're bringing him up tonight to lie in state in the Pro-cathedral! Collins! We'll be doubly glad to be going home, now, she said! Because of you, Papa, I suppose, says Dolly. Says Dolly, says Dolly, says Dolly, says Dolly . . .

Annie   Papa! Stop it!

He does. He stands still where he is, the sword loose in his grip. He breathes heavily. He sinks to his knees, offers **Annie** *the sword.*

Thomas   Please, child . . .

Annie   What now?

Thomas   I am quiet now, Annie. I ask you a simple favour.

Annie   What favour, Papa?

Thomas   Take the sword, Annie, and raise it up like a slash-hook, and bring it down on top of me like I was brambles, with all your might.

Annie *looks at him. She goes to him and pulls the sword roughly from him. Maybe she considers using it for a moment. She goes, taking the sword with her.* **Thomas** *stares after her. He closes his eyes and cries like a child. The fire fades away, and the colder light of his room in the Baltinglass home returns.* **Willie** *comes, his uniform flecked with gold.*

Thomas (*head down*)   Da Da, Ma Ma, Ba Ba . . . (*After a little, seeing his son.*) Oh, Willie . . . (*Humorously.*) The great appear great because we are on our knees. Let us rise.

Willie *holds out a hand to help him get up.* **Thomas** *is surprised to find it solid enough when he takes it.*

Thomas   Oh, Willie . . .

Willie *brings him over to the bed and helps him get in.*

Thomas   It's all topsy-turvy, Willie. (*After a little.*) Sure, Willie, I think the last order I gave to the men was to be sure and salute Mr Collins's coffin as it went by . . . (*After a little.*) One time, Willie, and it was Christmas time too, and I was a young fellow in Kiltegan, our dog Shep went missing for some days, as dogs in winter will. I was maybe ten or eleven, and I loved that Shep, and feared he was gone for ever. We had got him as a young dog that had been beaten somewhere, and broken, till he reached our haven, and uncoiled, and learned to bark like a baby learns to laugh, and he shone at his work.

Willie *gets up on the bed beside his father.*

Thomas   One morning early after a fall of snow I went out to break the ice on the rain-barrel to plash my face, and I saw his tracks in the snow going up the sloping field, high to the fringes of the wood, and I was greatly afeared, because there were drops of blood now and then as he went, little smears of it on the cleanly snow. So I followed him up, sinking here and there in the drifts, well used to it, well used to it, and on a piece of field we called the upper garden, because it was flat there and you could see across to Baltinglass and some said even to Shillelagh and the dark woods of Coollattin, I found our dog there with the carcass

of a ewe well eaten, only the hindquarters remaining. I saw
my father's blue sign on the wool and knew the worst. For
a dog that would kill a sheep would die himself. So in my
innocence I went down to my father and told him and he
instructed me, as was right and proper, to go back up with
a rope and lead Shep down so the killing could take place.
The loss of a ewe was a disaster, a disaster, there'd be pounds
of money gone into her. But I loved the dog so sorely, I
hesitated when I had the rope tied about him, and at length
led him off further up the hill, across the little stand of
scrubby pines, and on into the low woods dark with snow
and moss. And we went through by a snaking path I knew,
till we got to the other side, where there was a simple man
living, that made his living from the rabbits, and maybe had
need of a watchful dog. But he wouldn't take a dog that had
killed, though he was a tender man enough, and it behoved
me to retrace my steps back into the woods, now moving
along but slowly, and the dog sort of dragging behind, as if
he knew well his misdeed and his fate. And I stopped in the
centre of the trees, and do you know my young legs would
not go forward, they would not proceed, try as I might, and
there I was all that afternoon and night with the dog and
the hazels. How is it that the drear of winter didn't eat my
bones and murder me for my foolishness? Love of the dog
kept me standing there, as only a child can stand, without
moving, thinking, the poor dog whimpering with the cold.
About five o'clock I went on, because I heard calling over
the hill, here and there, and I could see black figures with
lights moving and calling, calling out to me and the dog to
come home. We came down the sloping field with the
neighbours about us, them not saying a word, maybe
marvelling at me, thinking I had been dead, and the torches
and lamps making everything crazy with light, the old crab
apple enlarging to the size of the field, its branches wild like
arms. Down at last into the yard we came, the dog skulking
on the rope just the same as the day he had arrived to us,
and my father came out from the house in his big clothes.
All brown with clothes and hair. It was as if I had never seen

him before, never looked at him in his entirety, from head to toe. And I knew then that the dog and me were for slaughter. My feet carried me on to where he stood, immortal you would say in the door. And he put his right hand on the back of my head, and pulled me to him so that my cheek rested against the buckle of his belt. And he raised his own face to the brightening sky and praised someone, in a crushed voice, God maybe, for my safety, and stroked my hair. And the dog's crime was never spoken of, but that he lived till he died. And I would call that the mercy of fathers, when the love that lies in them deeply like the glittering face of a well is betrayed by an emergency, and the child sees at last that he is loved, loved and needed and not to be lived without, and greatly.

He sleeps. **Willie** *lies in close to him. Sleeps. Music. Dark.*

Martin McDonagh

The Cripple of Inishmaan

The Cripple of Inishmaan was first performed in the Cottesloe auditorium of the Royal National Theatre on 12 December 1996. The cast was as follows:

Kate	Anita Reeves
Eileen	Dearbhla Molloy
Johnnypateenmike	Ray McBride
Billy	Ruaidhri Conroy
Bartley	Owen Sharpe
Helen	Aisling O'Sullivan
Babbybobby	Gary Lydon
Doctor	John Rogan
Mammy	Doreen Hepburn

Directed by   Nicholas Hytner
Designed by   Bob Crowley
Lighting by   Mark Henderson
Music by   Paddy Cunneen
Sound by   Simon Baker

Characters

very "physical" description.

Sister — **Kate**, *mid-sixties*
Eileen, *mid-sixties*
Johnnypateenmike, *mid-sixties*

Billy, *seventeen or eighteen, crippled*
Bartley, *sixteen or seventeen*
Helen, *seventeen or eighteen, pretty*
Babbybobby, *early thirties, handsome, muscular*
Doctor, *early forties*
Mammy, *early nineties*

Setting

The island of Inishmaan, 1934.

Scene One

A small country shop on the island of Inishmaan, circa 1934. Door in right wall. Counter along back, behind which hang shelves of canned goods, <u>mostly peas.</u> An old dusty cloth sack hangs to the right of these, and to the left a doorway leads off to an unseen back room. A mirror hangs on the left wall and a table and chair are situated a few yards away from it. As the play begins, **Eileen Osbourne**, *late sixties, is placing some more cans onto the shelves. Her sister* **Kate** *enters from the back room.*

Kate Is Billy not yet home?

Eileen Not yet is Billy home.

Kate I do worry awful about Billy when he's late returning home.

Eileen I banged me arm on a can of peas worrying about Cripple Billy.

Kate Was it your <u>bad arm?</u>

Eileen No, it was me other arm.

Kate It would have been worse if you'd banged your bad arm.

Eileen It would have been worse, although it still hurt.

Kate Now you have two bad arms.

Eileen Well, I have one bad arm and one arm with a knock.

Kate The knock will go away.

Eileen The knock will go away.

Kate And you'll be left with the one bad arm.

Eileen The <u>one bad arm will never go away.</u>

Kate Until the day you die.

Eileen   I should think about poor Billy, who has not only bad arms but bad legs too.

Kate   Billy has a host of troubles.

Eileen   Billy has a hundred troubles.

Kate   What time was this his appointment with McSharry was and his chest? *repetitive & confusing...*

Eileen   I don't know what time.

Kate   I do worry awful about Billy when he's late in returning, d'you know?

Eileen   Already once you've said that sentence.
↳ somewhat of an oxymoron.

Kate   Am I not allowed to repeat me sentences so when I'm worried?

Eileen   You are allowed.

Kate (*pause*)   Billy may've fell down a hole with them feet of his.

Eileen   Billy has sense enough not to fall down holes, sure. That's more like something Bartley McCormick'd do is fall down holes.   *↳ who is this kid? stupid?*

Kate   Do you remember the time Bartley McCormick fell down the hole?   *↳ Kate a Eileen share memories, almost.*

Eileen   Bartley McCormick's an awful thick.

Kate   He's either a thick or he doesn't look where he's going proper. (*Pause.*) Has the egg-man been?

Eileen   He has but he had no eggs.

Kate   A waste of time him coming, so.   *waste of name too.*

Eileen   Well it was nice of him to come and not have us waiting for eggs that would never arrive.   *absence of goods is still a signification*

Kate   If only Billy would pay us the same courtesy. Not with eggs but to come home quick and not have us worrying.

Eileen   Maybe Billy stopped to look at a cow like the other time.

Kate   A fool waste of time that is, looking at cows.

[handwritten: this is also a pun. fool/full]

Eileen   If it makes him happy, sure, what harm? There are a hundred worse things to occupy a lad's time than cow-watching. Things would land him up in hell. Not just late for his tea.

Kate   Kissing lasses.

Eileen   Kissing lasses.

Kate (*pause*)   Ah, no chance of that with poor Billy.

Eileen   Poor Billy'll never be getting kissed. Unless it was be a blind girl.

[handwritten: something weird abt two old women discussing a boy's kissing prospects.]

Kate   A blind girl or a backward girl.

Eileen   Or Jim Finnegan's daughter.

Kate   She'd kiss anything.

Eileen   She'd kiss a bald donkey.

Kate   She'd kiss a bald donkey. And she'd still probably draw the line at Billy. Poor Billy.

Eileen   A shame too.

Kate   A shame too, because Billy does have a sweet face if you ignore the rest of him.

Eileen   Well, he doesn't really.

Kate   He has a bit of a sweet face.

Eileen   Well, he doesn't really, Kate.

Kate   Or his *eyes*, I'm saying. They're nice enough.

Eileen   Not being cruel to Billy but you'd see nicer eyes on a goat. If he had a nice personality you'd say all well and good, but all Billy has is he goes around staring at cows.

[handwritten: somehow Billy = goat, donkey, cow cows.]

Kate   I'd like to ask him one day what good he gets, staring at cows.

Eileen   Staring at cows and <u>reading books</u> then.

this is not a virtue.

Kate   No one'll ever marry him. We'll be stuck with him till the day we die.

Eileen   We will. (*Pause.*) I don't mind being stuck with him.

Kate   *I* don't mind being stuck with him. Billy's a good gosawer, despiting the cows.

Eileen   I hope that the news from McSharry was nothing to worry o'er.

us?

Kate   I hope he gets home soon and not have us worrying. I do worry awful when Billy's late in returning.

The shop door opens and **Johnnypateenmike**, *an old man of about the same age as them, enters.*

Eileen   Johnnypateen<u>mike</u>.

Kate   Johnnypateen.   *why the compound name?*

Johnny   How is all? Johnnypateenmike does have three pieces of news to be telling ye this day . . .

Kate   You didn't see Cripple Billy on your travels now, Johnnypateen?

Johnny (*pause, put out*)   You have interrupted me pieces of news now, Mrs Osbourne, and the third piece of news was a great piece of news, but if you want to interrupt me with <u>fool</u> questions so be it. Aye, I saw Cripple Billy on me travels. I saw him sitting on the hedgebank, the bottom of Darcy's fields.

Kate   What was he doing sitting on the hedgebank?

Johnny   Well what does he usually be doing? He was looking at a cow. Do ye have any more interruptions?

Kate (*sadly*)   We don't.

no event in their lives.

Johnny   I will get on with me three pieces of news so.
I will leave me best piece of news till the end so's you will
be waiting for it. Me first piece of news, a fella o'er in
Lettermore stole a book out of another fella's house and
pegged it in the sea then

Eileen   Sure that's no news at all, sure.   *same story, repetition.*

Johnny   I suppose it's not, now, only that the fella was the *change of*
other fella's brother and the book he pegged was the *Holy   two words.*
Bible! Eh?   *→ suddenly*
it's big news.

Kate   Lord save us!

Johnny   Now is that no news at all?!

Eileen   That *is* news, Johnnypateen, and big news.

Johnny   I know well it's big news, and if I have any more
doubting of how big me news is I'll be off on the road to
somewhere me news is more appreciated.   *he's like a traveling news-man.*
like the egg-man, travels
Eileen   Your news *is* appreciated, Johnnypateenmike.   *even when*
there's no
Kate   We never once doubted how big your news was,   *news.'*
Johnnypateen.

Johnny   Me second piece of news, Jack Ellery's goose bit
Pat Brennan's cat on the tail and hurt that tail and Jack
Ellery didn't even apologise for that goose's biting, and now
Patty Brennan doesn't like Jack Ellery at all and Patty and
Jack used to be great friends. Oh aye.

Eileen (*pause*)   Is that the end of that piece of news?

Johnny   That *is* the end of that piece of news.

Eileen   Oh that's an awful big piece of news that is. Oh
aye.   *→ just to keep Johnny from leaving.*

Eileen *rolls her eyes to the ceiling.*

Johnny   That *is* an awful big piece of news. That goose
might start a feud. I *hope* that goose does start a feud. I like
a feud.   *seeking news.*

340   The Cripple of Inishmaan

Kate   I hope Patty and Jack do put it behind them and make up. Didn't they used walk hand-in-hand to school as ladeens?

Johnny   *There's* a woman speaking if ever I heard one. What news is there in putting things behind ya? No news. You want a good feud, or at least a Bible pegged about, or a thing like me third piece of news, which is about the biggest piece of news Johnnypateenmike has ever had . . .

[handwritten annotation: peace-seeking. no good for news.]
[handwritten annotation: → Interruption]

Billy, *seventeen, one arm and one leg crippled, enters, shuffling.*

Billy   I'm sorry I'm late, Aunty Kate and Aunty Eileen.

[handwritten annotation: "half"?]

Johnny   You've interrupted me news-telling, Cripple Billy.

Kate   What did the doctor say to you, Billy?

Billy   He said there was nothing on me chest at all but a bit of a wheeze and nothing but a bit of a wheeze.

Johnny   I didn't hear the lad had a wheeze. Why wasn't Johnnypateen informed? *[handwritten annotation: → only valuable as news.]*

Kate   Why are you so late home so, Billy? We was worried.

Billy   Oh, I just had a sit-down for meself in the sun there at Darcy's fields.

Kate   A sit-down and did what?

Billy   A sit-down and did nothing.

Kate   Did nothing at all?

Billy   Did nothing at all.

Kate (*to* **Johnny**)   Now!   *[handwritten annotation: doing nothing is such a scandal / grief.]*

Billy   Nothing at all but look at a couple of cows came over to me.

Kate *turns away from him.*

Johnny (*to* **Kate**)   Now who's nowing?! Eh?!

Eileen   Can't you just leave cows alone, Billy?

Billy   I was just looking at them cows.

Johnny   Excuse me, but wan't I talking . . . ?

Kate   There's <u>nothing to see</u> in cows! You're a grown
man!   *objective entertainment is subjective.*

Billy   Well I *like* looking at a nice cow, and I won't let
anybody tell me the differ.
                  authoritative.
Johnny (*screaming*)   Well if ye don't want to hear me news
I'll take it and go! Talking about cows with a fecking eej!

Billy   A fecking eej, is it?

Eileen   Tell us your news, now, Johnnypateenmike.

Johnny   If ye've finished with the cow-talk I'll tell you me
news, although I'm sure I'd get a better audience for it from
fried winkles.

Kate   We're a good audience for it . . .

Eileen   We're a good audience for it . . .

Billy   Don't pander to him.

Johnny   Pander, is it, Cripple Billy?

Billy   And <u>don't call me Cripple Billy</u>, you.   *defined by his crippledness.*
                                              → *very sharp. sees thru*
Johnny   For why? Isn't your name Billy and aren't you a   *wordplay &*
cripple?   *basic desire for*
                                                      drama.

Billy   Well, do I go calling you 'Johnnypateenmike with
the news that's so boring it'd bore the head off a dead bee'?

Johnny   Boring, is it? How is this for boring news, so . . .

Billy   At least you do agree it's boring news anyways.
That's one thing.

Johnny (*pause*)   From Hollywood, California, in America
they're coming, led be a Yank be the name of Robert
Flaherty, one of the most famous and richest Yanks there is.
Coming there to Inishmore they're coming and why are
they coming? I'll tell you why they're coming. To go making
repetitive speech.
      holy shit this long.

a moving picture film will cost o'er a million dollars, will be shown throughout the world, will show life how it's lived on the islands, will make film stars of whosoever should be chose to take part in it and will take them back to Hollywood then and be giving them a life free of work, or anyways only acting work which couldn't be called work at all, it's only talking. Colman King I know already they've chosen for a role, and a hundred dollars a week he's on, and if Colman King can play a role in a film anybody can play a role in a film, for Colman King is as ugly as a brick of baked shite and everybody agrees, and excuse me language but I'm only being descriptive. A little exodus Johnnypateenmike foresees to the big island so, of any lasses or lads in these parts with the looks of a film star about them wants to make their mark in America. That rules out all in this household, I know, it goes without saying, unless of course it's cripples and ingrates they're looking for. Me in me younger days they'd've been sure to've took, what with me blue eyes and me fine head of hair, and probably still today they'd be after taking me, what with me fine oratory skills could outdo any beggar on the Dublin stage, only, as ye know, I have me drunkard mammy to look after. *The Man of Aran* they're going calling the film, and Ireland mustn't be such a bad place so if the Yanks want to come to Ireland to do their filming.

Billy *sits on the side table, deep in thought.*

Johnny   That was Johnnypateen's third piece of news, and I'll ask you now, bad-leg-boy, if that was a boring piece of news?

Billy   That wasn't nearly a boring piece of news. That was the biggest piece of news I did ever hear.

Johnny   Well, if we've agreed on the bigness of me news … 'Bigness' isn't a word, I know, but I can't be bothered to think of a better one for the likes of ye … I will take me payment in kind for that piece of news, and me payment today will be a small boxeen of eggs for I do fancy an omelette, I do.

Eileen Oh.

Billy What 'oh'?

Eileen The egg-man came and he had no eggs.

Johnny No eggs?! I've gave you me big piece of news on top of me two smaller but almost as good pieces of news and ye've no eggs?!

Eileen He said the hens weren't laying and Slippy Helen dropped the only eggs he had.

Johnny What do ye have for me tea so?

Eileen We've peas.

Johnny Peas! Sure peas won't go far for a grown man's tea. Give me that bit of bacon there, so. That one there.

Eileen Which one? The lean one?

Johnny The lean one, aye.

Eileen Jeez, your news wasn't *that* bloody big, Johnnypateen.

B ∂ ask the payment or hi3 news being respected.

Johnny *stares at them* <u>*hatefully,*</u> *then exits, fuming.*

Eileen That fella.

Kate We oughtn't be getting on his wrong side, now, Eileen. How else will we know what's going on in the outside world but for Johnny?

Eileen But isn't that the first decent bit of news that fella's had in twenty years?

Kate Aye, and we might miss out on the next bit, now.

Eileen Coming with his egg extortions every week.

Billy That was an <u>interesting</u> bit of news, aye. why suddenly interested?

Kate *(approaching him)* You're not usually at all interested in Johnnypat's biteens of news, Billy.

Billy   Not when they're about frogs falling over, no. When they're about films and getting away from Inishmaan I am, aye.

Kate   You're not thinking about your poor mammy and daddy again, are ya?

Billy   No, now. I'm just thinking about general things for meself, now.

Eileen   Is he off again?

Kate (*sighing*)   He is.

Eileen   Off thinking?

Kate   That lad'll never be told.

Eileen   The doctor didn't look at your head when he looked at your chest did he, Billy?

Billy (*blankly*)   No.

Eileen   I think that's the next thing to go checking out is his head.

Kate   I think that's the next item on the agenda, aye.

The shop door bangs open. **Johnny** *sticks his head in.*

Johnny (*angrily*)   If ye aren't chasing after me I'll take your bloody peas, so!

Eileen *hands* **Johnny** *a can of peas.* **Johnny** *slams the door on his exit,* **Billy** *not noticing him at all, the women bemused. Blackout.*

Scene Two

Bartley, *sixteen, at the counter, looking over the penny-sweets in the two rectangular boxes* **Eileen** *is tilting up for him.* **Billy** *is sitting on the chair, reading.*

Bartley (*pause*)   Do ya have any Mintios?

Eileen   We have only what you see, Bartley McCormick.

Bartley   In <u>America</u> they do have Mintios.

Eileen   Go to America so.

Bartley   Me Aunty Mary did send me seven Mintios in a package.

Eileen   Good on your Aunty Mary.

Bartley   From Boston, Massachusetts.

Eileen   From Boston, Massachusetts, uh-huh.

Bartley   But you have none?

Eileen   We have only what you see.

Bartley   You should get some Mintios really, because Mintios are nice sweeties. You should order some in. You should get somebody from America to go sending you some. In a package. Now I'll have to be taking another look for meself.

Eileen   Take another look for yourself, aye.

Bartley *looks over the boxes again.* **Billy** *smiles at* **Eileen***, who rolls her eyes to the ceiling and smiles back.*

Bartley (*pause*)   Do ya have any Yalla-mallows?

Eileen (*pause*)   We have only what you see.

Bartley   They do have Yalla-mallows <u>in America</u>.

Eileen   Oh aye. I suppose your Aunty Mary did send you some in a package.

Bartley   No. <u>She sent me a photograph of some in a package</u>. The only proper sweeties she sent me were the seven Mintios. (*Pause.*) Really it would've been better if she'd only sent me *four* Mintios, and then put in three Yalla-mallows with them, so then I could've had like a selection. Or three Mintios and four Yalla-mallows. Aye. But, ah, I was happy enough with the seven Mintios if truth be told. <u>Mintios are nice sweeties.</u> Although the photograph of the Yalla-mallows did raise me curiosity about them. (*Pause.*) <u>But you have none?</u>

Eileen   Yalla-mallows?

Bartley   Eye.

Eileen   No.

Bartley   Oh.

Eileen   We have only what you see.

Bartley   I'll have to be taking another look for meself so. I want something to go sucking on. For the trip, y'know?

Billy   For what trip, Bartley?

The shop door bangs open and **Helen**, *a pretty girl of about seventeen, enters, shouting at* **Bartley**.

Helen   Are you fecking coming, you, fecker?!   *pretty girl bad m*

Bartley   I'm picking me sweeties.

Helen   Oh you and your fecking sweeties!

Eileen   Lasses swearing, now!

Helen   Lasses swearing, aye, and why shouldn't lasses be swearing when it's an hour for their eejit fecking brother it is they're kept waiting. Hello, Cripple Billy.

Billy   Hello there, Helen.

Helen   Is it another oul book you're going reading?

Billy   It is.

Helen   You never stop, do ya?   *always thinking.*

Billy   I don't. Or, I do *sometimes* stop . . .

Eileen   I heard you did drop all the eggs on the egg-man the other day, Helen, broke the lot of them.

Helen   I didn't drop them eggs at all. I went pegging them at Father Barratt, got him bang in the gob with fecking four of them.   *oh? for what?*

Eileen   You went pegging them at Father Barratt?   *confirmation for everything*

Helen   I did. Are you repeating me now, Mrs?

Eileen   Sure, pegging eggs at a priest, isn't it pure against God?

Helen   Oh, maybe it is, but if God went touching me arse in choir practice I'd peg eggs at that fecker too.

Eileen   Father Barratt went touching your . . . behind in choir pr—

Helen   Not me behind, no. Me *arse*, Mrs. Me *arse*.

Eileen   I don't believe you at all, Helen McCormick.

Helen   And what the feck d'you think I care what you believe?

Billy   Helen, now . . .

Bartley   The worst part of the entire affair, it was a sheer waste of eggs, because I do like a nice egg, I do, oh aye.

Helen   Are you entering the egg debate or are you buying your fecking sweeties, you?

Bartley (*to* **Eileen**)   Do you have any Chocky-top Drops, Mrs?

Eileen (*pause*)   You know what me answer's going to be, don't you, Bartley?

Bartley   Your answer's going to be ye have only what I see.

Eileen   We're getting somewhere now.

Bartley   I'll take another look for meself, so.

Helen *sighs, idles over to* **Billy**, *takes his book from him, looks at its cover, grimaces and gives it back.*

Billy   Are ye going on a trip, did Bartley say?

Helen   We're sailing o'er to Inishmore to be in this film they're filming.

Bartley   Ireland mustn't be such a bad place, so, if the Yanks want to come here to do their filming. *same words as Johnny*

Helen   From the entire of the world they chose Ireland, sure.

Bartley   There's a French fella living in Rosmuck nowadays, d'you know?

Eileen   Is there?

Bartley   What's this, now, that the French fella does do, Helen? Wasn't it some funny thing?

Helen   Dentist. *thinks it's unnecessary?*

Bartley   Dentist. He goes around speaking French at people too, and everybody just laughs at him. Behind his back, like, y'know?   *vs foreigner remaining foreign.*

Helen   Ireland mustn't be such a bad place if French fellas want to live in Ireland.

Billy   When is it you're going, so, Helen, to the filming?

Helen   The morning-tide tomorrow we're going.

Bartley   I can't wait to go acting in the film.

Helen   You, are you picking or are you talking?

Bartley   I'm picking *and* talking.

Helen   You'll be picking, talking and having your bollocks kicked for ya if ya back-talk me again, ya feck.

Bartley   Oh aye.

Billy   Sure, why would you think they'd let you be in the filming at all, Helen?

Helen   Sure, look at as pretty as I am. If I'm pretty enough to get clergymen groping me arse, it won't be too hard to wrap film fellas round me fingers.

Bartley   Sure, getting clergymen groping your arse doesn't take much skill. It isn't being pretty they go for. It's more being on your own and small. *that's not quite wrong.*

Helen   If it's being on your own and small, why so has Cripple Billy never had his arse groped be priests?

Bartley   You don't know at all Cripple Billy's never had his arse groped be priests.

Helen   Have you ever had your arse groped be priests, Cripple Billy?

Billy   No.

Helen   *Now.*

Bartley   I suppose they have to draw the line somewhere.

Helen   And you, you're small and often on your own. Have you ever had your arse groped be priests?

Bartley (*quietly*)   Not me arse, no. *→ dang.*

Helen   D'ya see?

Bartley (*to* **Eileen**)   Do ya have any Fripple-Frapples, Mrs?

Eileen *stares at him, puts the boxes down on the counter and exits into the back room.*

Bartley   Where are you going, Mrs? What about me sweeties, Mrs?

Helen   You've done it now, haven't ya?

Bartley   Your oul aunty's a mad woman, Cripple Billy. *can't understand the world doesn't revolve his way. thrice.*

Helen   Mrs Osbourne isn't Cripple Billy's aunty at all, anyways. She's only his pretend aunty, same as the other one. Isn't that right, Billy?

Billy   It is.

350   The Cripple of Inishmaan

Helen   They only took him in when Billy's mam and dad went and <u>drowned</u> themselves, when they found out Billy was born a cripple-boy.   *so they're not away & alive...*

Billy   They didn't go and drowned themselves.

Helen   Oh aye, aye . . .

Billy   They only fell o'erboard in rough seas.

Helen   Uh-huh. What were they doing sailing in rough seas, so, and wasn't it at night-time too?

Billy   Trying to get to America be the mainland they were.

that's so cruel.

Helen   No, trying to <u>get away from you</u> they were, be distance or be death, it made no differ to them.

Billy   Well how the hell would you know when you were just a babby at the time, the same as me?

as if Johnny = truth.

Helen   I gave Johnnypateen a cheesy praitie one time and he told me. Wasn't it him was left there holding ya, down be the waterside?

Billy   Well, what did he know was in their heads that night? He wasn't in that boat.

Helen   Sure didn't they have a sackful of stones tied between themselves?

Billy   That's pure gossip that they had a sackful of stones tied between themselves, and even Johnnypateen agrees on that one . . .

Bartley   Maybe he had a telescope. *that's also not wrong.*

Helen (*pause*)   Maybe who had a telescope?

Bartley   Maybe Johnnypateenmike had a telescope.

Helen   What differ would having a telescope have?

Bartley *thinks, then shrugs.*   → *verifying truth. there is a too*
↳ he doesn't fully see.

Helen   You and your fecking telescopes. You're always throwing telescopes into the fecking conversation.

Bartley   They do have a great array of telescopes in America now, d'know? You can see a worm a mile away.

Helen   Why would you want to see a worm a mile away?

Bartley   To see what he was up to.

Helen   What do worms usually be up to?

Bartley   Wriggling.

Helen   Wriggling. And how much do telescopes cost?

Bartley   Twelve dollars for a good one.

Helen   So you'd pay twelve dollars to find out worms go wriggling?

Bartley (*pause*)   Aye. I would.   *≈ Billy watching cows, in a way,*

Helen   You don't have twelve hairs on your bollocks, let alone twelve dollars.

Bartley   I don't have twelve dollars on me bollocks, no, you're right there. I saw no sense.

    again concedes pretty easily.

Helen *approaches him.*

Bartley   Don't, Helen . . .

Helen *punches him hard in the stomach.*

Bartley (*winded*)   Hurt me ribs that punch did.   *⌐ = contesting her view. she fights anything in her way.*

Helen   Feck your ribs. Using that kind of fecking language to me, eh? (*Pause.*) What was we talking about, Cripple Billy? Oh eye, your dead mammy and daddy.

Billy   They didn't go drowning themselves because of me. They loved me.

Helen   They loved you? Would *you* love you if you weren't you? You barely love you and you *are* you.

    some modern self-love type stuff

Bartley (*winded*)   At least Cripple Billy doesn't punch poor lads' ribs for them.

Helen   No, and why? Because he's too fecking feeble to. It'd feel like a punch from a wet goose.

Bartley (*excited*)   Did ye hear Jack Ellery's goose bit Patty Brennan's cat on the tail and hurt that tail . . .

Helen   We *did* hear.

Bartley   Oh. (*Pause.*) And Jack didn't even apologise for that goose's biting and now Patty Brennan . . .

doesn't listen.

Helen   Didn't I just say we fecking heard, sure?

Bartley   I thought Billy mightn't have heard.

Helen   Sure Billy's busy thinking about his drowned mammy and daddy, Bartley. He doesn't need any of your days-old goose-news. Aren't you thinking about your drowned mammy and daddy, Billy?

Billy   I am.

Helen   You've never been on the sea since the day they died, have you, Billy? Aren't you too scared?

Billy   I *am* too scared.   *very nonchalant, admitting all "flaws"*

Helen   What a big sissy-arse, eh, Bartley?

Bartley   Sure anybody with a brain is at least a biteen afraid of the sea.

Helen   *I'm* not a biteen afraid of the sea.

Bartley   Well there you go, now.   *← that was a smart joke.*

Billy *laughs.*

Helen   Eh? Was that an insult?!

→ did Bartley get it? some amound of mutual unders-

Bartley   How would that be an insult, saying you're not *ding.* afraid of the sea?

Helen   Why did Cripple Billy laugh so?

Bartley   Cripple Billy only laughed cos he's an <u>odd boy</u>. Isn't that right, Cripple Billy?

Billy   It is, aye. Oh, plain odd I am. *= façade.*

Helen *pauses, confused.*

Bartley   Is it true you got nigh on a hundred pounds insurance when your mammy and daddy drowned, Billy?

Billy   It is.

Bartley   Jeebies. Do ya still have it?

Billy   I have none of it. Didn't it all go on me medical bills at the time? *↳ true?*

Bartley   You don't have even a quarter of it?

Billy   I don't. Why?

Bartley   No, only if you had a quarter of it you could probably buy yourself a <u>pretty classy telescope</u>, d'you know? Oh, you could.

Helen   Do you have to bring telescopes into fecking everything, you?

Bartley   I don't, but I like to, ya bitch. Leave me!

Bartley *dashes out of the shop as* **Helen** *advances on him. Pause.*

Helen   I don't know where he gets the fecking cheek of him from, I don't.

Billy (*pause*)   How are ye two sailing to Inishmore, so, Helen? Ye've no boat.

Helen   We're getting Babbybobby Bennett to bring us in his boat. *what's up w. these names,*

Billy   Are you paying him? *↳ "pretty power"!*

Helen   Only in <u>kisses and a bit of a hold of his</u> hand, or I *hope* that it's only his hand I'll be holding. Although I've heard it's a big one. Jim Finnegan's daughter was telling me. She knows everybody's. I think she keeps a chart for herself. *↳ crude enjoyment.*

Billy   She doesn't know mine.

Helen   And you say that like you're proud. I suppose she wasn't sure whether you had one, as mangled and fecked as you are.

Billy (*sadly*)   I have one.

Helen   Congratulations, but would you keep it to yourself? In more ways than one. (*Pause.*) Me, the only ones I've seen belong to priests. They keep showing them to me. I don't know why. I can't say they whetted me appetite. All brown. (*Pause.*) What have you gone all mopy for?

Billy   I don't know, now, but I suppose you intimating me mammy and daddy preferred death to being stuck with me didn't help matters.

Helen   I wasn't intimating that at all. I was saying it outright.

Billy (*quietly*)   You don't know what was in their heads.

Helen   Uh-huh? And do you?

Billy *bows his head sadly. Pause.* **Helen** *flicks him hard in the cheek with her finger, then moves off.*

Billy   Helen? Would Babbybobby be letting me go sailing to Inishmore with ye?

Helen   What have you to offer Babbybobby, sure? He wouldn't want to go holding your mangled hand.

Billy   What has Bartley to offer Bobby, so, and he's still going with ye?

Helen   Bartley said he'd help with the rowing. Could you help with the rowing?

Billy *lowers his head again.*

Helen   What would you want to be coming for, anyways?

Billy (*shrugging*)   To be in the filming.

Helen   You?

She starts laughing, slowly, moving to the door.

I <u>shouldn</u>'t laugh at you, Billy . . . but I <u>will</u>. *deliberately mean.*

She exits laughing. Pause. **Eileen** *returns from the back room and slaps* **Billy** *across the head.*

Billy   What was that fer?!

Eileen   Over my dead body are you going to Inishmore filming, Billy Claven!

Billy   Ah, I was only thinking aloud, sure.

Eileen   Well, stop thinking aloud! Stop thinking aloud and stop thinking quiet! There's <u>too much oul thinking</u> done in this house with you around. Did you ever see the Virgin Mary going thinking aloud?

Billy   I didn't.

Eileen   Is right, you didn't. And it didn't do her any harm! *↱but no good either. bare minimum standards.*

Eileen *exits to the back room again. Pause.* **Billy** *gets up, shuffles to his mirror, looks himself over a moment, then sadly shuffles back to the table.* **Bartley** *opens the shop door and pops his head inside.* *↳kinda like Johnny?*

Bartley   Cripple Billy, will you tell your aunty or your pretend aunty, I'll be in for me Mintios later, or, not me Mintios but me sweeties generally.

Billy   I will, Bartley.

Bartley   Me sister just told me your idea of being in the filming with us and I did have an awful laugh. That was a <u>great joke</u>, Billy.

Billy   Good-oh, Bartley.

Bartley   They may even bring you to Hollywood after. They may make a (star) out of ya.

Billy   They might at that, Bartley. *→ takes it w. grace, a bit of truth...*

Bartley   A little <u>cripple star</u>. Heh. So you'll remind your *attached term.*
aunty I'll be in for me Mintios later, or, not me Mintios but me . . . *→repetition.*

Billy   Your sweeties generally.

Bartley   Me sweeties generally. Or if not later then tomorrow morning.

Billy   Goodbye, Bartley.

Bartley   Goodbye, Cripple Billy, or are you okay there, Cripple Billy, you do look a little bit sad for yourself?

Billy   I'm fine, Bartley.

Bartley   Good-oh.

Bartley *exits.* **Billy** *wheezes slightly, feeling his chest.*

Billy (*quietly*)   I'm fine, aye.

Pause. Blackout.

Scene Three

A shore at night. **Babbybobby** *fixing his curragh.* **Johnny** *enters, slightly drunk, walks up to him and watches a while.*

Johnny   I see you're getting your curragh ready, Babbybobby.

Bobby   I am, Johnnypateen.

Johnny (*pause*)   Are you getting your curragh ready so?

Bobby   Didn't I just say I was getting me curragh ready?

Johnny   You did, aye. (*Pause.*) So you're getting your curragh ready. (*Pause.*) All spick and span you're getting it. (*Pause.*) All nice and prepared like. (*Pause.*) All ready for a trip or something. (*Pause.*) That's a nice boat, that is. A nice boat for a tripeen. And it's even more nice now that you've got it all prepared for yourself. (*Pause.*) All prepared and ready.

Bobby   If it's a question you have to ask me, Johnnypateen, go ahead and ask me the question and don't be <u>beating around the bush</u> like some fool of an eejit schoolchild.

Johnny   I have no question to ask you. If Johnnypateen has a question to ask he comes right out and asks it. You don't see Johnnypateen beating around a bush. Oh no. *nottrue at all.* (*Pause.*) Just commenting on how nice your curragh is is all. (*Pause.*) How nice and ready you're getting it. (*Pause.*) Nice and ready for a trip or something. (*Pause. Angrily.*) Well, if you won't tell me where you're going I'll fecking be off with meself! *↳ bro just askin*

Bobby   Be off with yourself, aye.

Bobby   I gave you no treatment. *) is this just editing error? or a big pause?*

Johnny   You did give me treatment. <u>You never tell me any news.</u> *you ask* Your Mrs up and died of TB the other year, and who was the last to know? *I* was the last to know. I wasn't told until the day she died, and you knew for weeks and weeks, with not a thought for my feelings . . .

Bobby   I should've kicked her arse down the road to tell you, Johnnypateen, and, d'you know, I've regretted not doing so ever since.

Johnny   One more time I'll say it so. So you're getting your curragh ready. All nice and prepared for a *trip* or something, now.

Bobby   <u>Ask me a question outright</u> and I'll be pleased to give you the answer, Johnnypateen. *why is he so allergic to questions?*

Johnny *stares at* **Bobby** *a second, fuming, then storms off.*
Bobby *continues with the boat.*

Bobby (*quietly*)   Ya stupid fecking eej. (*Pause. Calling off left.*) Who's that shuffling on the stones?

Billy (*off*)   It's Billy Claven, Babbybobby.

Bobby   I should've guessed that. Who else shuffles?

Billy (*entering*)   No one, I suppose.

Bobby   Are your aunties not worried you're out this late, Cripple Billy?

Billy   They'd be worried if they knew, but I snuck out on them.

Bobby   You shouldn't sneak out on aunties, Cripple Billy. Even if they're funny aunties. _=mad._

Billy   Do you think they're funny aunties too, Babbybobby?

Bobby   I saw your Aunty Kate talking to a stone one time.

Billy   And she shouts at me for staring at cows.

Bobby   Well I wouldn't hold staring at cows up as the height of sanity, Billy.

Billy   Sure, I only stare at cows to get away from me aunties a while. It isn't for the fun of staring at cows. There _is_ no fun in staring at cows. They just stand there looking at you like fools.

Bobby   Do you never throw nothing at them cows? That might liven them up.

Billy   I wouldn't want to hurt them, sure.

Bobby   You're too kind-hearted is your trouble, Cripple Billy. Cows don't mind you throwing things at them. I threw a brick at a cow once and he didn't even moo, and I got him bang on the arse.

Billy   Sure that's no evidence. He may've been a quiet cow.

Bobby   He may've. And, sure, I'm not telling you to go pegging bricks at cows. I was drunk when this happened. Just if you get bored, I'm saying.

Billy   I usually bring a book with me anyways. I've no desire to injure livestock.

Bobby   You could throw the book at the cow.

Billy   I would rather to read the book, Bobby.

Bobby   It takes all kinds, as they say.

Billy   It does. (*Pause.*) Are you getting your curragh ready there, Babbybobby?

Bobby   Oh everybody's awful observant tonight, it does seem.

Billy   Ready to bring Helen and Bartley o'er to the filming?

Bobby *looks at* **Billy** *a moment, checks out right to make sure* **Johnny** *isn't around, then returns.*

↳ doesn't want his life exposed as news.

Bobby   How did you hear tell of Helen and Bartley's travelling?

Billy   Helen told me.

Bobby   Helen told you. Jeez, and I told Helen she'd get a punch if she let anyone in on the news.

Billy   I hear she's paying you in kisses for this boat trip.

Bobby   She is, and, sure, I didn't want paying at all. It was ~~Helen insisted on that clause.~~

Billy   Wouldn't you want to kiss Helen, so?

very truthful admitting he's scared of a

Bobby   Ah, I get a bit scared of Helen, I do. She's awful *young girl.*
fierce. (*Pause.*) Why, would you like to kiss Helen, Cripple *he's a full*
Billy? *adult.*

Billy *shrugs shyly, sadly.*

Billy   Ah, I can't see Helen ever wanting to kiss a boy like me, anyways. Can you, Bobby?

Bobby   No.

Billy (*pause*)   But so you'd've took the McCormicks without payment at all?

Bobby   I would. I wouldn't mind having a look at this filming business meself. What harm in taking passengers along?

Billy   Would you take me as a passenger too, so?

Bobby (*pause*)   No.

Billy   Why, now?

Bobby   I've no room.   *lie*

Billy   You've plenty of room.

Bobby   A cripple fella's bad luck in a boat, and everybody knows.   *truthful.*

Billy   Since when, now?

Bobby   Since Poteen-Larry took a cripple fella in his boat and it sank.

Billy   That's the most ridiculous thing I've ever heard, Babbybobby.

Bobby   Or if he wasn't a cripple fella he had a <u>bad leg</u> on him anyways.   *whats the diffen*

Billy   You're just prejudiced against cripples is all you are.

Bobby   I'm not at all prejudiced against cripples. I did kiss a cripple girl one time. Not only crippled but disfigured too. I was drunk, I didn't mind. You're not spoilt for pretty girls in Antrim.   *sassy. he seems a good guy, except drunk?*

Billy   Don't go changing the subject on me.

Bobby   Big green teeth. What subject?

Billy   The subject of taking me to the filming with ye.

Bobby   I thought we closed that subject.

Billy   We hardly opened that subject.

Bobby   Sure, what do you want to go to the filming for? They wouldn't want a cripple boy.

Billy   You don't know what they'd want.

Bobby   I don't, I suppose. No, you're right there. I did see a film there one time with a fella who not only had he no arms and no legs but he was a coloured fella too.

Billy   A coloured fella? I've never seen a coloured fella, let alone a crippled coloured fella. I didn't know you could get them.

Bobby   Oh, they'd give you a terrible scare.

Billy   Coloured fellas? Are they fierce?

Bobby   They're less fierce with no arms or legs on them, because they can't do much to ya, but even so they're still fierce.

Billy   I heard a coloured fella a year ago came to Dublin a week.

Bobby   Ireland mustn't be such a bad place, so, if coloured fellas want to come to Ireland.

[handwritten: approved not just from "better" folks but from "worse" folks as well]

Billy   It mustn't. (*Pause.*) Ar, Babbybobby, you've only brought up coloured fellas to put me off the subject again.

[handwritten: → he's acute. doesn't stray off like others]

Bobby   There's no cripple fellas coming in this boat, Billy. Maybe some day, in a year or two, like. If your feet straighten out on ya.

Billy   A year to two's no good to me, Bobby.

Bobby   Why so?

Billy *takes out a letter and hands it to* **Bobby***, who starts reading it.*

Bobby   What's this?

Billy   It's a letter from Doctor McSharry, and you've got to promise you'll not breathe a word of it to another living soul.

[handwritten: dying!]

Halfway through the letter, **Bobby***'s expression saddens. He glances at* **Billy***, then continues.*

Bobby   When did you get this?

Billy   Just a day ago I got it. (*Pause.*) Now will you let me come?

Bobby   Your aunties'll be upset at you going.

Billy   Well, is it their life or is it my life? I'll send word to them from over there. Ah, I may only be gone a day or two anyways. I get bored awful easy. (*Pause.*) Will you let me come?   *doesn't seem like a excuse.*

Bobby   Nine o'clock tomorrow morning be here.

Billy   Thank you, Bobby, I'll be here.

Bobby *gives him back the letter and* **Billy** *folds it away.* **Johnny** *quickly enters, his hand held out.*

Johnny   No, hang on there, now. What did the letter say?   *→ nosey fucker.*

Bobby   Ah, Johnnypateen, will you feck off home for yourself?

Johnny   Be showing Johnnypateen that letter now, you, cripple-boy.   *entitled to all "news".*

Billy   I won't be showing you me letter.

Johnny   What d'you mean you won't be showing me your letter? You showed *him* your letter. Be handing it over, now.

Billy   Did anybody ever tell you you're a biteen rude, Johnnypateenmike?

Johnny   *I'm* rude? *I'm* rude? With ye two standing there hogging letters, and letters from doctors is the most interesting kind of letters, and ye have the gall then to go calling *me* rude? Tell oul limpy to be handing over that letter, now, else there'll be things I heard here tonight that won't stay secret much longer.

Bobby   Things like what, now?

Johnny   Oh, things like you rowing schoolies to Inishmore and you kissing green-teeth-girls in Antrim is the kind of thing, now. Not that I'm threatening blackmail on ya or anything, or, alright, yes, I am threatening blackmail on ya, but a newsman has to obtain his news be hook or be crook. *immoral business.*

Bobby   Be hook or be crook, is it? Well have this for hook or be crook.

Bobby *grabs* **Johnny** *by the hair and wrenches his arm up behind his back.*

Johnny   Aargh! Be letting go of me arm there you, ya thug! I'll get the constabulary on ya.

Bobby   Be lying down on the sand there, you, for yourself.

Bobby *forces* **Johnny** *face down on the ground.*

Johnny   Be running for the polis now you, cripple-boy, or shuffling anyways.

Billy   I won't. I'll be standing here watching. *decision. fight.*

Johnny   An accomplice that makes ya.

Billy   Good-oh.

Johnny   I'm only an oul fella.

Bobby *steps up onto* **Johnny**'s *backside.*

Johnny   Aargh! Get off of me arse, you!

Bobby   Billy, go pick up somes stones for me.

Billy (*doing so*)   Big stones?

Bobby   Middling-size stones.

Johnny   What do you want stones for?

Bobby   To peg them at your head till you promise not to bandy me business about town.

Johnny   You'll never get me to make such a promise. I can withstand any torture. Like Kevin Barry I am.

Bobby *throws a stone at* **Johnny**'s *head.* *gruesome.*

Johnny   Aargh! I promise, I promise.

Bobby　On Christ ya promise?

Johnny　On Christ I promise.

Bobby　That withstanding didn't last fecking long.

Bobby *gets off* **Johnny**, *who stands back up, brushing himself off.*

Johnny　I wouldn't get that kind of treatment in England! And now I have sand in me ears. *why England? comm*

Bobby　Take that sand home with ya and show it to your drunken mammy so.

Johnny　You leave my drunken mammy out of it.

Bobby　And be remembering that promise.

Johnny　Under duress that promise was made.

Bobby　I don't care if it was made under a dog's arsehole. You'll be remembering it.

Johnny (*pause*)　Ya feckers, ya!

Johnny *storms off right, shaking his fist.*

Bobby　I've wanted to peg stones at that man's head for fifteen years. *why so long? since Billy's age.*

Billy　I'd never get up the courage to peg stones at his head.

Bobby　Ah, I suppose you shouldn't peg stones at an oul fella's head, but didn't he drive me to it? (*Pause.*) You got up the courage to travel to Inishmore anyways, and you scared of the sea.

Billy　I did. (*Pause.*) We'll meet at nine tomorrow so.

Bobby　Better make it eight, Cripple Billy, in case Johnnypateen lets the cat out of the bag.

Billy　Do you not trust him so?

Bobby　I'd trust him as much as I'd trust you to carry a pint for me without spilling it.

Billy　That's not a nice thing to say.
he's always frank about his feeling. without judgement.

Bobby   I'm a hard character, me.

Billy   You're not a hard character at all, Babbybobby. You're a soft character.

Bobby (*pause*)   My wife Annie died of the same thing, d'you know? TB. But at least I got a year to spend with her. Three months is no time.

Billy   I won't even see the summer in. (*Pause.*) D'you remember the time Annie made me the jam roly-poly when I had the chickenpox? And the smile she gave me then?

Bobby   Was it a nice jam roly-poly?

Billy (*reluctantly*)   Not really, Bobby.

Bobby   No. Poor Annie couldn't cook jam roly-polies to save the life of her. Ah, I still miss her, despite her awful puddings. (*Pause.*) I'm glad I was able to help you in some way anyways, Cripple Billy, in the time you've left.

Billy   Would you do me a favour, Babbybobby? Would you not call me Cripple Billy any more long?

Bobby   What do you want to be called so?

Billy   Well, just Billy.

Bobby   Oh. Okay so, Billy. *redefined.*

Billy   And you, would you rather just be called Bobby and not Babbybobby? *baby Bob.*

Bobby   For why?

Billy   I don't know why.

Bobby   I do like being called Babbybobby. What's wrong with it? → *why does he want to continue being a baby?*

Billy   Nothing at all, I suppose. I'll see you in the morning so, Babbybobby.

Bobby   See you in the morning so, Cripple Billy. Em, *Billy.*

Billy   Didn't I just say?

Bobby   I forgot. I'm sorry, Billy.

Billy *nods, then shuffles away.*

Bobby   Oh, and Billy?

Billy *looks back.* **Bobby** *makes a gesture with his hand.*

Bobby   I'm sorry.

Billy *bows his head, nods, and exits right. Pause.* **Bobby** *notices something in the surf, picks a Bible up out of it, looks at it a moment, then tosses it back into the sea and continues working on the boat. Blackout.*

[handwritten: ↳ sacrilege?]

[handwritten: news returning to news. gossip to gossip there is more truth to pursue.]

Scene Four

Bedroom of **Mammy O'Dougal**, **Johnny**'s *ninety-year-old mother.* **Mammy** *in bed,* **Doctor McSharry** *checking her with a stethoscope,* **Johnny** *hovering.*

Doctor   Have you been laying off the drink, Mrs O'Dougal?

Johnny   Did you not hear me question, Doctor?

Doctor   I did hear your question, but amn't I trying to examine your mammy without your fool questions?

Johnny   Fool questions, is it?

Doctor   Have you been laying off the drink, Mrs O'Dougal, I said?

[handwritten: ↷ clearly not,]

Mammy (*burps*)   I *have* been laying off the drink or I've sort of been laying off the drink. *[handwritten: ✓ contradiction.]*

Johnny   She has a pint of porter now and then is no harm at all.

Mammy   Is no harm at all.

Johnny   Is good for you!

Doctor   So long as you keep it at a pint of porter is the main thing so.

Mammy   It *is* the main thing, and a couple of whiskies now and then.   *contradiction.*

Johnny   Didn't I only just say not to mention the whiskies, ya thick?

Doctor   How often is now and then?

Johnny   Once in a blue moon.

Mammy   Once in a blue moon, and at breakfast sometimes.   *again.*

Johnny   'At breakfast', jeez . . .

Doctor   Johnnypateenmike, don't you know well not to go feeding a ninety-year-old woman whiskey for breakfast?

Johnny   Ah, she likes it, and doesn't it shut her up?

Mammy   I do like a drop of whiskey, me, I do.

Johnny   From the horse's mouth.

Mammy   Although I do prefer poteen.

Doctor   But you don't get given poteen?

Mammy   I don't get given poteen, no.

Johnny   *Now.*

Mammy   Only on special occasions.

Doctor   And what qualifies as a special occasion?

Mammy   A Friday, a Saturday or a Sunday.

Doctor   When your mammy's dead and gone, Johnnypateen, I'm going to cut out her liver and show it to you, the damage your fine care has done.

Johnny   You won't catch me looking at me mammy's liver. I can barely stomach the outside of her, let alone the inside.

Doctor   A fine thing that is for a fella to say in front of his mammy.

Mammy   I've heard worse.

Johnny   Leave me mammy alone now, you, with your mangling. If she's been trying to drink herself dead for sixty-five years with no luck, I wouldn't start worrying about her now. Sixty-five years. Feck, she can't do anything right.

Doctor   Why do you want to drink yourself dead, Mrs O'Dougal?

Mammy   I do miss me husband Donal. Ate be a shark.

Johnny   1871 he was ate be a shark.

Doctor   Oh, you should be trying to get over that now, Mrs O'Dougal.

Mammy   I've tried to, Doctor, but I can't. A lovely man he was. And living with this goose all these years, it just brings it back to me.

Johnny   Who are you calling a goose, ya hairy-lipped fool? Didn't I go out of me way to bring Doctor McSharry home to ya?

Mammy   Aye, but only to go nosing about Cripple Billy Claven is all.

Johnny   No, not . . . not . . . Ah, you always go spilling the beans, you, ya lump.

Mammy   I'm an honest woman, me, Johnnypateen.

Johnny   Honest me hairy hole.

Mammy   And you didn't get me drunk enough.

*The **Doctor** packs up his black bag.*

Doctor   If I'm only here under false pretences . . .

Johnny   You're not here under false pretences. Me mammy did seem awful bad earlier . . . Cough, Mammy . . .

Mammy *coughs.*

Johnny   But she seems to be over the worst of it, you're right there, although, now, while you're here, Doctor, what *is* all this about Cripple Billy? He wouldn't be in a terrible way, would he? Maybe something life-threatening, now? Oh, I suppose it must be something awful serious if you go writing letters to him. *pretense care*

Doctor (*pause*)   Did you ever hear of a thing called doctor-patient confidentiality, Johnnypateenmike?

Johnny   I did, and I think it's a great thing. Now tell me what's wrong with Cripple Billy, Doctor.

Doctor   I'm going to open up that head of yours one day, Johnnypateen, and find nothing inside it at all.

Johnny   Don't go straying off the subject now, you. Tell me what's wrong with . . . or was that a clue to the subject, now? There's something on the inside of his head that's wrong? A brain tumour? He has a brain tumour!

Doctor   I wasn't aware . . .

Johnny   Tell me he has a brain tumour, Doctor. Oh, that'd be awful big news.

Doctor   I'm off home, I thank you for wasting me precious time, but before I go I'll just say one thing, and that's I don't know where you got your information from this time o'er Cripple Billy, for it's usually such accurate information you do get, oh aye . . .   *reverse psychology.*

Johnny   Polio, polio. He has polio.

Doctor   But as far as I'm aware, apart from those deformities he's had since birth, there is nothing wrong with Billy Claven at all, and it would be better if you didn't go spreading fool gossip about him.

Johnny (*pause*)   TB. TB. Ah it must be TB.
won't he realize?

The **Doctor** *walks away.*

Johnny   Where are you off to? Don't go hogging all the decent news, you!

The **Doctor** *has exited.*

Johnny   Ya beggar! Is Billy in such good health that rowing to Inishmore in the freezing morning as he did this day'll do him no harm, so?

Pause. The **Doctor** *returns, thoughtful.* ~~bro...~~

Johnny   Didn't that get him running back quick?

Mammy   Like a cat with a worm up his arse.

Doctor   Billy's gone to Inishmore?

Johnny   He has. With the McCormicks and Babbybobby rowing them. Babbybobby who'll be arrested for grievous bodily harm the minute he returns, or grievous *headily* harm anyways, for it was me head he grievously harmed.

Doctor   They've gone to see the filming?

Johnny   To see the filming or to be in the filming, aye.

Doctor   But the filming finished yesterday, sure. It's only clearing the oul cameras and whatnot they are today. *(holy shit.)*

Johnny (*pause*)   I suppose they must've been given unreliable information somewhere along the way, so.

Mammy   Aye, be this goose. *(by it's him.)*

Johnny   Don't you be calling me goose, I said.

Mammy   Get me a drink, goose.

Johnny   If you retract goose I'll get you a dr—

Mammy   I retract goose.

Johnny *pours her a large whiskey, the* **Doctor** *aghast.*

Doctor   Don't . . . don't . . . (*Angrily.*) Have I been talking to meself all day?!

Johnny (*pause*)   Would you like a drink too, Doctor, after I have stunned you with me Cripple Billy revelation?

Doctor   What do I care about that arse-faced revelation?

[handwritten: ? not true. I mean Bobby agreed knowing his condition.]

Johnny   Heh. We'll see if your tune's the same when Billy returns home dead because of your secrecy, and you're drummed out of doctorhood and forced to scrape the skitter out of bent cows, is all you were ever really fit for anyways, oh we all know.

Doctor   Billy won't be returning home dead because there's nothing the matter with Billy but a wheeze.

Johnny   Are you persisting in that one, Doctor Useless?

Doctor   Shall I say it one more time, thicko? There is nothing wrong with Billy Claven. Okay?

The **Doctor** *exits.*

Johnny   Cancer! Cancer! Come back you! Would it be cancer? Tell me what it begins with. Is it a 'C'? Is it a 'P'?

Mammy   You're talking to thin air, ya fool.

Johnny (*calling*)   I'll get to the bottom of it one way or the other, McSharry! Be hook or be crook! A good newsman never takes no for an answer!

Mammy   No. You just take stones pegged at your head for an answer.

Johnny   Let the stone matter drop, I've told you twenty times, or I'll kick your black arse back to Antrim for you.

He sits on the bed, reading a newspaper. *[handwritten: another source of (real) news.]*

Mammy   You and your shitey-arsed news.

Johnny   My news isn't shitey-arsed. My news is great news. Did you hear Jack Ellery's goose and Pat Brennan's cat have both been missing a week? I suspect something awful's happened to them, or I *hope* something awful's happened to them.

Mammy   Even though you're me own son I'll say it, Johnnypateen, you're the most boring oul fecker in Ireland. And there's plenty of competition for that fecking post!

Johnny   There's a sheep here in Kerry with no ears, I'll have to make a note. → *"crippled" makes news.*

funny that "real" news is as gossipy as

Mammy (*pause*)   Give me the bottle if you're going *Johnny* bringing up sheep deformities.

He gives her the whiskey bottle.

Johnny   Sheep deformities is interesting news. Is the best kind of news. Excluding major illnesses anyways. (*Pause.*) And I want to see half that bottle gone be teatime.

→ murder by command.

Mammy   Poor Cripple Billy. The life that child's had. With that mam and dad of his, and that sackful of stones of theirs . . .

Johnny   Shut up about the sackful of stones.

Mammy   And now this. Although look at the life I've had too. First poor Donal bit in two, then you going thieving the hundred-pound floorboard money he'd worked all his life to save and only to piss it away in pubs. Then the beetroot fecking paella you go making every Tuesday on top of it.

Johnny   There's nothing the matter with beetroot paella, and hasn't half of that hundred pounds been poured down your dribbling gob the past sixty years, ya bollocks?

Mammy   Poor Billy. It's too many of the coffins of gosawers I've seen laid in the ground in me time.

Johnny   Drink up, so. You may save yourself the trouble this time.

Mammy   Ah, I'm holding out to see you in your coffin first, Johnnypat. Wouldn't that be a happy day?

Johnny   Isn't that funny, because I'd enjoy seeing *you* in *your* coffin the same as ya, if we can find a coffin big enough to squeeze your fat arse into. Course we may have to saw half the blubber off you first, oh there's not even a question.

Mammy   Oh, you've upset me awful with them harsh remarks, Johnnypateen, oh aye. (*Pause.*) Ya fecking eejit. (*Pause.*) Anything decent in the paper, read it out to me. But no sheep news.

Johnny   There's a fella here, riz to power in Germany, has an awful funny moustache on him.

Mammy   Let me see his funny moustache.

He shows her the photo.

That's a funny moustache.

Johnny   You'd think he'd either grow a proper moustache or else shave that poor biteen of a straggle off.

Mammy   That fella seems to be caught in two minds.

Johnny   Ah, he seems a nice enough fella, despite his funny moustache. Good luck to him. (*Pause.*) There's a German fella living out in Connemara now, d'you know? Out Leenane way.

Mammy   Ireland mustn't be such a bad place if German fellas want to come to Ireland.

Johnny   They all want to come to Ireland, sure. Germans, dentists, everybody.

Mammy   And why, I wonder?

Johnny   Because in Ireland the people are more friendly.

Mammy   They are, I suppose.

Johnny   Of course they are, sure. Everyone knows that. Sure, isn't it what we're famed for? (*Long pause.*) I'd bet money on cancer.

Johnny *nods, returning to his paper.*

Scene Five

The shop. A few dozen eggs stacked on counter.

Kate   Not a word. (*Pause.*) Not a word, not a word, not a word, not a word, not a word, not a word, not a word. (*Pause.*) Not a word. → *extreme repetition*.

Eileen   Oh how many more times are you going to say 'Not a word', Kate?

Kate   Am I not allowed to say 'Not a word' so, and me terrified o'er Billy's travellings?

Eileen   You *are* allowed to say 'Not a word', but one or two times and not ten times.

Kate   Billy's going to go the same way as his mammy and daddy went. Dead and buried be the age of twenty.

Eileen   Do you ever look on the optimistic side, you?

Kate   I do look on the optimistic side, but I fear I'll never see poor Billy alive again.

Eileen (*pause*)   Billy could've at least left a note that he was going to Inishmore, and not have us hear it from oul Johnnypateen.

Kate   Not a word. Not a word, not a word, not a word.

Eileen   And Johnnypateen revelling in his news-telling then, along with his intimating o'er letters and doctors.

Kate   I fear Johnnypateen knows something about Billy he's not telling.

Eileen   When has Johnnypateen ever known something and not told, sure? Johnnypateen tells if a horse farts.

Kate   Do you think?

Eileen   I know.

Kate   I still worry o'er Cripple Billy.

Eileen   Sure, if McSharry's right that the filming's o'er, it won't be long at all before Billy's home, and the rest of them with him.

Kate   You said that last week and they're still not home.

oh no.

Eileen   Maybe they stayed to see the sights.

Kate   On Inishmore? What sights? A fence and a hen?

Eileen   Maybe a cow came o'er to Cripple Billy and he lost track of time.

Kate   It doesn't take much time to look at a cow, sure.

Eileen   Well, you used to take an age in talking to stones, I remember.

same predicament.
except Billy is only feigning.

Kate   Them stone days were when I had trouble with me nerves and you know well they were, Eileen! Didn't we agree on never bringing the stones business up!

Eileen   We did, and I'm sorry for bringing the stones business up. It's only because I'm as worried as ya that I let them stones slip.

Kate   Because people who live in glass houses shouldn't throw stone-conversations at me.

Eileen   What glass house do I live in?

ooh! seeing is not all there is.

Kate   We had twenty Yalla-mallows in the ha'penny box the other day and I see they're all gone. How are we ever to make a profit if you keep eating the new sweeties before anybody's had a chance to see them?   → *not that detached from the Americas as it seems.*

Eileen   Ah, Kate. Sure with Yalla-mallows, when you eat one, there's no stopping ya.

Kate   It was the same excuse with the Mintios. Well, if you lay one finger on the Fripple-Frapples when they come in, you'll be for the high jump, I'm telling ya.

Eileen   I'm sorry, Kate. It's just all this worry o'er Billy didn't help matters.

Kate   I know it didn't, Eileen. I know you like to stuff your face when you're worried. Just try to keep a lid on it is all.

Eileen   I will. (*Pause.*) Ah sure, that Babbybobby's a decent enough fella. He'll be looking after Billy, I'm sure.

Kate   Why did he bring poor Billy off with him anyways so if he's such a decent fella? Didn't he know his aunties would be worrying?

Eileen   I don't know if he knew. *thats a bit odd.*

Kate   I'd like to hit Babbybobby in the teeth.

Eileen   I suppose he . . .

Kate   With a brick.

Eileen   I suppose he could've got Billy to send a note at the minimum.

Kate   Not a word. Not a word. (*Pause.*) Not a word, not a word, not a wor— *like staring at rocks, can't help.*

Eileen   Ah, Kate, don't be starting with your 'Not a word's again.

Kate*watches* **Eileen** *stacking the eggs a while.*

Kate   I see the egg-man's been.

Eileen   He has. The egg-man has a rake more eggs when Slippy Helen doesn't be working for him.

Kate   I don't see why he keeps Helen on at all.

Eileen   I think he's afraid of Helen. That or he's in love with Helen.   *same thing?*

Kate (*pause*)   I think Billy's in love with Helen on top of it.

Eileen   *I* think Billy's in love with Helen. It'll all end in tears.

Kate   Tears or death.

Eileen   We ought look on the bright side.

Kate   Tears, death or worse.   *adding on.*

Johnny *enters, strutting.*

Eileen   Johnnypateenmike.

Kate   Johnnypateenmike.

Johnny   Johnnypateen does have three pieces of news to be telling ye this day.   *repetition of the first day.*

Kate   Only tell us if it's happy news, Johnnypat, because we're a biteen depressed today, we are.

Johnny   I have a piece of news concerning the Inishmore trippers, but I will be saving that piece of news for me third piece of news.

Kate   Is Billy okay, Johnnypateen? Oh, tell us that piece of news first.

Eileen   Tell us that piece of news first, aye, Johnnypateen.

Johnny   Well, if ye're going arranging what order I tell me pieces of news in, I think I will turn on me heels and be off with me!   '

Kate   Don't go, Johnnypat! Don't go!

Johnny   Hah?

Eileen   Tell us your news in whatever order you like, Johnnypateen. Sure, aren't you the man who knows best about news-ordering?

Johnny   I *am* the man who knows best. I *know* I'm the man who knows best. That's no news. I see you have plenty of eggs in.

Eileen   We do, Johnnypateen.

Johnny   Uh-huh. Me first piece of news, there is a sheep out in Kerry with no ears at all on him.

Eileen (*pause*)   That's a great piece of news.

Johnny   Don't ask me how he hears because I don't know and I don't care. Me second piece of news, Patty Brennan's cat was found dead and Jack Ellery's goose was found dead and nobody in town is said to've seen anything, but we can all put two and two together, although not out loud because Jack Ellery's an awful tough.

Kate   That's a sad piece of news because now it sounds like a feud is starting.

Johnny   A feud is starting and won't be stopped till the one or the two of them finish up slaughtered. Good. I will take six eggs, Mrs, for the omelette I promised me mammy a fortnight ago.

Eileen   What was the third piece of news, Johnnypateen?

Johnny   I mention me mammy and nobody even asks as to how she is. Oh, it's the height of politeness in this quarter.

Kate   How is your mammy, Johnnypateen?

Johnny   Me mammy's fine, so she is, despite me best efforts.

Eileen   Are you still trying to kill your mammy with the drink, Johnnypateen?

Johnny   I am, but it's no use. A fortune in booze that bitch has cost me over the years. She'll never go. (*Pause.*) Well now, I have me eggs, I've told you me two pieces of news. I suppose that's me business finished here for the day.

Kate   The . . . the third piece of news, Johnnypateen?

Johnny   Oh, the third piece of news. Wasn't I almost forgetting? (*Pause.*) The third piece of news is Babbybobby's just pulled his boat up on the sands, at the headland there, and let the young adventurers off. Or, let *two* of the young adventurers off anyways, Helen and Bartley. There was no hide nor hair of Cripple Billy in that boat. (*Pause.*) I'm off to have Babbybobby arrested for throwing stones at me head. I thank you for the eggs.

Johnny exits. Pause. **Kate** sadly caresses the old sack hanging on the wall, then sits at the table.

Kate   He's gone from us, Eileen. He's gone from us.

Eileen   We don't know at all that he's gone from us.

Kate   I can feel it in me bones, Eileen. From the minute he left I knew. Cripple Billy's dead and gone.

Eileen   But didn't the doctor assure us five times there was nothing wrong with Cripple Billy?

Kate   Only so not to hurt us that assuring was. It was Johnnypat who had the real story all along, same as about Billy's mam and dad's drowning he always had the real story.

Eileen   Oh Lord, I see Babbybobby coming up the pathway towards us.

Kate   Does he look glum, Eileen?

Eileen   He does look glum, but Babbybobby usually looks glum.

Kate   Does he look glummer than he usually looks?

Eileen (*pause*)   He does.

Kate   Oh no.

Eileen   And he's taken the hat off him now.

Kate   That's an awful bad sign, taking the hat off ya.

Eileen   Maybe just being gentlemanly he is?

Kate   Babbybobby? Sure, Babbybobby pegs bricks at cows.

Bobby *enters, cap in hand.*

Bobby   Eileen, Kate.

Eileen   Babbybobby.

Bobby   Would you be sitting down a minute there for yourself, now, Eileen? I've news to be telling ye.

Eileen *sits at the table.*

Bobby   I've just brought the two McCormicks home, and I was supposed to bring yere Billy home, I know, but I couldn't bring yere Billy home because . . . because he's been taken to America for a screen test for a film they're making about a cripple fella. Or . . . I don't think the *whole* film will be about the cripple fella. The cripple fella'd only be a minor role. Aye. But it'd still be a good part, d'you know? (*Pause.*) Although, there's more important things in the world than good parts in Hollywood films about cripple fellas. Being around your family and your friends is more important, and I tried to tell Cripple Billy that, but he wouldn't listen to me, no matter how much I told him. Be boat this morning they left. Billy wrote a letter here he asked me to pass onto ye. (*Pause.*) Two or three months at minimum, Billy said probably he'd be gone. (*Pause.*) Ah, as he said to me, it's his life. I suppose it is, now. I hope he enjoys his time there anyways. (*Pause.*) That's all there is. (*Pause.*) I'll be seeing ye.

Eileen   Be seeing you, Babbybobby . . .

Kate   Be seeing you, Bobbybabbybobby.

Bobby *exits.* **Kate** *opens the letter.*

Eileen   What the devil's a screen test, Kate?

Kate   I don't know at all what a screen test is.

Eileen   Maybe in his letter it says.

Kate   Oh the awful handwriting he has.

Eileen   It's never improved.

Kate   'Dear Aunties, can ye guess what?' Yes, we *can* guess what. 'I am off to Hollywood to make a screen test for a film they're making, and if they like the look of me a contract they will give me and an actor then I'll be.' He doesn't explain at all what a screen test is.

Eileen   With all the thinking he does?

Kate   What's this now? I can't make out even two words in this sentence with his writing . . . 'But if it's a big success I am . . . it might only be two or three months before I am too busy with acting work to be getting in touch with ye too often at all . . . so if ye don't hear from me much from summertime on, don't be worrying about me. It'll only mean I'm happy and healthy and making a go of me life in America. <u>Making something of meself</u> for ye and Mammy and Daddy to be proud of. Give my love to everyone on the island except Johnnypateen, and take care of yourselves, Kate and Eileen. You <u>moan the world to me</u> . . . *mean the world to me.*' It looks like 'moan'. (*Pause.*) 'Yours sincerely . . . Billy Claven.' (*Pause.*) Turned his back on us, he has, Eileen.

[handwritten margin note: → like news deliverers. Say the news in pain.]

Eileen (*crying*)   And us worrying our heads off o'er him.

Eileen *goes to the counter and quietly fishes through the sweetie box.*

[handwritten margin note: → like a child.]

Kate   After all we've done for him down the years.

Eileen   We looked after him and didn't care that he was a cripple-boy at all. *[handwritten: → but you literally call him Cripple.]*

Kate   After all the shame he brought on us, staring at cows, and this is how he repays us.

Eileen   I hope the boat sinks before it ever gets him to America.

Kate   I hope he drowns like his mammy and daddy drowned before him. *[handwritten: welp.]*

Eileen (*pause*)   Or are we being too harsh on him?

Kate (*crying*)   We're being too harsh on him, but only because it's so upset about him we are. What are you eating?

Eileen   Oh Yalla-mallows and don't be starting on me.

Kate   I thought you'd ate all the Yalla-mallows.

Eileen   I'd put a couple of Yalla-mallows aside for emergencies.

Kate   Eat ahead, Eileen.

Eileen   Do you want one, Kate?

Kate   I don't. I have no stomach for eating at all, this day. Let alone eating Yalla-mallows.

Eileen (*pause*)   We'll see Cripple Billy again one day, won't we, Kate?

Kate   I fear we've more chance of seeing Jim Finnegan's daughter in a nunnery before we see Cripple Billy again. (*Pause.*) I'm not sure if I *want* to see Cripple Billy again.

Eileen   I'm not sure if *I* want to see Cripple Billy again. (*Pause.*) I want to see Cripple Billy again.

Kate   *I* want to see Cripple Billy again.

Pause. Blackout.

Interval.

Scene Six

The shop, summer, four months later. A couple of flyers for Man of Aran, *being shown at the church hall, hang on the walls. The sweetie boxes and a stone lie on the counter, beside which* **Bartley** *stands, pursing his lips dumbly and doing other stuff for a few moments to fill in time as he waits for* **Kate** *to return.* **Helen** *enters carrying a few dozen eggs.*

Helen   What are you waiting for?

Bartley   She's gone in the back to look for me Fripple-Frapples. → *Kate doesn't lie.*

Helen   Oh you and your fecking Fripple-Frapples.

Bartley   Fripple-Frapples are nice sweeties.

Helen *arranges the eggs on the counter.*

Bartley   I see you've brought the eggs up.

Helen   You, you're awful observant.

Bartley   I thought bringing the eggs was the egg-man's job.

Helen   It *was* the egg-man's job, but I did kick the egg-man in the shins this after and he didn't feel up to it.

strong & aggressive as ever.

Bartley   What did you kick the egg-man in the shins for?

Helen   He insinuated it was me murdered Jack Ellery's goose and Pat Brennan's cat for them.

Bartley   But it *was* you murdered Jack Ellery's goose and Pat Brennan's cat for them. → *oh? cheating news. profiting off like Johnny.*

Helen   I know it was, but if it gets bandied around town I'll never be getting paid.

Bartley   How much are you getting paid?

Helen   Eight bob for the goose and ten bob for the cat.

Bartley   Why did you charge extra for the cat?

Helen   Well, I had to pay Ray Darcy for the borrow of his axe. See, the goose I only had to stomp on him. It takes more than a stomp to polish a cat off.

Bartley   A plankeen of wood you could've used on the cat, and saved shelling out for the axe at all.

Helen   Sure, I wanted the job carried out <u>professional</u>, Bartley. A plank is the weapon of a flat-faced child. I wouldn't use a plank on a blue-arsed fly.

Bartley   What *would* you use on a blue-arsed fly?

Helen   I wouldn't use a thing on a blue-arsed fly. There's no money involved in killing blue-arsed flies.

Bartley   Jim Finnegan's daughter killed twelve worms one day.

Helen   Aye, be breathing on them.

Bartley   No, be sticking needles in their eyes.

Helen   Now there's the work of an amateur. (*Pause.*) I didn't even know worms had eyes. bright in one way, dim in another

Bartley   They don't after Jim Finnegan's daughter gets through with them.

Helen   What's this stone here for?

Bartley   I caught Mrs Osbourne <u>talking to that stone</u> when first I came in.

Helen   What was she saying to the stone?

Bartley   She was saying, 'How are you, stone?' and then fully adapted to her madne putting the stone to her ear like the stone was talking back to her.

Helen   That's awful strange behaviour.

Bartley   And asking the stone, then, if it knew how oul Cripple Billy was doing for himself in America.

Helen   And what did the stone say?

Bartley (*pause*)   The stone didn't say anything, Helen, because stones they don't say anything.

Helen   Oh, I thought you said Mrs Osbourne was doing the voice for the stone.

Bartley   No, Mrs Osbourne was just doing her own voice.

Helen   Maybe we should hide the stone and see if Mrs Osbourne has a nervous breakdown.

Bartley   Sure, that wouldn't be a very Christian thing to do, Helen.

Helen   It wouldn't be a very Christian thing to do, no, but it'd be awful funny.

Bartley   Ah, let's leave Mrs Osbourne's stone alone, Helen. Hasn't she enough on her mind worrying o'er Cripple Billy?

Helen   Cripple Billy's aunties should be *told* that Billy's dead or dying, and not have them waiting for a letter from him that'll never come. Four months, now, isn't it they've been waiting, and not a word, and them the only two on Inishmaan not been informed what Babbybobby knows.

Bartley   What good would it do, sure, informing them? At least this way they've the hope he's still alive. What help would Babbybobby's news be to them? And you never know but maybe a miracle's happened and Cripple Billy hasn't died in Hollywood at all. Maybe three months wasn't a fair estimate for Cripple Billy.

Helen   I hope Cripple Billy *has* died in Hollywood, after taking his place in Hollywood that was rightfully a pretty girl's place, when he knew full well he was about to kick the bucket.

Bartley   A pretty girl's place? What use would a pretty girl be in playing a cripple fella?

Helen   I could turn me hand to anything, me, given a chance.

Bartley   I've heard.

Helen   Heard what?

Bartley   I've heard Hollywood is chock-full of pretty girls, sure. It's cripple fellas they're crying out for.

Helen   What are you defending Cripple Billy for? Didn't he promise to send you a package of Yalla-mallows you've never seen a lick of?

Bartley   Maybe Cripple Billy died before he had a chance of sending me them Yalla-mallows.

Helen   It's any excuse for you, ya weed.

Bartley   But dying's an awful good excuse for not sending a fella the sweeties he promised.

Helen   Too kind-hearted you are. I'm ashamed to admit you're related to me sometimes.

Bartley   It doesn't hurt to be too kind-hearted.

Helen   Uh-huh. Does this hurt?

Helen *pinches* **Bartley**'s *arm.*   Finds joy in cruelty.

Bartley (*in pain*)   No.

Helen (*pause*)   Does this hurt?

Helen *gives him a Chinese burn on the forearm.*

Bartley (*in pain*)   No.

Helen (*pause*)   Does this hurt?

She picks up an egg and breaks it against his forehead.
↪ compromising her own business, no foresig
Bartley (*sighing*)   I'd better say yes before any further you go.

Helen   You should've said yes on the arm-pinch, would've been using your brain.

Bartley   I should've said yes but you'd still've broken an egg on me.

Helen   Now we'll never know.

Bartley   You're just a terror when you get around eggs.

Helen   I do like breaking eggs on fellas.

Bartley   I had guessed that somehow.

Helen   Or could you classify you as a fella? Isn't that going a biteen overboard?   *defining yourself.*

Bartley   I notice you never broke an egg on Babbybobby Bennett when he reneged on your kissing proposals.

Helen   We were in a row-boat a mile from land, sure. Where was I supposed to get an egg?

Bartley   Reneged because you're so witchy-looking.

Helen   Reneged because he was upset o'er Cripple Billy, and watch your 'witchy-looking' comments, you.

Bartley   Why is it runny eggs don't smell but boiled eggs do smell?

Helen   I don't know why. And I don't care why.

Bartley   Reneged because you look like one of them ragged-looking widow women waiting on the rocks for a rascal who'll never return to her. *bit of a poet.*

Helen   That sentence had an awful lot of Rs.

Bartley   It was insulting with it, on top of the Rs.

Helen   You've gotten awful cocky for a boy with egg running down his gob.

Bartley   Well, there comes a time for every Irishman to take a stand against his oppressors. *jokes. funny.*

Helen   Was it Michael Collins said that?

Bartley   It was some one of the fat ones anyways.

Helen   Do you want to play 'England versus Ireland'?

Bartley   I don't know how to play 'England versus Ireland'.

Helen   Stand here and close your eyes. You'll be Ireland.

Bartley *faces her and closes his eyes.*

Bartley   And what do you do?

Helen   I'll be England.

Helen *picks up three eggs from the counter and breaks the first against* **Bartley**'s *forehead.* **Bartley** *opens his eyes as the yolk runs down him, and stares at her sadly.* **Helen** *breaks the second egg on his forehead.*   doesn't really resist/fight.

Bartley   That wasn't a nice thing at all to . . .

Helen   Haven't finished.

Helen *breaks the third egg on* **Bartley**.

Bartley   That wasn't a nice thing at all to do, Helen.

Helen   I was giving you a lesson about Irish history, Bartley.

Bartley   I don't need a lesson about Irish history. (*Shouting.*) Or anyways not with eggs when I've only washed me hair!

Helen   There'll be worse casualties than eggy hair before Ireland's a nation once again, Bartley McCormick.

Bartley   And me best jumper, look at it!

Helen   It has egg on it.

Bartley   I know it has egg on it! I know well! And I was going to go wearing it to the showing of the film tomorrow, but you've put paid to that idea now, haven't ya?

Helen   I'm looking forward to the showing of the film tomorrow.

Bartley   I was looking forward to the showing of the film too until me jumper became destroyed.

Helen   I think I might go pegging eggs at the film tomorrow. The *Man of Aran* me arsehole. *The Lass of Aran* they could've had, and the *pretty* lass of Aran. Not some oul shite about thick fellas fecking fishing.

Bartley   Does everything you do have to involve egg-pegging, Helen?

Helen   I do take a pride in me egg-work, me. Is this bitch never bloody coming to pay for me eggs? (*Calling.*) You, stonewoman!

Bartley   She's taking an age to bring me Fripple-Frapples.

Helen   Ah, I can't waste me youth waiting for that mingy hole. You collect me egg-money, Bartley, and give it to the egg-man on the way home.

Bartley   I will, Helen, aye.

Helen *exits.*

Bartley   I will me fecking arse, ya shite-gobbed fecking bitch-fecker, ya . . .

Helen *pops her head back in.*

Helen   And don't let her dock you for the four you went and broke on me. ~~flipped~~

Bartley   I won't, Helen.

She exits again.

(*Sighing.*) Women.

Kate *slowly enters from the back room, absent-mindedly, noticing* **Bartley** *after a second.*

Kate   Hello there, Bartley. What can I be getting for ya?

Bartley (*pause, bemused*)   You were going in the back to look for your Fripple-Frapples, Mrs.

Kate *thinks to herself a moment, then slowly returns to the back room.*

Bartley *moans loudly in frustration, putting his head down on the counter. Slight pause, then* **Kate** *returns and picks up her stone.*

Kate   I'll bring me stone.

She exits to the back room again. Pause. **Bartley** *picks up a wooden mallet, smashes all the eggs on the counter with it and walks out, slamming the door. Blackout.*

Scene Seven

Sound of **Billy**'s *wheezing starts, as lights come up on him shivering alone on a chair in a squalid Hollywood hotel room. He wheezes slightly throughout.*

Billy   Mam? I fear I'm not longer for this world, Mam. Can't I hear the wail of the banshees for me, as far as I am from me barren island home? A home barren, aye, but proud and generous with it, yet turned me back on ye I did, to end up alone and dying in a one-dollar rooming-house, without a mother to wipe the cold sweat off me, nor a father to curse God o'er the death of me, nor a colleen fair to weep tears o'er the still body of me. A body still, aye, but a body noble and unbowed with it. An Irishman! (*Pause.*) Just an Irishman. With a decent heart on him, and a decent head on him, and a decent spirit not broken by a century's hunger and a lifetime's oppression! A spirit not broken, no . . . (*Coughing.*) but a body broken, and the lungs of him broken, and, if truth be told, the heart of him broken too, be a lass who never knew his true feelings, and now, sure, never will. What's this, Mammy, now, that you're saying to me?

He looks at a sheet of paper on the table.

Be writing home to her, I know, and make me feelings known. Ah, 'tis late, Mammy. Won't tomorrow be soon enough for that task?

He gets up and shuffles to the mirror left, quietly singing 'The Croppy Boy'.

> 'Farewell Father and Mother too,
> And sister Mary I have none but you.
> And for my brother, he's all alone.
> He's pointing pikes on the grinding stone.'

He stumbles, ill, crawls up onto the bed, wheezing, and looks at the photo on the dresser.

What would Heaven be like, Mammy? I've heard 'tis a beautiful place, <u>more beautiful than Ireland even</u>, but even if it is, sure, it wouldn't be near as beautiful as you. I do wonder would they let cripple boys into Heaven at all. Sure, wouldn't we only go uglifying the place?

He puts the photo back on the dresser.

> ''Twas in old Ireland this young man died,
> And in old Ireland his body's lain.
> All the good people that do pass by,
> May the Lord have mercy on this croppy boy.'

Oh it's a bad way the chest of me is in tonight, Mammy. I think it's a little sleep I should have now for meself. For there's mighty work in the railyard tomorrow to be done. (*Pause.*) What's that, Mammy? Me prayers? I know. Sure, would I be forgetting, as well as you taught them to me? (*Blesses himself.*) And now I lay me down to sleep, I pray to God my soul to keep. But if . . . (*Pause.*) But if I die before I wake . . . I pray to God . . . (*Tearfully.*) I pray to God . . .

Pause, recovering himself. He smiles.

Ara, don't worry, Mammy. 'Tis only to sleep it is that I'm going. 'Tis only to sleep.

Billy *lies down. His pained wheezes get worse and worse, until they suddenly stop with an anguished gasp, his eyes close, his head lolls to one side, and he lays there motionless. Fade to black.*

only scene 7 & 9.

Scene Eight

like a senure.

A church hall in semi-darkness. **Bobby**, **Mammy** (*bottle in hand*), **Johnny**, **Helen**, **Bartley**, **Eileen** *and* **Kate** *sitting. All are staring up at the film* Man of Aran *being projected. The film is nearing its end, and its sound track is either very low or not heard at all.*

Mammy   What's this that's happening?

Johnny   What does it look like that's happening?

Bartley   Aren't they going catching a shark, Mrs, and a big shark?

Mammy   Are they?

Johnny   Shut up and drink, you.

Mammy   I will, goosey.

Bobby   I hope only water it is that's in that bottle. Johnnypateenmike.

Johnny   Of course it's only water. (*Whispered.*) Don't be breathing out near Babbybobby, Mammy.

Mammy   I won't be.

Johnny   And mind the 'goosey'. like the goose that got killed.

Bobby   Has your Johnny been thieving any more of your life savings lately, Mrs O'Dougal?

Johnny   I never ever thieved me mammy's life savings. I only borrowed them, short-term.

Mammy   Since 1914 this fecker's borrowed them short-term.

Johnny   Well, that's me definition of short-term.

Kate (*pause*)   That's a big fish.

Eileen   'Tis a shark, Kate.

Kate   'Tis a wha?

Eileen   A shark, a shark!

Helen   Have you forgot what a shark is, on top of talking to stones?

Bartley   It's mostly off America you do get sharks, Mrs, and a host of sharks, and so close to shore sometimes they come, sure, you wouldn't even need a telescope to spot them, oh no . . .

Helen   Oh telescopes, Jesus . . . !

Bartley   It's rare that off Ireland you get sharks. This is the first shark I've ever seen off Ireland. → *fictional Ireland. then what abt. Mammy? that shark was real... but past.*

Johnny   Ireland mustn't be such a bad place so if sharks want to come to Ireland.

Bartley (*pause*)   Babbybobby, you weren't in long with the polis at all when you was took down for Johnnypat's headstoning, how comes?

Bobby   Oh, the guard just laughed when he heard about Johnnypat's head-stoning. 'Use a brick next time,' he said. 'Stop piddling around with stones.'

Johnny   That guard wants drumming out of the polis. Or at least to have spiteful rumours spread about him.

Bobby   And we all know who the man for that job'll be.

Johnny   He beats his wife with a poker, d'you know?

Helen   Sure, is that news? They don't let you in the polis *unless* you beat your wife with a poker.

Bobby   And that's an outright lie anyways about the guard beating his wife with a poker. (*Pause.*) A biteen of a rubber hose was all he used.

Kate (*pause*)   Not a word. Not a word from him.

Helen   Is stony off again?

Eileen   She is.   *It's a name now.*

Helen   Hey, stony!

Eileen   Ah, leave her, Helen, will ya?

Helen (*pause*)   Ah, they're never going to be catching this fecking shark. A fecking hour they've been at it now, it seems like.

Bartley   Uh-huh. Three minutes would be more accurate.

Helen   If it was *me* had a role in this film the fecker wouldn't have lasted as long. One good clobber and we could all go home.

Bartley   One good clobber with Ray Darcy's axe, I suppose.

Helen   Cut the axe-talk, you.

Bartley   Doesn't shark-clobbering take a sight more effort than cat-besecting?

Johnny   What's this that Johnnypateen hears?

Helen *grabs* **Bartley** *by the hair and wrenches his head around as* **Johnny** *makes a note in a pocket book.*

Helen   Just you wait till I fecking get you home. Just you fecking wait . . .

Bartley   Ah that hurts, Helen, that hurts . . .

Helen   Of course it hurts. It's supposed to fecking hurt.

Bobby   Be leaving Bartley alone now, Helen.

Helen   Up your arse you, Babbybobby Bennett, you fecking kiss-reneger. Would *you* like to step outside with me?

Bobby   I wouldn't like to.

Helen   Shut your hole so.

Bobby   Not if there was to be kissing involved, anyways.

Helen *releases* **Bartley** *roughly.*

Johnny   A little noteen, now, Johnnypateen has made for himself. A side of lamb at minimum this news'll get me, off Patty Brennan or Jack Ellery anyways. Eheh.

Helen   You'll be eating that lamb with a broken neck, so, if that news gets bandied about before Jack and Pat've paid up, ya feck.

Johnny   Oh aye.

Bartley (*pause*)   Look at the <u>size of that fella's nose</u>. (*Pause*.)
Look at the size of that fella's nose, I said.   → why is that his interest.

Kate   Have you been falling down any holes since, Bartley?

oh! so it's not even that relevant.

Bartley   Oh Mrs, sure <u>wasn't I seven</u> when I fell down the   they say
bloody hole I fell down? D'ya have to keep dragging that up   as if it's
every year?   immediate.

Helen (*pause*)   Oh, they still haven't caught this fecking
shark! How hard is it?

Helen *throws an egg at the screen.*

Bobby   Oh, don't be pegging any more eggs at the film,
Helen. Weren't the five you pegged at the poor woman in it
enough?

Helen   Not nearly enough. I never got her in the gob even
once, the bitch. She keeps moving.

Bobby   You'll ruin the egg-man's bedsheet anyways.

Helen   Ah, the egg-man's bedsheet is used to being eggy.

Bartley   How do you know the egg-man's bedsheets are
used to being eggy, Helen?

unreliable

Helen   <u>E</u>m, Jim Finnegan's daughter was telling me.

Mammy (*pause*)   Ah, why don't they just leave the poor
shark alone? He was doing no harm.

Johnny   Sure what manner of a ⟨story⟩ would that be,
leaving a shark alone! You want a dead shark.

Bobby   A dead shark, aye, or a shark with no ears on him.

Johnny   A dead shark, aye, or a shark kissed a green-
teethed girl in Antrim.

Bobby   Do you want a belt, you, mentioning green-teeth
girls?

Johnny   Well, you interrupted me and me mammy's shark debate.

Mammy   They should give the shark a belt, then leave the poor gosawer alone.

Johnny   Why are you in love with sharks all of a sudden? Wasn't it a shark ate Daddy?

Mammy   It *was* a shark ate Daddy, but Jaysus says you should forgive and forget.

Johnny   He doesn't say you should forgive and forget sharks.

Bartley (*pause*)   Sharks have no ears to begin with, anyways.
Pause. They look at him.

→ observational, matter of fact

Babbybobby was saying a shark with no ears. (*Pause.*) Sharks have no ears to begin with, anyways.

Johnny   We've moved on from ears-talk, you, ya thick.

Bartley   What are we onto now?

↝ but can't follow the news...

Johnny   We're onto Jaysus forgiving sharks.

Bartley   Oh aye, that's an awful great topic for conversation.

Helen   I always preferred Pontius Pilate to Jesus. Jesus always seemed full of himself.

Bartley   Jesus drove a thousand pigs into the sea one time, did you ever hear tell of that story? <u>Drowned the lot of the poor devils.</u> They always seem to gloss o'er that one in school. ↳ he's always concerned w. animal & nature

Kate   I didn't know Jesus could drive.

Helen   Mrs? You've gone loopy, haven't you, Mrs? Haven't you gone loopy?

Kate   I haven't gone loopy.

Helen   You have. Your stone was telling me earlier.

Kate   What did me stone say?

Helen   Did you hear that one, Bartley? 'What did me stone say?'

Johnny   Of course poor Kate's gone loopy, Helen, with the gosawer she raised and loved sixteen year preferring to take his TB to Hollywood for his dying than bear be in the company of her.

Eileen *stands with her hands to her head and turns to face* **Johnny**, *as does* **Bobby**.

Eileen (*stunned*)   *⌒ Oh no.*   Wha? Wha?

Johnny   Em, whoops.

Bobby *grabs* **Johnny** *roughly and drags him up.*

Bobby   Didn't I say to ya?! Didn't I say to ya?!

Johnny   Sure, don't they have a right to know about their dying foster-babby, stabbed them in the back without a by-your-leave?

Bobby   Can't you keep anything to yourself?

Johnny   Johnnypateenmike was never a man for secrets.

Bobby   Outside with ya, so, and see if you can keep this beating a secret.

Johnny   You'll frighten me mammy, Babbybobby, you'll frighten me mammy . . .

Mammy   Ah you won't, Bobby. Go on and give him a good beating for yourself.

Johnny   That was the last omelette you'll ever eat in my house, ya bitch!

Mammy   Carrot omelettes don't go, anyways.

Johnny   You never like anything adventurous!

Johnny *is dragged off right by* **Bobby**. *Sound of his yelps getting more and more distant.* **Eileen** *is standing in front of* **Bartley**, *hands still to her head.*

Eileen What was this Johnnypateen was saying about . . .

Bartley Would you mind out of me way, Mrs, I can't see.

Eileen *moves over to* **Mammy**.

Helen What's to fecking see anyways but more wet fellas with awful jumpers on them?

Eileen Mrs O'Dougal, what now was this that your Johnny was saying?

Mammy (*pause*) TB they say your Cripple Billy has, Eileen.

Eileen No . . . !

Mammy Or, they say he *had* anyways. Four months ago Billy was told, and told he had only three months left in him.

Bartley That means he's probably been dead a month, Mrs. Simple subtraction that is. Three from four.

Eileen Ah sure, if this is only your Johnnypateen's oul gossiping I wouldn't believe you at all . . .

Mammy Aye, if it was Johnnypat's gossiping you wouldn't need to care a skitter about it, but Babbybobby's news this is. Cripple Billy showed him a letter from McSharry the night before they sailed. Sure, Babbybobby would never've taken Cripple Billy, only his heart went out to him. Didn't Bobby's Annie die of the same thing?

Eileen She did, and in agony she died. Oh, Cripple Billy. The days and nights I've cursed him for not writing us, when how could he write us at all?

Helen When he was buried six feet under. Aye, that'd be an awful hard task.

Eileen   But . . . but Doctor McSharry five or six times I've asked, and nothing at all wrong with Billy did McSharry say there was.

Mammy   Sure, I suppose he was only trying not to hurt you, Eileen, same as everyone around. (*Pause.*) I'm sorry, Eileen.

Helen *and* **Bartley** *stand and stretch, as the film ends.* **Eileen** *sits, tearfully.*

Helen   Oh, thank Christ the fecker's over. A pile of fecking shite.

Bartley   And not a telescope in sight.

The film winds out, leaving the screen blank. A light goes on behind it, illuminating the silhouette of **Cripple Billy** *on the screen, which only* **Kate** *sees. She stands and stares at it.*

Mammy (*wheeling herself away*)   Did they catch the shark in the end, so, Helen?

Helen   Ah, it wasn't even a shark at all, Mrs. It was a tall fella in a grey donkey jacket.

Mammy   How do you know, Helen?

Helen   Didn't I give the fella a couple of kisses to promise to put me in his next film, and didn't I stamp on the bollocks of him when his promise turned out untrue?

Mammy   All that fuss o'er a fella in a grey donkey jacket. I don't know.

Helen   He won't be playing any more sharks for a while anyways, Mrs, the stamp I gave the feck.

Helen *and* **Mammy** *exit.* **Bartley** *stands staring at* **Billy**'s *silhouette, having just spotted it.* **Eileen**, *crying, still has her back to it.* **Kate** *pulls back the sheet, revealing* **Billy**, *alive and well.*

Helen (*off, calling out*)   Are you coming, you, fecker?

Bartley   In a minute I'm coming.

Billy   I didn't want to disturb ye till the film was o'er.

Eileen *turns, sees him, stunned.* **Kate** *drops her stone and embraces* **Billy**.

Bartley   Hello there, Cripple Billy.

how is he back?

Billy   Hello there, Bartley.

Bartley   Just back from America are ya?

Billy   I am.

Bartley   Uh-huh. (*Pause.*) Did you get me me Yalla-mallows?

Billy   I didn't, Bartley.

Bartley   Ar, ya fecking promised, Billy.

Billy   They had only Fripple-Frapples.

Billy *tosses* **Bartley** *a packet of sweets.*

Bartley   Ah jeebies, Fripple-Frapples'll do just as fine. Thank you, Cripple Billy.

Kate   You're not dead at all, are you, Billy?

Billy   I'm not, Aunty Kate.

Kate   Well, that's good.

Bartley   What was it so, Billy? Did you write that doctor's letter yourself and only to fool Babbybobby into rowing ya, when there wasn't a single thing the matter with the health of you at all?

Billy   I did, Bartley. *bro!*

Bartley   You're awful clever for a cripple-boy, Billy. Was it out of *Biggles goes to Borneo* you got that idea? When Biggles tells the cannonball he has the measles so the cannonball won't eat Biggles at all?

children's book series. adventure.

originality? or copied from fiction?

Billy   No, I made the idea up meself, Bartley.

Bartley   Well now, it sounds awful similar, Billy.

Billy   Well, I made the idea up meself, Bartley. *repeat*

Bartley   Well, you're even more clever than I thought you was so, Billy . You've made a laughing stock of every beggar on Inishmaan, all thought you'd gone and croaked it, like eejits, me included. Fair play to ya. *threatening presence*

Eileen   Not everyone on Inishmaan. Some us of only believed you'd run off, and run off because you couldn't stomach the sight of the ones who raised you.

Billy   Not for a second was that true, Aunty Eileen, and wasn't the reason I returned that I couldn't bear to be parted from ye any longer? Didn't I take me screen test not a month ago and have the Yanks say to me the part was mine? But I had to tell them it was no go, no matter how much money they offered me, because I know now it isn't Hollywood that's the place for me. It's here on Inishmaan, with the people who love me, and the people I love back. *or Bobby said.* *phrasing is very dramatic.*

Kate *kisses him.*

Bartley   Ireland can't be such a bad place, so, if cripple fellas turn down Hollywood to come to Ireland. *again.*

Billy   To tell you the truth, Bartley, it wasn't an awful big thing at all to turn down Hollywood, with the arse-faced lines they had me reading for them. 'Can I not hear the wail of the banshees for me, as far as I am from me barren island home.'

Bartley *laughs.*

Billy   'An Irishman I am, begora! With a heart and a spirit on me not crushed be a hundred years of oppression. I'll be getting me shillelagh out next, wait'll you see.' A rake of shite. And had me singing the fecking 'Croppy Boy' then. *all stereotyped.*

Kate   Sure, I think he'd make a great little actoreen, don't you, Eileen? *→ they recognize something in him, potential?*

Bartley   Them was funny lines, Cripple Billy. Do them again. *but they he does it here too.*

Kate   I'll be off home and air your room out for you, Billy.

Bartley   Em, you've forgot your stone, there, Mrs. Mighn't you want a chat on the way, now?

Kate   Ah, I'll leave me stone. I have me Billy-boy back now to talk to, don't I, Billy?

Billy   You do, Aunty.

Kate *exits.*

Billy   Oh, she hasn't started up with the bloody stones again, has she?

Bartley   She has. Talks to them day and night, and everybody laughs at her, me included.

Billy   You shouldn't laugh at other people's misfortunes, Bartley.

Bartley (*confused*)   Why? *doesn't understand morality. different compass*

Billy   I don't know why. Just that you shouldn't is all.

lots of things unexplained here

Bartley   But it's awful funny.

Billy   Even so.

Bartley   We-ell, I disagree with you there, but you've got me me Fripple-Frapples so I won't argue the point. Will you tell me all about how great America is later, Cripple Billy?

Billy   I will, Bartley.

Bartley   Did you see any telescopes while you were over there?

Billy   I didn't.

Bartley (*disappointed*)   Oh. How about me Aunty Mary in Boston, Massachusetts? Did you see her? She has funny brown hair on her.

Billy   I didn't, Bartley.

Bartley   Oh. (*Pause.*) Well, I'm glad you're not dead anyways, Cripple Billy.

Bartley *exits.*

Billy (*pause*)   That's all Bartley wants to hear is how great America is.

Eileen   Is it not so?

Billy   It's just the same as Ireland really. Full of fat women with beards.

Eileen *gets up, goes over to* **Billy** *and slaps him across the head.*

Billy   Aargh! What was that fer?!

Eileen   Forget fat women with beards! Would it have killed you to write a letter all the time you were away? No, it wouldn't, and not a word. Not a blessed word!

Billy   Ah Aunty, I was awful busy. *really offered role?*

Eileen   Uh-huh. Too busy to write your aunties were worried sick about you, but not too busy to go buying Fripple-Frapples for an eejit gosawer and only to show off the big man you think you are.

Billy   Ah, it only takes a minute to buy Fripple-Frapples, sure. Is that a fair comparison?

Eileen   Don't you go big-wording me when you know you're in the wrong.

Billy   Sure, 'comparison' isn't a big word.

Eileen   Mr Yankee-high-and-mighty now, I see it is.

Billy   And I found the American postal system awful complicated. *he speaks like an enlightened traveler.*

Eileen   It's any excuse for you. Well don't expect me to be forgiving and forgetting as quick as that one. She's only forgiven cos she's gone half doolally because of ya. You won't be catching me out so easy!

Billy   Ah, don't be like that, Aunty.

Eileen (*exiting*)   I *will* be like that. I *will* be like that.

Long pause, **Billy**'s *head lowered.* **Eileen** *sticks her head back in.*

Eileen   And I suppose you'll be wanting praitie cakes for your tea too?!

Billy   I would, Aunty.

Eileen   Taahhh!

She exits again. Pause. **Billy** *looks at the sheet/screen, pulls it back across to its original dimensions and stands there <u>staring at it, caressing it slightly</u>, deep in thought.* **Bobby** *quietly enters right,* **Billy** *noticing him after a moment.*

[*margin note:* wishing he were on it >O what doesh e want?]

[*margin note:* ~very premeditated. planned.]
[*margin note:* almost prep a bigger f?]

Billy   Babbybobby. I daresay I owe you an explanation.

[*margin note:* what will dow?]

Bobby   There's no need to explain, Billy.

[*margin note:* >already knows what he's gonna do.]

Billy   I want to, Bobby. See, I never thought at all this day would come when I'd have to explain. I'd hoped I'd disappear for ever to America. And I would've too, if they'd wanted me there. If they'd wanted me for the filming. But they didn't want me. A blond lad from Fort Lauderdale they hired instead of me. He wasn't crippled at all, but the Yank said, 'Ah, better to get a normal fella who can act crippled than a crippled fella who can't fecking act at all.' Except he said it ruder. (*Pause.*) I thought I'd done alright for meself with me acting. Hours I practised in me hotel there. And all for nothing. (*Pause.*) I gave it a go anyways. I had to give it a go. I had to get away from this place, Babbybobby, be any means, just like me mammy and daddy had to get away from this place. (*Pause.*) Going drowning meself I'd often think of when I was here, just to . . . just to end the laughing at me, and the sniping at me, and the life of nothing but shuffling to the doctor's and shuffling back from the doctor's and pawing over the same oul books and finding any other way to piss another day away. Another day of sniggering, or the patting me on the head like a broken-brained gosawer. The village orphan. The village cripple, and nothing more. Well, there are plenty round here just as crippled as me, only it isn't on the outside it shows. (*Pause.*) But the thing is,

[*margin note:* contradicting sf?]
[*margin note:* what will ppl. take as true?]
[*margin note:* why all the pauses?]
[*margin note:* this is his mind. bitterness. → unable to conceal in his acting.]
[*margin note:* >turn of logic. But you are r he was getting here all alo but to get here he had to catch himself.]

Is everyone else aware of their "explanation"?

you're not one of them, Babbybobby, nor never were.
You've a kind heart on you. I suppose that's why it was so
easy to cod you with the TB letter, but that's why I was so
sorry for codding you at the time and why I'm just as sorry
now. Especially for codding you with the same thing your
Mrs passed from. Just I thought that would be more effective.
But, in the long run, I thought, or I hoped, that if you had
a choice between you being codded a while and me doing
away with meself, once your anger had died down anyways,
you'd choose you being codded every time. Was I wrong,
Babbybobby? Was I?   *= tricked. not just intentionally used. unknowingly...*

he took advantage of Bobby's soft point.
can an apology cure that? clever...

Bobby *slowly walks over to* **Billy***, stops just in front of him, and
lets a length of lead piping slide down his sleeve into his hand.*

Bobby   Aye.   *what is the use of this speech when there is such
great physical power/violence waiting?*

Bobby *raises the pipe . . .*

Billy   No, Bobby, no . . . !

bringing Billy "down" to reality.

Billy *covers up as the pipe scythes down. Blackout, with the sounds
of* **Billy***'s pained screams and the pipe scything down again and
again.*

Scene Nine

The shop, late evening. The **Doctor** *tending to* **Billy***'s bruised and
bloody face.* **Kate** *at the counter,* **Eileen** *at the door, looking out.*

Eileen   Johnnypateenmike's near enough running o'er the
island with his news of Billy's return to us.

Kate   This is a big day for news.

Eileen   He has a loaf in one hand and a leg o'mutton
neath each armeen.

Kate   Billy's return and Babbybobby's arrest and Jim
Finnegan's daughter joining the nunnery then. That was the
biggest surprise.   *by that's unrelated & surprising.
a real "when pigs fly"!*

Eileen   The nuns must be after anybody if they let Jim Finnegan's daughter join them.

Kate   The nuns' standards must have dropped.

Billy   Sure why shouldn't Jim Finnegan's daughter become a nun? It's only pure gossip that Jim Finnegan's daughter is a slut.

Doctor   No, Jim Finnegan's daughter *is* a slut.

Billy   Is she?   *↪ funny for a doctor to say*

Doctor   Aye.

Billy   How do you know?

Doctor   Just take me word.

Eileen   Isn't he a doctor?

Billy (*pause*)   Just I don't like people gossiping about people is all. Haven't I had enough of that meself to last me a lifetime?

Doctor   But aren't you the one who started half the gossiping about you, with your forging of letters from me you'll yet have to answer for?

Billy   I'm sorry about the letter business, Doctor, but wasn't it the only avenue left open to me?

Eileen   It's 'avenues' now, do ya hear?

Kate   It's always big talk when from America they return.

Eileen   'Avenues'. I don't know.

Billy   Aunties, I think the doctor might be wanting a mug of tea, would ye's both go and get him one?

Eileen   Is it getting rid of us you're after? If it is, just say so.

Billy   It's getting rid of ye I'm after.   *he's franker.*

Eileen *stares at him a moment, then the two moodily exit to the back room.*

Doctor   You shouldn't talk to them like that, now, Billy.

Billy   Ah, they keep going on and on.

Doctor   I know they do, but they're women.

Billy   I suppose. (*Pause.*) Would you tell me something, Doctor? What do you remember of me mammy and daddy, the people they were?

Doctor   Why do you ask?

Billy   Oh, just when I was in America there I often thought of them, what they'd have done if they'd got there. Wasn't that where they were heading the night they drowned?

Doctor   They say it was. (*Pause.*) As far as I can remember, they weren't the nicest of people. Your daddy was an oul drunken tough, would rarely take a break from his fighting.

Billy   I've heard me mammy was a beautiful woman.

Doctor   No, no, she was awful ugly.

Billy   Was she?

Doctor   Oh, she'd scare a pig. But, ah, she seemed a pleasant enough woman, despite her looks, although the breath on her, well, it would knock you.

Billy   They say it was that Dad punched Mammy while she was heavy with me was why I turned out the way I did.

Doctor   Disease caused you to turn out the way you did, Billy. Not punching at all. Don't go romanticising it.

Billy *coughs/wheezes slightly.*   tragic backstory is not granted.

Doctor   I see you still have your wheeze.

Billy   I still have a bit of me wheeze.

Doctor   That wheeze is taking a long time to go.

He uses a stethoscope to check **Billy***'s chest.*

Doctor   Has worse or better it got since your travelling? Breathe in.

Billy   Maybe a biteen worse.

*The **Doctor** listens to **Billy**'s back.*

Doctor   But blood you haven't been coughing up, ah no.

Billy   Ah, a biteen of blood. (*Pause.*) Now and again.

Doctor   Breathe out. How often is now and again, Billy?

Billy (*pause*)   Most days. (*Pause.*) The TB is it?

Doctor   I'll have to be doing more tests.

Billy   But the TB it looks like?   that's a ... fate.

Doctor   The TB it looks like.

Billy (*quietly*)   There's a coincidence.

bread, lamb, passover = celebration of exodus. plenty of violence.

Johnny *enters quietly, having been listening at the door, loaf in hand, a leg of lamb under each arm, which he carries throughout.*

Johnny   It's the TB after all?

Doctor   Oh Johnnypateen, will you ever stop listening at doors?

Johnny   Lord save us, but from God I'm sure that TB was sent Cripple Billy, for claiming he had TB when he had no TB, and making Johnnypateen's news seem unreliable.

Doctor   God doesn't send people TB, Johnnypateen.

Johnny   He *does* send people TB.

Doctor   He doesn't, now.

Johnny   Well, didn't he send the Egyptians boils is just as bad?

Doctor   Well, boils is different from tuberculosis, Johnnypateen, and *no*, he *didn't* send the Egyptians boils.

Johnny   In Egyptian times.

Doctor   No, he didn't.

Johnny   Well he did something to the fecking Egyptians!

Billy   He killed their first-born sons.

Johnny   He killed their first-born sons and dropped frogs on them, aye. There's a boy knows his scripture. Do your aunties know you have TB yet, Cripple Billy?

Billy   No, they don't know, and you're not to tell them.

Johnny   Sure, it's me job to tell them!

Billy   It isn't your job at all to tell them, and don't you have enough news for one day? Can't you do me a favour for once in your life?

Johnny   For once in me life, is it? (*Sighing.*) Ah, I won't tell them so.

Billy   Thank you, Johnnypateen.

Johnny   Johnnypateen's a kind-hearted, Christian man.

Doctor   I heard you were feeding your mammy poteen at the showing of the film today, Johnnypateen.

Johnny   I don't know where she got hold of that poteen. She's a devil, d'you know?

Doctor   Where's your mammy now?

Johnny   At home she is. (*Pause.*) Lying at the foot of me stairs.

Doctor   What's she doing lying at the foot of your stairs?

Johnny   Nothing. Just lying. Ah, she seems happy enough. She has a pint with her.

Doctor   How did she *get* lying at the foot of your stairs?

Johnny   Be falling down them! How d'ya usually get lying at the foot of a fella's stairs?

Doctor   And you just left her there?

Johnny   Is it my job to go picking her up?

Doctor   It is!

Johnny   Sure, didn't I have work to do with me news-divulging? I have better things to do than picking mammies up. D'you see the two legs of lamb I got, and a loafeen too? This is a great day.

*The **Doctor** packs up his black bag, stunned, as **Johnny** admires his meat.*

Doctor   I'm off now, Billy, to Johnnypateen's house, to see if his mammy's dead or alive. Will you come see me tomorrow, for those further tests?

Billy   I will, Doctor.

*The **Doctor** exits, staring at **Johnny** all the way. **Johnny** sits down beside **Billy**.*

Johnny   Me mammy isn't lying at the foot of me stairs at all. It's just I can't stand the company of that boring feck.

Billy   That wasn't a <u>nice</u> thing to do, Johnnypateen.

Johnny   Well, you're hardly the world's authority on nice things to do, now, are you, Cripple Billy?

Billy   I'm not at that, I suppose.

Johnny   Ah, what harm? Do what you want and feck everybody else is Johnnypateenmichael's motto.

Billy   Did you hear McSharry talking about my mammy when you were listening at the door?

Johnny   A bit of it.

Billy   Was he accurate about her?

Johnny *shrugs.*

Billy   Oh, isn't it always on this subject your lips stay sealed, yet on every other subject from feuds o'er geese to ewe-maiming be lonely fellas, your lips go flapping like a cabbage in the breeze?

Johnny   Now, on the subject of feuds over geese, have you heard the latest?

Billy *sighs.*

Johnny   Well, we all thought Jack Ellery and Patty Brennan were apt to go killing each other o'er the slaughter of their cat and their goose, but now d'you know what? A child seen them, just this morning there, <u>kissing the faces off each other in a haybarn</u>. I can't make it out for the life of me. Two fellas kissing, and two fellas who don't even like each other.   ↱oh? no feud as he'd hoped.

Billy (*pause*)   You've changed the subject, Johnnypateen.

Johnny   I'm great at changing subjects, me. What was the subject? Oh, your drowned mammy and daddy.

Billy   Were they gets like McSharry says?

Johnny   They weren't at all gets.

Billy   No? And yet they still left me behind when they sailed off.

Eileen *returns with mug of tea.*

Eileen   I've the Doctor's tea.

Billy   The Doctor's gone.

Eileen   Without having his tea?

Billy   Evidently.

Eileen   Don't you be big-wording me again, Billy Claven.

Johnny   I'll have the Doctor's tea so, if it'll save a family dispute.

She gives him the tea.

Johnnypateen goes out of his way to help people out, and do you have any biscuits there, Mrs?

Billy   You're changing the subject again, aren't ya?

Johnny   I'm not changing the subject. I want a biscuit.

Eileen   We have no biscuits.

Johnny   I'll bet you have a rake of biscuits. What do you have on the shelves behind them peas, there?

Eileen   We have more peas.

Johnny   You order too many peas. A fella can't go having peas with his tea. Unless he was an odd fella. (*Adjusting lamb.*) And there's no way you could describe Johnnypateenmike as an odd fella. Oh no.

Billy   Johnnypateen. Me mammy and daddy. Their sailing.

Eileen   Oh, that's ancient news, Billy. Just leave it alone . . .

Johnny   Sure, if the boy wants to hear, let him hear. Isn't he grown up and travelled enough now to be hearing?

Eileen   You're not going telling him?

Johnny *stares at her a moment.*

Johnny   It was on the sands I met them that night, staring off into the black, the water roaring, and I wouldn't've thought a single thing more of it, if I hadn't seen the sack full of stones tied to the hands of them there, as they heaved it into the boat. A big old hemp sack like one of them there, it was. And they handed you to me then, then started rowing, to deep water.

Billy   So they *did* kill themselves o'er me?

Johnny   They killed themselves, aye, but not for the reasons you think. D'you think it was to get away from ya?

Billy   Why else, sure?

Johnny   Will I tell him?

Eileen *nods.*

Johnny   A week before this it was they'd first been told you'd be dying if they couldn't get you to the Regional Hospital and medicines down you. But a hundred pounds or near this treatment'd cost. They didn't have the like of a hundred pounds. I know you know it was their death insurance paid for the treatment saved you. But did you know it was the same day I met them on the sands there they had taken their insurance policy out?

Billy (*pause*)   It was for me they killed themselves?

Johnny   The insurance paid up a week after, and you were given the all-clear afore a month was out.

Billy   So they *did* love me, in spite of everything.

Eileen   They did love you *because* of everything, Billy.

Johnny   Isn't that news?

Billy   That is news. I needed good news this day. Thank you, Johnnypateen.   *why was this concealed?*
                              Johnny's asset...?
They shake hands and **Billy** *sits.*

Johnny   You're welcome, Cripple Billy.

Billy   *Billy.*
                change.
Johnny   Billy. (*Pause.*) Well, I'm off home to me mammy. Hopefully she'll have dropped down dead when the doctor barged in and we'll both have had good news this day. (*Pause.*) Mrs, d'you have any payment there for Johnnypateen's good news and not peas?

Eileen   There's Yalla-mallows.

Johnny (*looking at packet*)   What are Yalla-mallows?

Eileen   They're mallows that are yalla.

Johnny (*pause; after considering*)   I'll leave them.

Johnny *exits. Long pause.*   .

Billy   You should have told me before, Aunty.

Eileen   I wasn't sure how you'd take the news, Billy.

Billy   You still should've told me. The truth is always less hard than you fear it's going to be.

Eileen   I'm sorry, Billy.

Pause. **Billy** *lets her cuddle him slightly.*

Billy   And I'm sorry for using 'evidently' on ya.

Eileen   And so you should be.

She gently slaps his face, smiling. **Helen** *enters.*

Eileen   Hello, Helen. What can I get you?

Helen   No, I've just come to look at Cripple Billy's wounds. I've heard they're deep.

Billy   Hello, Helen.

Helen   You look a fecking fool in all that get-up, Cripple Billy.

Billy   I do, I suppose. Em, Aunty, is that the kettle, now, I hear boiling in the back?

Eileen   Eh? No. Oh. (*Tuts.*) Aye.   *nice. kinda farcical.*

Eileen *exits to back room, as* **Helen** *pulls up* **Billy**'s *bandages to look under them.*

Billy   Hurts a bit that picking does, Helen.

Helen   Ar, don't be such a fecking girl, Cripple Billy. How was America?

Billy   Fine, fine.

Helen   Did you see any girls over there as pretty as me?

Billy   Not a one.

Helen   Or almost as pretty as me?

Billy   Not a one.

Helen   Or even a hundred times *less* pretty than me?

Billy   Well, maybe a couple, now.

Helen *pokes him hard in the face.*

Billy (*in pain*)   Aargh! Not a one, I mean.

Helen   You just watch yourself you, Cripple Billy.

Billy   Do ya have to be so violent, Helen?

Helen   I do have to be so violent, or if I'm not to be taken advantage of anyways I have to be so violent.

Billy   Sure, nobody's taken advantage of you since the age of seven, Helen.

Helen   Six is nearer the mark. I ruptured a curate at six.

Billy   So couldn't you tone down a bit of your violence and be more of a sweet girl?

Helen   I could, you're right there. And the day after I could shove a bent spike up me arse. (*Pause.*) I've just lost me job with the egg-man. *→ why? actual reflection. well, Billys right...!*

Billy   Why did you lose your job with the egg-man, Helen?

Helen   D'you know, I can't for the life of me figure out why. Maybe it was me lack of punctuality. Or me breaking all the egg-man's eggs. Or me giving him a good kick whenever I felt like it. But you couldn't call them decent reasons.

Billy   You couldn't at all, sure.

Helen   Or me spitting on the egg-man's wife, but you couldn't call that a decent reason.

Billy   What did you spit on the egg-man's wife for, Helen?

Helen   Ah, the egg-man's wife just deserves spitting on. (*Pause.*) I still haven't given you a good kick for your taking your place in Hollywood that was rightfully mine. Didn't I have to kiss four of the film directors on Inishmore to book me place you took without a single kiss?

Billy   But there was only *one* film director on Inishmore that time, Helen. The man Flaherty. And I didn't see you near him at all.

Helen   Who was it I was kissing so?

Billy   I think it was mostly stable-boys who could do an American accent. *willing & getting tricked. welp.*

Helen   The bastards! Couldn't you've warned me?

Billy   I was going to warn you, but you seemed to be enjoying yourself.

Helen   You do get a decent kiss off a stable-boy is true enough. I would probably go stepping out with a stable-boy if truth be told, if it wasn't for the smell of pig-shite you get off them.

Billy   Are you not stepping out with anyone at the moment, so?

Helen   I'm not.

Billy (*pause*)   Me, I've never been kissed.

Helen   Of course you've never been kissed. You're a funny-looking cripple-boy.

Billy (*pause*)   It's funny, but when I was in America I tried to think of all the things I'd miss about home if I had to stay in America. Would I miss the scenery, I thought? The stone walls, and the lanes, and the green, and the sea? No, I wouldn't miss them. Would I miss the food? The peas, the praities, the peas, the praities and the peas? No, I wouldn't miss it. Would I miss the people?

Helen   Is this speech going to go on for more long?

Billy   I've nearly finished it. (*Pause.*) What was me last bit? You've put me off . . .

Helen   'Would I miss the people?'

Billy   Would I miss the people? Well, I'd miss me aunties, or a *bit* I'd miss me aunties. I wouldn't miss Babbybobby with his lead stick or Johnnypateen with his daft news. Or all the lads used to laugh at me at school, or all the lasses used to cry if I even spoke to them. Thinking over it, if Inishmaan sank in the sea tomorrow, and everybody on it up and drowned, there isn't especially anybody I'd really miss. Anybody other than you, that is, Helen.

Helen (*pause*)   You'd miss the cows you go staring at.

Billy   Oh, that cow business was blown up out of all proportion. What I was trying to build up to, Helen, was . . .

Helen   Oh, was you trying to build up to something, Cripple Billy?

Billy   I was, but you keep interrupting me.

Helen   Build up ahead so.

Billy   I was trying to build up to. . . There comes a time in every fella's life when he has to take his heart in his hands and make a try for something, and even though he knows it's a one in a million chance of him getting it, he has to chance it still, else why be alive at all? So, I was wondering Helen, if maybe sometime, y'know, when you're not too busy or something, if maybe . . . and I know well I'm no great shakes to look at, but I was wondering if maybe you might want to go out walking with me some evening. Y'know, in a week or two or something? *that's a feeble date for a grand speech*

Helen (*pause*)   Sure what would I want to go out walking with a cripple-boy for? It isn't out walking you'd be anyways, it would be out shuffling, because you can't walk. I'd have to be waiting for ya every five yards. What would you and me want to be out shuffling for?

Billy   For the company.

Helen   For the company?   *in some way Billy allows Helen to realize there is another option beyond cruelty → function of fart...*

Billy   And . . .

Helen   And what?

Billy   And for the way sweethearts be.   *laughing at Billy or ? his speech?*

Helen *looks at him a second, then slowly and quietly starts laughing/ sniggering through her nose, as she gets up and goes to the door. Once there she turns, looks at* **Billy** *again, laughs again and exits.* **Billy** *is left staring down at the floor as* **Kate** *quietly enters from the back room.*   *same reaction only she doesn't say m...*

Kate   She's not a very nice girl anyways, Billy.

Billy   Was you listening, Aunty Kate?

Kate   I wasn't listening, or alright I was a biteen listening. (*Pause.*) You wait for a nice girl to come along, Billy. A girl who doesn't mind at all what you look like. Just sees your heart.

Billy   How long will I be waiting for a girl like that to come along, Aunty?

Kate   Ah, not long at all, Billy. Maybe a year or two. Or at the outside five.

Billy   Five years . . .

Billy *nods, gets up, wheezes slightly, and exits into the back room.*

Kate *starts tidying and closing up the shop.* **Eileen** *enters, helping her. Sound of* **Billy** *coughing distantly in the house now and then.*

Eileen   What's Cripple Billy looking so glum for?

Kate   Billy asked Slippy Helen to go out walking with him, and Helen said she'd rather go out walking with a broken-headed ape.

Eileen   That was a descriptive turn of phrase for Slippy Helen.

Kate   Well, I've tarted it up a bit.

Eileen   I was thinking. (*Pause.*) Cripple Billy wants to aim lower than Helen, really.

Kate   Cripple Billy *does* want to aim lower than Helen.

Eileen   Billy wants to aim at ugly girls who are thick, then work his way up.

Kate   Billy should go to Antrim really. He'd be well away. (*Pause.*) But Billy probably doesn't like ugly girls who are thick.

Eileen   Sure there's no pleasing Billy.

Kate   None.

Eileen (*pause*)   And you missed the story Johnnypateen spun, Kate, about Billy's mam and daddy tying a sack of

stones to their hands and drowning themselves for their
insurance money that saved him.

Kate   The stories Johnnypateen spins. When it was poor
Billy they tied in that sack of stones, and Billy would still be
at the bottom of the sea to this day, if it hadn't been for
Johnnypateen swimming out to save him. And stealing his
mammy's hundred pounds then to pay for Billy's hospital
treatment.

oh! all these truth man.

Eileen   We should tell Billy the true story some day, Kate.

Kate   Sure, that story might only make Cripple Billy sad,
or something, Eileen.

should we know the truth?

Eileen   Do you think? Ah there's plenty of time to tell
Billy that story anyways.

Kate   There is.

The two finish their closing up, **Eileen** *locking the door,* **Kate**
turning the oil lamp low.

Kate   This'll be the first decent night's sleep in many a
month I've had, Eileen.

Eileen   I know it will, Kate. Have you finished for good
with your stone shenanigans now?

Kate   I *have.* They only crop up when I've been worrying,
and, you know, I know I hide it well, but I do worry awful
about Billy when he's away from us.

Eileen   I do worry awful about Billy when he's away from
us too, but I try not to let stones enter into it.

Kate   Ah, let's forget about stones. We have our Billy back
with us now.

Eileen   We *do* have our Billy back with us. Back for good.

Kate   Back for good.

The two smile and exit to the back room, arm in arm. After a pause,
Billy *comes in from the back, sniffling, and turns the oil lamp up,*

revealing his bloodshot eyes and tear-stained cheeks. He quietly takes the sack down from the wall, places inside it numerous cans of peas until it's very heavy, then ties the cords at the top of the bag tightly around one of his hands. This done, he pauses in thought a moment, then shuffles to the door. There is a knock on it. **Billy** *dries his cheeks, hides the sack behind him and opens the door.* **Helen** *pops her head in.*

Helen (*forcefully*)   All right so, I'll go out walking with ya, but only somewheres no fecker would see us and when it's dark and no kissing or groping, cos I don't want you ruining me fecking reputation.

Billy   Oh. Okay, Helen.

Helen   Or anyways not much kissing or groping.

Billy   Would tomorrow suit?

Helen   Tomorrow wouldn't at all suit. Isn't it Bartley's fecking birthday tomorrow?

Billy   Is it? What have you got him?

Helen   I got him . . . and for the life of me I don't know why I did, because I know now he'll never stop fecking jabbering on about it or anyways won't stop jabbering till I give him a big thump in the fecking face for himself and even then he probably won't stop, but didn't I get the fecker a telescope?

Billy   That was awful nice of ya, Helen.

Helen   I think I must be getting soft in me old age.

Billy   I think so too.

Helen   Do ya?

Billy   Aye.

Helen (*coyly*)   Do ya really, Billy?

Billy   I do.

Helen   Uh-huh. Does this feel soft?

Helen *pokes* **Billy** *hard in the bandaged face.* **Billy** *yelps in pain.*

Billy   Aargh! No, it doesn't feel soft!

Helen   Good-oh. I'll see you the day after tomorrow for our fecking walk, so.

Billy   You will.

Helen *kisses* **Billy** *briefly, winks at him, and pulls the door behind her as she exits.* **Billy** *is left standing there stunned a moment, then remembers the sack tied to his hand. Pause. He unties it, replaces the cans on the shelves and hangs the sack back up on the wall, stroking* again. *it a moment. He shuffles over towards the back room, smiling, but stops as he gets there, coughing heavily, his hand to his mouth. After the coughing stops he takes his hand away and looks down at it for a moment. It's covered in blood.* **Billy** loses his smile, *turns the oil lamp down and exits to the back room. Fade to black.*

will for life fluctuates so easy.
(what makes life worth it for him?
→ fake death in sc.7 → real death in sc. 9.
"dumbing down" → deliberate? value?   Is this real?

originality
↳ beetroot paella / carrot omelette / peas in tea...
what new thing can we make w. old ingredients?

Bloomsbury Methuen Drama Student Editions

Jean Anouilh *Antigone* • John Arden *Serjeant Musgrave's Dance*
Alan Ayckbourn *Confusions* • Aphra Behn *The Rover* • Edward Bond
Lear • *Saved* • Bertolt Brecht *The Caucasian Chalk Circle* • *Fear and
Misery in the Third Reich* • *The Good Person of Szechwan* • *Life of Galileo* •
Mother Courage and her Children • *The Resistible Rise of Arturo Ui* • *The
Threepenny Opera* • Anton Chekhov *The Cherry Orchard* • *The Seagull* •
Three Sisters • *Uncle Vanya* • Caryl Churchill *Serious Money* • *Top Girls*
• Shelagh Delaney *A Taste of Honey* • Euripides *Elektra* • *Medea* •
Dario Fo *Accidental Death of an Anarchist* • Michael Frayn *Copenhagen*
• John Galsworthy *Strife* • Nikolai Gogol *The Government Inspector* •
Robert Holman *Across Oka* • Henrik Ibsen *A Doll's House* • *Ghosts* •
Hedda Gabler • Charlotte Keatley *My Mother Said I Never Should* •
Bernard Kops *Dreams of Anne Frank* • Federico García Lorca *Blood
Wedding* • *Doña Rosita the Spinster* (bilingual edition) • *The House of
Bernarda Alba* • (bilingual edition) • *Yerma* (bilingual edition) • David
Mamet *Glengarry Glen Ross* • *Oleanna* • Patrick Marber *Closer* • John
Marston *Malcontent* • Martin McDonagh *The Lieutenant of Inishmore* •
Joe Orton *Loot* • Luigi Pirandello *Six Characters in Search of an Author*
• Mark Ravenhill *Shopping and F***ing* • Willy Russell *Blood Brothers*
• *Educating Rita* • Sophocles *Antigone* • *Oedipus the King* • Wole
Soyinka *Death and the King's Horseman* • Shelagh Stephenson *The
Memory of Water* • August Strindberg *Miss Julie* • J. M. Synge *The
Playboy of the Western World* • Theatre Workshop *Oh What a Lovely
War* Timberlake Wertenbaker *Our Country's Good* • Arnold Wesker
The Merchant • Oscar Wilde *The Importance of Being Earnest* •
Tennessee Williams *A Streetcar Named Desire* • *The Glass Menagerie*

Bloomsbury Methuen Drama Modern Plays

include work by

Edward Albee	Howard Korder
Jean Anouilh	Robert Lepage
John Arden	Doug Lucie
Margaretta D'Arcy	Martin McDonagh
Peter Barnes	John McGrath
Sebastian Barry	Terrence McNally
Brendan Behan	David Mamet
Dermot Bolger	Patrick Marber
Edward Bond	Arthur Miller
Bertolt Brecht	Mtwa, Ngema & Simon
Howard Brenton	Tom Murphy
Anthony Burgess	Phyllis Nagy
Simon Burke	Peter Nichols
Jim Cartwright	Sean O'Brien
Caryl Churchill	Joseph O'Connor
Complicite	Joe Orton
Noël Coward	Louise Page
Lucinda Coxon	Joe Penhall
Sarah Daniels	Luigi Pirandello
Nick Darke	Stephen Poliakoff
Nick Dear	Franca Rame
Shelagh Delaney	Mark Ravenhill
David Edgar	Philip Ridley
David Eldridge	Reginald Rose
Dario Fo	Willy Russell
Michael Frayn	Jean-Paul Sartre
John Godber	Sam Shepard
Paul Godfrey	Wole Soyinka
David Greig	Simon Stephens
John Guare	Shelagh Stephenson
Peter Handke	Peter Straughan
David Harrower	C. P. Taylor
Jonathan Harvey	Theatre Workshop
Iain Heggie	Sue Townsend
Declan Hughes	Judy Upton
Terry Johnson	Timberlake Wertenbaker
Sarah Kane	Roy Williams
Charlotte Keatley	Snoo Wilson
Barrie Keeffe	Victoria Wood

Bloomsbury Methuen Drama Contemporary Dramatists
include

John Arden (two volumes)
Arden & D'Arcy
Peter Barnes (three volumes)
Sebastian Barry
Dermot Bolger
Edward Bond (eight volumes)
Howard Brenton
   (two volumes)
Richard Cameron
Jim Cartwright
Caryl Churchill (two volumes)
Sarah Daniels (two volumes)
Nick Darke
David Edgar (three volumes)
David Eldridge
Ben Elton
Dario Fo (two volumes)
Michael Frayn (three volumes)
David Greig
John Godber (four volumes)
Paul Godfrey
John Guare
Lee Hall (two volumes)
Peter Handke
Jonathan Harvey
   (two volumes)
Declan Hughes
Terry Johnson (three volumes)
Sarah Kane
Barrie Keeffe
Bernard-Marie Koltès
   (two volumes)
Franz Xaver Kroetz
David Lan
Bryony Lavery
Deborah Levy
Doug Lucie

David Mamet (four volumes)
Martin McDonagh
Duncan McLean
Anthony Minghella
   (two volumes)
Tom Murphy (six volumes)
Phyllis Nagy
Anthony Neilsen (two volumes)
Philip Osment
Gary Owen
Louise Page
Stewart Parker (two volumes)
Joe Penhall (two volumes)
Stephen Poliakoff
   (three volumes)
David Rabe (two volumes)
Mark Ravenhill (two volumes)
Christina Reid
Philip Ridley
Willy Russell
Eric-Emmanuel Schmitt
Ntozake Shange
Sam Shepard (two volumes)
Wole Soyinka (two volumes)
Simon Stephens (two volumes)
Shelagh Stephenson
David Storey (three volumes)
Sue Townsend
Judy Upton
Michel Vinaver
   (two volumes)
Arnold Wesker (two volumes)
Michael Wilcox
Roy Williams (three volumes)
Snoo Wilson (two volumes)
David Wood (two volumes)
Victoria Wood

Bloomsbury Methuen Drama World Classics

include

Jean Anouilh (two volumes)
Brendan Behan
Aphra Behn
Bertolt Brecht (eight volumes)
Büchner
Bulgakov
Calderón
Čapek
Anton Chekhov
Noël Coward (eight volumes)
Feydeau (two volumes)
Eduardo De Filippo
Max Frisch
John Galsworthy
Gogol
Gorky (two volumes)
Harley Granville Barker
  (two volumes)
Victor Hugo
Henrik Ibsen (six volumes)
Jarry

Lorca (three volumes)
Marivaux
Mustapha Matura
David Mercer (two volumes)
Arthur Miller (six volumes)
Molière
Musset
Peter Nichols (two volumes)
Joe Orton
A. W. Pinero
Luigi Pirandello
Terence Rattigan
  (two volumes)
W. Somerset Maugham
  (two volumes)
August Strindberg
  (three volumes)
J. M. Synge
Ramón del Valle-Inclán
Frank Wedekind
Oscar Wilde

Bloomsbury Methuen Drama Classical Greek Dramatists

include

Aeschylus Plays: One
(Persians, Seven Against Thebes, Suppliants,
Prometheus Bound)

Aeschylus Plays: Two
(Oresteia: Agamemnon, Libation-Bearers, Eumenides)

Aristophanes Plays: One
(Acharnians, Knights, Peace, Lysistrata)

Aristophanes Plays: Two
(Wasps, Clouds, Birds, Festival Time, Frogs)

Aristophanes & Menander: New Comedy
(Women in Power, Wealth, The Malcontent,
The Woman from Samos)

Euripides Plays: One
(Medea, The Phoenician Women, Bacchae)

Euripides Plays: Two
(Hecuba, The Women of Troy,
Iphigeneia at Aulis, Cyclops)

Euripides Plays: Three
(Alkestis, Helen, Ion)

Euripides Plays: Four
(Elektra, Orestes, Iphigeneia in Tauris)

Euripides Plays: Five
(Andromache, Herakles' Children, Herakles)

Euripides Plays: Six
(Hippolytos, Suppliants, Rhesos)

Sophocles Plays: One
(Oedipus the King, Oedipus at Colonus, Antigone)

Sophocles Plays: Two
(Ajax, Women of Trachis, Electra, Philoctetes)

For a complete listing of Bloomsbury
Methuen Drama titles, visit:
www.bloomsbury.com/drama

Follow us on Twitter and keep up to date
with our news and publications
@MethuenDrama

CPSIA information can be obtained
at www.ICGtesting.com
Printed in the USA
LVHW011830220723
753127LV00001B/51

9 781408 106785